TWO WEEKS EVERY SUMMER

A volume in the series
American Institutions and Society
Edited by Brian Balogh and Jonathan Zimmerman

A full list of titles in the series is available at www.cornellpress.cornell.edu.

TWO WEEKS EVERY SUMMER

Fresh Air Children and the
Problem of Race in America

Tobin Miller Shearer

CORNELL UNIVERSITY PRESS   **ITHACA AND LONDON**

First published 2017 by Cornell University Press
Printed in the United States of America

Library of Congress Cataloging-in-Publication Data

Names: Shearer, Tobin Miller, author.
Title: Two weeks every summer: fresh air children and the problem of race in
    America / Tobin Miller Shearer.
Other titles: American institutions and society.
Description: Ithaca; London: Cornell University Press, 2017. | Series: American
    institutions and society | Includes bibliographical references and index.
Identifiers: LCCN 2016047308 (print) | LCCN 2016049195 (ebook) | ISBN
    9781501707452 (cloth: alk. paper) | ISBN 9781501708459 (epub/mobi) | ISBN
    9781501708466 (pdf)
Subjects: LCSH: Fresh-air charity—United States. | African American children—
    Social conditions. | Race relations—United States.
Classification: LCC HV934 .S54 2017 (print) | LCC HV934 (ebook) | DDC
    362.71—dc23
LC record available at https:// lccn.loc.gov/2016047308

Cornell University Press strives to use environmentally responsible suppliers
and materials to the fullest extent possible in the publishing of its books. Such
materials include vegetable-based, low-VOC inks and acid-free papers that are
recycled, totally chlorine-free, or partly composed of nonwood fibers. For further
information, visit our website at www.cornellpress.cornell.edu.

Contents

Preface

Ten years ago, when I was working in the record room of Eastern Mennonite Missions (EMM), an agency supported primarily by Lancaster Mennonite Conference congregations in Pennsylvania, I encountered a photo that grabbed my attention (see figure 1).

It was most likely taken by volunteer host Anna Denlinger to help promote the Children's Visitation Program, an initiative begun on October 11, 1949, to bring—in the now dated and problematic language of the day—"colored children of our city missions" into church member homes.[1] The program copied the much older and larger initiative known as the *Herald Tribune* Fresh Air Fund or the Friendly Town Program. The Fresh Air Fund had since 1877 brought children from New York City to the country and suburbs for one- to two-week summer vacations at little or no cost to the children or their parents. Dozens of cities along the Eastern Seaboard, the Midwest, and some portions of the West Coast had replicated the model, and by 1962 well over a million children had participated. Urban congregations, social service agencies, settlement houses, and other nonprofit organizations vetted the children while rural churches, civic organizations, and women's groups organized the home stays and camp visits. Although originally designed to restore malnourished white ethnic children to health, by the early 1970s white hosts and African American and Latino guests dominated the program. The Lancaster-based initiative had focused on African American and Latino children from its inception.

But it was the image itself that arrested me. When I first saw the photo, I wondered how such an event came to pass. Who had proposed sending African

FIGURE 1.   Edith and John Boll of Easter Mennonite Missions with unidentified Fresh Air participant at Lancaster City, Pennsylvania, train station, circa late 1950s. Used by permission of Eastern Mennonite Missions, Salunga, PA.

American children from the city to spend time with white people in the country? Why was the girl so young? Where were her parents? What motivated the white hosts to flock in such large numbers to the pickup point? What was awry? What caused the expressions of consternation? Had the young girl's hosts failed to show up? Were the white adults and the girl simply uncomfortable being photographed? And why were the girl's eyes closed? Was she imagining a more familiar place than the one where a crowd of religiously garbed white women and children—along with one man, out in front, holding some document—hovered around her? I set out to discover more.

As I began to present my initial findings at conferences and public lectures, I often featured this photo. Every time I presented my research, without exception, someone in the audience had either hosted a Fresh Air child or had been one. Often, both former hosts and guests came up to me after a talk. The vast majority of the hosts expressed positive memories about picking up their guests at train stations like the one featured in the photo. However, the former Fresh Air children spoke with far more ambivalence. Some shed tears because of the feelings evoked by their Fresh Air memories; a few grew quite angry as they recalled insults and indignities like the ID tag draped around the girl's neck. One Fresh Air child said such tags made her feel like she was the subject of a "slave auction"; others expressed gratitude for their hosts' generosity even while raising questions about the programs' disparagement of the city.[2]

Reactions to my first forays into writing about Fresh Air were likewise mixed. Some readers found the research fascinating and sent me photographs and newspaper clippings from Fresh Air programs in their communities. Others found my critical stance unfair. A few reprimanded me for writing about the program at all because they felt it was just too important of a resource to bring under academic scrutiny. But the vast majority of readers wanted to know more.

So I kept on writing. I continued to travel to archives and interview participants. This book is the result of a decade's worth of research that began when I first encountered that photo in the EMM record room.

As I near the completion of this book, I realize that I know much more about the white people featured in the photo than I do about the African American girl. I do not know exactly when it was taken, but most probably in the late 1950s. Although I do not know the names of the white crowd members, I do know that John Boll, a Mennonite farmer and businessman from Manheim, Pennsylvania, holds papers in his hands as his wife, Edith Boll, cradles one of their children in her arms. Like many white Mennonites in southeastern Pennsylvania, the Bolls hosted children connected to Mennonite urban congregations. However, I know much less about the Fresh Air girl. She appears to be fairly young—perhaps seven or eight—although not as young as some participants. I do know that the photo was taken at the train station in Lancaster, Pennsylvania, soon after her arrival from New York City. The tag around her neck indicates that she has been labeled for pickup at a location far removed from friends and family who could identify her on sight. I have not been able to discover her name.

Hundreds of thousands of children like the girl featured in this photo spent summer vacations away from their families in ventures fueled by anecdotes alone. All those involved in promoting and organizing the programs asserted that a two-week stay in the country had a meaningful impact on the life of a city child. However, these promoters used only anecdotes and carefully crafted stories to defend their practice. At no point between 1939 and 1979 did any of the programs present convincing, research-based evidence that the programs improved children's lives.[3] The assumption that fourteen days of interracial connection had enough power to transform the lives of children had widespread support but little empirical grounding.

The white volunteers pictured in the photo represent the rural and suburban residents who hosted Fresh Air children for decades and saw themselves as champions of the downtrodden. Through the 1940s, many hosts participated in order to offer a simple act of charity to white ethnic children of city tenements. Beginning in the 1950s, many more signed on to host an African American, Asian American, or Latino child as part of a massive, widespread race relations effort. During the height of the Cold War, still others sought to take part in—as Fresh Air Fund administrator Bud Lewis came to call it—an experiment in the production of democracy. Volunteers poured countless hours into transport, hosting, entertainment, and relationship building. Those most committed maintained some kind of connection with the children they welcomed into their homes, even if only by the occasional letter, phone call, or visit to the city. The hosts used the relational, conceptual, and social tools that they had available at the time, ones that left them ill-equipped to address the underlying issues of power and privilege that separated them from the children they hosted. They focused first and foremost on the publicity material fashioned by eager boosters about a popular program, one in which children reported that "they liked . . . the smell of the air, . . . the green trees . . . the flowers . . . even . . . [the] frogs."[4]

The photo thus captures a multilayered moment. On one level, the photo depicts a local group of charitable, white Pennsylvania Mennonites hosting a destitute, black urban child. Yet the photo also reveals the inner workings of an interlocking array of white-led, child-centered institutions intent on ending poverty and racism through one-on-one acts of charity.[5] At the same time, the photo illustrates an example of national white neoliberalism in the latter half of the twentieth century, one focused on privatization, minimal government, and reduced appropriations for social services. This book explores all three levels of the Fresh Air story: the local, the institutional, and the national.

When I first encountered this photo of the Fresh Air girl surrounded by well-meaning white people, I was not just intrigued; I was also discomfited. I was left unsure about how I felt about the photo. Should I excoriate it as did many critics in the 1960s and 1970s as yet another example of the paternalistic excess of naïve white people wanting so desperately to do something about the state of race relations in America but lacking the will and resources—whether social, historical, or political—to offer a more nuanced response? Should I draw attention to the deliberate separation of child from parent? Should I ask for pity for the black girl, as did most of the white boosters involved in the programs? Should I highlight the courage, fortitude, and creativity of the children who learned how to negotiate racial boundaries at a very young age? Or should I ignore the photo and focus instead on happier images that affirm the kindness of white hosts who took black and brown children into their homes?

The photo still leaves me unsettled, but I also think it is an evocative and accurate reflection of a multivalent Fresh Air movement. And so I return to the photo yet again. It is a complex image, one that is replete with notions of place, race, and identity. One that touches on prejudice, fear, innocence, and superiority. It is an image that asks how we decide whose lives matter inside our national household. The photo resonates with any political moment—which is to say most of them—in which we struggle to determine both boundaries of exclusion and gates of welcome.

Acknowledgments

As with all intellectual enterprises, a book arises in the midst of many conversations. I am grateful for those who have engaged with this project. My colleagues in the history department, African American Studies program, and women's, gender, and sexuality studies program at the University of Montana have offered unwavering encouragement and insightful feedback. I am especially thankful for splendid interlocutors like Robert Greene, Anya Jabour, Mike Mayer, Jody Pavilack, Kyle Volk, and Jeff Wiltse. During his all-too-brief sojourn with us before heading back to New York, Christopher Pastore also provided excellent counsel about the craft of writing itself. The provost's office at UM awarded me a sabbatical to complete this manuscript, and the University Research and Creativity Committee funded a trip to the Northeast during which I visited multiple archives and encountered some of my most important sources. Peter Staudenmaier, Geeta Raval, my brother Jud Shearer, and his partner, Sue Ann Foster, provided wonderful hospitality each evening after I was done flitting from archive to archive during the day.

Scholars in the fields of childhood and environmental history have been incredibly helpful—Pamela Riney-Kehrberg and Barry Ross Muchnick provided especially astute feedback—as have colleagues in the Afro-American Religious History group of the American Academy of Religion and the Association for the Study of African American Life and History. The 2014 Fannie Lou Hamer National Institute on Citizenship and Democracy in Jackson, Mississippi, also provided conversation partners and interlocutors extraordinaire. Special thanks go to Jeff Kolnick, Barry Lee, Jolie Sheffer, Jervette Ward, and Dwana Waugh for their particularly insightful commentary. Courtney Bender, Josef Sorett, and participants in the Religion and Politics in American Public Life lecture series at Columbia University provided me with the opportunity to develop key components of my argument for a lecture there. In the same way, lecture invitations from Provost Fred Kniss at Eastern Mennonite University and Stacy Keogh George from Whitworth University allowed me to hone the interpretive frame I have employed in this book.

The archivists and librarians at the institutions listed in the appendix have been unfailingly supportive. In particular, Linnea Anderson at the Elmer L. Andersen Library, Simone Horst at the Menno Simons Historical Library, Wayne Kempton at the archives of the Episcopal Diocese of New York, and John Thiesen at the Mennonite Library and Archives of Bethel College provided essential support. The staff of UM's interlibrary loan department also served above and beyond the call of duty. I likewise owe a debt of gratitude for the on-site assistance offered by Andrew Jungclaus at Columbia University, Ian Lewenstein at the University of Minnesota, and James Ward at the Library of Virginia when I could not travel in person to these collections. James Lont organized and recorded a conversation of former Fresh Air hosts in Graafschap, Michigan, after only one phone call from me. And Molly Williams, my intrepid work-study student from 2013 through 2015, diligently assisted me in the tedious task of documenting Fresh Air hosting locations.

I am furthermore thankful for all those who spoke with my colleagues and me about various Fresh Air experiences. They were unfailingly forthcoming, honest, and courageous in relating stories that were, in many cases, difficult to tell.

My editors at Cornell—Brian Balogh, Michael J. McGandy, and Jonathan Zimmerman—have been steadfastly professional, consistently perceptive, and more percipient than I sometimes wished (although I always came to appreciate their feedback).

Two additional groups have earned my deep gratitude. First, the members of our weekly supper club—now meeting in its eighth year—have offered delicious food, spirited conversation, and tons of teasing. I don't know what I would do without you all—Beth and Britta Baker, Brad Clough, Julie and Steve Edwards, Mark and Kara Hansen, Clary Loisel, and Ken Thompson. Finally, I am ever grateful for the support, encouragement, and droll badinage that my life partner, Cheryl, and our two sons—Dylan and Zach—brought to me in the midst of writing this book. They kept me grounded, balanced, and laughing out loud.

TWO WEEKS EVERY SUMMER

Introduction

A RECKONING OF CHILDHOOD, RACE, AND NEOLIBERALISM

Gee, it smells good to be home.

Unidentified Fresh Air Fund boy, New York City, 1972

Since 1877, Fresh Air programs from Maine to Montana brought hundreds of thousands of urban children to rural homes and camps for summer vacations. Through the 1950s, few had criticized the annual ventures. That changed in the 1960s. In 1963 a resident of Bennington, Vermont, noted that African American Fresh Air children became an "economic and social threat" to their former hosts after they reached adolescence. Although younger children could share intimate home space, white residents "repulsed" black teens.[1] Three years later another critic called such social service programs "paternalistic arrogance."[2] By 1967, black and Latino residents from the Chelsea neighborhood of Manhattan labeled programs like Fresh Air "irrelevant, discriminatory, and not really committed to integrating."[3]

But it was not until the 1970s that the most intense criticism erupted. When the National Association of Black Social Workers declared in 1971 that placement of black children in white homes for fosterage and adoption was cultural "genocide," Fresh Air critics intensified their rhetoric.[4] In addition to ironically calling for city-based "stale-air" vacation programs directed at white suburban children, critics asserted that taking black and brown children out of the city was, in fact, "psychologically damaging."[5] Busing children to the country or suburbs, asserted the critics, harmed the children by instilling false expectations about their ability to relocate to such nonurban settings. That same year a blistering critique of the Cleveland "Friendly Town" Fresh Air program appeared in the pages of the historic black newspaper *Call and Post* excoriating the Inner City

Protestant Parish for transporting children to "areas which lock them out" the rest of the year. Under the heading "Brushing up on Paternalism," reporter Ellen Delmonte mocked not only the short duration of the suburban vacations but also the "magnanimous" gift of a new toothbrush given to each child as she or he climbed aboard buses bound for southern Ohio, western Pennsylvania, and rural New York. As Delmonte queried, "[W]as this their way of showing how they love all the little 'cullud' kids?"[6]

Such acerbic criticism marks one end of the Fresh Air movement's narrative arc. *Two Weeks Every Summer: Fresh Air Children and the Problem of Race in America* tells the story of the Fresh Air movement's efforts to bring city children to the country for summer vacations in homes and camps from the onset of World War II through the end of the 1970s. In addition to the words and actions of both adult hosts and critics, the exploits and insights of the Fresh Air children guide this narrative.[7] Together they tell the story of a movement that was active in twenty states, that was based out of more than thirty-five cities, and that connected with more than one and a half million children from its inception through 1979.[8]

That Fresh Air story hinges on four themes. First is the centrality of nature discourse to the Fresh Air enterprise. Promoters returned time and again to the notion that city children had never encountered lawns or green space. In the process, they promoted the countryside by disparaging the city. A second theme focuses on the multiple ways in which guest children protected their interests even while the adult hosts and administrators dismissed their actions as simple recalcitrance. The children surprised their hosts by their politeness as much as their truculence but had to face racial bias about their standards of behavior at every turn. The third central theme, the pursuit and promotion of innocence through age caps, follows from the second. Hosts preferred younger children because the older the guests became, the more problems the hosts perceived. A final theme emerges from the adult promoters' persistent concern about sex. Program administrators fixated on the children's knowledge of intimate matters as they tried to keep interracial romance from blossoming. Each chapter expands on these themes and introduces related topics such as health care, religion, swimming, finance, and power.

At some point in the forty years analyzed here, nearly every major urban center in the Northeast and Midwest hosted an initiative to offer short summer stays for children from the city. Although rarely found in the Deep South, each of those programs based in Baltimore, Chicago, Cleveland, New York, Pittsburgh, Seattle, and elsewhere sent children out and collected them back (see figure 2).

The thousands of Fresh Air households who responded to invitations to join in Fresh Air work were usually white, rural or suburban. The hosts were usually

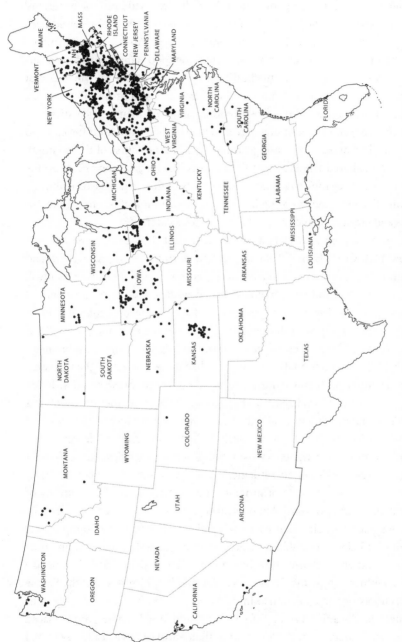

FIGURE 2. This map locates more than 1,100 hosting sites from 1939 to 1979, culled from archival sources, newspaper accounts, and publicity materials. The Fresh Air Fund alone claimed more than 2,500 hosting sites but would not provide a list of those locations. Map designed by Bill Nelson based on data compiled by Molly Williams.

home owners with their own children tended by a stay-at-home parent—most often the mother. Although poor white ethnic children had been the programs' original beneficiaries, the hundreds of thousands of children who received invitations for summer vacations in host homes or Fresh Air–run camps usually were—after the 1950s—black or brown, came from poor families, had been vetted by both social service and medical providers, and (in the vast majority of the cases) lived inside a city's limits. The cadre of organizers, administrators, boosters, and volunteers who wrote promotional pieces, managed logistics, vetted the children, and raised funds were also white, came from both the city and the country, had become increasingly professional in the course of the twentieth century, and believed fervently that their efforts had long-lasting effects on the children's lives. They took a far more positive view of the programs, contributing to an initiative designed "to bring inspiration, education and fun to children of all races and creeds trapped in . . . [the city's] stone caverns."[9]

Four types of programs structured the movement. Those run by newspapers like New York City's *Herald Tribune* emerged during the Progressive Era and outlasted other sponsors. Originally concerned both with generating goodwill for the paper and combating malnutrition, newspapers dropped their official sponsorships by the 1960s as budgets tightened and nonprofits professionalized. The independent nonprofits that remained made nature, race, and poverty their chief concern amid the effects of the second Great Migration and the subsequent white flight. Denominational-run programs like those offered by the Christian Reformed Church proliferated during the middle of the twentieth century, driven by a concern for child evangelism. Throughout the four decades on which this book concentrates, religiously affiliated programs became increasingly focused on racial matters as church groups dealt with the aftermath of desegregation and the advent of civil rights activism. Social service agencies and settlement houses like New York's Union Settlement Association included Fresh Air vacations among the broad range of programs they offered from the beginning of the twentieth century onward. Although also providing city-based summer programming, such agencies focused more on day trips and longer camp excursions but did help send children to private homes as well, usually in an effort to expose children to nature and white norms. Civic-religious associations like the joint venture run by the Ecumenical Metropolitan Ministry and the Seattle Public Schools or the cooperative initiatives organized by local congregations and Rotary or Kiwanis clubs appeared after World War I. These groups placed racial and class concerns at the forefront of their efforts as civic leaders searched for ways to respond to growing racial foment and urban unrest.

The interlocking but organizationally distinct groups that made up the movement used the same terminology and program design to market their initiatives.

As the oldest, largest, and highest-profile rural hosting program, the *Herald Tribune* Fresh Air Fund provided the model, and others copied it. Independent groups like Chicago's City Missionary Society and the Episcopal Diocese of New York adopted the *Tribune*'s "Fresh Air" label to describe their overall efforts and borrowed the "Friendly Town" title to publicize the home-based portion of their initiatives. All involved treated the home stays and camp stays as part of a single effort to save children from the city.[10] To indicate this programmatic unity, "Fresh Air movement," "Fresh Air program," or simply "Fresh Air" will refer to the full breadth of rural hosting ventures for children from the city, including both those that sent children to homes and those that sent them to camps. At the same time, the term "Fresh Air Fund" or simply the "Fund" will be reserved for the *Herald Tribune*'s program. Independent sponsors will be noted where indicated.

The children's experience during the summer vacations varied widely. Some children returned to the same host family for more than one summer, in a small number of cases as many as six or seven times. About half the children returned to the same home at least twice, but only about 10 percent returned to the same home more than two times. In other communities, hosts rarely offered re-invitations. A smaller percentage got to stay for extended visits of a month or longer, and some programs only offered a week or weekend vacation, but the vast majority returned home after two weeks. Between 1939 and 1979, an overwhelming majority of the children stayed in homes rather than camps. Upon occasion a select group—at most 10 percent of the total participants—spent Christmas vacation with their rural hosts. And although sponsors rarely found it difficult to recruit children interested in participating in the programs, a familial and social rumor network relayed cautionary tales about what to do and what to avoid doing when traveling to the country.

Despite strong interest from the children, many critics joined the vitriolic columnist from Cleveland in raising questions about Fresh Air. Even the director of the *Herald Tribune* program acknowledged the "perennial and persistent" criticism that their programs did "more harm than good," an assessment in keeping with similar criticisms of white-led social service programs by African American and Latino urban leaders during the 1960s and 1970s. The children, said the critics, would "become disillusioned" and "embittered by sampling a much better life."[11] As another queried, "What is the good of exposing these youngsters to the comfort and pleasure of country life and then sending them back to the same dismal slums?"[12]

The emergence of such criticism coincided with the shift to hosting children of color. This book begins with the onset of World War II, in 1939, when the hosting of a child of color in a white home was still a rarity and ends in 1979, the year that staff and local organizers at the Fresh Air Fund admitted that racial prejudice and a "rising tide of suburban apathy" had dramatically curtailed their volunteer host base.[13] Within the space of forty years, the Fresh Air movement transitioned from a program that brought an almost exclusively white group of children to stay with white families to a program that brought an almost exclusively black and brown group to stay with white families. As urban racial demographics shifted, so did the various programs' goals. Rather than restore the children's health and counter malnutrition, Fresh Air ventures became much more focused on bridging the racial divide and introducing children to middle-class suburban values. That transition to serving children of color offered Fresh Air programmers their most daunting challenge. The story of how they responded spans the middle four decades of the twentieth century while also tracing the shifts and patterns in the discourse about childhood innocence and its often ironic intertwining with racism in the United States. In sum, *Two Weeks Every Summer* examines the racially transformative years between 1939 and 1979 in order to explore how one-on-one models of social change influenced patterns of racial subordination.

The tensions evident in a program both lauded and excoriated for its race relations record reveal the social forces at play from the beginning of the 1940s through the end of the 1970s. In particular, the qualities of childhood innocence reiterated by promoters and lambasted by critics served political purposes—in this case, to promote a particular response to mid-century racial conflict.[14] Fresh Air promoters did not just offer their ventures alongside other, more confrontational efforts to address racial inequity; they also argued that their measures were superior. Comparing their hosting ventures to those of the 1961 civil rights Freedom Riders, one promoter insisted that Fresh Air initiatives created "better relationships and better understandings."[15]

And the boosters had a point. By comparison to other interracial initiatives, the rural summer visits offered greater intimacy, more interaction, and less risk for white participants. During civil rights marches, black and white activists rubbed shoulders for several hours but usually returned home to separate living rooms. The activists who crossed racial lines in the early years of the Student Nonviolent Coordinating Committee's integration efforts and voter registration drives lived together for a time, but these interracial practices generally came to an end by 1966. Schoolchildren who attended interracial classes did connect across racial lines, but those relationships frequently snagged on the controversies surrounding school desegregation during the 1950s and 1960s and busing during the 1970s. Other interracial venues like military barracks and sports locker rooms did build interracial bridges but affected proportionately fewer individuals.[16] By contrast, Fresh Air programs integrated living rooms, lasted for decades, and bused black and brown children to white communities with no legal interference.

Boosters, administrators, and volunteers in the thousands countered their critics by telling a nonthreatening story. They focused on crafting a narrative about black and brown children restored to full health and well-being through short stays in the country.[17] The rhetoric worked. Although hosting efforts waned by the end of the 1970s, during the peak years between 1968 and 1975 white hosts welcomed upwards of 16,000 children per summer—the vast majority of them African American and Latino—in the Fresh Air Fund's program alone. Many of those children, once on site at their hosting locale, disrupted the story told about them by wrinkling their noses at the smell of manure, complaining about bugs, and growing homesick for their urban homes. Yet the children's efforts to challenge the racism they encountered and participate in the programs on their own terms could not entirely refute the rhetoric of innocence that brought them out of the city. During the period of peak civil rights activity in the 1950s and 1960s, leaders of the Fresh Air movement stuck tenaciously to a common narrative, a story focused on individual change, told by well-intentioned white people, featured in the media, and divorced from demonstration. Most Fresh Air hosts and organizers genuinely desired an end to racial strife. They believed that hosting children of different racial groups for two weeks in the country could solve the country's racial problems one child at a time. In so doing, the hosts' feelings dictated the national narrative about Fresh Air vacationing.

When approached from the perspective of the children, however, a different story emerges. This narrative, one that few adults recognized at the time, shows how the young Fresh Air visitors engaged in their own civil rights struggle. In far more intimate settings than those entered by Martin Luther King Jr. and his associates, the children integrated racially segregated neighborhoods, challenged racist stereotypes, and demanded respect. Even though most ventured into white communities for short, two-week stints at a time, they nonetheless confronted crank phone calls, stood up to racial epithets, and dealt with verbal harassment in living rooms and camp cabins where no reporters witnessed their efforts. Sometimes the children fought back with words. Other times, with their fists. Whether withholding information about their home life, objecting to rules that excluded teenagers, or refusing to spend their vacations working without pay, the children did not always conform to their hosts' visions of cooperative, well-mannered, compliant innocents. The hosts viewed them, in short, as sassy. But the children's actions speak more of nascent activism than disrespectful behavior.

By paying attention to these three interlocking narratives—of the boosters, critics, and children—this book expands and refines much of what has been written about U.S. racism by revealing the complex negotiations involved in the hosting of children across racial lines. Some authors have attempted to explain why racial inequity persisted through the 1970s by examining voting rights, presidential elections, and congressional acts.[18] Others have focused on interracial marriage, housing patterns, and cultural stereotypes.[19] Without question, historians need to analyze public policy and social and cultural patterns to understand racism's longevity. For example, activists and elected representatives shaped the outcomes of the civil rights struggle. Yet the Fresh Air movement's well-meaning hosts, trenchant critics, and redoubtable children also helped determine what would and would not change in the country's racial constellation. Hosts focused energy on integrating their homes and neighborhoods through carefully structured, time-limited visits. Critics called foul at one-way, white-led, parent-demeaning programming. Guest children challenged the attitudes and actions of the white adults they encountered and the host children they befriended.

In addition to revealing the complexities of mid-twentieth-century racial negotiation, the Fresh Air story also shows the close association that Americans have posited between nature and childhood innocence, a notion employed by adults throughout this period first and foremost as a quality of untroubled naïveté about sex. Although innocence could also refer to freedom from the demands of work, politics, and culture, intimate matters remained most salient. Throughout the nineteenth century, artists, writers, and philosophers linked the idea of childhood innocence with nature and the country.[20] Historians such as Sarah Burns have suggested that this nature-centric impulse intensified as adults pined for forgotten youth in the face of industrialization.[21] Yet Fresh Air promoters attempted, and in many ways succeeded, in extending the linkage of nature and childhood innocence far into the twentieth century. In donor campaigns such as the Fresh Air Fund's 1962 "give summer to a child" advertising blitz, publicists and administrators effectively froze in time and space the idea of childhood wonder before all things natural.[22] Rapturous prose about the children's immersion in nature appeared as frequently in the 1970s as it did in the 1940s. Although various scholars have warned against making claims about innocence devoid of the particularities of time and place, participants in the Fresh Air movement stabilized the linkage between nature and childhood through sheer force of repetition.[23]

Innocence in Fresh Air programs also involved sex. To be certain, promoters evoked innocence as they extolled the country and sought to keep the children under control. Likewise, critics touched on innocence as they denounced programs that cut black and brown adults out of the equation. But it was sex and the hosts' attendant fears of interracial romance that generated sustained attention. The Fresh Air story reveals just how central concerns about interracial sexual attraction—even concerning prepubescent children—remained during the middle three decades of the twentieth century.[24] In keeping with the tradition of Romantics like William Wordsworth who emphasized the holiness and redemptive capacity of children, most Fresh Air promoters countered all hints of sexuality by describing the children as wholesome waifs whenever possible.[25] Critics shied away from addressing the issue at all. And the children, especially preteens and adolescents, fell in love, tested sexual boundaries, and in too many instances dealt with adult sexual predators in homes they had been told would be safe havens. Although program promoters invested significant energy in shielding white households from the perceived threat of black teenagers, in truth white men proved far more threatening to the guest children.

Grounded by the 1960s in a rhetoric of sexless, nature-bound, hope-filled, health-infused, race-based innocence, Fresh Air provided a model by which white suburbanites and rural residents judged other racial exchanges. During what Martin Luther King Jr. called "the most segregated hour" of 11:00 on Sunday mornings, hosts proudly pointed out the "shiny black faces" scattered through their sanctuaries during a 1960 Fresh Air venture.[26] In 1963 a church leader from Newton, Kansas, claimed that sending mission groups to the South did not confront white prejudice as effectively as did hosting black Fresh Air children.[27] When racial rebellions erupted in urban centers in 1968, reporters noted the concern expressed by the white suburban hosts for the safety of their young guests who had returned to the city.[28] As one host asserted in 1962, because "a mixture of all races" lived "together peaceably" during Fresh Air trips, adults should be able to do the same.[29] Although evidence of the long-term effects of hosting Fresh Air children remains as scant as evidence of the effects of being hosted, the claims that Fresh Air programs improved the racial order for all involved received widespread attention, influencing opinion across the country. The extent of the national coverage suggests that positive sentiment about white-led Fresh Air ventures prompted at least some white suburbanites to more readily criticize black-led activism. Contemporary scholars have simply ignored the race relations benchmarks established by Fresh Air programs.[30]

Six thematically focused chapters tell the story of the Fresh Air movement. Chapter 1, "Knowledge, Girl, Nature: Fresh Air Tensions prior to World War II," examines foundational stressors in the early Fresh Air programs. During the late nineteenth century, adults participated in the movement in part because the programs allowed them to exercise a modicum of control over their lives in the face of ever more impersonal bureaucratic forces. The concrete and accessible design of the program prompted white, middle-class hosts to bring urban children—the vast majority of them poor, white ethnics from immigrant families—into their homes. Those children came to embody three central tensions within the movement during this period: knowledge against ignorance, girl against boy, and nature against city. Adults in the programs claimed more knowledge than their charges, preferred female guests, and trumpeted the superiority of the country over urban environs. In response the children resisted discipline, expressed preferences for placement, and renewed their hosts' appreciation of nature. As they negotiated these innocence-inflected pressures, children and promoters drew national attention to their efforts and garnered far-reaching support for continuing the summer vacation programs.

The next four chapters focus on the movement's defining themes during the central period under study, the four-decade spread between 1939 and 1979. Fresh Air hosting was never just about programs that directed well-meaning adults down a particular path of service; children also played an important role in defining program outcomes. The first of these chapters emphasizes the children's responses to their white hosts.[31] In chapter 2—"Church, Concrete, Pond: How Innocence Got Disrupted," the children emerge as independent actors.[32] Rather than conform to the arc of a redemption tale in which the country saves the city by the intervention of well-meaning adults, the children themselves expressed their love of urban pastimes, streetscapes, and swimming. As they sat in pews and relaxed in camp cabins, the children told stories about themselves and the world around them that disrupted the Fresh Air narrative. In swimming, girls and boys especially found freedom from adult control even as they confronted racial barriers blocking their access to aquatic adventure.

"Grass, Color, Sass: How the Children Shaped Fresh Air," the third chapter, explores three of the central arenas in which children found ways to shape the programs. Program promoters certainly managed to present the hosts and guests as unblemished pairs. Yet, within the discourse about the beauty of the natural world, the value of good race relations, and positive behavioral conduct, children subverted these messages by spurning nature's wonders, taking on the role of teacher to their hosts, and refusing to cooperate with their hosts' directives. In the midst of the storm of criticism arising from the black and brown freedom struggles, some of the children pushed back against white control despite disciplinary measures instituted to heighten the adults' authority. Rather than being passive recipients of white largesse, the children practiced their own racial code of conduct that at times frustrated and astounded hosting families and camp staff. In the course of their visits to the country, the children acted out race relations struggles, mirroring the social issues on the nightly news.

Chapter 4, "Sex, Seven, Sick: How Adults Kept the Children in Check," analyzes how the children's bold responses met the primary control mechanisms employed by Fresh Air administrators. In response to children who schooled their hosts, distrusted rural environments, and reworked the stories of redemption being told about them, adults involved in Fresh Air put in place strict gender segregation and age caps. Those in charge of the programs also instituted rigor-ous medical vetting procedures designed to protect hosts from contagious illness and sexually transmitted diseases by screening out unhealthy children; the hosts and their children received no such scrutiny. By the end of the period, promot-ers included black and brown children in their rhetoric about innocence but only for those children deemed medically fit and preadolescent. Once the specter of interracial sex appeared, administrators removed children from any setting where they might become romantically involved with a member of the opposite sex. In the end, the adults instituted control mechanisms at odds with their goal of "interracial harmony."[33]

The fifth chapter, "Milk, Money, Power: How Fresh Air Sold Its Programs," demonstrates the ways in which adult boosters packaged and sold the cultural, social, and democratic relevancy of the Fresh Air ventures to national audiences. Those efforts resulted in a thoroughly American institution, one associated with pristine symbols of the country, backed by the financial engines of capitalism, and associated with power brokers in politics, entertainment, business, and the military. A potent blend of volunteerism, charity, agrarian husbandry, and high-profile endorsements laid a foundation for long-term success despite criti-cism of contradictions implicit in the boosters' egalitarian narrative and restric-tive policies. In the process, a set of social service organizations kept the public's attention on interpersonal, short-term, charity-based programs rather than on institutional equality and systemic change.

The final chapter, "Greeting, Gone, Good: Racialized Reunion and Rejection in Fresh Air," tells the contrasting stories of two Fresh Air children in order to highlight the breadth of the children's experience. Luis Diaz cherished the memories of carefree summers spent with families. However, Janice Batts found the trips traumatic, harmful, and filled with troubling memories of events she continued to unpack long into her adulthood. The prevailing legacies of the mid-twentieth-century Fresh Air movement lie somewhere in the midst of these twin tales. Diaz embodies the program's "greeting" or *racialized reunion*, the idea that racial freedom could be realized if everyone got along as well as did Fresh Air participants. Batts embodies the departures—i.e., "gone"—or *racialized rejection*, the idea that interracial relationships were not worth supporting once children became equals. Fresh Air movement leaders carried both legacies into the twenty-first century. Images of racialized reunion peppered publicity; age caps fostered racialized rejection. Despite the good will, interpersonal connec-tions, and childhood initiative fostered by the programs, the Fresh Air movement remained bound by these two themes. Participating organizations relied on both reunion and rejection to foster the exchange—i.e., the "good"—between white adults and black and brown children, a historical insight which suggests that the

black and brown freedom struggles depended as much on ideas of racial separation as on the notion of a racially integrated "beloved community."[34]

Two Weeks Every Summer concludes with an epilogue that connects the end of
the 1970s with the present.

Back in the Municipal Stadium parking lot in 1971, where Fresh Air children
prepared to leave Cleveland with a free toothbrush in hand, all the players made
their bids. The organizers directed children on to the correct buses, hoping that
all would arrive safely at their assigned suburban homes. The critics wrote an
editorial intended to expose the program's paternalistic underbelly. The children
sought the benefit of a vacation, even knowing they were headed toward always
unfamiliar, many times unwelcoming, and sometimes hostile white communities. And the parents of the children—often reluctant, frequently suspicious, and
invariably pushed to the margins of the Fresh Air story—were also present, many
times instructing their children on what to say and what not to say to the strange
white people that they would soon meet.

The photographer who snapped a picture of the blonde and blue-eyed
emissary laden with new toothbrushes for each child captured a tableau of
twentieth-century neoliberalism. A thorough history of the racially focused
strands of that liberalism requires the perspectives of those the photographer
featured: white liberals like the Pro Brush representative, her employers, and the
Fresh Air organizers. But the perspectives of those outside the frame—the children, their parents, the critics—help craft a much more complex history. The
story told here examines deeply intimate spaces where connections at the level
of family, home, and sex were both fostered and severed. It allows us to identify
the widespread anxieties that limited true social reorganization. It prepares the
ground for a more honest reckoning of the promises and failures of civil rights
era programs. This history, in the end, assesses the themes of nature, control,
inequality, and innocence in order to present a clearer picture of the problem of
race in America.

KNOWLEDGE, GIRL, NATURE
Fresh Air Tensions prior to World War II

Prolific illustrator James Montgomery Flagg, best known for his patriotic posters of Uncle Sam, captured Fresh Air appeal in a pencil drawing. Flagg depicted a nine-year-old girl preparing her five-year-old brother for a Fresh Air trip to the country. In the sketch, the young girl washes her brother's face. Flagg penned a caption to accompany the drawing: "You must be washed, dear, we're goin' ter the country an' you might get the beautiful flowers dirty."[1] In his 1910 drawing, Flagg featured the themes most central to Fresh Air narratives prior to World War II: the naïveté of children, the prominence of girls, and the restorative power of nature. He portrayed two young urbanites who knew little of country life, offered a sympathetic portrayal of a girl taking charge of her brother, and referred to an abundance of natural flowers. Like the fund-raisers who solicited his artwork, Flagg sold Fresh Air based on depictions of nature-centric, female-centered, naïveté-dependent children.

Flagg had good company. Between 1877 and 1938, Fresh Air boosters described children from the city in sweeping generalities that emphasized the young visitors' nature-centered condition. In promotional accounts the children's innocent state—one defined by freedom from adult responsibility, lack of sexual knowledge, and proximity to the divine—turned on their simple union with nature. A staple of Fresh Air literature of the late nineteenth and early twentieth century, the image of children at play in the sun-drenched, tree-filled, grass-strewn countryside filled the pages of newspapers and magazines. For instance, in 1912 Fresh Air enthusiast Alexander Hynd-Lindsay effused over "a band of little children . . .

out under the deep blue of God's sky, playing upon Nature's own green carpet."
He described the children's laughter as "sweeter than an angel's song," emphasized their "innocent vision," and recounted their "marvel . . . wonder . . . and . . .
joy" as the "sweets of Nature" enveloped them.[2] Whether or not the children's
voices filled the accounts, program promoters like Flagg and Hynd-Lindsay peppered their reports with assurances of the children's unsullied state.

Promoters featured such accounts from the Gilded Age through the eve of
World War II. During these first sixty-one years, promoters, hosts, and the guest
children themselves contributed to the growth and development of a program
few anticipated would have the staying power and cultural reach to rival vener-
able charities such as the American Red Cross. The varied interactions between
the rural adult hosts and their urban guests reveal three dichotomies at the programs' roots: naïveté/knowledge, girl/boy, and city/country. Those three dichotomies remained consistent as the movement grew and developed in the midst of
increasing urbanization, the rise and fall of the Progressive Era, and an awak-
ened conscience regarding race relations among white northern churchgoers.
The combination of ideas about the children's innocence and the overt historical
forces of urbanization, industrialization, and bureaucratization prompted hosts
to invite children of all ethnic and racial backgrounds into the intimate environments of kitchens, parlors, and bedrooms. Presented as ignorant of country ways,
free of sexual knowledge, and enraptured with nature, the children who stood in
such apparent wonder before nature's glory offered hundreds of thousands of
adults a way to counter a growing sense of helplessness in the face of ever more
impersonal charity, encroaching federal bureaucracy, and the fading memory of
a rural way of life.[3] By taking in credulous children but not their worldly wise
parents, the hosts felt that they could make a difference. In the midst of offering
their hosts fresh hope, the children also took hesitant steps toward establishing
their own agency.

The ambitious project of relocating children to the country and returning
them to the city drew on a variety of intellectual resources. Early Gilded Age
reformers focused on notions of natural bliss. By the turn of the century, promoters focused on hygienic purity. Later Progressive Era activists drew on patriotic ideals to assimilate foreign children into the nation.[4] Yet the dichotomies of
naïveté/knowledge, girl/boy, and city/country reveal how consistently program
promoters used and shaped the idea of innocence through 1938.

And they crafted the idea carefully. The boosters first brought Christian-infused
ideals of freedom from knowledge of sin, sexuality, and ethical responsibility to
their interactions with the children. But as they promoted Fresh Air programs
they also linked innocence to nature, focused on fund-raising, and negotiated
race, class, and gender. Only tangentially did they connect their ideas about

innocence to the actions taken by the children during their country visits. In their passion to bring as many children as possible to the country, the promoters declared that the innocence they had crafted was not just a condition; it was also a location, one found outside the city. By the time World War II began, Fresh Air promoters had long practice in emphasizing the children's naïveté, focusing on the white and feminine, and immersing the children in nature.

Knowledge

An exploration of the rhetoric and response to children's knowledge first requires a brief recap of the breadth, growth, and development of Fresh Air programs during their initial sixty years. Prior to the founding of the Fresh Air movement, various organizations in Britain, Germany, and the United States had transported children from the city to the country. Some children became indentured to rural employers; others joined farm families as foster children.[5] By 1854, the Children's Aid Society (CAS), under the leadership of Charles Loring Brace, had instituted a "placing out" system—also known as "orphan trains"—in which children from New York City traveled west by train until chosen by farm families. In return for room, board, schooling, and religious instruction, the children worked on the farms, but, unlike indenture, the arrangements remained informal.[6] The host family could request a replacement at any time, and the CAS agent could remove the child if the host family proved unsatisfactory.[7] Although fraught with problems ranging from neglect to abuse and burdened by controversy over whether institutions or home placements offered more benefit to destitute children, the placing out movement brought as many as 350,000 children from the city to the country from the mid-nineteenth century through the end of the Progressive Era.[8] Although focused on long-term work placements rather than short-term vacation stays, the orphan trains provided an early example of how to take children out of the city and bring them to rural settings.

One organization led all others in building on such rural placement models to establish Fresh Air practice, reach, and popularity. The *Herald Tribune* Fresh Air Fund, so named by 1882 in honor of its primary publicity partner, developed the movement and established its most enduring practices.[9] Originating seven years prior to the Fund's founding in 1877, Country Week of Boston and the Country Week Association of Philadelphia offered week-long visits to the country for poor children; however, the Fund was the first to provide two-week stays.[10] Because of the efforts of Willard Parsons, a Presbyterian minister who served as the organization's executive director through 1906, the organization grew to provide country sojourns for as many as 13,000 children per summer by his retirement.[11] Working alongside leaders from other Progressive Era organizations like the Children's Aid Society, the National Playground Association, and the Camp Fire Girls, Parsons joined efforts to protect children from the city. According to Parsons and his contemporaries, as the embodiment of the nation's future the children needed saving.[12] A series of capable administrators followed Parsons and initiated camping programs, promoted home visitations under the "Friendly Town" slogan, and saw the organization through the 1916 polio epidemic, the stock market crash of 1929, and the influenza outbreaks of 1918 and 1930.[13] Despite such setbacks, by 1931 the organization had doubled its clientele base with the help of a vibrant network of religious institutions, social service agencies, and civic organizations that selected and registered potential Fresh Air visitors.

Developing in an era defined by both burgeoning bureaucracy and an increasing emphasis on "democratic, affectionate, and child-centered" family life, the initiative flourished.[14] From 1920 through 1939, the *Herald Tribune*'s Fresh Air Fund served an average of 14,628 children per year, with a low of 9,740 in 1920 and a high of 17,514 in 1925. By 1939, the Fund served about 14,000 children in a year. Through the 1930s roughly half of the children ended up in homes and half in Fresh Air camps, a split that would become more and more weighted toward home stays following World War II. As sustained by frequent reports in a host of media outlets, the Fresh Air Fund defined the field of rural hosting from its inception through the start of World War II and beyond.

The Fresh Air Fund's predominance at points obscured a host of programs operating under the "Fresh Air" name. Some, like the *Herald Tribune*'s primary competitor, the *New York Times*, challenged the *Herald Tribune*'s leading role by claiming in 1890 that it had originated the Fresh Air work, an unfounded assertion.[15] Others forged ahead by the middle of the 1890s with their own versions of the program such as the *Christian Herald*'s Montlawn summer home for tenement children in Nyack, only a few miles north of New York City on the Hudson River.[16] The Summer Outing Program of the Charity Organization Society mirrored the Fresh Air efforts at the end of the nineteenth century by placing children in country homes so that the youngsters could benefit from the "mental uplift which comes from the sight of waving grain and swaying corn."[17] Philanthropic organizations like the Salvation Army and the Volunteers of America likewise developed their own Fresh Air initiatives. Day picnics, steamboat rides, and camping trips rather than home visits typified these programs, which were active through the first two decades of the twentieth century, but the scale of the day-long endeavors outmatched many of the Fresh Air Fund's highest-profile efforts. In Chicago, for example, the Volunteers of America sponsored a summer picnic in Washington Park that attracted as many as 25,000 children to the 1896 festivities.[18] Altogether, groups in New York City provided 188,742 outings in 1895, a number more than matched by the 356,531 combined outings provided in other cities that same year.[19] By that time, city children also had the opportunity to attend Fresh Air camps sponsored by the Boy Scouts, the Camp Fire Girls, the Sons of Daniel Boone, and the Woodcraft Indians.[20]

Fresh Air work proved popular in the international community as well. Dutch reformers initiated a program in the 1870s.[21] Canadians marked the founding of another Fresh Air fund in Toronto in 1901.[22] Even more prominently, yet another organization, separate from both the New York- and Toronto-based programs but carrying the same name, operated out of Great Britain beginning in 1892 under the auspices of newspaper publisher C. Arthur Pearson.[23] Active throughout the twentieth century, this Fresh Air Fund purported to serve more than a quarter million children in a single year by 1913, the vast majority of them sent on day trips to the country.[24] Other programs eventually began in Scotland and France as well, often in response to articles featuring the Fund's work.[25]

The Fresh Air ventures thus grew at a phenomenal rate amid this breadth of international programming. The *Christian Herald*'s Montlawn program had hosted 40,000 children by 1913.[26] In New York City the Harlem Children's Fresh Air Fund, a smaller program sponsored by the African American community with the backing of the historic black newspaper the *Amsterdam News*, served a thousand children at a time through day-long outings in metropolitan parks in 1927.[27] Although the numbers vacillated somewhat because of the economic constraints of the Great Depression, the Fresh Air Fund alone served more than 600,000 children prior to World War II.

Such growth stemmed in part from the Progressive Era shift away from church-based charity toward professional relief organizations. Organizations like the Fresh Air Fund and its many imitators readily integrated modern business practices to organize and implement the massive logistical undertaking involved in transporting tens of thousands of children from the city to the country and back again. No longer focused on saving souls for the church, charity leaders believed that they could end poverty itself if they designed organizations according to scientific principles and good business practices.[28] Sending children to the country in as efficient and sustainable manner as possible became a hallmark of the modern business practices that Progressive Era reformers held so dear.

The Fresh Air programs that would come to sponsor children like the girl who busily cleaned her brother's cheeks operated in much the same way. Most centrally, the initiatives aimed to save children from the harmful effects—identified in social and physical terms—of the ever more industrial city.[29] Adults need not apply. Fresh Air and other charity workers maintained that the city had damaged adults beyond repair.[30] As a result, from 1877 through the beginning of World

War II the programs publicized their efforts by abasing the city and valorizing the country. Whether in Boston or Seattle, reformers sought to provide children with a healthier environment for their development.[31] Such efforts flourished across the long Progressive Era wherever concern for protecting childhood coincided with efficient bureaucracies and transportation networks capable of managing the logistics of shuttling thousands of children to and from the countryside.

Yet time and region diversified the movement. Gilded Age evangelical Fresh Air programs focused on redeeming children weakened by malnutrition through no fault of their own. During the Progressive Era, a more scientific approach attempted to mold children and shape them—especially at camps—to pursue civic goals that would save the entire city. By World War I, Fresh Air programs had become a packaged commodity focused on exposing children to middle-class values.[32] Following the Great Migration, the programs took on the additional burden of bridging the racial divide.

This chronological shift from recuperative redemption to racial reconciliation unfolded amid limited regional diversity. Some cities simply started later than others. The Fresh Air hub in and around New York City set trends picked up in other metropolitan centers. By 1897, twenty-four cities representing thirteen states reported Fresh Air programs. Fresh Air programs flourished in Connecticut, Illinois, Indiana, Maine, Maryland, Massachusetts, Michigan, Minnesota, Missouri, Ohio, Pennsylvania, and Wisconsin. All these efforts began after the founding of the Fresh Air Fund. For example, initiatives in Chicago started only after New York organizations had tested their programs for a decade.[33]

However, regional differences in chronology and size did not lead to substantial program variations. Some planners offered longer stays than others but not according to any discernible regional pattern. Midwest and West Coast hosting ventures included proportionately more religiously sponsored programs and fewer newspaper-funded initiatives than in the Northeast, but this trend had as much to do with date of program founding as with geographical spread. Only when looking to the South did significant regional differences appear.

Southerners rarely joined in Fresh Air exchanges. Excepting anomalies like a few placements in Virginian households, a racially segregated camp-based program in Florence, South Carolina, and a denominationally sponsored initiative to bring children from Gulfport, Mississippi, to the upper Midwest, few southerners participated. From the 1950s onward, northern organizers attributed the lack of southern participation to racial prejudice on the part of rural hosts, a plausible explanation. It was not by accident that the Gulfport program sent participants on 24-hour-long bus rides to the North in order to find willing hosts. At the same time, unlike most white, middle-class suburbanites and rural residents in the Northeast and Midwest, white southerners had opportunities for home-based contact across racial lines, often through employer-employee relationships with cleaning and other domestic staff. In the South, intimate racial contact offered little novelty.

The relative absence of southerners in Fresh Air programming underscores the centrality of race to the hosting ventures. Already in 1882–1884, the pages of the *Christian Recorder*, a Philadelphia-based newspaper published by the African Methodist Episcopal Church, included conflicting accounts about whether the Fresh Air Fund allowed "colored children" in its program. At first, T. Thomas Fortune, editor and publisher of the short-lived African American newspaper the *New York Globe*, informed *Recorder* staff in 1882 that he had made inquiries at the *Herald Tribune*. According to Fortune, Fresh Air staff admitted that African American children had "not enjoyed the benefit of the fund" up to that date, but they planned to include a "limited number" in a subsequent trip.[34] A year later, however, editors at the *Recorder* asserted that the *Herald Tribune* had "refused to allow colored children to share the benefit of the Fund," an accusation repeated the following year.[35] At this early stage, African American children rarely took part in Fresh Air ventures, a pattern consistent with other late-nineteenth-century initiatives like the orphan trains.[36] Starting in the 1930s, the Children's Aid Society's Camp Wallkill provided vacation opportunities for black children, but the workers there did so on a strictly segregated basis and reached only a small fraction of New York City's 50,000 African American children.[37] Like most Progressive Era charities, Fresh Air programs followed the segregationist patterns prevalent at the time.[38]

Historic black newspapers then stepped into the void. The editors at the *Freeman* in Indianapolis published an appeal by William Johnson in 1896 that called for the formation of a "Fresh Air Guild" to serve the "helpless waifs" from "indigent" African American neighborhoods.[39] By 1908, some communities had formed their own programs, often with the backing of local black newspapers. With the support of the *Amsterdam News* and the leadership of long-time program director Guilford A. Crawford, the Harlem Children's Fresh Air Fund conducted frequent fund-raisers to send African American children to camp by the 1920s. Through the 1920s, these and related groups maintained separate camps for African American children in facilities within driving distance of New York, Pittsburgh, and Chicago.[40] In some locations, upper-crust African American families from New England sent their children to camps as well appointed as those frequented by the children of wealthy white families.[41] However, most of the camp-based Fresh Air programs sponsored by African American newspapers and charitable organizations focused on poorer children. Despite these efforts, camping options for African American children remained few and far between through the middle of the twentieth century.

Policy makers at the Fresh Air Fund modified their approach even as the racially segregated programs developed. By 1919, they claimed to serve "poor children of Greater New York, without respect to color, creed or nationality."[42] Editors at the *Chicago Defender*, one of the country's oldest and most influential black newspapers, praised the Fund for establishing racially integrated facilities and encouraged their readers to support the effort.[43] Through 1938, however, the Fund had no black directors, permanent staff people, or board members, and no record exists of African American hosts participating in the program. Furthermore, the Fund sent African American, Latino/a, or Asian American children only if a host requested them. Concurrent with most other white social service workers at the time, those few Fresh Air sponsors who focused on racial contact believed more in their ability to take control of and correct the black community than they did in racial equality.[44] As a result, movement toward racially egalitarian programming inched forward through the 1930s.

In sum, more than fifty organizations offered Fresh Air programs during the Gilded Age and Progressive Era. Although an exact figure remains elusive given a lack of official record keeping in the smaller organizations, average service rates suggest that well over two million children participated in a Fresh Air venture of a day or more in length through 1939. Amid such momentum and institutional vibrancy, administrators in white-led organizations only haltingly included African American children; black-led hosting organizations then founded their own programs. Such numerical growth and racial segregation became intertwined with promotion of the children's lack of awareness about the world around them. Turning to a discussion of the first of three promotional dichotomies prominent prior to World War II—naïveté/knowledge—reveals how sponsors controlled the children's image and the children themselves by making sure that the young visitors looked like they knew nothing about the country.

Fresh Air promoters called city children naïve at a time when new child labor laws led to changes in the notion of childhood. Since the middle of the nineteenth century, activists had lobbied for child labor regulation. After repeated attempts, reformers finally saw passage of the Fair Labor Standards Act in 1938, legislation that regulated child workers' ages and hours. No longer would children work all day in sweatshops. Except in the case of farms or other family-owned businesses, the instance of adults and children working side by side dissipated quickly. Even in rural settings, by 1918 all states required that children attend school at least through their elementary years. Although legislators included additional exceptions for newspaper delivery, domestic service in private homes, and the entertainment industry, the prospect of children toiling in dangerous, machine-intensive, industrial workplaces had begun to disappear. Rather than worldly wise laborers familiar with workplace banter and tavern talk, the children appeared more ignorant about worldly matters as they worked less and studied more.

Legislative shifts led to changes in conceptions of childhood itself. During the latter part of the eighteenth century, adults began to view children as "innocent, malleable, and fragile" and thus in need of protection. Rather than a time of forced labor, childhood had become a period of sheltering "from contamination."[45] In 1905 Chicago Hull House resident and child labor activist Florence Kelley coined the phrase "a right to childhood."[46] The slogan implied that children should be able to spend time in play and exploration free of the need to garner wages. Such notions drew on Elizabethan conceptions of childhood as an unencumbered period of frolicking in the grass. With the onset of World War I, however, these romanticized, European ideals grew out of favor.[47] Instead, during and after the 1920s, movie marketers and commercial vendors propagated images of "cute and loving children."[48] As the presentations of childhood spread, so did the assumption that children from all backgrounds, not just those depicted on the silver screen or products for purchase, first and foremost knew little of adult affairs; although they would gain awareness as they grew older, the line between them and adults hardened. As the twentieth century opened, the boundary separating children from adults grew ever more distinct.[49] Childhood had become its own country. Adults only gazed on it from afar.

The administrators' attempts to maintain the image of perfectly paired guests and hosts relied on an increasing measure of scientifically based control. Following the growing attention to efficiency, bureaucracy, and rational design made famous by Frederick W. Taylor and other Progressive Era reformers, camp and home hosts touted the "scientific management" principles used to order their programs and combat the social evils that they so disdained.[50] Hosts and camp directors applied such bureaucratic tenets with particular enthusiasm as they tracked the children's weight gain.[51] Upon the children's arrival, usually in public and often at the train station, through the 1930s local organizers lined the children up in front of a scale, weighed them, and recorded the data. They repeated the process upon departure and noted the increases with great satisfaction. "In nearly every case an increase in weight was shown," declared one administrator of a Baltimore program in 1901.[52] Parents in the 1920s also participated in the shift toward science as they increasingly relied on psychologists to help them manage bed-wetting, recalcitrance, and other behavioral issues.[53] Fresh Air staff soon did the same. The adults likewise supervised children with an intensity that countered a trend toward "free play" present in the 1930s. Rather than reject earlier efforts to mold children from working-class immigrant communities into proper Americans, Fresh Air staff kept the children under "constant watch."[54] Whether in monitoring weight gain, drawing on psychological expertise, or supervising recreational activities, boosters managed the children as if the young travelers had no knowledge of the adults' interest in shaping their bodies and their minds.[55]

Fresh Air promoters marketed their programs based on the children's naïveté. In winsome accounts, boosters emphasized the children's lack of knowledge in all matters but especially regarding the country. Some simply reported that the children had never seen "green pastures, cows, chickens and other everyday sights" of the country.[56] Others told stories about the children's humorous misadventures, a common tendency in children's programming at the time.[57] One Fresh Air veteran explained to a host in 1899 that he had seen many chickens before but only "generally . . . after they was peeled."[58] In 1907 a reporter featured the exclamation of a young girl who mistook a greenhouse for an "onion factory."[59] In droll tones another reporter quoted Fergus McArdle, a Fresh Air traveler in 1935 who carried "a brand new fishing-rod all poised for action" but did not know the names of his quarry other than that he wanted to catch "fish—just little green fish, that's all."[60] In every instance, Fresh Air promoters invited hosts to educate their city guests. In return, the hosts told stories of the children's naïveté and the wonder exhibited by their urban guests. As one account noted in 1934, many of the children had "never seen the typical signs of country life and marveled at the sights they saw from the windows of their train."[61] Hosts relished the children's awe at newfound country sights.

Administrators fostered that sense of awe by carefully selecting the children. Second only to fund-raising and transportation logistics, the vetting of children demanded the bulk of staff time. In essence, Fresh Air programs focused on sending only certain children to the country. They did not welcome all. It was not enough for a child to desire to go to the country; that child had to fit agency criteria to be awarded a vacation. Despite the thousands served, many thousands more did not pass through the screens. Those not selected for a summer vacation joined summer day camps, participated in settlement house recreational clubs, swam in city pools, or played in the streets and sidewalks. For example, the Children's Aid Society sent white children on day boat outings and maintained the Harlem's Children Center to serve African American children through a robust offering of basketball, boxing, singing, cooking, carpentry, drama, and arts.[62]

Despite such attractive city-based options, a trip to the country remained a sought-after prize. Upon hearing reports from their siblings and friends about the country trips, others asked to be included. Given that the children's demand for vacations was consistently greater than host supply, Fresh Air administrators could pick and choose whom they wanted to send.

This highly selective process allowed administrators to imagine ideal exchanges between hosts and children. Even as program promoters sought "ideal surroundings" and "ideal locations," they also sought ideal children.[63] Staff identified specific criteria during this period. The children had to live in the city, be connected with a sending agency, come from an impoverished home, be free of contagious disease, have no record of disciplinary problems, and be of sound body and mind. In short, children had to be "deserving" of charity and free of both physical and moral defect.[64] Selected children could then "gain" from their hosts' "nobler," "new ideals."[65] In the exchange presented by boosters, the children's naïve state fit the hosts' informed condition. A knowledgeable, country host would be found to carefully correct the naïve nine-year-old girl who had expressed such concern about making flowers dirty with city grime.

The rigorous vetting process also attracted donors. The subsequent reports of contagion-free children visiting rural-wise hosts made charming stories. Fresh Air founder Willard Parsons wrote such copy for decades. The news coverage that he and other boosters generated hinged on the children's naïveté. Any child who demonstrated knowledge of adult affairs, whether sexual or criminal, or who challenged adult authority would not travel to the country. Only those most likely to accept host discipline and learn from their knowledge of the countryside passed the vetting screens. In addition, childhood reformers' "beliefs in children's potential, the restorative power of the outdoors, and a child's right to play" supported the ideal of an uninformed child.[66] From the program's inception through the beginning of World War II, narratives about children's naïveté piqued the interest of donors anxious about social instability.[67]

Girl

Discussions about gender also helped bring Fresh Air children to the country. During the first sixty years of the movement, gender trumped race and class as hosts focused on whether to invite a girl or boy. As had been the case when program promoters sought to establish the children's naïveté, the hosts who selected girls more often than boys also helped promote the program.

The preference for girls permeated Fresh Air ventures. Re-invitations highlighted the pattern. Notably, during the 1930s only girls appear as re-invited guests in available published reports.[68] More broadly, rural hosts expressed a preference for girls regardless of the decade or region.[69] As a reporter in 1934 mentioned in passing, "Evidently girls were more popular in Frederick County" by a ratio of three to one.[70] Although an Ohio-based day outing program did plan a "stag" picnic for Fresh Air boys, local police officers, and firefighters in 1937, such male-centered programming remained rare.[71] Whether because of conceptions about preadolescent girls being easier to manage than preadolescent boys or the ability of girls to develop stronger host relationships, girls dominated both first-time and re-invitation lists.

However, boys populated Fresh Air camp rosters. As noted, rural hosts preferred to invite girls. Because hosts could choose the age, the gender—and until the 1960s—the race and the religion of their guests, the trend toward inviting girls meant that many boys did not receive invitations to visit country homes. Instead, organizers sent them to camps. The Brooklyn Urban League announced in 1926 that it had sent 25 "children to private homes" while intending to transport 150 "boys to camp."[72] Business groups such as the Rotary Club supported efforts to send city youngsters to boys-only camps.[73] In the late 1930s a group of 33 boys who had received neither home invitations nor camp scholarships traveled to a lakeside camp for a weekend in mid-September as a consolation prize.[74] Although unwelcome in many homes, boys enjoyed camps even if for only a weekend.

The drive to place boys in a camping environment stemmed in part from G. Stanley Hall's recapitulation theory. In the early twentieth century, Hall, a developmental psychologist, provided educators and social reform advocates with new ideas to reinvigorate their efforts.[75] Most significantly, he argued that children repeated—hence recapitulated—the trajectory of human evolution as they transitioned "from savagery through barbarism to civilization."[76] This recapitulation process, Hall contended, could only come to fruition in white people because the darker, less well developed, and inferior races had not yet advanced to full civilization.[77] As such, Hall asserted that a childhood devoid of savagery made white boys incapable of coping with the demands of adulthood. To counter this civilized coddling, they needed to run wild and be exposed to nature in the raw.[78] Camp provided white boys with just such an opportunity.

Hall's ideas then dovetailed with concerns about the domestic environment and inexpert parenting. Following Hall, during the late nineteenth and early twentieth centuries, summer camp directors sought to protect boys from becoming too feminized. Rather than spend summertime with their mothers in the country while their fathers stayed in the city to work, boys went to camp to escape female pampering.[79] By the 1920s, the wilderness models on which many camp directors based their programs also began to draw on masculine notions of the frontier, lending further support to the premise that boys best became men when kept away from women.[80] By the 1930s, developmental psychologists had raised the alarm that the home environment did not offer the scientific parenting methods found in camp settings.[81] In short, through the 1930s, camps protected boys from their mothers.

The hosts who preferred girls over boys could count on receiving a white female guest unless they specifically requested otherwise. As already noted, the inclusion of children of color in the programs' early years had been anemic. Selecting a girl for a Fresh Air visit prior to the onset of World War II meant bringing a white girl from a particular ethnic community. With black and brown children so seldom included, organizers paid much more attention to whether an Italian, Slavic, Polish, or Scandinavian child would be entering a host home. Even though a 1933 newspaper editorial exclaimed over the "poverty, overcrowding, disease, and unemployment" disproportionately affecting African American children in communities like Harlem, and the Children's Aid Society raised similar concerns, few hosts responded by asking for black girls in their homes.[82]

Racial selection thus undergirded gender preference. In addition to institutional records and newspaper accounts, fiction of the era and host testimony made clear that rural farmers and small town residents favored girls. The descriptions they offered of golden-locked, curly-haired, sun-dressed city visitors frolicking in the grass emphasized that the young girls posed no threat to their hosts.[83] As white girls proliferated in homes and white boys and African American children in camps, these gender-differentiated, race-specific components of the Fresh Air movement depended upon the presentation of nonthreatening girls. Hosts chose guests they thought to be naïve, cooperative, nonsexualized, and female. Prior to 1939, those fundamental choices shaped donor perceptions of the programs' foundational values. Hosts and program promoters alike strove to allow golden-haired girls to adorn green grasses while keeping both white boys and African American children out of hosts' homes. As they did so, the adults placed a premium on the one environment that in their view engendered leisure, simplicity, and wonder; they valorized nature.

Nature

Above all else, program promoters emphasized the theme of city and country. More than naïveté against knowledge or girl against boy, the comparison of city and country drove the Fresh Air movement forward. Boosters repeatedly contrasted urban and rural environs to demonstrate the superiority of the country and its ability to restore children to a state of wholeness, health, and purity. If not for the belief that the city harmed children and the country saved them, the Fresh Air program would mostly have remained a backwater curiosity.

Those writing about Fresh Air programs rarely nuanced the urban/rural dichotomy. As established by the muckraking enterprises of journalist Jacob Riis, Progressive Era reformers depicted the city as unhealthy, dirty, crowded, and morally corrupting.[84] In 1901 the president of Baltimore's Fresh Air Society reported that the city teemed with "poverty and squalor," while the country pulsed with "abundance and . . . elevating influences."[85] According to a 1908 account from Denton, Maryland, the "musty city streets" oppressed children cut off from the "smell of clover and buckwheat and the fragrant odor of apples."[86] And in 1924, an enthusiastic reporter exclaimed that the "noise, . . . confusion and . . . abnormalcy" of the city dulled the senses of children deprived of the country's "peace and quiet."[87] Like others reacting to an increasingly urban world, Fresh Air promoters claimed that distance from the city brought safety, quiet, cleanliness, and freedom from disease, congestion, and crime.

The idea that the country held restorative properties gained much of its potency from nostalgic representations of nature untrammeled. This idea had been a central tenet of the environmental movement from its inception in the late nineteenth century.[88] In order to promote remedies to urban ills, Progressive Era reformers had long drawn on urban dwellers' nostalgia for country towns.[89] For example, Chicago's Charity Organization Society sought to renew the nation by infusing "small-town values" into urban communities.[90] With a practiced hand, reformers in social service agencies and cultural institutions continued to draw on misty-eyed memories of the country when describing children's journeys from the city.[91] In an 1883 account, a fictional Fresh Air child named Dot listened to her mother describe memories of the country, a place with "wide, clean streets, . . . big trees and blue sky and flowers."[92] Above all else, grassy green stood for the country. In multiple Fresh Air reports, children walked on, ran across, scampered around, and gazed at "the green grass."[93] The "wholesome" country contained no ills.[94]

Nonetheless, city children spent their days much like their country counterparts. In the eyes of reformers, the city children lived in wretched conditions. The statistics support their impression. In an era of burgeoning urbanization, human density increased, and temperatures rose. Entire families crowded into rooms meant for single occupancy.[95] The all-too-recent memory of yellow fever epidemics enhanced the impression of tenement districts as disease-ridden pits of despair.[96] Yet children also played games, did chores, worked with adults, developed friendships, gossiped about relationships, and dealt with parents. Reformers in the city parks and playground movements built spaces where children could have access to green spaces and recreational equipment.[97] These activities did not vary tremendously in form and function from those of children in the country. The similarities of the city and country children's lives did not impress program promoters, however, as much as did the contrasts between home environments in urban tenements and rural towns.

The promoters also asserted that the city further damaged children by distorting the natural order. Once immersed in the country, claimed one 1924 report, Fresh Air children could finally relish their "first experience of real existence." By contrast, the city's "canyons" contained a "dazzling, dizzying brilliancy" and dusty, choking fumes that left urbanites confused and disoriented amid "the abnormalcy of a great city."[98] According to the unidentified writer, city children came from a place so artificial and polluted that it could no longer be called real. From this perspective, an abnormal, unreal environment would warp the children and stunt their development.

The very supporters who emphasized the unreal nature of the children's city homes often lived in urban settings themselves. The bulk of those who contributed to, wrote about, and administered the programs lived in the same cities as did the children. Although rural hosts also contributed financially, the highest-profile donors came from the city itself. Those wealthy donors, like many upper-crust urbanites from the late nineteenth century onward, had long practiced summer vacationing, often for extended stays, outside the city proper.[99] They, too, tried to get away from the city's summer heat. In essence, the donors paid for the children to do what they themselves did in an August swelter.

Yet the urban donors did not actually live in the same city as the children. Through fund-raising and publicity efforts, two cities emerged: the city of the children and the city of the donors. To be certain, by the turn of the century, many wealthy city dwellers had themselves relocated to the suburbs that had begun to ring the inner city.[100] The proliferation of the automobile accelerated the process but did not remove all donors from the urban settings where they worked, socialized, and read the newspapers that sustained the programs. As such, the city from which boosters helped the Fresh Air children "escape" meant one thing and the city peopled by Fresh Air donors meant another.[101] The tenements of the immigrant-populated community of the Lower East Side never met the park-front mansion properties of the Upper East Side. Children in the former community prompted Fresh Air Fund founder Parsons to start the program.[102] Residents of the latter included industrialist Andrew Carnegie and various members of the wealthy Vanderbilt family who avidly supported Fresh Air ventures.[103]

Regardless of where they lived, donors gave to a program based on exposing poor city children to the country, not on exposing them to the wealthy. Even though the country families who hosted Fresh Air children had more financial resources and material wealth than did their urban visitors, program promoters highlighted the contrast between country and city and downplayed the difference between wealth and poverty. In a nation that by the 1930s celebrated self-made millionaires even while underplaying class differences, promoters had little to gain by highlighting class.[104] Rather, they contributed to the voyeurism of the emerging social journalism field in which reporters like Jacob Riis described the destitution of the urban poor for the benefit of a wealthy reading public.[105]

The apparent inattention to class did not extend to matters of health and disease. If avoiding class defined Fresh Air administrators' approach to the city up until World War II, focusing on contagion defined their approach to the country. From the onset of the programs, Fresh Air workers assured hosts that every child sent from the city had been examined thoroughly to ensure that they carried no "contagious disease" or "vermin."[106] In the late nineteenth century, one Fresh Air chronicler claimed that only a third of the 15,000 children inspected by physicians "passed muster" for passage to the country.[107] By the 1920s and 1930s, nearly every publicity article written about a Fresh Air program pointed out that the children were "thoroughly inspected for disease," often twice, with the second examination taking place either as the children boarded the train or within twenty-four hours of their departure.[108] The practice, common at the time among camp programs and charity organizations like the Children's Aid Society, could also include checks for venereal disease, often offered with little or no explanation to the parents or children.[109] Program promoters made certain that the children they sent to the country would not infect their hosts.

Such disease-prevention measures went only one way. Program promoters did not require hosts or their children to undergo medical examinations. Even as promoters assumed that guest children would carry disease, they assumed that hosts would not. The hosts who welcomed guests like the young girl and boy depicted in James Montgomery Flagg's drawing never had to fill out a medical form, go to a doctor's office, or have their house examined for disease. According to available records from the program's first sixty years, administrators simply assumed that homes in the country harbored no contagion. By Fresh Air fiat, country homes thus countered city sickness. As such, few considered that possibility that country people also took ill. By the 1930s, none took measures to ensure that a visitor to a farm, for example, did not bring back a case of measles or scarlet fever to tenement apartments.

At least one physician in the Fresh Air movement challenged the assumption of urban contagion. Dr. Charles R. Conklin, the Children's Aid Society medical director in 1936, reported that children from the tenements of Manhattan who traveled to the country were "actually healthier than the country boys and girls who lived on the nearby farms." He explained that, contrary to popular perception, city children resisted disease better than country children because of more-sanitary water supplies, easier access to health care, and more-robust immune systems. Exposure to urban pollution, he claimed, allowed city children to build up "anti-bodies, immunities and tolerances to microbes and other dangerous conditions."[110] To further support his argument, he noted that whooping cough, small pox, typhoid, influenza, and malaria occurred more frequently in rural populations.

Despite such evidence, Fresh Air promoters rarely substantiated their claims about rural superiority. The rhetorical contrast proved far easier to maintain than a fact-based comparison of the respective health benefits of city and country. Anecdotes describing sickly anemic waifs turned into ruddy-cheeked robust cherubs dominated press copy. Convalescent homes set up in the country furthered the image even though the facilities themselves offered good medical care that had little to do with their location.[111] In those cases where the children had more access to food while on country vacations, health did improve. Yet children could be fed anywhere. Improvement came from better nutrition, not the rural environs themselves. Moreover, those who valorized the country during the first decades of the twentieth century felt that the "purity of nature would protect and preserve the purity of childhood."[112] The country could thus mend both body and soul. In essence, promoters claimed that the city was inferior to the country because the country was better than the city.

Claims about the country's curative powers returned repeatedly to the food available there. Progressive Era reformers focused on three central childhood concerns: child labor, juvenile justice, and childhood health.[113] Fresh Air organizers attended to the third. To improve Fresh Air children's health, hosts put food before their guests in copious quantities. Well before the Progressive Era, in the second year of Parsons' initiative, a booster described the parcels of food taken home by the children that held "apples, pumpkins, butter, eggs, mosses, leaves, vines, ferns, clubs, melons, beechnuts, butternuts, ripe tomatoes, grapes, crab-apples, gourds, plums, and sticks of black birch."[114] More than thirty years later, reporters still described the "beefsteak, potatoes, vegetables and milk" offered to the undernourished children.[115] The message was clear: In the country, food abounded.

That abundance came to be represented by wholesome and nutritional milk. Just as grass stood in for nature, milk stood in for food. More so than any other foodstuff, references to milk proliferated throughout the first fifty years of the Fresh Air programs and, as chapter 5 will demonstrate, for many years to follow.[116] The reporters who referred again and again to "pure rich milk" created a symbol of the wholesome experience and nutritional value that organizers desired for the children.[117] As a cultural icon firmly established within North American culture by the end of the 1930s, the mention of milk evoked rustic farmers squatting on stools before cows' udders; tall, cool glasses filled with white liquid; and the assurance of a pure product free of all taint and contagion.[118]

Promoters intensified their grass-covered, milk-fed, city-country rhetoric during the summer. The administrators asserted that their young charges most needed rescue when temperatures soared. Although mid-twentieth-century Fresh Air staff would appeal to hosts based on far more romantic descriptions of summer, through the 1930s boosters associated July and August with discomfort and danger to the children. At times the depictions of the season verged on the piteous as boosters described children "who drag their weary little limbs across the hot sun-baked pavements."[119] In contrast to the humid, sleep-depriving conditions of summer in the city, the country offered safe, comfortable "summer glories" where "the undefiled air of summer blows with health and vigor."[120] Fresh Air promoters promised that, amid fresh breezes, the children would be energized, enjoy sunny skies, and embrace the wonders of the country.

The Fresh Air narrative thus told the story of nature rescuing children from the city through full immersion in the country. In 1883 one child "ran nearly wild with delight" as she "reveled among the daisies in the deep soft grass."[121] By 1905, children still embraced "the joy of wallowing" in the green turf.[122] Seven years later, the rhetoric had changed little as "children steeped in the sweets of Nature" played "upon Nature's own green carpet."[123] Because they had been so doused in daisies, grass, and "sweet air," the children knew no evil, a conviction consistent with the popular conception—in place by the end of the nineteenth century—of childhood as a time of innocence and freedom.[124] Whether suffused with "God's . . . bounty and purity," "akin to Nature" in "innocence, purity, simplicity, modesty, credulity and humility," or enraptured with "the great world of Nature" that imbued them with an "innocent vision," the children who embraced the natural world nearly glowed with goodness.[125] Although such romanticized descriptions proliferated from the 1880s through the 1910s, they continued through the 1930s as rural nostalgia found a home in Fresh Air programs.[126] By virtue of such depictions, the children came to represent an innocence defined by freedom from the burdens of knowledge, sex, and urban complexity.

Upon occasion, however, organizers let slip that the casual access to nature provided by rural hosts could not bestow this tripartite goodness on all children. Those deemed medically fit but socially troubled required fuller immersion. Personnel from the Fresh Air Fund made clear in 1934 that they sent "incorrigibles" and "rougher types" to camps rather than homes.[127] In the more controlled and rustic environments offered by camps during this early stage of Fresh Air program development, these difficult cases met nature unrefined. Even in Fresh Air sites modeled after military boot camps, some campers could not be saved by nature as staff deemed them "too tough" and sent them home.[128] Those who did stay found facilities where camp directors took great pains to leave nature intact. In a move common to camps through the interwar period, designers of a Salvation Army Fresh Air camp kept much of their site in a "natural wooded condition."[129] The children sent to the camps played, hiked, ate, and in some cases slept out of doors. As one director exclaimed about her campgrounds, "I've never seen the woods so sweet. The grass has never been so green, I'm sure."[130]

Such nature-centered rhetoric often concealed the children's efforts to shape their vacation trips. Newspaper accounts like those describing Fresh Air children concerned about dirtying country flowers made the children look like passive recipients of adult largesse. Yet at least some children pushed back. To counter assumptions about their poverty, a few children made up stories about the size and beauty of their city homes.[131] Others attempted, not always successfully, to determine their own bathing schedule. One girl resisted a scheduled shampooing but, after a spirited debated with her host, finally relented.[132] Still others wrote to their former hosts asking to be given the chance to return the following year.[133] Given the children's frequent preference for the familiar, the possibility also remains that at least some of the "incorrigible" children may have preferred the structured environment of a camp to a home stay and so manipulated the vetting process to ensure their placement on camp grounds.[134] Whether by expressing preferences or resisting discipline, some children participated in creating what the organizers assured them would be "the thrill of a lifetime."[135]

Only when discussing nature did promoters highlight the children's role in shaping the programs. In the midst of contrasting the city and country, boosters acknowledged that the children helped their hosts notice nature anew. More typically, through the 1930s Fresh Air staff and administrators viewed the children's attempts to order their own lives as material for gentle ridicule. Those who exaggerated about the grandeur of their city homes protected their egos by reflex. The girl who did not want to shampoo her hair demonstrated the city children's ignorance about proper hygiene. The ones who requested return visits simply responded to their hosts' beneficence. Yet when it came to the country, staff and volunteers acknowledged the children's agency by pointing out that the young guests helped their hosts appreciate their rural surroundings. As Willard Parsons' eulogist declared in 1912, by serving as "a wholesome object lesson in benevolence," the children "taught" their hosts that they had "something which the city can never give" in their "green fields and running brooks, pure sweet fresh air, and that pastoral peace which is Nature's tonic to a weary brain."[136]

The Benefits of Naïveté

Fresh Air boosters thus linked appreciation of nature to the children's naïveté and goodness. As the program supporters described the children's influence on their hosts, they emphasized that the children evoked new awareness and elicited fresh compassion from their adult hosts because the children knew so little. At the same time, the boosters rarely discussed the children's willful resistance. Worldly wise, recalcitrant children did not move the hearts of donors; naïve but cooperative children did. Children capable of manipulating a system designed to save them could not serve as passive conduits of wonder for their hosts' benefit. They knew too much. By emphasizing time and time again that the children lacked all knowledge of the country, exercised no volition of their own, and stood ready to be amazed by the beauty of the countryside, the boosters built a loyal donor base.

No wonder then that adults were enthusiastic about Fresh Air. The innocence that these programs had crafted offered an alternative to a growing sense of collective loss. Cities may have been expanding, but donors and hosts could yet put children in contact with nature's remains. Charities may have otherwise become ever more impersonal, but Fresh Air programs offered hands-on contact with poor people grateful for the service and "deserving" of the opportunity.[137] Even as bureaucracies grew more complex, Fresh Air stayed simple. In the face of growing cities, professionalizing social services, and burgeoning bureaucracies, a program focused on doing only one thing well offered a hopeful contrast. Even the hard-boiled editors of New York's Communist Party paper *Daily Worker* called in 1937 for the city to set up dozens of Fresh Air camps so that every child in New York could experience "health and happiness" in the country.[138] Within the confines of Fresh Air during the programs' first sixty years, the adults who worried about controlling their own lives could at least take a child into their home—or by giving make it possible for others to do so—and so better the world.

The anecdote that starts this chapter captures the most foundational of the themes prior to 1939. What could be more appealing than a Fresh Air child concerned about sullying flowers with city dirt? The image of this child so deliberately crafted by Flagg gave adult donors and potential hosts clear evidence of her naïveté, her nonthreatening gender, and her nature-focused purity. Such a girl and her very young brother proved so attractive because promoters promised that they would be rigorously vetted before being brought into their hosts' homes: not too old, well off, sick, misbehaved, or dark skinned. In essence, the boosters had crafted the innocence that the sketch evoked. Such a presentation—one wrapped in summer, bedecked with nature, girded by fundraising, and embedded in the countryside—would eventually be recast by future boosters and called by other names. As chapter 2 makes evident, the children themselves would also disrupt the stories told about them. The young visitors made choices that knowledge, girl, and nature did not always obscure.

CHURCH, CONCRETE, POND
How Innocence Got Disrupted

The Fresh Air story began in church, came out of concrete, and ended in ponds. Without religion's support, the city's contrast, or swimming's attraction, the redemption story at the center of Fresh Air would have appealed to few. To sell Fresh Air to donors, promoters told the same tale again and again. It went like this: Susie—or Buster or Johnny or Jane—suffered from living in the hot, dirty, dangerous city where she—or he—was boxed in by concrete walls and pavement-covered streets. However, little did Susie know that a group of upstanding Christian—though sometimes Jewish—citizens were preparing to invite her to suburban homes and country camps. When Susie escaped from the city, she brought a swimsuit with her because she had been told she would get to swim—every day if she wanted. And swim she did, leaving her cares behind as she splashed in a pond—or lake or pool—often with minimal adult supervision. She had been redeemed from the burden of concrete, buoyed up by the wonder of water.

That story had little room for complication. Donors wanted a simple story free of any disruption. They had no interest in hearing that hosts and their guests did not always meet the expectations of the Fresh Air redemption tale. Few desired more details about the freedoms and advantages of living in the city. Rarely did a supporter want to know why the children talked so much about swimming. The redemption story succeeded because those who crafted the narrative edited out the children's disruption.

A closer examination of the themes of church, concrete, and pond reveals a different, more complex story. Churches and synagogues did provide the most widespread foundation for the programs, but Fresh Air children resisted the very religious expectations meant to save them from the city. Even widely lauded Mennonite and Amish hosts often failed in their efforts to redeem the children. Multiple anecdotes gave plenty of evidence that the city could be an uncomfortable place to live, but Fresh Air narrators seldom drew on equally ample evidence that city children delighted in their urban environment. All signs indicate that the vast majority of Fresh Air children reveled in swimming, but those who donned swimming suits with such excitement did so as much for the opportunity to frolic without adults directing them as for the refreshment of water play. Fresh Air children complicated the story told about them by doing what children have always done: They sought out spaces of their own, free of adult oversight.[1] In the end, the children's disruptions of an oft-told Fresh Air tale reveal more about the conceptions of innocence prominent in this period than they do about redemption.

Church

The story told by Fresh Air supporters flowed from and fed into intellectual currents about innocence long present in Western thought. Christian theology proved particularly influential. Much of the promotional copy echoed early Christian sentiment that one must become like a child "to enter into heaven." According to Clement of Alexandria and other early church patriarchs of the first and second centuries, "uncontaminated" children set an example for adults in that they had no interest in or knowledge of sexual pleasure and thus centered all their affection on the divine.[2] During the late fourth and early fifth centuries, Saint Augustine developed the doctrine of "original sin," which maintained that infants bore the "taint of sin" and could be saved only through baptismal rites. By the time of the Reformation, Martin Luther continued to promote a version of original sin but also maintained that children embodied innocence up until they reached the age of five or six.[3] Members of the Radical Reformation, those who would go on to found Anabaptist groups such as the Mennonites and Amish, opted for the notion of "complex innocence": Children were culpable as inheritors of original sin but did not yet actively sin and so were covered over by God's grace until the age of accountability, a perspective extended to all children, not just the children of believers.[4]

Fresh Air promotional copy also echoed eighteenth-century romantic notions popularized by Jean-Jacques Rousseau. The Swiss-French philosopher maintained in his 1762 novel *Émile* that society corrupted children over time but that children entered the world with none of the depravity claimed by proponents of original sin.[5] Highly influential in both secular and sacred circles, Rousseau's thought amplified the stream of Christian doctrine already present in the work of Clement of Alexandria and later developed by German theologian Friedrich Schleiermacher, both of whom supported childhood innocence.[6] However, Rousseau's intervention did not eradicate the idea that children came into the world bearing evil and depravity. The duality of Christian thought as represented by these competing claims about children's evil and innocence continued to echo through the twentieth century.[7]

Cast into a role of cooperative protagonists by the church's redemption stories, Fresh Air children often played against type. Despite religion's powerful influence on the movement, many children challenged the instruction they received. One camper simply refused to attend planned religious services in 1948.[8] During the 1950s, others did not attend Sunday School regularly enough in their home community in order to be "worthy" of a Fresh Air trip.[9] Through the 1970s, Fresh Air visitors also interrupted worship services that they had been required to attend, got into arguments with their hosts over religious matters, and came to doubt their hosts' religious dictates.[10] In short, during the post–World War II period, Fresh Air children consistently disrupted the religious narrative told about them.

The Fresh Air movement's story began in a church. As told repeatedly in press accounts and promotional materials, the Reverend Willard Parsons invited members of his Presbyterian congregation to host children from tenements made "unbearable" by the heat of the city.[11] In a sermon given early in the summer of 1877, Parsons reflected on the time he had spent at Union Theological Seminary in New York City and enjoined his congregants to welcome "the least of these" into their homes.[12] Although a secular newspaper eventually sponsored the program that he started, those who followed after him celebrated these religious roots. In every decade of this study, multiple published accounts referred to Parsons and his congregation.[13]

Parsons emerged from a long tradition of Protestant ministry to urban children. During the Progressive Era, evangelical organizations and their secular partners lobbied against child labor and sought to provide good nutrition, health care, and religious instruction.[14] Even when employed by the *Herald Tribune*, Parsons and subsequent Progressive Era directors valorized the inspirational influence of Christian role models and households.[15] By the middle of the twentieth century, churches responded to the perceived threat of juvenile delinquency by offering athletic programs, games, arts and crafts, drama clubs, bible studies, and "moral, social, and health education."[16] Parsons' own denomination administered an extensive program for city children in San Francisco in the 1960s that included a bagpipe player parading on sidewalks to usher children to "songs, games, and class."[17] Fresh Air programs replicated those activities—including religious instruction—but did so in the country at both homes and camps.[18]

Parsons also inspired rural and suburban congregations to support their urban counterparts by organizing, promoting, and funding Fresh Air ventures—a pattern of rural support for urban ministry that lasted through the 1970s. Clergy headed local hosting committees.[19] Ministers recruited hosts and donations by offering appeals "from their pulpits."[20] Entire congregations in rural communities near Boston, Chicago, and Des Moines oversaw the transportation of thousands of city children to the country.[21] Church leaders of the small town of Olean, New York, collaborated with their mayor to proclaim Sunday, June 13, 1948, as "Fresh Air Children's Sunday" in honor of the children hosted in their community.[22]

Religious groups also did far more to implement Fresh Air visits than did civic organizations, businesses, or public personalities. Service organizations like the Kiwanis, Rotary, and Lions would sometimes sponsor local Fresh Air ventures, but in turn relied on churches for publicity and logistical support.[23] Businesses and related foundations provided in-kind donations and grants, yet rarely became involved in the actual execution of the programs. Politicians and celebrities lent their status, names, and dollars to Fresh Air programs, but they also avoided logistical work. Through the 1970s, the Amish, Episcopalians, Lutherans, Mennonites, Methodists, Presbyterians, Roman Catholics, and members of nondenominational congregations continued to promote, organize, and sponsor Fresh Air visits. Even the ostensibly secular Fresh Air Fund relied on donations of time and money from congregations and religious organizations such as Catholic Charities, the East Harlem Protestant Parish, Glad Tidings Mennonite Church, and the True Life Lutheran Chinese Church.[24] As church attendance rates dropped across the country, religion remained integral to the Fresh Air world.[25]

The religious leaders who organized Fresh Air operated within a post–Great Depression realignment of faith-based charity assumptions. In the early twentieth century, social gospel proponents like Walter Rauschenbusch urged mainline denominations to become involved in ministry to the poor based on the assumption that their efforts could eventually bring an end to poverty. Government intervention was not necessary. The scope of economic hardship during the Great Depression led many in the church community to recognize the insufficiency of resources available through private charities and religious communities; government resources needed to be marshaled as well.[26] Even as government programs began to address long-term poverty through President Lyndon B. Johnson's War on Poverty, however, church leaders backed away from calling for systemic transformation.[27] The Fresh Air model dovetailed well with the post-Depression mind-set that churches had a mission to serve the poor, but the scope of that mission need not extend beyond short-term, relationally focused, charity-based programs.

In the context of that foreshortened scope of ministry, religious leaders held more sway as gatekeepers than as organizers. In order to shield hosts from children deemed uncooperative, problematic, or "real delinquents," all Fresh Air programs carefully vetted guest applicants.[28] While health care professionals screened potential Fresh Air candidates for medical conditions, church workers and social service personnel screened the children for behavioral problems. In Chicago during the 1960s, parish ministers "selected" which children would get "to participate in the program."[29] In New York City in 1970, church staff offered their "recommendation" as to which children would best benefit from a country vacation.[30] One year later in Cleveland, staff of the Emmanuel Episcopal Church "helped recruit and prepare" the children for their visits.[31] Although at least one religious leader claimed in 1976 that he and his colleagues did not dangle the prospect of a summer vacation in front of children "as bait" to lure them into church, other church leaders made clear that children who misbehaved during worship or proved unfaithful "in attending Sunday School" would be denied summer vacation visits.[32] Further amplified by the practice of requiring rural hosts to get the signature of a "minister, priest or rabbi" in order to participate, the power and influence of the religious community within the Fresh Air movement had no parallel.[33]

Christianity's central role influenced hosts' and reporters' expectations. A 1946 report stressed that, "as the fundamental units of society," Fresh Air homes offered children "their first spiritual impressions."[34] In 1955 a local organizer claimed that hosts put their "Christianity to work" by opening their homes.[35] Participants in a 1962 Fresh Air meeting in southeast Pennsylvania concluded by singing "Jesus loves the little children of the world."[36] In 1975 a reporter echoed religious themes when remarking that a trip to the country "could amount almost to salvation."[37] Through 1979, reporters highlighted hosts' Christian identity.[38] In addition to making Jewish participants invisible, such descriptions made Christian emphasis on and interpretation of innocence normative.

And denominationally based programs made much of the children's unsullied state. In 1946 a Mennonite author praised the "sacredness of childhood" by equating the face of a child with the face of an angel.[39] In 1961 an Episcopalian editor captioned a photo of a boy on a playground swing as "The Innocent Years."[40] Such innocence claims influenced the broader movement. In 1955 a small-town newspaper editor in Oneonta, New York, featured a photo of a young girl kneeling in prayer for a summer home visit to emphasize her innocence and piety.[41] In 1971 a Fresh Air recruiter assured potential hosts that "these are little children, innocent kids."[42] Although in the early 1970s an alternative narrative suggested that "little kids" from the city were "no longer little kids," religious and secular promoters stuck to the message that the children came to host homes free of worldly knowledge, untainted by sexual activity, and open to religious devotion.[43]

Through the early 1970s organizers undergirded their religiously focused narrative by allowing hosts to select their guests' religious affiliation. Already in 1949, Fresh Air Fund staff told potential hosts that they could "specify the age, color, and religion" of the child that they would bring into their home.[44] In 1966 a Boston-based program assured hosts that Protestant children would be "placed with Protestant families, Roman Catholic children with Roman Catholic families."[45] Chicago organizers discontinued race selection in 1968 while allowing hosts to continue selecting their guests' religious affiliation.[46] After 1971, however, the Fresh Air Fund stopped permitting hosts to designate religion and race in an effort to remove bias from the placement process.[47] Religiously based programs continued to vet children through their mission agencies and thus made sure that the majority of sponsored children had at least a degree of familiarity with the basic tenets of their faith. Although religious vetting had ended, religious instruction continued in many Fresh Air homes.[48]

Some Fresh Air children enjoyed that religious instruction. In the 1940s and 1950s, campers listened to formal religious instruction from camp staff or off-site clergy.[49] Those sent on home visits had a wider range of experiences, with some attending Bible school, others kneeling for bedtime prayers, and still others accompanying their host families to church and Sunday school.[50] In addition, hosts asked their guests to memorize Bible passages and religious songs for later recitation during church services and family devotions.[51] Through the 1970s, some children participated eagerly and highlighted churchgoing as a favorite activity.[52] Looking back on her experience as a Fresh Air child with a Huntingdon, Pennsylvania, family, Peggy Saporato wrote, "The thing I think I liked best of all was going to church."[53]

Other children countered the story told about them. In particular, Fresh Air children placed in Mennonite and Amish homes disrupted the redemption tale. Like their counterparts in the Christian Reformed Church, the Episcopal Church, and several ecumenical partnerships, Mennonites and Amish followed the model first created by Parsons. Children from the city—or in the case of one Mennonite-sponsored program, the rural South—traveled to suburban or country homes for one- to two-week stays often described as vacations. The designation of age ranges, program purposes, and strategies for dealing with issues like homesickness likewise followed Parsons' model. The primary difference came in the form of specific religious practices that shaped and molded both guests and hosts.

Members of the Mennonite and Amish communities brought historical, cultural, and religious particularities to their Fresh Air work. Emerging from the Radical Reformation in early-sixteenth-century Europe, the Anabaptist movement that would eventually give rise to both Mennonites and Amish as well as the Hutterites and Brethren focused on adult confession of faith—hence the term *Anabaptist* or *rebaptizers* because most early believers had been baptized as infants into the Catholic Church—communal discernment of the scriptures, the refusal to bear arms, and nonconformity to the standards of the secular world. Mennonites gained their name from an early church leader, Menno Simons, and the Amish took their label from Jakob Ammann, the leader of a group who separated from the larger Mennonite community in 1693 following a disagreement over how best to practice church discipline. Fleeing persecution for their faith, Mennonites arrived in Pennsylvania in the late seventeenth century and had constructed their first meetinghouse by 1708 in Germantown. The Amish likewise moved out of the Palatinate region of western Germany in the eighteenth century and settled in Pennsylvania as well as neighboring states before moving south and west in search of land.

Decades of religious persecution instilled a separatist identity in both groups. Visible in prayer veils, straw hats, and horse-drawn buggies, the Anabaptists and their value of nonconformity became as well-known to the broader public as the community's penchant for barn raising and pacifism. Although committed to spiritual and social separation from worldly influences, Mennonites and Amish also cherished a strong service ethic that prompted them to provide practical assistance to those afflicted by natural disasters or other tragedies.

A desire to serve the less fortunate coupled with an impulse to proselytize the unchurched prompted Mennonites and Amish to participate eagerly and often in Fresh Air ventures. They did so in two ways. First, several Mennonite groups ran their own Fresh Air programs. In 1896 a group of Chicago mission churches started a program that ran somewhat sporadically through the 1960s.[54] Mennonites from Lancaster, Pennsylvania, founded their own program in 1949 focused on bringing "Negro children" from urban mission sites to rural Mennonite homes.[55] Another group of Mennonites serving in a variety of social service projects in Gulfport, Mississippi, began transporting groups of African American children by bus to Kansas, South Dakota, and Michigan in 1959.[56] In all three of these sites, Mennonite participants enthusiastically brought "the mission field" into their homes by hosting city children.[57]

Second, an even larger group of Mennonites and Amish participated in the *Herald Tribune*'s Fresh Air program, where they received unabashed accolades for their work. In Paradise and Mount Joy, Pennsylvania, Mennonites Emma Denlinger and Gertrude M. Spangler organized local Fresh Air hosting committees for nearly a quarter of a century between them.[58] In 1964 the Fresh Air Fund released *Summer's Children*, a promotional film that featured children hosted in Mennonite homes.[59] For almost thirty years, Alice Trissel, a Mennonite from Harrisonburg, Virginia, coordinated Fund activities in one of their few active southern sites, where she sent thousands of children to Mennonite homes.[60] Administrators from the New York-based program heaped praise on the groups; executive director Lisa Pulling said that Mennonite hosts made Pennsylvania "the most popular place to go," and another administrator exclaimed that the "Amish are fantastic for taking children."[61] In addition, staff from the Fund noted that children sent to Mennonite and Amish families had re-invitation rates as high as 80 percent, a significant increase over other groups, which often reached only 50 percent.[62] As presented to the public, the Mennonites and Amish were "good and generous and kind" hosts who "refused plaques and scrolls and requests to be photographed for publicity."[63]

Public opinions about the Mennonites and Amish who hosted Fresh Air children mirrored those expressed about the decency and goodness of plain people in general as well as the children who visited them. The Amish in particular garnered the distinction of being "innocent, pure, plain" people.[64] Both groups' "plain" dress patterns furthermore cast them as leading characters in "the myth of white racial purity."[65] Just as Fresh Air promoters assured hosts that the children knew nothing of worldly matters—whether sex, race, or political matters—those same administrators assured the broader public that their best hosts were equally untainted. According to reports that most donors encountered in the course of a fund-raising season, the meeting of plain people with city children matched innocence with innocence. Neither group would be sullied or made worldly by the encounters.

In these Anabaptist settings the children's disruptions became most evident. Following pietistic commitments of their community, Mennonites and Amish renounced dancing, wearing makeup, listening to the radio, or participating in the occult. Despite being informed of these strictures, the young guests in Mennonite and Amish homes often refused to cooperate with the restrictive dictates. One guest received a scolding for dancing.[66] Another young girl from Harlem by the name of Margie Middleton learned to resist the messages her hosts gave her about proper conduct when she returned to the city from visits with Mennonite families. Her hosts decried listening to the radio, dancing, going to the movies, putting on lipstick, and wearing earrings. Only after talking with her mother, who engaged in all the activities her hosts condemned, did Middleton decide that "God judges the heart" as much as external appearances.[67] Yet another child told scary stories about "spooks and ghosts" to his host siblings, causing much consternation in the household.[68]

In other instances, tensions emerged around Mennonite and Amish dress customs. Although many children came to their host homes wearing new clothing purchased by their parents or given by donors prior to their arrival, rarely did a child have a wardrobe that included Amish prayer veils or cape dresses in bold primary colors. When placed in a conservative Mennonite or Amish home, many guests looked for ways to blend into their environment. Although few boys sported wide-brimmed straw hats or wore suspenders in the Amish style, some girls adopted local dress patterns in order to look like their hosts. As one local organizer from Lancaster, Pennsylvania, noted, "We end up sending them back to New York dressed like the Amish. Their hair is parted in the middle with the girls in long, brightly colored dresses and black aprons." Although they could not change other aspects of their appearance, dress did afford the young girls a measure of camouflage so that they would not look "different" while on their summer sojourn.[69] In at least one instance, Amish costume even made Natasha Brown feel glamorous, "with the deep maroon color against her dark skin, her almond-shaped Polynesian eyes, and her hair gleaming in tight braids under the bright white covering."[70]

Yet the decision about whether to dress in a conservative fashion distressed some guests. Middleton remembered that both she and her friend Pat had "accepted Christ" as their savior at the Mennonite church they attended in New York City, but only Pat had decided to wear a prayer covering as a sign of that commitment. As a result, the Mennonite family in Lancaster who had hosted them both the previous summer extended a re-invitation to Pat but not to Middleton.[71] The host family rejected the young city guest who would not conform to their ways. Decades later, Middleton still carried with her the memory of the rejection and separation from her best friend.

The Mennonites and Amish who received such accolades for the quality of their hosting had a mixed record. In addition to condemning many of the children's behaviors and excluding those who did not conform to their practices, some hosts put the children to work as inexpensive farm hands, rejected children once they became teenagers, and used racial epithets.[72] In more than one area, members of the Anabaptist community physically and sexually abused their guests, a reality examined at greater length in chapter 4.[73] By assuming that Mennonite and Amish hosts would never harm a child, administrators deflected attention away from such problems and increased the likelihood that abuse would recur.

Here again the children disrupted the prevailing narrative. In a hosting movement that presented children as free of moral corruption, adults expected their guests to conform to their religious precepts. Children like Middleton chose alternate paths based on their parents' instructions, their own preferences, and the sheer love of dancing or telling scary stories. Even among hosts lauded for their generosity and wholesomeness, or perhaps especially in those settings, Fresh Air children did not conform to their sponsors' script.

Concrete

Every Fresh Air visit concluded with concrete. The programs did not permanently remove the children from the city; they took them away in order to bring them back. Although foster care was sometimes an option in the late nineteenth and early twentieth centuries, by the mid-twentieth century hosts rarely adopted or extended foster care to Fresh Air guests. And so, nearly all the children came back to the cement-filled environs that purportedly threatened, oppressed, and limited their horizons.

The return home nonetheless delighted many of the children. Upon emerging from the subway into the streets above, one boy sniffed the air, turned to his escort, and exclaimed, "Gee, it smells good to be home."[74] Another adult chaperone recalled how frequently she witnessed train cars full of Fresh Air children cheer when they pulled into Penn Station in New York City.[75] The instance of homesick children longing to return to their families and more familiar surroundings likewise speaks to children enamored with a place said to do them great harm.[76] For example, David Son, a "Chinese guest" of the Schilling family of Salisbury, Maryland, returned home early because he missed his city home.[77] Although the young age of many of the Fresh Air guests and their attachment to parents and siblings were certainly factors, those labeled as homesick knew the city as a place of comfort and familiarity.

Such fondness for the urban center counters widely held notions of the city as a site of deviance and moral decadence. From 1920 onward, more than 50 percent of the U.S. populace lived in cities, and so those social reformers who advocated for children to be exposed to the country in order to receive a "normal childhood" in truth pushed for access to an abnormal one.[78] Many influential historians through the 1960s emphasized the wholesomeness and normality of the countryside, while casting city spaces as "impure."[79] Reformers expanded on this notion with a lexicon of "overlapping idioms" they used to describe the "industrial city": "vicious destroyer of the common good," "necessary mirror of American civilization," and "a threat to democracy, Protestantism, and virtue alike."[80] In particular, New York City embodied Americans' fears of urban perils, a perception not incidental to the success of the *Tribune* Fresh Air program.[81] Although also a site of redemption because of the very depravity hosted therein, the urban environment became by the middle of the twentieth century a place where bad things came from, not where good people went.[82]

The children's delight in returning to the city disrupted the central message of the Fresh Air movement. Promoters made the point that the country held the power to restore and rejuvenate children, but this idea depended first on the conviction that the city had the power to oppress the children. If the city did not look bad, the children had nothing from which they needed rescue. Fresh Air promoters cast the ugly, threatening city as a troll, the antagonist in their story. References to children enjoying their return to the city appear so anomalous not only because they countered the prevailing narrative but also because they made it into the written record.

Cities stood at the center of the Fresh Air project from their inception. By the end of the 1960s, programs varied in how much they emphasized cross-racial connections or urban/suburban ones, but none of the initiatives lost their primary focus on the city as the children's point of origin. As of 1970, the list of sponsoring cities included Denver, Des Moines, Los Angeles, Minneapolis, and Toledo, in addition to the long-term sites of Boston, Chicago, Cleveland, New York, and Philadelphia.[83] Other than the city itself, a Fresh Air program needed only two other ingredients to thrive: transportation to take the children away from city streets and suburban or rural homes in which to welcome them.

Those who whisked the children out of the city employed the same narrative line. First and most consistently, program promoters noted that the city held heat. Whether facing "baking," "blistering," "unbearable," "oppressive," "torrid," or "sweltering" conditions, children stayed "trapped in the high-wall heat of the city" until cooled by country environs.[84] Children also escaped crowds. According to promotional accounts, crowded streets and cramped housing made life miserable and play nearly impossible.[85] Fresh Air accounts by the 1970s described neighborhoods defined first by drugs, crime, and gangs.[86] In such urban communities, overwhelming cacophony, drab aesthetics, and street fights created what Fresh Air recruiter Shelby Howatt deemed "a jungle atmosphere."[87] Howatt's description invoked a racial blackness that further alienated the city from white Fresh Air sponsors (see figure 3).

Publicity materials continued to emphasize the city's heat, overcrowding, danger, ugliness, dirt, noise, and cement through the 1960s, even as some of the earlier tropes disappeared. Although concern for children's malnutrition in the late nineteenth and early twentieth centuries had been a Fresh Air hallmark, few programs described the city as a place of hunger after the 1950s. Likewise, post-1960, most authors stopped using labels like "bad" or "evil" to describe the city as such moral contrasts had become clichés.[88] After the 1960s, descriptions of housing projects began to replace those of tenements and "slums," and fewer authors described the city as a prison.[89] Those seeking to promote Fresh Air programs had become more careful in how they described urban environments, but

FIGURE 3.   Unidentified participants from the Henry Street Settlement House in New York City prepare for a trip to the country, 1965. Used by permission of Henry Street Settlement House, New York, NY. Social Welfare History Archives, University of Minnesota Libraries.

their underlying judgment remained. As a college student and child of long-time hosts declared in 1967, children from the city lived "dreary, disorganized, hollow and uninspired" lives.[90]

Such small changes in promotional rhetoric echoed larger shifts brought about by urban renewal. The 1949 Housing Act channeled federal dollars into programs designed to eradicate substandard housing. Given an increasingly urban population, much of that money went to tearing down tenements and building in excess of 800,000 new public housing units. The 1956 Federal-Aid Highway Act likewise altered cityscapes as contractors demolished homes and split neighborhoods in order to construct elevated highways to the suburbs.[91] As a result, suburbs erupted: Chicago's suburbs charted a 117 percent increase, and New York City's outer ring posted a 195 percent increase at the same time that both urban centers lost residents.[92] The designers of the housing projects that arose above the rubble of historic neighborhoods seldom took into account residents' physical needs, comfort, or safety. Compounded by substandard construction materials and inadequate maintenance budgets, the housing developments quickly deteriorated at sites such as Cabrini-Green in Chicago and Pruitt-Igoe in St. Louis.[93]

The promoters stayed on message amid this urban change. In the Fresh Air narrative, the city had always made its residents uncomfortable. Urban denizens, depicted as primal and uncivilized through repeated references to the "jungle" of the city core, had suffered in the heat for all time.[94] In perpetuity, the masses shoved and pushed their way through city streets, leaving little room for children to play. Quiet never settled on the streets. At no point did city dwellers smell sweet air, walk safely on the sidewalk, or enjoy trash-free stoops. The lives of urban children had always been "bound by the crowded, blistering streets."[95] Frozen in time, devoid of attraction, a monolith of "din and dirt," in Fresh Air stories the city did not change.[96]

Youthful participants in Fresh Air ventures began to reflect a similar negative mind-set about the city. In 1952 a young camper wrote his counselor after returning home to complain that it was "to [sic] hot in the city and dirty."[97] One reporter described the words of Carlos Rivera, a twelve-year-old from the Bronx who had spent four summers with a family in Schenectady, New York, as he expounded in 1971 on the Fresh Air experience to a group of first-time travelers: "It's better out there. . . . Here they's junkies everywhere. There. . . . It's clean, man, it's clean. Anywhere you go, you don't run into trouble. And one more thing, it don't smell."[98] Nine-year-old Jaquelyn Schofield had a similar perspective in 1975. She explained that in comparison to her Queens home, Troy, New York, felt "much colder and not as hot" and was "clean," not "dirty and polluted."[99] Through the 1970s, other Fresh Air children commented on "burned houses," noise, and crime; too often they described their neighborhoods accurately.[100]

Rooting out the source of such sentiment may not be possible. The children certainly heard program promoters and administrators speaking in negative terms. Even their host siblings asserted that "real life" could be found only in the country.[101] Structurally the programs made these kinds of unflattering comparisons implicit. The children did, after all, leave the city behind. They did not simply commute to another borough. Staff and administrators likewise ensured that the children visited stable, middle-class homes in the suburbs and country where the contrast with the city would be even more apparent. And the process of changing to a different environment, living with different people, and getting to do new activities made the old and familiar less appealing.

Some children grew so dissatisfied with the city that they left it at their first opportunity. Looking back on her experience as a Fresh Air child during the 1950s, Helen Regenbogen said, "It was my dream my whole life to get out of the city and move to the country."[102] She not only realized that dream but went on to host Fresh Air children of her own. Former Brooklyn resident James Hinton left the city for a while during a tour of duty with the Marines, moved back to a "crowded section of Brooklyn" to start a family, but aimed in 1966 to bring his wife and three sons "back to Fresh Air country, to live."[103] In 1978 a former Fresh Air participant relocated from Brooklyn to Croton-on-Hudson, about forty-five miles north of New York City, in order to live with his host family and attend high school. Although he grew homesick midyear for the city's "action," he stayed with his mother for only a few weeks before returning to Croton.[104]

At the same time, adult critics and some children pushed back against the rhetoric perpetuating urban stereotypes. A few children explained to their hosts that they had in fact seen trees in the city and knew how to climb them.[105] Others, by simply showing that they were not addicted to drugs, engaged in crime, or pursuing sex, countered sentiments such as those held by a thirteen-year-old host who claimed in 1956 that 90 percent of New York's school-age children drank "strong drink."[106] Adults also challenged prevailing anti-urban sentiment when they, like Margie Middleton's mother, stated plainly that the host parents "shouldn't implant" in the minds of the children "that the city was wicked."[107]

Black Power activists in the 1960s intensified the criticism. For nearly a century, few observers had publicly criticized Fresh Air programs. Under scrutiny by black activists, however, many white-led social service programs found themselves under attack. Fresh Air was no exception. As noted in the introduction to this book, critics denounced the practice of busing children to the country because it instilled false expectations about their ability to relocate to the suburbs. In keeping with the damage imagery used by liberal reformers and black activists in their efforts to counter societal racism, still more critics claimed that the programs and others like them exuded paternalism, wreaked psychological havoc, and needed to be revised so that white suburban kids could be transported to the inner city.[108] The intensity of the criticism emerged from a sense that white liberals sought to undermine the black community in particular by attempting to influence the children at an early age. Black Nationalist critics and their white and Latino allies asserted that white liberals targeted the most vulnerable members of their community rather than speaking as equals with adults.[109] In an era when Black Power calls for self-determination rocked many a white-led service agency, the Fresh Air movement faced such blunt criticism through the middle of the 1970s.

Promoters and organizers responded by changing their rhetoric and promotional techniques. First, they brought parents of Fresh Air children before audiences of prospective hosts to testify that the programs "had done more to inspire than to hinder."[110] Prior to the 1960s, urban parents had played little to no role in the program as a whole, let alone in promotional efforts. In a similarly innovative move, at least some promoters dropped, however temporarily, the language of naïveté and began asserting that the children knew more than their hosts about racial and class dynamics. Rosemary Sandusky, a host and promoter in the town of Elk Grove, Illinois, claimed that the children visiting her and other hosts in the Chicago suburbs were "very wary" of their hosts and recognized that they would be able to stay only for a two-week visit. Moreover, she asserted that the children "are far more realistic than the people into whose homes they come."[111] Along similar lines, *Herald Tribune* Fresh Air executive director Frederick Lewis said that the children had enough savvy not to become bitter or full of despair but rather that they gained confidence from the visits to "face this world and make something" of themselves.[112] A 1979 self-study for the Fund likewise emphasized that children returned from their vacations having matured and having become more aware of the world around them.[113] Instead of ingenuous waifs, suddenly the children appeared knowledgeable and wise.

The city, too, got a facelift. In the aftermath of the most intense criticism and following leadership changes at the Fresh Air Fund, promotional copy and program initiatives presented the city in a far more positive light. In addition to including references to those who cheered upon pulling into Penn Station or took a deep breath of city air, other organizers referenced children chattering about "playing stick ball" or "walking the dog" when they returned home.[114] Barbara King, a local organizer from Garden City, about thirty miles east of New York, admitted, "The city is where their friends are. It is where they are loved."[115] A photo of Fresh Air child Savina Arenas hugging her mother upon her return home sent a similar message.[116] In an even bolder move, the Fresh Air Fund celebrated its centennial in 1977 by initiating programs to "get our kids to appreciate the city where they spend most of the year." Although the Fund did not discontinue its normal rural-focused programming, it hosted children at baseball games, led them on historic tours of their neighborhoods, and took them to the Dance Theater of Harlem.[117] For at least a short while, the city became beautiful in the eyes of the leaders of the Fresh Air movement.

Many Fresh Air children had known of the city's pleasures long before administrators like Lewis included their perspectives in their promotional package. During the 1940s, neighborhood children flocked to summertime athletic competitions organized by settlement houses.[118] Other social service groups planned city-focused adventures. In one example, a group of young Italian immigrant boys hiked through city streets in the summer of 1940 and climbed eight floors to the top of "Mount Roof" in Manhattan, where they enjoyed a corn feast, set up tents, and camped overnight.[119] A photographer captured the sentiment of at least one New York graffiti artist in the middle of the twentieth century who scrawled on a brick wall, "Summer in the City is Fun."[120] By the late 1970s, Fresh Air promoters admitted that it sometimes took "encouragement" to get children to leave the city.[121] In addition, other children decided not to leave so that they could participate in local baseball programs or find summer employment.[122] Nicol Roberts, a youthful correspondent for the "To Kids from Kids" column in the New York *Amsterdam News*, responded to a letter writer's query by asserting, "The city may be hot, dirty and muggy to you, but I always find things to do in it. You can too. Good luck!"[123] In the course of the 1970s, both promoters and children disrupted the corrupted city discourse.

Other programs kept children in the urban neighborhoods they loved. For example, New York's Union Settlement Association ran a summer day camp during the 1950s that took children to zoos, baseball games, swimming pools, and local parks within the city limits.[124] Staff of the "Summer in the City" program offered social and artistic activities for children and their parents in New York City in the late 1960s. Funded by the federal Office of Economic Opportunity, the program staffed thirty-nine offices in Manhattan and the Bronx in order to connect the children "with their own richnesses and with those of their neighbors."[125] Participants sculpted papier-mâché, painted wall murals, decorated playgrounds, and performed in plays.[126] In contrast to the home- and backyard-based activities common in the suburbs, programs like "Summer in the City" celebrated the front stoop- and sidewalk-centered culture of many of the urban communities.[127]

Fresh Air administrators kept sending children out of the city even as they temporarily moderated their urban negativity. Promoters had long emphasized the city's depravity in order to sell a story of rescue and relief. But in the face of harsh criticism, Fresh Air administrators took note. They had begun to pay attention to a barrage of criticism that was "if not frontal, then at least questioning."[128] Peter F. Carlton, the director who followed Lewis in 1972, questioned whether the program should even continue "as a 'distribution conduit'" for children.[129] At a time when Fresh Air programs across the country experienced a drop in their hosting volunteer base, administrators experimented with telling a different story about the city, one not quite so dependent on calling it and those who lived there awful.[130]

The positive take on the urban environment proved short-lived. Two years after the Fund's centennial program celebrated the city, promoters started to disparage the urban core once more. Children again received a "wonderful break from the hot and noisy city streets."[131] They again escaped lives spent "surrounded by concrete and asphalt."[132] Once more they received "respite" from "deteriorating" neighborhoods.[133] Even as late as 2005, promotional materials continued to emphasize the need to save children from the "hot, noisy, dangerous streets of our city's poorest neighborhoods."[134]

The old tropes resurfaced in part because the most critical voices turned quiet. Following the deliberate suppression of Black Power activists by local and federal authorities and the concomitant breakdown of a unified black political platform in the aftermath of the highly contentious 1974 National Black Political Convention in Little Rock, Arkansas, a concerted critique of the Fresh Air movement disappeared.[135] With less vocal criticism to answer, promoters continued to offer "street-wise, country-innocent" children a break from the city that purportedly oppressed them.[136] Those children who celebrated their return home disrupted the city's disparagement but did not stop it altogether.

Pond

Roosevelt "Teddy" Mayes loved to swim. During a 1970 Fresh Air trip to a host family in one of Chicago's northwest suburbs, he longed to take a dip in the local municipal pool. However, his hosts at the time could not take him. At eleven years old, Mayes decided that his hosts' schedules would not interfere with his summer fun. According to his host the following year, the young boy from the south side of Chicago went to the pool by himself.[137] Mayes wanted to swim, and he made certain that he did.

Mayes's independence and love of swimming represent a site of great freedom for hosted children amid Fresh Air programs' many restrictions. Of all the sites that children from the city visited while vacationing, swimming ponds, pools, and lakes received the most consistent praise. Although adults often watched over them from the periphery and sometimes joined in aquatic adventure, the children expressed their independence while swimming. Despite facing real danger from drowning, having to negotiate racial boundaries at the waterfront, and listening to still more derision directed at the city, Fresh Air children made the pond and all such swimming sites their own.

Public pools have a long history as sites of social contestation. Up until the 1920s, municipal pools brought together white and black laborers across racial lines but remained segregated by gender and class. During the following three decades, city leaders segregated pools by excluding African Americans while simultaneously bringing bathers together across class and gender lines.[138] Starting in the mid-1940s, African American swimmers and their white allies successfully agitated for admission to municipal pools.[139] White flight from cities, white refusal to swim in integrated settings, and an eroding urban tax base by the 1970s led to many municipal pools crumbling in disrepair.[140]

Yet suburban and small-town swimming opportunities never disappeared. In segregated settings, municipal pools remained vibrant. Where municipal pools became integrated, new private swimming clubs sprung up, a phenomenon especially common after 1950 in suburbs populated by white families fleeing cities in which public pools had become integrated.[141] Backyard pools also became more common from the 1950s onward as income increased, pool construction became more affordable, and white suburban families vied for even more control over their swimming partners.[142] As hundreds of thousands of water enthusiasts switched from municipal to private swimming, race remained central to their decisions.

Children like Teddy Mayes came to love swimming regardless of racial stereotypes that discouraged black and brown children from water sport. Despite sustained interest in summer swimming, few African Americans found their way into pool-based athletics. Although the actual reasons primarily lie in cultural tradition, role modeling, and lack of access to swimming facilities, physiologists of the time attempted to explain black absence from aquatic competition by creating theories about buoyancy, body type, lung capacity, and specific gravity.[143] Such conjecture, stamped with the authority of science, drew popular attention away from racial discrimination at swimming pools by suggesting that African Americans were biologically unsuited for water sport.

Mayes and his city playmates nonetheless dealt with remote, crowded pools as they clamored to swim. Prior to the desegregation of public pools in the 1940s and 1950s in the Northeast and Midwest, where Fresh Air programs proliferated, African American and Latino swimmers in Harlem, for example, had to travel up to three miles to the Colonial Park pool because white managers at the nearby Jefferson Park pool denied them entrance.[144] During the 1960s and 1970s the few pools available to children in major urban centers drew so many swimmers on a hot day that some waited more than an hour for a chance to splash in shallow, tepid water.[145] Ten-year-old Lauren "Flip" Bailey told a reporter in 1977 that swimming pools near her home in the Bronx grew "so crowded it was impossible to swim."[146] Alexander Cruz, a Fresh Air participant from Brooklyn, hesitated to accept his host's offer to swim simply because he was used to crowded swimming facilities and "no one else was in" the backyard pool when his host invited him to take a dip.[147]

Interest in swimming only increased on a Fresh Air vacation. When asked to describe the highlights of a trip to camp or home, the children referred to swimming more than any other activity. Some also enjoyed riding bikes, playing baseball, or romping with pets and farm animals.[148] A few highlighted the opportunity to make money by harvesting onions or blueberries.[149] However, the overwhelming majority simply said, as did "Santiago" in a letter describing his visit to the home of "Mis Blomson" in the early 1950s, "I like to go swimming."[150] Another camper, identified only as Floyd, wrote in 1969 that "most of all I liked . . . swimming."[151] A decade later, nine-year-old Troy declared that he most looked forward to "swimming every day" on his upcoming trip.[152] A Fresh Air camp director summarized the children's sentiment by noting, "[S]wimming is the most important activity during a vacation."[153]

Few children expressed disdain for getting in the water. Those who did prove the rule. One camper explained his refusal to swim in 1948 as a dislike of cold water.[154] In 1951 a five-year-old camper informed his counselor that he did not want to go swimming because he would have to expose his body.[155] Yet expressions of such dislike rarely appear in the written record or individual participants' recollections. The vast majority of the children demanded more time in the water rather than less.

Swimming attracted so many Fresh Air children largely because of the independence it afforded them. In their bid for freedom from adult control, the children joined a long tradition of swimming pool autonomy. Administrators of swimming pools in the latter half of the nineteenth century found they could not curtail the rowdy behavior of the working-class boys who flocked to municipal pools.[156] In the same way, Fresh Air guests joined groups of local children who left adult supervision to have, as one host mother noted, "a grand time . . . going to some swimming hole of theirs."[157] At some camps, children convinced their counselors to let them hike to a swimming pond and go for midnight swims, activities that demonstrated the increasing autonomy and agency demonstrated by children while at camp.[158] With the advent of backyard pools by the 1970s, others took full advantage of the ease and proximity of the swimming facility. Kevin Miller, an eleven-year-old from West Harlem, reported that the family he stayed with in Pennsylvania let him swim in their pool whenever it took his fancy.[159] Although hosts had to sometimes supply bathing suits, the children literally dove into pools and away from adult control once properly attired.

The Fresh Air Fund took swimming independence to another level through its program for physically disabled children at Camp Hidden Valley. Nestled in the wooded expanse of the Fund's Sharpe Reservation near Fishkill, some seventy miles north of New York City, the facility catered to children with a variety of conditions, including "congenital amputations, cerebral palsy, post-polio, muscular dystrophy, epilepsy, rheumatic fever and spina bifida."[160] Regardless of their condition, all Hidden Valley campers spent time in the pool, as per camp requirements.[161] The professionally designed pool allowed "both handicapped and able-bodied children" to play together.[162] After being allowed to swim and play on their own in the water, many children returned home with a new sense of adventure that often surprised their parents.[163] The experience of solo swimming prompted the campers to seek other forms of independence as well.

Yet watery depths could prove perilous. In 1951, and again in 1962, 1963, and 1967, Fresh Air children drowned while visiting hosts.[164] Although they experienced drowning rates well below the national averages at that time of 5.1 per 100,000, or .005%—according to available data, Fresh Air drowning rates reached the .005% figure only four times in a two-decade spread—parents of the children who drowned dealt with the additional trauma arising from the circumstances of the tragedy: Their child died in the care of hosts that the family of origin had never met in a distant location that most of them had never visited.[165] One young host described a tale of swimming trauma. The young girl's older brother abandoned her and a Fresh Air visitor in the middle of a deep swimming hole until her guest "started yelling with all her might . . . as if she would never stop."[166] At least one other former Fresh Air participant in the 1960s "nearly drowned" while swimming in Lake Michigan.[167] Given the prevalence of water sport, other unreported water accidents seem likely. Amid complications born of economic, racial, and cultural dislocation, the very aquatic activity that enlivened so many Fresh Air visitors often proved deadly. Tragically, the danger continued past the 1970s. A 2006 study revealed that African Americans, like many of those endangered by swimming during Fresh Air visits, had been "disproportionately victims of accidental drowning" because of limited access to pools and proper training in water safety.[168]

Fresh Air administrators responded to these deaths though an aggressive education campaign. Beginning in the 1950s, these water safety initiatives reflected a social shift toward viewing children as priceless rather than replaceable as the twentieth century progressed.[169] In 1964 a Red Cross safety director spoke to Fresh Air coordinators at their annual gathering in New York.[170] The same year that George Bonilla drowned while visiting Winchester, Massachusetts, in 1967, the *Herald Tribune* Fund had informed every host about the importance of providing children with proper swimming supervision.[171] From the mid-1960s onward, individual hosts also enrolled their guests in swimming classes during their stays.[172] By 1978, Fresh Air camps provided swimming instruction to all campers who needed it as staff and administrators recognized that "more than 90 percent of the youngsters cannot swim."[173] Because of such concerted efforts, the danger of death by swimming while on a Fresh Air venture diminished.

Racial tensions also made swimming treacherous. Since the 1930s, the prospect of interracial swimming at municipal pools had fomented discord across the country.[174] While public protests against Fresh Air children integrating swimming sites rarely, if ever, took place, African American and Latino children nonetheless faced overt racism in the midst of water play. In the early 1960s, Fresh Air host Kathy Knoll Larson went to the Graafschap beach in Michigan along with her parents and brother only to be told that Harvey, their African American guest from New York, could play on the beach but would not be allowed in the water. The entire family and their guest left in protest.[175] Other children endured comments about their "wonderful tan[s]" and dealt with racist taunts and harassment from children in the pool or pond.[176] Given instances of racial harassment of African American children by white children well into the early 1990s, Fresh Air children in the middle decades of the twentieth century probably underreported instances of racial harassment while swimming.[177]

Few local residents objected to Fresh Air swimmers because staff kept the dose small and segregated by sex. Although some communities hosted upwards of fifty guests at a time, more typically administrators dispersed the children in small batches. Given their short stay and limited numbers, the African American and Latino children who showed up to swim at municipal pools posed little threat. Problems emerged at public pools only when permanent residents vied for swimming space. In the early 1950s, around the time that activists forcibly integrated many northern swimming pools, Fresh Air camp personnel voluntarily followed suit but reduced the threat of interracial, cross-gender contact by scheduling separate swimming periods for girls and boys. Promotional materials through the 1970s featured photos of lakes and ponds integrated by race but seldom by gender.[178] Exceptions include a photo of a white, female water safety instructor teaching two young male African American campers how to swim and one of an integrated group of very young Fresh Air campers splashing in a wading pool.[179] In these latter instances, the slim chance of sexual contact across racial lines threatened few.

The proliferation of backyard pools also reduced racial tension. As the number of backyard pools increased from 575,000 to 800,000 between 1965 and 1970, Fresh Air children began to speak of swimming at their hosts' homes.[180] Through the 1970s, the guest children continued to comment on the delights of backyard swimming.[181] Fewer instances of racial harassment took place in these backyard swimming sites, where hosts could temper racial animus. Given that most guests came from African American and Latino homes, by the time that private pools became common, hosts had decided to allow dark-skinned children into their pools long before the children arrived on the doorsteps of their "domestic haven."[182] By inviting the children to swim at home, the hosts could demonstrate their racial largesse without compromising the privacy and status of their backyard oasis.[183]

Even class tensions submerged when Fresh Air children took a dip. Given the high status bestowed upon suburban pool owners and the low status attributed to urban children who relied on charity to obtain swimwear, class tension should have increased whenever swimming came up in conversation.[184] Even as more middle-class families purchased and installed swimming pools, more poor families turned to public assistance. Between 1960 and 1970, the number of people receiving some form of welfare doubled.[185] In the midst of that economic disparity, a few tensions surfaced. One reporter overheard a Fresh Air guest exclaiming, "I've got a new pair of swim trunks," only to hear his host brother reply, "And I've got a new swimming pool at home." Although the reporter treated the exchange as evidence of the two boys "thinking along the same lines," the guests noticed the difference in economic station.[186] Lawrence Phifer, a ten-year-old from Brooklyn, also noted class differences when he declared to his train seatmate, "I told you we were getting near when you start seeing the swimming pools."[187] Yet most of the guest children set aside talk of economic inequity in favor of immersing themselves in the luxury of a "backyard pool."[188]

A willingness to diffuse class differences, countenance racial discomfort, brave physical danger, and visit unfamiliar places in order to swim to their heart's content suggests that the children paid little attention to what promoters claimed about their aquatic fixation. From the 1950s through the 1970s, Fresh Air publications featured nostalgic descriptions of swimming in the summer as promoters attempted to keep revenue streams strong in the face of cuts to social programs. The publicity copy also highlighted the wonders of rowing boats, milking cows, hiking trails, and riding horses, but swimming received first mention (see figure 4).[189] In 1975 the Fresh Air Fund's executive director Lisa Pulling went so

FIGURE 4. Two boys demonstrate their rowing prowess in 1949 at a Fresh Air Camp sponsored by the New York Episcopal Diocese. Used by permission of the New York Episcopal Diocese, New York, NY (Episcopal Diocese of New York, Records of the Protestant Episcopal City Mission Society, Box: Summer Camp Photos 1940's—1960's, SC7423, SC 7400 Series, dated July 1949, Elko Lake Camps, Parksville, New York).

far as to claim that learning to swim while on a Fresh Air trip prevented juvenile delinquency.[190] Through the 1970s, even more references to the delights of swimming in ponds and lakes appeared despite evidence that most children by that time swam in pools when on a Fresh Air vacation.[191] Regardless of the adults' nostalgia, the children celebrated rare freedom in the water.

Fire hydrants highlight the independence children found in getting wet. When denied access to swimming pools, city residents often beat the heat by turning on fire hydrants. Fresh Air promoters regularly derided the practice as an inferior substitute for country swimming. In 1948, rather than "splattering under a hydrant on a dirty street," Fresh Air participants could take "a long swim in a clear, country stream."[192] A local organizer in 1976 pitied city children who "would go through the summer without going swimming—except for an occasional fire-hydrant spray."[193] But Fresh Air participants seldom felt deprived by fire hydrant frolics. According to one eyewitness in 1962, children darted "in and out of the gushing fountain" of a fire hydrant and sat "down, beaming joyfully beneath it" even while keeping an eye out for the police.[194] Just as was the case when swimming in a pool or pond, the children found freedom in the streaming water as they danced, shouted, screamed, and even roller-skated through the cascading torrent. In a conversation with a travel chaperone during a return trip home, one Fresh Air participant explained that he had missed "the fire hydrants with sprinkler caps" in his neighborhood.[195]

That love of water independence even helped shift national priorities. In 1966 children frolicked in an open fire hydrant on Chicago's West Side. When two police officers shut down the stream, local residents objected and defied the police order by reopening the hydrant before the police had left the block. Asserting that only black neighborhoods saw the citywide ban enforced, residents threw debris at the officers as they arrested Donald Henry, the man who had reopened the fire hydrant. Only after Illinois Governor Otto Kerner sent in 1,500 National Guardsmen did the subsequent three days of rioting and rebellion come to an end. In the aftermath, city officials in Chicago and other major urban centers followed the lead of President Lyndon Johnson in announcing plans to construct new swimming pools. Although most of that new construction resulted in small, shallow, and overcrowded pools, the children had changed their surroundings by standing before a fire hydrant.[196]

Fresh Air children made sure they got to swim. Some, like Teddy Mayes, ventured to local community pools on their own. Others confronted overt racial discrimination when doing so. Still others learned to swim in order to tame the water's dangers. Many ignored class tension in order to swim all they wanted. Regardless of what promoters wrote about them and their love of swimming, Mayes and his companions dove into water where they splashed, dunked, paddled, and moved their bodies as they desired. In such a watery environment, from the 1940s through the 1970s, Fresh Air children claimed pool and pond as their own. Adults may have segregated them by sex or set lifeguards to hover nearby, but children ruled the waters when they swam.

A Disrupted Redemption Story

Those who told the story of religiously motivated families saving children from the city to swim in country ponds based their redemption tale on a changing notion of innocence. Prior to World War II, the innocence used by Fresh Air promoters had suggested naïveté, femininity, and natural wonder. In the postwar period, movement leaders continued to call the children innocent but used the term to indicate sexual inexperience, religious piety, obedience, and general receptivity to host instruction. The rest of the redemption story followed suit. Hosts had to be faultless to exercise redemption. Children had to be wholesome to shed the city's contagion. Ponds had to be pure to cleanse those who swam in deep waters. The Fresh Air redemption story fell apart if host families were imperfect, the city not so bad, and ponds irrelevant as sites of purification. Although few of the principal storytellers, people such as Frederick Lewis, discussed how much they depended upon innocence to fund their programs, it remained a staple of the movement across four decades and beyond.

The repeated telling of this redemption tale obscured underlying narrative disruptions. In the church's case, the Fresh Air redemption story drew much of its legitimacy from Protestant-inflected idioms of innocence, but leaders from that same religious community often failed in their efforts to shape the children according to their core values. Religious leaders vetted children on one end and, to a lesser extent, hosts on the other in order to block contagion from either direction. The efforts proved futile. Even though hosts selected the children's religion and prescribed Christocentric instruction, the children did not cooperate. Mennonite and Amish hosts, the most persuasive and upright of the hosting corps, still found that many guests resisted their ideas. Although religious practitioners offered innocence in idiom, they could not offer innocence in fact.

Concrete also disrupted the redemption tale. Despite decades spent describing the city as unremittingly hot, crowded, dangerous, ugly, and uncomfortable, administrators and publicists could not hide that children grew homesick for the city, loved the games they played on cement sidewalks, and cherished neighborhoods where everyone knew them. In response to the Black Nationalist critics who excoriated the programs from the mid-1960s through the mid-1970s, boosters and other Fresh Air supporters began to celebrate the city as they spoke of the sage counsel that the children brought the suburbs. Yet even as organizers turned away from such urban adoration and again lambasted the city, children continued to cheer when they returned home and sniffed the air with satisfaction. Those children who rejoiced in all things metropolitan undermined the redemption story by making the country appear less virtuous and the city look less evil.

Even pristine ponds could disrupt the redemption tale. Concepts of purity—and by extension innocence—depend upon clear separation. Something cannot be innocent or pure unless it is separated from something else that is corrupt or dirty. Dirt is itself nothing more than matter out of place.[197] Innocence means little if those who use it do not maintain conceptual order, structure, and boundaries. In the racially contested sites of swimming pools and ponds, children of color from the mid-1950s onward disrupted Fresh Air's innocence rhetoric by crossing the boundaries intended to separate black from white and city from country. In their bid for independent play and physical relief from heat in the city, children swam through dangers both imagined and real as they faced death by drowning, racial harassment, and economic inequity.

And so the children disrupted a redemption story told about them. They did not accept their religious instruction, misbehaved in church, and challenged belief. They flipped the script on calling the city bad. And they did all they could to find freedom in the water regardless of what program executives said about them. Yet the promoters covered over their disruptions by telling the redemption story again and again. From their perspective, it was the only story that mattered—the only one that they found to be true.

In the end, the Fresh Air model could not achieve the redemption it claimed or the freedom it offered because the children always went back home. Two weeks of focused religious instruction, country environs, and swimming in ponds was never quite enough. Because they returned to the city, the children again risked urban corruption. And so the redemption story proved self-defeating. Fresh Air saved children from the city but only for a while. The organizers then returned them to the very urban monster they had imagined in their bid to save them in the first place. Church, country, and pond could not fully save.

But that was not the only story.

Amid the themes of grass, color, and sass, another story emerged. As chapter 3 will show, even where manicured lawns purported to welcome all regardless of race, the children found ways to challenge adult authority and tell another tale that only got whispered on the margins of the Fresh Air community. In the contested space where black and brown children interacted with white adults, an alternative vision of the meaning of Fresh Air emerged. In the midst of adult limitations on their behaviors, Fresh Air children entered a racial freedom struggle on their own.

GRASS, COLOR, SASS
How the Children Shaped Fresh Air

Sonia and Laelia had had enough. Fresh Air camp offered them none of the attractions they enjoyed back home in Brooklyn and Manhattan. Even though their counselors encouraged them to relish "the birds and plants, have scavenger hunts, and picnics, and go home with suitcases full of speckled rocks and swimming citations," the girls would have none of it. They longed to watch movies and spin on merry-go-rounds in their home community. Rather than put up with a nature-filled environment they detested, the girls decided to catch a bus back to New York. Although foiled by a quick-acting counselor who spotted the girls as they scrambled through bushes in their bid for freedom, the girls acted anything but innocent. One counselor noted that campers like Sonia and Laelia were "more grown up . . . assertive . . . hostile . . . unsatisfied . . . hard to handle" and got into fights and caused trouble.[1] At the age of ten in the summer of 1971, the girls had—in the opinion of their minders—gotten sassy.

Fresh Air participants like Sonia and Laelia shaped Fresh Air programs as they dealt with adults focused on nature, race, and behavior. Even as Fresh Air boosters and administrators linked the children with grass in a bid to market carefree summer vacations, the children disrupted the adults' promotional plans by expressing less enthusiasm for nature than their hosts desired. Those same Fresh Air promoters who described the children as blissfully ignorant of racial dynamics overlooked the sophisticated racial code of conduct practiced by the children in often racially hostile communities. In the midst of such unwelcoming environments, those children who made it through the strict vetting process meant to winnow out delinquents prompted their adult caretakers to expend as much energy on behavioral modification as relationship building. Thought only to be sassy—with all the racial baggage of the period attached to the term—the children responded with an often-uncredited complexity.

The children thus helped craft a hosting program that had become the dominant model of positive race relations in the country. Despite a history of overt prejudice and racism in Friendly Towns during the 1950s and 1960s, to host a black or brown Fresh Air child by the 1970s was to strike a blow against "racism," "racial prejudice," and "racial misunderstanding."[2] Even as urbanization amplified the boosters' rhetoric about the countryside restoring children to a state of uncorrupted naïveté, children of color from the city became instructors and teachers to the white hosts who took them into their homes. In the process, the children engaged in their own freedom struggle.

Grass

Fresh Air boosters loved grass. They used it in 1959 when they wrote of the children's desire "to run in the grass, like angels with green footprints on the good earth."[3] They used it in 1962 to attract donors interested in supporting children who frolicked "in what they delight in calling their 'running-around grass'" and left "symbolic little impressions of their bare feet as they run—green footprints of happiness."[4] Even when the word had taken on a double meaning, adult supporters still turned to grass in 1974 as the centerpiece of their development campaign. As a full-page ad in *Forbes* magazine declared, "This summer nice city kids will get into some really good grass." After a visual space to let the pun sink in, the ad continued, "The kind that tickles your toes when you walk through it barefoot." In a photo above the text, one white boy, one Latino boy, two Latina girls, two African American boys, and one African American girl run together in "the grass, the sun and fresh air." This kind of restorative grass, the ad writers assured the wealthy *Forbes* readers, gave "a kid a clear head for the rest of the year."[5]

Not every Fresh Air child shared the boosters' enthusiasm. In 1956 one unnamed Fresh Air participant arrived at a camp run by Episcopalians from New York City. As he looked out at well-tended lawns, a lake large enough for boating, and tall trees next to "shimmering" waters, the "city boy" was not impressed. He declared, "So what's the big deal, I've seen grass before."[6] Like many other Fresh Air children who played regularly in New York's extensive park system, he knew what grass looked like. Regardless of what the Fresh Air promoters may have imagined, many of the children who came to the country knew of nature before they ever set foot off the bus, train, or plane.

The theme of grass reveals how children shaped the Fresh Air narrative. When describing the programs' benefits, promoters used grass as a metonym for nature to cast the children as compliant recipients of the adults' largesse. Many of the children did enjoy the freedom to roam among trees, lawns, and lakes. Yet others found their encounters with nature repellent rather than attractive. As Fresh Air guests both affirmed and countered pro-grass sentiment, they forced hosts and boosters to protect their turf. The adults responded to the children's diverse opinions by increasing grassy promotions, disregarding the racial dynamics of lawn-centric enclaves, and intensifying their rhetoric about nature's restorative capacity. Regardless of their intent, the children helped shaped the Fresh Air program simply by talking about sod.

The symbolic power of suburban lawns fertilized such grass-filled narratives. By the end of World War II, the modern lawn had taken on its familiar form, a carefully trimmed expanse of grassy green. With roots in the landed estates of English aristocracy, lawns marked class status as suburbs proliferated from the mid-nineteenth century onward.[7] Homeowners demonstrated civic commitment by maintaining their lawns while at the same time offering proof of upright moral standing and commitment to the Protestant work ethic.[8] Lawns came to carry even more symbolic freight in the post–World War II period as they signified retreat from the pressures and intrusions of the surrounding world.[9]

The weight of this symbolic significance led to the first of two ironies present in postwar lawn culture. A pristine lawn evoked nature's romance even though suburbanites destroyed natural habitats to develop manicured greens.[10] Homeowners invested time, energy, and money to avoid the social opprobrium visited on those who did not mow their grass.[11] There was nothing natural about it. In other words, the very sign of nature that would come to be valued by so many hosts and guests in the Fresh Air program actually represented a constructed artifice supported by mass-produced machines, petrochemicals, and urban industries.

Secondly, suburban homeowners invited African American and Latino children to frolic on lawns purchased with restrictive covenants. Such deeds of sale stipulated that a given property could be sold to or inhabited by white people only.[12] The provisions gained support from both private sellers and the U.S. government as the Federal Housing Administration sought to maintain racially homogenous communities in order to protect property values.[13] Even though the Supreme Court outlawed the judicial enforcement of the practice with *Shelley v. Kraemer* (1948) and again in *Barrows v. Jackson* (1953), neither the courts nor the federal government sought to halt the actual practice of racially restrictive covenants until civil rights activists achieved legislative reforms in the 1960s.[14] When black and brown Fresh Air children arrived to play on the grass, they entered territory from which they had been deliberately and intentionally barred.

Amid these unacknowledged ironies of nature and race, Fresh Air boosters and hosts exulted in claiming that the children had never before laid eyes on grass. For a span of forty years, host after host exclaimed that the children had "never seen" grass prior to arriving at their Fresh Air destination.[15] Although the boosters moderated their claims upon occasion by noting it was "the first green grass" the child "*may* have ever seen" or "*some* of the youngsters had seen," they repeated the assertion with impressive consistency.[16] As late as 1979, a *New York Times* reporter again declared that many of the children on a country visit had "never seen a field of grass."[17] These recurrent claims of "firsts" likewise shared a common tone of awe and excitement in the children's discovery. A 1943 report emphasized that watching children set eyes on grass for the first time "provided as much entertainment for the host as for the child."[18] Others were thrilled to offer children their first exposure to grass.[19] As was the case with stories about the children's first encounters with cows, boosters echoed one of the pre–World War II themes of natural wonder by underscoring how little knowledge the children had of the countryside.

Hosts waxed even more rhapsodic about the freedom and sensory immersion afforded by grass. A 1944 promotional film depicted a young girl turning cartwheels in a grassy field.[20] Reinforcing the nineteenth-century trope of children frolicking barefoot in nature, one host wrote a poem in 1955 about a guest who, "wondering at so much that grows, . . . scuffed the grass with his bare toes."[21] Another exclaimed in 1963 over the "abundance of clean, sweet grass in which to tumble and frolic."[22] Others noted that their guests asked permission to take off their shoes to walk in the grass, cavorted in lawns, and fondled blades of green.[23] A host from Vermont in 1961 described how Ruth, a six-year-old African American girl who purportedly had never before laid eyes on grass, would spend long hours lying prone in the yard caressing the grass with her fingers. The host's children thought their guest "unbalanced to be so enthralled with green grass."[24] A 1979 editorial in the *New York Times* captured the grassy rapture by quoting former Fresh Air child Mario Puzo, author of *The Godfather*. Puzo wrote that he "'nearly went crazy' with the joy of smelling the grass and flowers" while on a Fresh Air visit.[25]

The hosts' and boosters' references to the children's love of grass served as a metonym for nature as a whole. As was the case in other programs like the Boy Scouts and private summer camping programs, Fresh Air boosters waxed eloquent about the wonders of nature writ large, not just grassy plains.[26] Whether evoking burbling brooks, depicting summer breezes over a gleaming lake, or quoting Henry Wadsworth Longfellow to describe whispering pines, promoters such as Fresh Air Fund public information director Richard Crandell saw only good in nature.[27] Here again Crandell and other professional Fresh Air promoters

followed a script that reformers in the nineteenth century had used to romanti-
cize the country amid the uncertainty of burgeoning industrialization.[28] Rather
than curtailing their rhetoric in a purportedly less sentimental age, the Fresh
Air boosters turned up the romantic tones. Nature had "eternal rhythms" that
beat through "precious greenery" in, as New York governor Nelson A. Rockefeller claimed, a "wonderful and beautiful and wholesome" environment.[29] By the
mid-1960s, the threat of a nature-consuming "megapolis . . . stretching from Boston to Richmond, Va." prompted Fresh Air leaders to enlist children in conservation initiatives such as seeking out and destroying gypsy moths.[30] Such efforts
only served to intensify the boosters' praise of nature's benefits.

Fresh Air guests in some cases confirmed claims made about them. One youngster started his description of a "wonderful" vacation by noting that "the grass was
soft and clean."[31] Looking back on her experience as a child, a former Fresh Air
participant recalled that the "most amazing thing" about being in the country was
"being able to play in the grass and run outside."[32] Yet the children rarely claimed
that they had never before seen grass. Like the boy at the Episcopal camp in 1956,
Fresh Air visitors knew what grass looked like. None needed an explanation. They
could exclaim, as one guest did in 1954, "Gee the grass is so green" without requiring anyone to point it out to them.[33] Their comments typically revolved around
requesting permission to walk on the grass or exclaiming over the amount of grass
rather than stating that they had never before laid eyes on it.[34]

The children knew about grass because they came from cities that had
well-developed park systems. According to the vast majority of the children's
hosts, the cities from which the children came had no discernible green space. As
is explored in chapter 2, Fresh Air promoters prompted donations by creating a
stark contrast between "garbage strewn alley[s]" and "the grassy green of a backyard."[35] In the process of that comparison, they did not mention the green spaces
available to many city children. Most major urban centers had park systems in
place by 1920.[36] Initiated by Progressive Era reformers interested in establishing
moral order in the face of what they deemed degeneracy and chaos in the city, the
parks also served the purpose of exposing children and adults to nature in order
to nourish the former and refresh the latter.[37] By the end of the 1900s, urban
residents themselves celebrated parks where "the grass is always green" and frequented recreation areas filled with grass and trees.[38] Even though Judith Thiede,
a Fresh Air organizer from Suffolk, New Jersey, may have meant well when she
exclaimed in 1976, "The city is just not the place for children during the summer,"
she ignored those children who were already feeling a "little grass under their
feet" where they lived in the city.[39]

The young urbanites further contested their hosts' nature-centric claims
by also letting their dislike of the country be known. Alternately annoyed and

provoked by the deerflies and mosquitoes he encountered while visiting Pittsfield, Massachusetts, twelve-year-old Jack from New York City exclaimed in 1956, "Bugs. . . . Everywhere I go there's bugs."[40] Jack was not alone. Many children from the city complained about the insects they encountered in the country.[41] Others were frightened by looming trees, a sight that caused one young girl to exclaim, "It's so dark and scary here. Let's go back!"[42] Another young guest reported in 1961 of being frightened to walk barefoot on "dewy grass."[43] A year later, still another ran frantic and breathless into his host's kitchen and exclaimed, "A butterfly was chasing me!"[44] On the drive home from her pickup point in Connecticut in 1962, a young guest by the name of Ernestine confessed her fear of what might happen to her when first she encountered the unknown specter of fresh air. Referring to her host mother, she said, "Mommie, what do fresh air mean? I get kind of skeered."[45] Although hosts often told such tales for humorous effect or to stress the children's ignorance of rural life and their eventual acculturation to it, the children nonetheless expressed as much fear and dislike of nature as they did appreciation for it. At the very least, as in the case of the Fresh Air boy who wrinkled his nose at an odiferous cattle barn upon his arrival and wondered where all the fresh air had gone, guests found that their first encounter with nature—whether with grass or those that crawled between its blades—sometimes did not live up to its billing.[46]

Reports of the children's reaction to nature varied by race. Hosts attributed negative comments about trees, bugs, and farm odors almost exclusively to African American and Puerto Rican children. Of the negative comments featured thus far, all came from children of color except the anecdote about the butterfly in hot pursuit. Reports about white children's encounters with nature invariably focused on the positive. In 1956, for example, a host mother in Pittsfield, Massachusetts, described how a New York City guest originally from Estonia would sit in the grass looking out at the "panorama of hills" for fifteen minutes at a time. When queried why he did so, he replied, "I like to look around at all the green stuff and thank God for letting me stay here a while."[47] Hosts also reported on African American and Latino children who enjoyed picking blackberries, looking at the bright stars at night, and going on picnics.[48] However, the consistency with which the accounts centered on African American and Latino children pestered by bugs or afraid of looming trees suggests as much about racially selective reporting on the part of the hosts as it does about racially distinct reactions on the part of the children. Through the 1960s and into the 1970s, as children of color came to dominate the Fresh Air guests and boosters sought to promote their programs in the midst of that racial sea change, stories about the children's encounters with nature—both good and bad—proliferated. In the midst of that increase in nature-centric reporting, the hosts did lock on to dark-skinned city kids complaining about insects.

The children thus shaped Fresh Air by both reveling in nature and being revolted by it. Both responses provided program boosters with publicity material. When children delighted in all things natural, news reports, advertisements, and brochures teemed with their quotations; a donating public that grew every more nostalgic for rural Edens responded enthusiastically. When other children spoke their minds about the damp, buzzing, smelly, and grassy outdoors, publicity pieces suggested that the children would soon adapt and learn to appreciate green lawns and dense woods no matter how buggy. In both cases the adults returned to accounts of children enraptured with grass. The Fresh Air Fund even introduced a new logo in 1958 based on the impression of a child's footprint in the grass.[49] The children had left footprints on the lawn, but some did so while running away from nature rather than toward it.

Those who developed the 1974 ad campaign that riffed on grass as marijuana appealed to rural nostalgia based on the assumption that the children would not get the joke. The children were, as the ad proclaimed, "nice city kids."[50] The ad showed them in a classic stance of unburdened abandon running hand in hand across a grass-covered plain. It suggested that the grass would tickle their toes. It evoked them walking barefoot. Such children would be free of the knowledge that "pot," "weed," "reefer," and "Mary Jane" also went by "grass." The gift of a "clear head" from country exposure would, the ad suggested, keep them from the influences of real drugs. Evidently the ad designers either did not know about or chose to ignore the highly publicized drug raid of a Fresh Air camp in Baltimore two years previously in which state troopers arrested sixteen counselors and the camp director for "smoking marijuana all summer."[51] If the children knew about "really good grass" of the *High Times* kind, the ad would lose its appeal. The children needed to be presented as naïve for the humor to succeed.

Yet such naïveté was unlikely among the children but not among the adults. Children like those featured in the ad knew far more about urban realities than did their hosts. Few by the 1970s would have been ignorant of drug culture slang.[52] Yet the boosters and program promoters—as well as the publicity team that crafted the *Forbes* ad—seem to have been convinced of the children's ignorance. However, rural hosts knew far less about the city in this instance than did their urban guests. By sending the message that children vetted by the program would be naïve, unthreatening, and malleable, such ads obscured the adult hosts' ignorance about the children's world. As the following section will show, the young travelers from the city shaped the program that they loved not only by expressing both their enjoyment of and displeasure with nature but also by teaching their hosts about race and the urban worlds from which they came.

Color

Those who promoted Fresh Air programs had long taken pride in their race relations record. In 1954 Frederick Lewis shared a peer's praise with his board members. The executive director of the New York Urban League had complimented the Fresh Air program for "doing the most outstanding job in the country" of integrating its camps. Lewis began his end-of-year report with that accolade.[53] Others joined Lewis in expressing confidence that Fresh Air exchanges could bring about racial change. An organizer for the Fresh Air program of the Community Renewal Society of Chicago claimed in 1968 that the program was the "best way to get to know the Negro."[54] Others averred that the programs were "the most positive form of charity in this country [, in which] there are absolutely no barriers of race, color or creed," and that they offered the "best possible experience" for blacks and whites "to live together and get to know one another."[55]

Such tributes rarely took into account what the African American, Latino, and Asian American children experienced when they arrived in white hosting communities. Gregory and William, ages nine and five, respectively, traveled to Harrisburg, Pennsylvania, from New York in 1963. While staying with their hosts, the Steger family, the two boys went shopping with their host mother and sister. At the store, they overheard two other shoppers exclaim, "I wonder if they're her children—isn't it terrible" and "I bet they are Fresh Air kids. I wouldn't want them sleeping in my beds." Others offered similar comments during visits to the local playground. As their host mother admitted, the two African American boys would not have been allowed to swim at the local Hershey Pool only a few years previously.[56]

The adults' claims and the children's experiences together describe what supporters nonetheless insisted was the dominant race relations model of the civil rights era. To be certain, Fresh Air programs brought more white, rural people from the Northeast and Midwest into intimate contact with people of color than any other social organization, governmental program, or grassroots initiative. Although the largest of the Fresh Air programs prolonged the transition, once it made the shift the Fresh Air Fund joined the dozens of other programs that had focused on racial and ethnic exchange from their founding. Boosters took pride in a program that could accurately boast of being more intimate than schools, more far-reaching than the military, more integrated than churches, and more sustained than marches. Fresh Air boosters touted a model of one way that race relations could work.

Yet critics pointed out the limits on integration inherent in the Fresh Air model. They noted that even as it brought racial groups together, the programs required long-distance travel, set up power imbalances, and curtailed the length of interaction. Moreover, black social workers decried the psychological damage done by immersing children of color in white communities where they ended up with debilitating "white psyches."[57] Despite acknowledging this criticism, as the programs became more integrated, administrators kept the same model in place. Although program promoters like Lewis touted their race relations record, they had much less to say about the complex, problematic, and contradictory process of black and brown children teaching white adults about racism in the midst of an often racially threatening environment.

A review of the history of interracial contact within the Fresh Air movement brings the dissatisfaction of Black Power activists into a new light. The children of color who began to populate the Fresh Air ranks at the onset of World War II entered a program dominated by white, impoverished children. In his original vision for the program, Willard Parsons emphasized the spiritual purity of the poor, malnourished immigrant children he sent to the country. Progressive Era reformers turned more toward civic instruction of untutored immigrants but continued to focus on the children's virtue in the midst of a blighted, foreigner-infused city.[58] By contrast, African American, Latino, and Asian American children were an afterthought, a difficult but necessary demand of doing business in an increasingly multihued city. To be a Fresh Air child at the start of World War II was to be presented as spiritually and ethically faultless because of one's prepubescence and openness to assimilation and instruction. The shift from this class- and ethnicity-based rhetoric of innocence to a race-based narrative would be decades in the making.

The transition to a program defined by black and brown children thus got off to a slow start. Under way already by the 1920s, the efforts of the historic black newspaper *Amsterdam News* to fund Fresh Air trips for the children of Harlem opened a limited number of pathways for African American children to spend time in the country at friendly facilities, but these efforts reached relatively few. Most white-run camps, with the exception of those "red" camps affiliated with communist and socialist groups, excluded black and brown children from joining their programs through the 1930s and beyond.[59] During the 1940s no significant Fresh Air programs existed in the Midwest, and the few programs active in the South served only white children.[60] By 1947, only 30 percent of the Fund's 10,000 sponsored children were African American, with no mention made of Asian American or Latino children in the mix.[61] Even though city-based recreation programs run by the National Council of Churches, the YMCA, and private organizations catered directly to African American and Latino youths, administrators at the Fresh Air Fund touted their race relations record only in the more controlled and less intimate campground programs.[62] According to camp program directors and home-hosting organizers in 1948, "race, creed or color" was never a "matter of any moment." In fact, despite the lower number of invitations for African American children, promoters still claimed "many whites prefer Negro children for these vacations."[63]

The social reality for people of color proved far harsher than the rosy picture painted by Fresh Air promoters. The tensions present from the ongoing influx of African American families from the South into major urban centers like New York and Detroit boiled over in riots and rebellions. Forty people died in Detroit in 1942 when a white mob attempted to take back housing set aside for black families.[64] Despite the release of Gunnar Myrdal's *An American Dilemma* in 1944, which asserted that the problem of race resided with white prejudice rather than black inferiority, and a growing consensus in the scientific community to expose the "evils of racism," popular notions about black inferiority remained.[65] Even in the aftermath of the 1967 urban rebellions, when the Kerner Commission faulted governmental agencies for failing to provide adequate education, housing, and social services to urban populations, elected officials invested more in the police than in increasing economic opportunities.[66]

The racial tensions present in northern urban centers sprang from major demographic shifts. Even as suburban developers used restrictive covenants to set up white enclaves, African Americans migrated to the city. From 1950 to 1970, five million African Americans moved into metropolitan neighborhoods at the same time that seven million white people left them. In the first ten years of that time, New York's African American population increased by 46 percent while the white population dropped by 7 percent; Chicago's black population skyrocketed by 65 percent while the white population plummeted by 13 percent. During the same time the Puerto Rican population climbed in Chicago and New York, and Asian Americans settled in large numbers in New York, Los Angeles, and San Francisco.[67]

The initial shift toward serving children of color began in the 1940s and 1950s, concurrent with changing urban demographics. In the broader camping community, some northern groups like the New York City YMCA founded interracial camps in 1944 while southern YMCA affiliates integrated their camps much later, in at least one instance not until the mid-1960s.[68] In the *Herald Tribune* camping program, participating partners signed a policy statement in 1950 indicating that they would help ensure that the Fund would not sponsor "either an all-white or all-Negro camp population at any camp at any time."[69] Although staff abided by the integration policy through the period, in 1951 they considered establishing "Camp George Washington Carver" for black children but never realized the plan.[70] Even though African American children had fewer options for attending camp than did white children, the call for racial integration was too strong during the period for staff to create a separate facility.[71] Other Fresh Air camping initiatives such as the Warrensdale program near Pittsburgh also integrated their facilities in the early 1950s.[72]

However, staff at the Fresh Air Fund found it more difficult to integrate homes. Despite their efforts to "encourage invitations for Negroes and Puerto Ricans," by 1953 the ratio of white to "dark skinned youngsters" was only five to one.[73] Through the decade, hosts could indicate their preference for a child's race, a practice that, although discouraged by staff, hampered racial integration.[74] Other Fresh Air programs founded in the 1950s such as a program run by Mennonites in southeast Pennsylvania also had selection clauses and, as a result, transitioned slowly to an integrated service model. Interestingly, on a local basis enough children of color had begun to frequent white homes that by 1956 at least one reporter assumed that Fresh Air programs served "mostly Negro and Puerto Ricans," an assertion that may have been true in a few communities but had not yet become the dominant reality by the end of the 1950s.[75]

Many Fresh Air promoters lumped African American and Puerto Rican children together in the same way the reporter did in 1956. Although administrators kept track of four primary racial groups—white, black, Hispanic, and Asian—for statistical purposes, they wrote about and referred to essentially two groups: white and black. Frequently, hosts made little effort to distinguish the rich cultural diversity within black and Latino communities. The common practice of isolating single guests in host homes further racialized the children.

The slow move to integrate camps and homes matched national integration efforts. Following the 1954 *Brown v. Board of Education* decision, many white parents in the North and South opposed the racial integration of their children's schools. Despite the success of the 1956 Montgomery bus boycott, positive media coverage, and northern political support, those white people required to integrate their social space did so reluctantly or not at all. A declaration of support for integrating a southern city's public transportation system did not always translate into an invitation to dinner for an African American acquaintance.

Fresh Air hosts overcame their initial reluctance and helped transform the hosting programs into the primary site of intimate racial exchange by the end of the 1960s. In 1965 only a third of the children sponsored by the *Herald Tribune* Fund came from white families.[76] The following year Friendly Town coordinator Ralph B. Dwinell reported that the *Herald Tribune* had served more "non-white" children than ever before as he noted participation rates of "35 percent Negro; 28 percent Puerto Rican; . . . and 3 percent Chinese."[77] Although the *Herald Tribune* kept the racial selection option in place through the 1960s, by 1968 enough adults had become convinced of the benefits of hosting African American and Latino children that staffers reported receiving "more invitations for blacks than for whites, except below the Mason and Dixon line"; most of their camps had also become dominated by "black and Puerto Rican children."[78] Other Fresh Air programs founded in the 1960s focused exclusively or primarily on African American children. Programs in Chicago and Seattle joined programs such as the Ames, Iowa, effort that transported "Negro children from urban slums and place[d] them [for] two weeks with white families in other towns."[79] By 1966, a reporter from the *Amsterdam News* thought it significant to mention only that the *Herald Tribune* Fund sent "over 17,000 Negro and Puerto Rican children" to the country.[80] Although the overwhelming majority of hosts continued to be white, middle-class, heterosexual, two-parent families located in racially homogenous suburbs and rural communities, in 1969 the Cleveland-based program featured an African American host of an African American child.[81] No longer a Fresh Air sideline, race had become the programs' cause célèbre.

So central had race relations become to the Fresh Air model that program promoters began to suggest that the rural hosting programs could calm racial foment. Urban dwellers in the Northeast, Midwest, and West witnessed large-scale racially motivated rebellions marked by destruction of both private and public property. Whether Cambridge in 1963, Watts in 1965, Newark in 1967, or Baltimore, Chicago, Kansas City, Washington, D.C., and others in 1968, urban unrest rocked the nation. To stop the "racial violence," those committed to the Fresh Air model such as Jonathan Dwyer of Bennington, Vermont, suggested in 1968 that "Negroes from New York and white Vermonters . . . live together and get to know one another." According to Dwyer, such contact would end "blind prejudice" because Fresh Air children had never "tried to burn down any buildings in our fair state."[82] That same year, *Herald Tribune* Fresh Air president Blancke Noyes used the occasion of a fund-raising letter to assert that sending "Negro and Puerto Rican" children to the country could "prevent . . . pent-up frustrations from erupting during the hot summer months."[83]

The racial violence of the 1960s segued into a decade of normalizing home-based racial contact through Fresh Air ventures. During the 1970s, the term "Fresh Air child" became synonymous with a black or brown urban visitor in nearly every area of the country. By 1978, the *Herald Tribune* program reported that black and Puerto Rican children constituted 85 percent of its served population while programs in Seattle and Chicago focused exclusively on "minority" and "negro" children being hosted in white homes.[84] The Fresh Air movement had arrived at the racial paradigm that it would hold through the decade and beyond. Press accounts and accompanying photographs in Montana, New York, North Dakota, Pennsylvania, and Vermont focused on white host children and adults in proximity to dark-skinned children from the city.[85] Because of the legacy of racially segregated suburbs and white-dominated hosting committees, few African American or Latino hosts followed the example of the black Cleveland host in 1969. Whether displaying children in the act of fishing, eating food, or walking side by side through a parking lot, reporters and many cartoonists turned repeatedly to scenes of inoffensive integration in which African American children and white hosts figured prominently (see figure 5).[86]

FIGURE 5. "At right, Melanie Hinkle of Penn Laird (right) shepherds her new friend Bernadette Dorsey toward the family car. Melanie is the daughter of Mr. and Mrs. Donald Hinkle" (original caption). Used by permission of the *Daily News-Record*, Harrisonburg, VA ("Holiday Begins," *Daily News-Record*, July 14, 1978, 13).

So intensely did promoters focus on racial integration that they appear to have forgotten their history. Although the Fresh Air Fund—no longer affiliated with the then defunct *Herald Tribune*—continued its practice of allowing hosts to designate the race of their prospective guests until 1971, five years later a reporter, clearly drawing on materials provided by the Fund's publicity staff, claimed that the Fund had provided "one million vacations for boys and girls, based on need and without sectarian or racial restrictions."[87] The claim disregarded the decades-long practice in which staff from the Fund had allowed hosts to restrict race and religion even though other programs had long discontinued or never instituted the practice. Despite efforts of administrators in cities like Cleveland and New York to recruit African American and interracial hosts to the program, throughout the 1970s the program remained committed to a white host/black or brown guest model.[88]

The Fresh Air programs that became linked with white suburbanites hosting black and brown city children based their publicity on a string of heartwarming anecdotes. Consistent with the postwar celebration of liberal cultural pluralism that prompted white people to develop interracial relationships, by the middle of the 1950s Fresh Air publicists had begun to promote the racial benefits of their programs.[89] According to the accounts, African American and Latino children and their hosts shared playthings, held hands, and accepted each other without condescension or paternalism.[90] A 1956 host mother reported that her visitor's "shy smile" immediately rid her of all race prejudice.[91] Even as the 1960s push for school integration gave way before Supreme Court reversals in the 1970s, the signs of happy integration continued. Whether the children who won over a prejudiced neighbor in 1968, those who referred to their hosts as their "family" in 1973, or the guest named Flip Bailey who shared "secrets and stuff" with her host sister Lisa Cantella in 1977, these African American and Latino children righted racial wrongs, crossed racial boundaries, and solved racially tinged problems during two-week country visits.[92]

Yet some children encountered a very different racial landscape through their participation in black-run summer camps. In the main, black families in the city expressed enthusiasm about camping yet had few options to offer their children.[93] Rather than spend time in a white suburbanite home or at a camp run by any one of the many white-dominated Fresh Air programs, a small selection of African American children attended one of the few camps run and funded by the black community. In New York, for example, wealthier black children visited exclusive health resorts such as the Perdeux Health Farm, Donhaven Country Club, and the Nungesser Chateau.[94] Those with fewer financial resources went to camps run or sponsored by the Harlem Children's Fresh Air Fund or participated in camps sponsored by evangelical groups like Camp Pioneer in Pearl, Mississippi.[95]

Although often similar in form to white-run camps, the black-run camps offered children a substantively different experience. Two camps—one that catered to wealthier black children and one that served African American children from middle- and lower-class homes—reveal the racial differences.

Camp Atwater in Brookfield, Massachusetts, accommodated the black elite. Founded in 1921 by Dr. William De Berry as St. John's Camp, the retreat center changed names in 1926 to honor Dr. David Fisher Atwater, a highly respected physician in the Brookfield community and father of major donor Mary Atwater.[96] Through the 1960s, the camp offered elite children of lawyers, judges, and other black professionals a venue where they could socialize with their peers.[97] In 1954 a columnist described the cachet ascribed to Camp Atwater alums by asserting that "[b]eing a Camp Atwater alumnus is the equivalent of being a Harvard grad, a Yale grad and goodness knows what all rolled into one."[98] Another reporter noted in 1961 that "a certain amount of distinction" afforded those who attended the camp.[99] A parent added in 1966 that Atwater campers represented the "cream of the crop" from the black community.[100] In addition to offering social connections for the youths, Camp Atwater staff provided recreation opportunities seldom seen at white-run Fresh Air camps, such as ballet, tennis, and horseback riding.[101] Although staff at Atwater scheduled sex-segregated camp sessions and focused on outdoor activities as did Fresh Air staff, Atwater personnel allowed campers to attend until they turned eighteen, awarded "cultured" conduct, and organized camper alumni reunions.[102] Atwater personnel focused on creating an environment in which black children felt at ease and where counselors from their communities who were themselves often Atwater alums provided positive role models.

Camp Bryton Rock in Allaben, New York, offered camping opportunities for middle- and low-income children in a similar African American enclave nestled in the Catskill Mountains. Founded and directed by Reginald and Lillybelle McHugh, the camp served as an extension of their ministry at First Emmanuel, a congregation that worshipped in nearby Kingston but had deep connections in Harlem.[103] Founded in the mid-1930s, the camp brought together children who could not otherwise afford to leave the city for a summer camp outing and also those whose parents had the resources to cover the summer fee. Like Camp Atwater, Camp Bryton Rock provided a similar array of outdoor activities, including swimming, baseball, camping, tennis, and horseback riding.[104] Although Bryton Rock staff did not segregate their camps by gender, like Atwater personnel they offered multiple-week stays and invited campers back through their teen years. Listed as a facility friendly to African American families in the *Green Book* guide for "Negro travelers," Bryton Rock not only hired counselors who themselves came from Harlem—including several who would go on to distinguished careers such as Harry Belafonte and Cicely Tyson—but also took children on field trips to learn about black historical leaders such as abolitionist and women's rights activist Sojourner Truth.[105] Beginning in the 1960s, Rev. and Mrs. McHugh also brought a smaller group of children from the camp to stay with them for a few weeks in the exclusive Martha's Vineyard resort community.[106]

The differences between black-run camps like Atwater and Bryton Rock and white-run facilities like the Fresh Air Fund's Sharpe Reservation run deeper than racial demographics. At black-run camps, children and teenagers encountered adults who acknowledged, celebrated, and fostered their racial identities and who assumed they would succeed in life. Counselors and administrators at white-run camps also worked hard to foster positive self-images in their charges but usually did so while ignoring racial identities. Yet, in addition to providing an implicitly inclusive environment, black-run camps rarely debased the city. Promotional materials for Atwater and Bryton Rock touted the benefits of their respective natural settings but did not degrade the city in the process. Some African American leaders did engage in antiurban rhetoric, such as the *Pittsburgh Courier* columnist who in 1965 lauded rural communities with their "wide open spaces and fresh air not available in the slums."[107] By contrast, a 1960 advertisement for Bryton Rock simply focused on the numerous activities offered by a "Camp That Inspires Youth."[108] In the same way, promotional articles about Camp Atwater in both 1941 and 1961 made no mention of the city's deficiencies but instead focused on a long list of the activities enjoyed by campers, including "tennis, archery, riflery, croquet, swimming, fencing, volleyball, baseball, folk dancing and other games."[109]

The small slice of Fresh Air children who attended black-run camps opens a window into a different racial camping experience. To be certain, only a fraction of the African American children who spent time in summer camps ended up in black-run programs. In 1965, for example, the Fresh Air Fund sent 4,000 African American children on home stays and another 800 to the Fund's Sharpe Reservation campgrounds.[110] Other Fresh Air groups sent thousands more black children to white homes that year.[111] By comparison, Camp Atwater averaged well under 500 campers in its entire season.[112] An even smaller percentage of African American children attended black-run camps after white-run facilities began to integrate in the 1950s and 1960s.[113] Nonetheless, those who attended black-run camps faced far less racial discrimination and bias against the city than those who ventured into white-led space.

Given the relative lack of camps like Atwater and Bryton Rock, some African American families chose to support white-led Fresh Air efforts. Members of Antioch Baptist, one of the oldest African American Baptist congregations in Cleveland, contributed money and clothing to the Fresh Air program in 1967.[114]

In New York, the *Amsterdam News*, having long since discontinued its own Fresh Air project once the *Herald Tribune* began serving African American children in earnest, held fund-raisers for and helped publicize the programs of the Fresh Air Fund by the end of the 1960s.[115] Other socialites from New York's African American community participated in planning a Fresh Air fund-raiser in 1969 after the Fresh Air Fund board indicated its interest in "attaining funds from minority groups" three years previously.[116] Although such overtly integrated fund-raising efforts appear to have peaked at the end of the 1960s, these fund-raising initiatives show that at least some adult members of the African American community cared enough about Fresh Air ventures to contribute both their children and their money. In the main, however, these more well-heeled African American boosters did not register their children for Fresh Air vacations.

Some mothers of Fresh Air children did join leaders from the African American and Latino communities in affirming the programs. Boosters touted their accolades with enthusiasm. The racially focused testimonies of mothers of Fresh Air children received some of the most sustained and positive coverage in Fresh Air press accounts from the middle of the 1960s onward. Following the urban street violence of the summer of 1964, several newspapers reprinted an article featuring excerpts of a letter from Marian Kirton of Brooklyn, New York, praising her son George's hosts for opening their "door to Negro children" and, by doing so, demonstrating that "white people, like every other people on earth, are not all alike—there are good and there are bad."[117] Kirton's commentary echoed many such post–World War II declarations of the need to help young people lose their prejudices.[118] Other mothers of Fresh Air children in the late 1960s and 1970s acknowledged that they held doubts about "do gooder" programs run by white families in the suburbs but concluded in the end that the programs would be safe and beneficial for their children.[119] Reports likewise mentioned mothers of Fresh Air children who commented on bursts of piety, improved manners, and general exclamations of delight from their children upon return from a Fresh Air visit in the country.[120] Although such positive testimonies from Fresh Air mothers appeared less frequently than did accounts from the host mothers, boosters widely distributed comments made by mothers of Fresh Air children. Notably, comments from fathers of Fresh Air children rarely if ever found their way into promotional pieces.

Yet the most effusive claims about the racial benefits of Fresh Air programs came not from the home-based initiatives but the white-led Fresh Air camps. Already in the 1940s, New York's Union Settlement Association proudly documented the integration of its camps.[121] In step with other white camps interested in integration at the time, the Fresh Air Fund received praise from the Anti-Defamation League in 1954 for the "absence of prejudice" in its staff and the ease with which its camps had become racially integrated.[122] Not only did camp staff claim that they brought together "whites, Negroes, and Puerto Ricans" from an embattled Manhattan high school "without the slightest difficulty whatsoever," they also asserted that they fostered positive relationships between Arab and Jewish staff members.[123] One year later, a report on a camp run by the United Neighborhood Houses of New York avowed that its interracial staff "worked together in friendship and warmth of inter-personal relations."[124] Publicity materials from the camps provided ample evidence that white and black children did indeed dance, swim, ride horses, chase frogs, and practice archery together.[125] Although the assertions of interracial harmony among campers dropped off after the 1960s, when African American and Latino children had come to dominate most of the Fresh Air camps and "problems of the city [and] . . . of race" began to surface, publicists still lauded the positive relationships between white counselors and their black and brown charges.[126]

Other evidence belies these testimonies about interracial bliss. Camps had long been sites of minstrel shows, segregation, and overt racism.[127] For example, a 1920 "Camp Standards" manual for the United Neighborhood Houses of New York included instructions on how to play a dodgeball variation in which "the person hit is the 'nigger baby.'"[128] During the pre–World War II period, white camp children also played games such as "white man and Indian" and "nigger-in-the-hole."[129] Although directors had discontinued some of the most overtly racist practices by the end of the 1940s, a 1953 study by the National Social Welfare Assembly's Committee on Camping documented widespread ignorance and naïveté about interracial issues among white staff, underrepresentation of blacks and Jews in leadership positions, and overrepresentation of the same groups in food service jobs. Home visits often compounded the situation. In 1958 a social worker for the Hudson Guild commented, "In actuality, *Herald Tribune* Friendly Towns are not so friendly" because "most friendly town folk apparently prefer White children." He went on to describe efforts to "pass off Spanish children as 'white'" so that they could receive vacations.[130] More generally, through the 1970s people of color who visited rural white communities encountered widespread racial prejudice and ignorance.[131]

Despite publicity practices focused on filtering negative experiences before they appeared in print, some less than ideal references did make it into the public record. A few reports only hinted at troubles born of interracial contact. When pressed, hosts and administrators would occasionally admit to "problems."[132] Although rarely being specific, those who did expand on the nature of the difficulties prefaced their comments by noting that they were "very minor" or the "usual challenges" faced by young children.[133] In 1976 one reporter attributed the negative experiences of a few children to "a kind of cultural shock" triggered by displacement and exposure to an unfamiliar environment.[134] If more-entrenched issues remained after a child's return home, the Cleveland-based program sought to bring host and guest families together for face-to-face conversation.[135] According to these accounts, interracial problems that emerged during Fresh Air visits barely deserved mention or could be easily managed.

Those who dismissed the racial issues as minor or irrelevant failed to grasp how often Fresh Air children encountered overt prejudice and racism during their visits. The children entered communities inundated with advertising images that depicted African American children as overly sexualized, vacuous, unintelligent, and suited only for menial labor.[136] On the virulent end of the spectrum, in 1961 one African American child listened at the pickup point as his assigned host in Plattsburgh, New York, exclaimed to the local Fresh Air organizer, "You didn't tell us this kid was gonna be no nigger."[137] Although another host intervened and brought the child to her home, the trauma remained. Oral histories from former Fresh Air children make clear that local residents frequently used racial epithets and hate speech in front of the visiting children.[138] Other incidents proved just as troubling. One resident from a small town in Michigan registered his opposition to a Fresh Air program in 1960 because he thought that the African American children visiting from New York might relocate to his neighborhood on a permanent basis. At the same location, the managers of a local beach banned an African American visitor from entering the water.[139] In New Jersey in 1964, the parents of neighborhood children prohibited them from playing with two Fresh Air visitors of "mixed Puerto Rican and Negro parentage" and declared that "under no circumstances" were the guests "to put as much as one foot" on their property.[140] At Hudson Guild Farm that same year, staff rued the racial animosity faced by African Americans from other Fresh Air participants.[141] Children also encountered hostile stares while out in public, overheard crank calls by residents opposed to the program, suffered racist comments from adult neighbors, and listened to other children call them names.[142] Although some guests did not report overt prejudice, the prevalence of accounts like these even in reports meant to promote the programs suggests that most children encountered racial animus at some point in their stay.[143]

The children who faced overt prejudice also dealt with hosts who treated them as exotic. Whether commenting on a "mouthful of white, white teeth," the visiting children's use of "different expressions," their musical talents, or their consumption of melons and corn on the cob, hosts frequently emphasized their Latino and African American guests' otherness based on common racial stereotypes.[144] The few children of Chinese descent who participated in Fresh Air programs received extra attention throughout the 1950s and 1960s as promoters featured them prominently in articles and photos.[145]

The Fresh Air guests who encountered overt racism, stereotypes, and paternalistic attitudes responded on their own terms. Rather than passive innocents unable to shape the environments in which they lived, the children appear as informed and often cagey actors who dealt with their hosts' preconceptions by instructing the adults about the realities of race in America. In short, the children influenced those around them as much as they were themselves influenced. At a time when children had begun to resist adult supervision of their play and form strong peer groups, Fresh Air children from Latino and African American communities shared a common transcript in responding to the racism they encountered.[146]

Most hosts incorrectly assumed that their guests knew little about life in general and the realities of race in particular. In a striking display of ignorance about racial identity development, one reporter claimed that a seven-year-old African American girl from the east side of Manhattan would have no awareness of "race tension, of sit-downs and wade-ins, of manifestations of prejudice."[147] Contrary to the reporter's assertions, children as young as three and four from all racial groups throughout the twentieth century learned to respond to racial, physical, and cultural markers, a skill far more developed and sophisticated in children of color than in white children.[148] While comments from white host children about the "nice tan" of their visiting guests ring true, the assertion that children of color who traveled to the suburbs knew little about the dynamics of race attests to host naïveté.[149] A more informed account comes from an unnamed Fresh Air girl who told her chaperone that the house she would be staying in was "white." The chaperone at first queried if the girl referred to paint color. "No, that's not what I mean," she replied. "The family I'm going to is white."[150]

Such racially aware children countered racial stereotypes by first and foremost modeling the respectable behavior taught them by their parents. During the late nineteenth and twentieth centuries, some African American families resisted the effects of Jim Crow and racial prejudice by embracing white, middle-class standards of propriety.[151] In this way, proponents of "proper" conduct claimed that those who embodied respectability thwarted racial stereotypes that described African Americans and Latinos as lazy, unkempt, undereducated, and ill mannered (see figure 6).[152] A majority of the Fresh Air children selected for the country visits had imbibed the ethic of respectability and demonstrated it during their home visits. Prior to departure, the children's parents gave final instructions on good manners and made sure that the children arrived on site wearing their best outfits.[153] Photos from the era show African American children greeting their hosts while wearing their "Sunday suit" or dress.[154]

One Fresh Air registrar speculated that some African American parents sent their children to relatives in the South rather than white suburbs in the North

FIGURE 6. In 1960 Fresh Air host Mark Stucky of the Newton, Kansas, community shakes hands with Thomas Flowers from Gulfport, Mississippi, as Doris Zerger Stucky—Mark's mother—watches. Used by permission of the Mennonite Library and Archives, Bethel College, North Newton, KS (Mennonite Library & Archives, Bethel, Kansas: Photo collection; folder: "Mississippi—Gulfport").

because it required less money to be spent on clothing.[155] Those who found their way into white homes took their parents' instructions seriously as hosts and counselors commented on how clean, neat, "well mannered," "obedient," "considerate," and "extremely polite" the children were, comments that recurred in every Fresh Air location from the onset of World War II through the end of the 1970s.[156]

The children's careful conduct changed many of the hosts' perceptions. For example, one Iowan host parent admitted in 1968 to thinking that "all children from slum areas had no manners" and "were all gangster types" but found that her Fresh Air guest was "better behaved than our own children."[157] Other hosts expressed similar surprise that their guests did not exhibit "ignorance, resentment, or sloth" but rather "faultless manners" and a "passion for cleanliness."[158] Another host mother testified that the children's "manners are unbelievable" given the context of their upbringing and, as a result, other hosts should not "be afraid their children will be 'polluted'" by the Fresh Air visitors.[159]

The children maintained their polite demeanor even when refusing to reveal details of their home environment. In the main, hosts rarely had direct contact with Fresh Air parents. As a result, the children fielded multiple queries, many of them quite pointed, as hosts attempted to glean information about the children's home life. For the most part, the children politely refused to answer, a decision that hosts interpreted as stubbornness, mistrust, or introversion.[160] In their silence, the children again followed their parents' instructions. As one former Fresh Air child later revealed, "Our parents had prepared us for the questions: 'Any questions they ask you about your home life, don't answer them. If they persist, tell them what goes on in our house stays in our house.'"[161] Given that many of the children's parents had to negotiate the often dehumanizing and frequently racist demands of the social service system, they knew that a stray word about a detail of home life could have direct financial ramifications if a social worker overheard it.[162] The children recognized that they needed to keep quiet about what happened at home, a pattern that continued at least into the 1980s.[163]

Such circumspection could also be found in the Fresh Air children's response to local law enforcement officials. Hilton Cobb Jr., a seven-year-old African American Brooklynite visiting Syracuse, New York, in 1965, lost his way while bike riding. Having observed Cobb's confusion, adult onlookers flagged down a police cruiser. Despite the officers' willingness to escort him around the neighborhood, Cobb "refused to go with [the] police," opting instead to drive through the neighborhood with an adult who had earned his trust.[164] Cobb and others like him knew that law enforcement officials regularly harassed, intimidated, and used violence against African American and Latino residents in their home communities.[165]

Fresh Air guests further challenged their hosts' preconceived notions by adhering to their own ethical framework. One host summed up the differing worldviews when she noted that her guests "had very different ideas about the meaning of words such as 'cheat' and 'fair' and 'share' and 'lie.'"[166] Those differing ideas showed up most often around notions of private property. One family accused a Fresh Air guest of having stolen a tie clasp even though the boy asserted that he had only borrowed it and had not taken it home.[167] After they found the tie clasp, the family later admitted that their guest had been telling the truth.[168] The children in these instances knew about theft: Although a few admitted to pilfering an item of sentimental value, more commonly the children had themselves been robbed.[169] One girl brought home a bicycle given to her by her hosts only to have it stolen three days after she returned to the city.[170] Other Fresh Air children expressed amazement that their hosts left toys and other personal possessions outside at night with no fear that someone would steal them.[171] Here again, the children held their ground when accused of theft and attempted to instruct their hosts on how to take better care of personal property.

Taken together, the children's respectable behavior, refusal to share information about their home environments, mistrust of police, and defense of their ideas about personal property constituted a racial code of conduct. Under this code, children from African American and Latino communities responded to the racial prejudice and naïveté of their white rural and suburban hosts by being polite, withholding information, mistrusting the police, and thwarting theft. By contrast, white guests—regardless of their economic class—exhibited a wider spread of manners, shared more information about their home lives, trusted the police more consistently, and seldom discussed personal property. Although neither written nor formalized, this code among children of color remained remarkably consistent during the height of the civil rights movement. The children further refined their conduct through a robust rumor network built up by returning children sharing their experiences with those not yet departed for the country.[172] The children cooperated when asked to do so but also knew when to stand their ground, draw back, or remain silent. As they spoke with older children who had experience with Fresh Air vacations, listened to their parents give them instructions about how to relate to white people, and talked with one another about what had transpired in these strange, white, rural homes, they responded with a consistency across region and time all the more remarkable for the generally chaotic and unorganized nature of children's interactions with adults.

This racial code of conduct often prompted the children to become teachers for their adult hosts. For much of the twentieth century, white novelists, reporters, and advertisers portrayed African American children as impish tricksters impervious to pain, adorable playmates devoid of intelligence, or simply as passive receptacles, waiting to receive charity.[173] The shift to viewing black children as instructors to white adults departed from this prior practice. By the 1950s, hosts had begun to reference the racial lessons they learned from their guests, a pattern that continued through the 1970s. Whether offering glowing testimony about how much they gained from hosting a child of a different race or simply stating that their children's worldviews had been stretched, host after host noted that bringing African American and Latino children into their homes changed their perspective.[174] As one organizer declared, changes in the hosts' "narrow point of view" took place because "the [Fresh Air] children are doing it."[175] Some hosts said that they became color-blind; others said that they recognized the universality of the human condition; still others said that they learned about their own prejudice and that of other white people.[176] A group of white suburbanites even traveled to Harlem in 1968 to see if they could recruit African American members to relocate to their community in Long Island. The African American Fresh Air children who had visited them had helped them realize that they and their children "were being deprived of black culture" and therefore were "impoverished, culturally."[177]

The shift toward white host education corresponded with a growing awareness of white complicity in racial oppression. Stemming from the decades-long struggle of African American organizers and educators like Mary McCleod Bethune, W. E. B. DuBois, and Carter G. Woodson, recognition of white responsibility for racism intensified during the 1950s, and Fresh Air advocates began to echo the sentiment that whites in the suburbs were "the ones with much to learn" by the 1960s.[178] The programs soon centered on white-black exchanges and offered glowing reports in which hosts wept at the children's departures, neighbors welcomed dark-skinned guests, and the children lessened "bigotry, prejudice and deprivation in the country" in order to "bring the dawn."[179] By 1965, as white resistance to housing rights and affirmative action picked up steam, many Fresh Air initiatives focused on educating the white hosts as much as on improving the children.

Organizers first isolated the guests. Most Fresh Air programs cautioned against sending multiple guests to the same home. As one promoter noted, "Two children often invited to one family is not advisable." Although intended to increase host involvement and keep guests from "cling[ing] together," the policy isolated African American and Latino children in settings where they alone represented their community.[180] A 1949 children's story referred to Fresh Air children as goodwill ambassadors who represented "the thirteen million colored people of America."[181] Publicity materials furthermore emphasized the bridge-building capacity of these solo ambassadors. From the mid-1960s onward, promoters promised that the programs would foster friendships, develop relationships, and, as asserted by a local organizer in Illinois in 1969, "bridge many of the false notions about persons of different ethnic and racial backgrounds."[182] In return, the hosts reiterated the Fresh Air bromide that "people are just people."[183] Yet it fell to the children to "foster a better understanding of attitudes and beliefs of inner-city people by their hosts."[184] The children could rely on no one else when separated from their friends and family.

Across the country, children also offered much more practical instruction. In 1961 Isla, a Fresh Air child visiting Moundridge, Kansas, from Gulfport, Mississippi, taught her hosts several household cleaning tricks.[185] Another child in Pennsylvania helped her host overcome an aversion to touching the child's dark, thickly textured hair.[186] Although some guests like Bronx resident Lauren "Flip" Baily suffered her Connecticut host mother's inept attempt at hair braiding, other guests like a girl from Harlem named Wendy taught her northern Michigan hosts how to care for her hair.[187] In 1967 a seven-year-old girl from Cleveland staying with the Rauschenberg family in Athens, Ohio, shared with her hosts what she knew about fending off potential burglars.[188] Ten years later, Theresa, a seven-year-old New Yorker, likewise told her suburban hosts that they would "probably be all right" if they looked straight ahead when followed by teenage boys while walking home late one evening.[189] Whether offering instruction on the rudiments of race relations or more practical matters, the children took on the role of teacher, one that many seemed to enjoy. As one Fresh Air child declared proudly upon her return home to Mississippi in 1963, "I taught them to cook red beans and corn bread."[190] In few other settings could African American and Latino children instruct white adults in an area of their own expertise.

A few children took their teaching responsibilities to another level during the foment of the later half of the 1960s, when Black Nationalist and La Raza rhetoric captured the imagination of many urban residents. As adults criticized "discriminatory" practices of sponsoring organizations like New York's Hudson Guild and demanded that "neighborhood youth be regularly consulted and involved in their own program planning," the children also spoke out.[191] In 1966 an Episcopalian Fresh Air summer day camper asserted that rather than being "culturally deprived," the campers had their own culture replete with "soul music" and "Spanish slang."[192] Two years later, a participant in a Fresh Air Fund camp informed her two counselors, one of whom was white and the other black, that she would "get the NAACP" after them if they disciplined her. That same year, a seven-year-old boy informed his host father, "I don't like white people."[193] Although the intensity of the rhetoric waned in the following decade and some of the children dropped their bluster once they learned to know their hosts, Fresh Air children contributed their voices to the persistent critique of white liberal paternalism typically associated with much older racial activists.

The long-term effects on children who educated their hosts after traveling far and facing racism remained mixed. Through the 1970s, critics continued to emphasize the harm done to the children by exposing them to rural comforts and then returning them to urban confines.[194] At the same time, some Fresh Air alumni did leave the city; Cindy Vanderkodde, a former participant in a Fresh Air program run by a Christian Reformed congregation in New York City, moved to the same Michigan community that had hosted her as a child.[195] Still more critics asserted that "real education" would take place only when white suburban youths stayed with urban African American and Latino families.[196] Proponents countered that Fresh Air did far more to "inspire than to hinder" the children and, again, that urban hosting was not financially practical.[197] Other boosters emphasized that Fresh Air alumni went on to accomplished careers as social workers, lawyers, corporate CEOs, doctors, and artists.[198] Some of the former Fresh Air guests credited the programs for giving them a sense that "there could be something better out there."[199]

In the end, the racial legacy of the Fresh Air program is unclear. To be certain, children educated their hosts and resisted the paternalism of the era and, by doing so, initiated some of the few conversations about racism that white rural residents ever had. By 1967, Philip Chinn, a member of the Wheaton (Illinois) Human Relations Council, claimed that visits by Fresh Air children made racial integration in their community possible.[200] At the same time, only a few Fresh Air programs responded to the 1971 suggestion by John Powell, a Black Nationalist religious leader, to set up "stale air" vacations in which white kids from the suburbs spent time with African American and Latino families in the inner city.[201] From the 1950s onward, the internal conflict between the efforts of the children and initiatives of the adults suffused the Fresh Air movement, a process supported by equally tension-filled concerns about the children's behavior.

Sass

Sonia and Laelia, the two girls thwarted in their attempt to run away from camp, fit the profile of uncooperative, ill-behaved guests. They took no pleasure in nature, despised the activities prepared for them, and resented the authority of their hosts. At ten years old in 1971, they had one desire while visiting the Fresh Air Fund's Sharpe Reservation. According to Laelia, they wanted to get "back on the street." By contrast, cooperative guests loved to hike, relished swimming, and adored their hosts. Rather than pine for cityscapes, well-behaved guests grew "tearful at the thought of returning to New York." Whether the two girls eventually found some measure of fulfillment amid the camp regimen, whether they grew to appreciate their counselors, or whether they came to find nature attractive remains unknown. We have only the image of them sitting on the ground, bereft, "defeated," still longing for the streets of Brooklyn and Manhattan.[202]

The girls could, in this instance, be described as sassy. In contrast to the black middle-class strategy of cooperation and polite behavior, an equally robust tradition of resistance to white authority through deliberate insolence had also shaped members of the African American community. Labeled "sass" by slave owners and white southerners intent on maintaining white hegemony in the aftermath of the Civil War, the behavior encompassed intentional disrespect, refusal to act in a subservient manner, and an unbowed, intransigent demeanor. African Americans took risks to establish their humanity and equality through disrespectful behavior as well.[203] Misbehaving children like Sonia and Laelia reflected this less accommodating tradition of resistance to white authority.

The girls' apparent failure to escape nonetheless shaped Fresh Air. Like many other girls and boys sent to homes and camps outside the city, Sonia and Laelia forced their hosts to invest time and energy on disciplinary matters. The same program promoters who claimed that Fresh Air held the key to solving the country's race relations problems made similar claims about the program's efficacy in addressing juvenile delinquency. However, strict vetting procedures kept those deemed intractable in the city, unable to access Fresh Air's resources. Those who made it through the screens created enough problems that Fresh Air still had to find ways to deal with uncooperative children, a challenge that increased over time.

Concerns about juvenile delinquency among the entire youth population, boys and girls alike, intensified following World War II.[204] In the first decades of the twentieth century, pundits claimed that wayward youths' delinquency stemmed from low intelligence, familial neglect, and inadequate education. As juvenile court cases tripled in the twelve years prior to 1962, however, adults began to recognize that youths, regardless of their IQs, family situation, or level of ignorance, could still become delinquent as a result of psychological disorders.[205] Explanations eventually focused on economic, social, and political deprivation as the root cause of juvenile delinquency.[206] The unrest and disruption born of efforts to desegregate schools and oppose the Vietnam War further created fear and uncertainty among adults troubled about unruly youths.[207] By 1961, the Kennedy Administration acted on the growing concern and passed legislation to address the issue.[208] In keeping with a long-term pattern of adults focusing their anxiety on children when social changes erupt, Fresh Air organizers joined the chorus of adults lamenting the wayward state of the next generation.[209]

Fresh Air program administrators followed and in some cases led efforts to combat juvenile delinquency as part of their effort to manage youthful passage to suburban retreats. They did so by first assuring hosts that they had screened out both delinquent and emotionally troubled young people. In their rush to assuage potential fears, the boosters employed at times jarring terminology. In 1948 one press release declared that referring agencies screened out all "delinquent, psychopathic . . . [and] intellectually sub-normal" children.[210] By the 1960s, as youths became even more antagonistic toward adult authority, the description had changed only slightly with the assurance that "[n]one of the children are emotionally disturbed or delinquent."[211] Exercising more moderate language, by 1979 administrators noted that the children "are screened very carefully" so that none arrived with "emotional or behavioral problems."[212] Although their rhetoric shifted somewhat over time, the social workers and church volunteers tasked with selecting children continued to screen out "real delinquents" from the eager children waiting to participate.[213]

The very program administrators who invested so much time and energy in eliminating troublemakers during the screening process also sought to curtail juvenile delinquency through their efforts. Rather than deal with youths actually involved in crime, drug dealing, or other illicit behavior, the programs intervened before children turned to such activity. In 1950 the Fresh Air program of the Episcopal Diocese of New York aimed to work with "children of trouble ... ready for a turn toward delinquency" but not yet walking down that path.[214] That same year, a Mennonite group that sponsored Fresh Air programs evoked FBI director J. Edgar Hoover by claiming that he said, "Boys and girls who go to Bible school [and, by doing so, go on Fresh Air vacations] DO NOT GO TO JAIL!"[215] In addition to religious figures, politicians also used Fresh Air programs to make points about juvenile delinquency. New York Governor Thomas E. Dewey asserted in 1953 that the *Herald Tribune* Fresh Air Fund deterred "juvenile unrest," an issue that his secretary of health, education, and welfare said was "one of the nation's most urgent problems."[216] Fresh Air Fund director Frederick Lewis joined the politicians by announcing two years later that "[e]very newspaper deplores youthful delinquency. The *Tribune* not only writes about it but does something about it."[217]

Claims about countering juvenile delinquency continued for the next two decades. Whether professing to save children from "juvenile gang-infested sections" of the city in 1960 or, one year later, "to prevent juvenile delinquency by showing the children another side of life and offering them the security of a real home," Fresh Air organizers rarely nuanced their assertions.[218] But they did contradict themselves. In a bid to tailor his message to fit his audience, Lewis first touted his organization's efforts to solve the "complicated problem" of juvenile delinquency in 1962 only to report to a funder several months later that his organization had never considered itself an "anti juvenile delinquency" program.[219] Subsequent reports at the *Herald Tribune* Fund and in other programs through the 1960s repeated claims that they prevented juvenile delinquency by removing youths from bad influences in their home communities.[220]

Promoters expanded and intensified their claims in the 1970s. In sync with the cultural and political backlash against the freewheeling excesses of the 1960s, they maintained that juvenile delinquency programming also improved manners and, in some cases, rescued children from lives already gone bad. Because of the love and attention heaped upon him, an eleven-year-old Fresh Air camper stopped verbally harassing his fellow campers in 1972 as he discovered a "newfound incentive to behave." That same year Frederick Gibson, a New York City police detective volunteering at a Fresh Air camp, added that the program not only prevented children from joining gangs in the first place but also allowed some to "break away" after they had become members.[221] Lisa Pulling, the Fresh Air Fund's director in 1975, highlighted the "preventative aspect" of keeping "16,000 children off the street each summer," a theme repeated throughout the decade.[222]

In addition, at least one parent mentioned in 1977 that her child learned "table manners while he was away" and started teaching his sisters and brothers when he returned home.[223]

Yet the bulk of the children who went on Fresh Air trips had already proven their ability to play by the rules. As already noted, the children had often been taught to behave in a respectful manner by their parents.[224] Representing the ethic of respectability that had been a pillar of middle- and upper-class blacks' bid for racial equality at least since the end of the nineteenth century, they came prepared to be polite and impressed many a host with their "faultless" manners, "passion for cleanliness," and "unconscious, easy courtesy."[225] In particular, many African American children understood that polite behavior towards white people could reap certain rewards. Well-behaved children stood the best chance of passing the multiple vetting screens maintained by Fresh Air programs.

Fresh Air connections with well-mannered children buttressed city-based efforts to reduce the threat of juvenile delinquency but did less substantive work of their own. Given the careful parenting evidenced by the children's behavior, many had strong familial support. Likewise, only those children already connected to sponsoring agencies passed the vetting screens. The majority of those sponsors, groups like urban churches, social service agencies, and boys and girls clubs, offered their own programs designed to keep children out of trouble. Unlike the Fresh Air ventures, the city-based programs usually ran year round. At best, Fresh Air initiatives augmented the efforts of the churches and agencies that partnered with them but—given their vigorous vetting and short-term design—seldom dealt with the children most likely to end up on a juvenile court docket.

The disobedience that did take place received little public scrutiny. As can be expected, promoters preferred to keep such stories quiet. They did not publicize camp counselors' reports about infighting, cursing, aggression, or disruptive behavior.[226] The girl who claimed in 1956 that her counselor slapped her for misbehaving received no public redress.[227] Boosters did not publicize the antics of a child who repeatedly put kittens in his hosts' mailbox or accounts of "fighting, yelling, and biting" at home and during vacation bible school.[228] Descriptions of campers who refused to kiss their counselor good night, swore in Spanish, and "wanted to do everything" by themselves did not compel donors.[229] Although children in both homes and camps had long tested adult authority through small acts of rebellion, publicists included only the most general of references to misbehavior.[230] As one host wrote in 1961, "We understand there were a few isolated cases where problems arose" but had no specifics to offer.[231] In 1976 another host mentioned that she had "heard people have problems" but again did not add any detail.[232] Otherwise, reports simply informed hosts that they should contact local organizers or the national office if problems arose.[233]

Once contacted, Fresh Air staff used a variety of strategies to deal with discipline issues, beginning with sending the children home. As a 1954 report assured potential hosts, "any child who misbehaves is sent back to New York immediately at the expense of the Fresh Air Fund."[234] Seven years later a pair of girls hosted by a family in Michigan found the same policy in effect in a program sponsored by the Christian Reformed Church. The girls traveled home early because they could not get along with each other or their hosts.[235] Although staff rarely made such statistics public, a *Reader's Digest* article did mention that staff in the *Herald Tribune*'s Friendly Town program sent home 75 children out of the 9,000 they served in 1962.[236] As in the case of homesickness, the additional expense and logistical challenge of sending disobedient children home early made this option the least desirable of all those available.

Discipline problems also prompted hosts to stop re-inviting guests. After Luis Diaz got into a "little tiff" with his host mother over a religious matter, he stopped coming to the home of the Cooley family even though he had traveled from New York to New Jersey every summer for almost ten years.[237] A Fresh Air program run out of Gulfport, Mississippi, had to find new hosting communities in Kansas, Michigan, and South Dakota every couple of years because the organizers found it difficult to recruit hosts willing to re-invite guests. (See figure 7.)

FIGURE 7.   In 1960 a group of children from Gulfport, Mississippi, prepares to travel twenty-four hours to rural homes in Kansas for two-week Fresh Air stays. Used by permission of the Mennonite Library and Archives, Bethel College, North Newton, KS (Mennonite Library & Archives, Bethel, Kansas: Photo collection; folder: "Mississippi—Gulfport").

Rumors about purported theft and misbehavior caused hosts to withdraw.[238] Although those hosts who did not extend re-invitations—usually about 50 percent of the participants each year—left little record of their reasons for declining, the experience of Diaz and the Gulfport children suggests that problems related to disobedience played a major role.

Program administrators used camps as a repository for misbehaving children. Frederick Lewis explained the process in 1963. In hopes of avoiding "a black eye" and "ruin[ing] for a decade" future Fresh Air placements by sending a "difficult child" to a host home, Fund staff sent children with "strong anti-social tendencies" to one of their camps.[239] In that setting, as another administrator in the program later explained, "unruly" children "buckled under the camp's discipline requirements." Disciplinary practices ranged from simply removing dangerous items from campers—such as the meat cleaver and switchblades that showed up in the luggage of one camping group—to withholding swimming privileges.[240] Although in some instances, such as at a camp run by the New York Episcopal diocese in 1971, staff admitted to taking "a switch to boys" who were not cooperating, in the main Fresh Air camp staff enforced strict policies against corporal punishment.[241] In order to manage the disciplinary challenge, some camps segregated their programming so as to hold a week of camp for urban Fresh Air children and another week for children from the country.[242] By default, this practice also kept racial groups from extended contact.

Policies that concentrated unruly children in the camps created problems unanticipated by Fresh Air staff. When compounded with the unrest and Black Nationalist foment of the late 1960s and early 1970s, the disciplinary policy resulted in staff like Fresh Air Fund camp manager Larry Mickolic complaining about "hostile and unsatisfied" campers who fought, caused trouble, and proved "hard to handle."[243] A college-age camp counselor by the name of Thomas David added in 1971 that black and brown urban Fresh Air campers, unlike cooperative white children from the suburbs, challenged and resented the counselors' authority.[244]

Administrators responded by hiring former campers familiar with such impudence. In 1969 the Fresh Air Fund hired twenty-six former campers for its two-hundred-member counseling corps.[245] By 1973, the same organization had hired a former camper by the name of Tom Palmgren as the director of Camp Pioneer, a site focused on immersing "boys from slum areas in New York City" in nature. A self-described "bad camper" who had "created a lot of problems," Palmgren knew how to manage his charges.[246] Here again the campers had shaped the program by requiring administrators to change how they hired staff.

Because of their purportedly sassy disposition, Fresh Air participants like Sonia, Laelia, and even Palmgren in his day forced the hand of the adult programmers. Although declarations about ending juvenile delinquency continued, children

from the middle of the 1960s onward nonetheless challenged the authority figures around them. Some did cooperate at the behest of parents concerned about
respectability. However, others did not. Even when confined to camps, those who
misbehaved and tried to run away prompted new hiring patterns and disciplinary
techniques. Entire programs had to relocate in order to find hosts willing to bring
unruly children into their homes. Willard Parsons may have been the architect of
Fresh Air, but through actions like these the children became its builders.

Other Kinds of Activists

Sonia, Laelia, and the hundreds of thousands like them who traveled to suburban
and rural homes become civil rights activists in the midst of their Fresh Air activity. The African American and Latino/a children who spent time in white homes
educated their hosts and ventured into communities where racial epithets, prejudice, and negative assumptions proliferated. If nothing else, the hosts' ignorance
about the extent of prejudice in their own communities made the children all the
more vulnerable because the hosts rarely protected their guests. Simply by brav-
ing these racist conditions, the children challenged the assumptions of the adults
around them. If anything, the demands placed upon black and brown children
became more intense from the 1940s through the 1970s as the various Fresh Air
initiatives focused attention on the value of racial exchange. Although earlier
organizers had called the children ambassadors of their race, by the 1970s they
called them bridge builders.[247] The expectation in the 1940s was that the children represent their entire racial community, an onerous burden in itself. In the
1970s the rhetoric employed by promoters demanded that the children not only
represent their race but shoulder the responsibility of bringing together racial
groups separated by physical, economic, and cultural distance. Some cooperated
and others did not, but, simply by making the choice to participate, they earned
the name of activists.

White children also became activists but of a different sort. In the programs'
earliest years, they arrived at host homes where messages about their malnutrition, stunted development, and poverty had preceded them. When they did
not give sufficient evidence of their impoverishment, hosts protested that the
children in their care needed to be needier. The dignity displayed by children
who stayed and won over their hosts despite doubts about them speaks of the
deliberation and courage that such actions required. As white children became
the minority of those sent out each summer by the 1970s, they countered the
ever-growing assumption that all Fresh Air children were black and brown. In
essence, the white children took steps as activists by staying in a program that
quickly became associated with children of color alone. Indeed, some programs,

such as the Chicago-based Missionary Society program, served children only from African American and Latino communities. By showing up and participating, the white children challenged the assumption that poverty had a dark face.

These young activists and their adult hosts together inhabited a rare if short-lived space in the middle of the twentieth century. In pursuit of adventure and the oft-repeated value of friendship, guests and hosts lived in intimate contact across both class and race lines. Although some African American and Latino domestics lived with their white employers in the South and the West, white rural families in the Midwest and the Northeast had little to no contact with those from other racial or economic groups. All the problems evident in southern domestic arrangements, including but not limited to paternalism, unequal power relationships, and the danger and actuality of sexual abuse, showed up in critics' comments about Fresh Air hosting ventures as well. At the same time, children did challenge assumptions, especially those based in ignorance about other racial groups, when they dressed better, worked harder, and proved smarter than their hosts expected. Whether such challenges resulted in substantive change in the hosts' attitudes remains somewhat doubtful. As social contact theorists have shown, greater proximity does not lead automatically to a reduction in prejudice.[248] The very rarity of the intimate spaces opened up by the Fresh Air movement helped sustain interest in them and, because so few had experience in translating short-term visits into long-term change, kept them relatively non-threatening. White adults hosting black and brown children may have drawn thousands of headlines but brought about only the most modest of changes in the racial and class order.

The children in the end shaped Fresh Air most foundationally by contradicting adult claims about them. Many children already had knowledge of grass, both the mowing and the smoking kind, and did not always find nature as blissfully welcoming as their benefactors claimed. The majority of African American and Latino children knew much more about racial dynamics than did their hosts, practiced their own racial code of conduct, and frequently taught the adults important lessons about prejudice, racism, and urban life. Even the children deemed well enough behaved to earn a summer vacation to the country sassed counselors, ran away, and got into fights with their host siblings.

Nestled among the themes of grass, color, and sass lay another triad: sex, seven, and sick. As chapter 4 shows, in response to children shaping the Fresh Air movement, adults kept boys and girls separate, set strict age caps, and instituted rigorous medical screening practices. Through these actions the adults protected the public image they had worked so hard to develop. They polished the Fresh Air reputation to perfection. Although largely successful in doing so, they also ended up limiting the very opportunities they sought to give the children.

SEX, SEVEN, SICK

How Adults Kept the Children in Check

Macy Thomas thought about falling in love. At eleven years old, she looked ahead to her future and imagined living in the Kishacoquillas Valley of central Pennsylvania, a community she had traveled to for five consecutive summers as a Fresh Air child. Although as an African American Macy stood out among the overwhelmingly white population of Mifflin and Huntingdon counties, she still dreamed of returning to the site of many summer pleasures, marrying a local boy, and having a family. Her mother, Jolene Thomas, listened to her daughter describe her "obsession" but could not share her enthusiasm.[1] She knew, as did every parent of a Fresh Air child, that most guests could no longer travel to the country once they turned thirteen. Macy's wish to live in the Kishacoquillas Valley, however fervent and sincere, had little chance of coming to fruition. The age limits and strict behavioral vetting that kept the threat of interracial romance at bay thwarted Thomas's desires.

Together the themes of forbidden love, managed adolescence, and medical vetting explain both the Fresh Air movement's longevity and the children's varied and at times contradictory response to it. Some, but not nearly all, of the visits resulted in hosts inviting their guests back over the course of many years. Children usually, but not in every instance, responded positively to the invitations to return. As long as the children cooperated with their adult hosts, avoided any romantic entanglements, and accepted second-class status, they could craft long-term relationships that advanced their careers and increased their chances of financial stability. Only when they disrupted their hosts' suburban equanimity by agitating to be sent home, becoming entangled in romantic attachments, or claiming equal status did the relationships end and the re-invitations discontinue. In a careful exercise of social control, hosts and program administrators selected children's genders, set campground policy, and protected hosts from infection as prepubescent children morphed into teenagers all too capable of romantic entanglement.

Sex

Parents and social reformers have long sought to control children's sexuality. As the middle class grew in Europe and the United States during the nineteenth century, the idea of adolescence became more widely recognized. With increasing pressure to delay marriage until one had earned enough to establish financial independence, the period between childhood and adulthood lengthened. Parents in turn attempted to repress children's sexual urges, whether to masturbate or experiment, in hopes of establishing patterns that would extend into the risky period before one married and earned one's fortune.[2] Although they would rarely dare to do so to adults, members of both the religious and medical communities felt free to moralize about the sexual habits of children and youths.[3] Such ready intervention into the private lives of children signified a larger cultural concern for self-control—especially evident among "neo-Puritans" in the United States who "saved the hottest jeremiads for pelvic matters."[4] Childhood innocence had become linked with the absence of sexuality.[5] Adults sought to keep it that way. Ultimately, the interest in controlling children's sexuality served as one component of a broader project to exercise dominance and control throughout the nineteenth and twentieth centuries.[6]

Such repressive interests remained the responsibility of parents until psychologist Sigmund Freud called into question the innocence of children. By the end of the nineteenth century, children faced moral condemnation and social disapprobation anytime they engaged in sexual activity. A child who masturbated invited rebuke from ministers concerned about the eternal well-being of the child's soul and from social reformers attempting to maintain the foundations of society itself.[7] However, Freud attempted to cast aside such moralizing pursuits by positing that, rather than being free of sexual knowledge, children had already begun to integrate and process sexual information.[8] A new class of experts emerged in the first half of the twentieth century who knew better than parents how to liberate children from unhealthy sexual strictures. By the middle of the twentieth century, schools, children's activity centers, and various child professionals had supplanted parents—and especially mothers—as the purveyors of sexual education.[9]

The shift to sex education in the schools did not reduce sexual repression in Fresh Air host homes. Rural and suburban residents did engage in variant sexual practices, but the cover of social respectability often repressed libertarian impulses unleashed elsewhere by Freud and related behaviorists. Given the religious foundations of the Fresh Air movement, theological assertions about children's malleability also influenced participating hosts. In particular, Protestant families described children as both impressionable and impervious.[10] On the one hand, a good Creator engendered children who needed only gentle encouragement to flower. On the other, as creatures of a sinful world, children resisted discipline meant to foster good behavior. Although contradictory, these twin tenets led to the same ends. Whether to nurture or to force acceptable behaviors, parents influenced by these doctrines prohibited sexual expression in their guests and children. As suburban mothers entered the workforce and ideas about natural sexual development influenced the religious community, many parents moderated their control, but at least through the end of the 1970s, Fresh Air children encountered more sexual repression than liberation.[11]

The entry of children from African American and Latino communities into white host families in the mid-1950s and afterward introduced the threat of racial mixing. U.S. history makes evident that "[n]o American issue ever ignited as much fire as amalgamation, mixing races."[12] The nationally publicized 1958 "kissing case" drives home the point. White mobs and police officers terrorized two black boys, one eight, the other ten, for playing a kissing game with three white girls.[13] After the milestone *Brown* decision, segregationists revealed deep-seated fears that interracial schools would lead to interracial sex; as white youths listened to black music replete with sexual themes, the segregationists' worries intensified.[14] To be certain, not all white southerners opposed school integration.[15] Yet in those places where "massive resistance" did emerge, concerns about interracial sex set the stage for school integration battles across the country.[16] In the North and the Midwest, where most Fresh Air children spent summer vacations, host concerns about interracial sex paralleled southern passions in intent if not in form. At root, northern white suburban parents through the 1970s had no more interest in their children marrying across racial lines than did their southern counterparts. Comments from white antibusing activists in cities such as Boston reveal similar fears about interracial sex.[17]

Organizers of Fresh Air ventures assuaged these fears of racial intermixing by presenting physical intimacy in as nonthreatening a manner as possible. During the 1950s, when interracial hosting first became common, publicity shots featured white hosts touching African American children as they welcomed or comforted them. The white hosts often appear uncomfortable. A 1956 photo shows three white host mothers standing stiffly behind their African American guests. No physical contact is apparent. More typically, photos showed hosts laying a hand on a guest's shoulder or touching a homesick child.[18] As African American children came to dominate the program in the 1960s, publicity materials featured host parents kissing their guests goodnight, holding their guests' hands while walking to the car, or snuggling with their guest on the sofa while reading a bedtime story.[19] Only at the end of the sixties did images proliferate in which guests and their host siblings draped arms around one another's shoulders, tossed one another in the pool, or built an interracial human pyramid.[20] By the 1970s, photographers focused on black guests hugging or holding hands with their white host siblings but only in same-sex pairs.[21] At no time did promoters allow even the suggestion of physical contact across race and gender lines except in such endearing cases as when a white male host is shown cradling a napping African American girl.[22]

Those who set up Fresh Air visits designed a second simple, yet effective, method to curtail unwanted romance. Program administrators allowed hosts to select whether a boy or girl would visit their home. For decades, hosts could choose the gender of their guest.[23] Although program administrators no longer allowed hosts to select the children's race or religion by the beginning of the 1970s, not a single program surveyed here—whether run by newspaper companies, social service agencies, schools, denominational agencies, or congregations—stopped hosts from selecting their guests' gender. In this way, hosts reduced or eliminated opportunities for their children to become romantically attached to a guest of another racial group.

A preference for girls continued. In many programs, invitations for girls led boys by a ratio of two to one.[24] As the percentage of African American and Latino children grew, so did the balance in favor of girls over boys. In response, by the mid-1960s the Fresh Air Fund had set numerical goals to increase invitations for boys.[25] By the early 1970s, Veronica Anthony, the Fresh Air Fund's Friendly Town Director, stopped short of naming the sexual root of the problem when she declared, "People think boys are harder to manage; that they cause trouble and may be a risk. . . . [Some] say they'd rather have no guests than take a boy." To attract host interest, she described "little boys sitting on the stoop all summer long," notably emphasizing the boys' young age and, presumably, less risky state.[26] Despite Anthony's efforts, appeals for hosts to invite boys only grew more insistent through the 1970s.[27] Although publicly unspecified, the prospect that black and brown boys would threaten the social and sexual equilibrium of the hosting communities mirrored similar attitudes toward black and brown men. As comments and reactions from white suburbanites made evident through the 1970s, a single African American or Latino man moving into an all-white community projected a threat to white women, whereas a single African American or Latino woman in the same setting presented a target for white men.[28]

Yet gender selection did not stop romance from blossoming. Private correspondence to Fresh Air administrators revealed host concerns about interracial attraction. As one local host wrote, "One of your [black] boys was much interested in our white girls"; another expressed the opinion that "it would also be wise if the older [black] boys could be placed in homes where there are no girls their age."[29] Still another local organizer stated his concern even more obliquely by suggesting that Fresh Air children be placed in different homes each summer because "[f]amiliarity in this case might lead to certain problems."[30] Looking back on his years as a Fresh Air child in the 1970s, Luis Diaz remembered falling in love with two different local girls and regretting that he never had the opportunity to really tell them how he felt.[31] Even though few accounts became public, Fresh Air children of color and the white children they met while on vacation still fell in love. Like Macy Thomas, who traveled to the Kishacoquillas Valley and expressed interest in the white boys who lived there, or the young white woman from that community who fell in love with a Fresh Air visitor, married him, and moved to Queens, hosts and guests, male and female, crossed the romantic color line despite the wishes of the adults around them.[32]

Cross-class romance had not threatened hosts or organizers to the same degree. Novels and movies had long idealized working-class heroes and heroines falling in love with members of the upper class.[33] Although sometimes offered with a dose of caution that marrying above one's station would require giving up friends and family in exchange for comfort, ease, and luxury, popular culture familiarized the idea of cross-class romance.[34] Prior to the shift to interracial hosting, Fresh Air promoters celebrated such romantic attachments. A 1948 article told the charming story of an Otego, New York, family who hosted two Fresh Air girls and their single mother. A few months later, the girls' mother married their hosts' oldest son.[35] In the mid-1950s the Fresh Air Fund still proclaimed that many visitors married romantic partners they met while on a summer visit.[36] Such proclamations disappeared from promotional materials from that point onward.

Romances that crossed both class and race lines simply proved too threatening. By program policy instituted at the vast majority of Fresh Air initiatives, children who traveled to the country came from impoverished families. From the mid-1950s onward, most of them came from African American or Latino families. By contrast, hosting families had enough financial stability to bring an additional diner to the table without undue financial hardship; with few exceptions, all were white. Even though movies such as Stanley Kramer's *Guess Who's Coming to Dinner* (1967), starring Spencer Tracey, Katherine Hepburn, and—most significantly, Sidney Poitier—began to make the prospect of interracial attraction somewhat less taboo, such films still addressed interracial romance only. Poitier's character was a doctor, not a working-class laborer. Those responsible for pub-licizing Fresh Air programs made the decision to avoid all mention of romance in light of the multiple dynamics at play. They could not script a scenario where only race proved salient.

The prevailing conservatism of both Fresh Air programs and the rural host-ing communities muted any record of gay and lesbian attraction. While Fresh Air children recognized same-sex relationships and often understood them to be a normal part of city life, they did not make their sexual preferences evident to their hosts if they strayed from heterosexual norms.[37] Through the 1970s, state and social repression of the gay and lesbian community fostered silence and covert behavior.[38] Despite that silence, Fresh Air children and their hosts found ways to express affection within gender lines that did not require public disclosure or invite punishment. At least one Fresh Air participant recalled being taught to masturbate by her host sister while they lay together in the bedroom.[39]

Organizers also hid abuse during this period. Consistent with the record of many religious communities, Fresh Air leaders initially invested far more resources in protecting hosts from dangerous children than in protecting children from dangerous hosts.[40] Through the 1970s, program administrators halfheartedly vetted hosts while rigorously vetting children. Given the relatively lax process for approving hosts, home visits could easily prove treacherous. An accurate assess-ment of how often abuse took place is difficult to make given the historical mis-trust of law enforcement within many of the urban neighborhoods from which Fresh Air children came and the significant power imbalance between program administrators and participant families.[41] Many instances of abuse never made it into the written record.

Yet some did. Instances ranged from the host who hit her guest on the back in 1956 to the host who fondled his guest in the 1960s and forced her to perform sexual acts.[42] In other instances that came to light only in the early 1980s, white hosts in Vermont beat and tormented a five-year-old girl from East Harlem dur-ing a four-week stay, and a counselor at a Fresh Air camp sexually assaulted a ten-year-old boy.[43] As a result of these latter cases and the lawsuits they prompted, the Fresh Air Fund "admitted it had been naïve," began participating in efforts to prosecute abusive hosts, and changed its vetting procedures.[44] But it did not do so until the 1980s. Through the course of the period under scrutiny here, the children remained vulnerable to sexual predators and could not rely on Fresh Air personnel to support them if they registered any kind of abuse complaint.

Overall, Fresh Air hosts and administrators invested far more energy in assuag-ing donor fears and curtailing sexual contact across racial lines than in preventing sexual assault. Publicizing interracial visits with photos of chaste hugs, goodnight kisses, and tender hand-holding presented the programs as safe, nonthreatening undertakings. Allowing hosts to choose the gender of their guest avoided complications around sleeping and privacy in the home while also greatly reducing the number of African American and Latino boys who received invitations. At any point, administrators could have modified gender-selection policies just as they had modified the selection of race and religion. The fact that none of the programs did so serves as yet another confirmation that fears about interracial sex presented the greatest challenge to the Fresh Air movement, and the resulting policy decisions proved the most essential to the movement's long-term success. Like most other social service providers at the time, those same administrators offered little public comment or concern about the safety of the children in the intimate spaces of bedrooms and camp cabins.

The adults' efforts to squash budding romance did prove effective but not foolproof. Macy Thomas most likely did not marry someone from her favorite summer vacation spot. Cultural, racial, and class chasms ran deep between New York City and the Kishacoquillas Valley. A few children of color ventured across those gaps, married Fresh Air romantic partners, and relocated to their former hosting communities.[45] Interestingly, those with light skin tones, whether white people or those from Puerto Rican or Dominican backgrounds, relocated most often.[46] Local residents, like many other white Americans, found people with lighter skin tones less threatening.[47]

The few children who returned to hosting communities did so without Fresh Air support. Only guests who received special invitations from their hosts got to go back after they became teenagers and, in many of the programs, could return only if their hosts paid their way. In some instances, children drawn by romance or nostalgia revisited without an invitation. When they returned, no one could deny their sexuality. At points the reunions turned awkward. The story that follows explains how Fresh Air organizers kept older children from returning by joining age caps with gender selection.

Seven

Laurence Mickolic revealed much when he explained gender inequity in the Fresh Air camp program. For twenty-three years, Mickolic had directed camps for the Fresh Air Fund. Although in 1960 he enthused over the ability of his staff to transform a group of "rowdy teenage girls," by the early 1970s that enthusiasm had begun to wane. He referred to girls who ran away and others who, along with some boys, were "hard to handle" because "they fight and . . . cause trouble."[48] By 1978, Mickolic had found ways to deal with troublesome boys because he allowed them to attend camps until the age of sixteen. Girls, however, had to stop attending once they turned thirteen. As he explained to a reporter, Fresh Air camps served girls only through the age of twelve because "[t]hey're a little too sophisticated these days."[49] He did not need to clarify his point. His concern had little to do with the girls' knowledge of the classics, their erudition, or their ability to engage in polite conversation. He referred to the onset of menarche and the girls' understanding of and interest in sex. Rather than grapple with those issues directly, Mickolic set an age cap.

Mickolic's policy of rejecting adolescent females unified Fresh Air homes and camps. Home-based programs had put a similar limitation in place on girls and boys for much of the twentieth century. By putting the age cap in place for girls in camp settings as well as homes, Mickolic and other Fresh Air administrators joined in the project of simultaneously shielding girls from sexual advances and reducing the threat of their unchecked sexuality.[50] As in the case of hosts who exercised the option to select their guest's gender, Fresh Air programs often allowed hosts to select their guest's age and extend re-invitations to former guests through their mid-teens. The policy of host preference again forestalled concerns about sexual contact between adolescents and dovetailed with a practice of shuttling older children and those with behavioral issues to the camp environment. Hosts' preference for younger children likewise emphasized their reluctance to engage guests who had lost the sexual naïveté of a seven-year-old.

A discussion of age selection begins first with the parameters set by the sponsoring organizations. In general, as program administrators gained experience with sending children on summer vacations, they usually raised the lower age limit. Already in 1897, a survey of the twenty-four Fresh Air programs active at that time found that the vast majority accepted children when they turned six.[51] Others did not follow that practice. In the 1950s a Fresh Air counselor commented on the "baby actions" of a two-and-a-half-year-old camper.[52] As late as 1972, a Fresh Air program in Ames, Iowa, allowed four-year-old children to participate.[53] Mickolic's program raised the entry age to five by 1949 and kept it there for the next three decades.[54] The only home-based program to have set the entry age above seven did so by disallowing any child younger than eight in order to address the "problem of homesickness."[55] Across region and time, children could most commonly participate once they turned five, six, or seven.

Home-based programs more consistently set the upper age limit at twelve. In 1897, well over three-quarters of the children transported out of the city were younger than thirteen, but it should be noted that, prior to the shift away from hosting white ethnic children, a small number of programs allowed teens to continue participating.[56] By 1922, the Fresh Air Fund had settled on twelve as the standard age cap, although local communities occasionally lowered it to ten.[57] Rarely did local communities raise the upper age limit.[58] As the African American and Latino children came to dominate the programs, publicity materials more and more consistently stated, "A child is no longer eligible to participate in this program after age 12."[59] During the early 1970s, programs in Boston, Chicago, and Des Moines did allow a few youths in their early teens to travel to local homes, but even these initiatives emphasized that most of their participants, as was the case in Boston, fell "between 5 to 12 years of age."[60]

Some programs allowed children who had developed an especially close relationship with their host family to be re-invited until they turned sixteen. Children could be placed with new hosts until they turned twelve, but after that point Fresh Air staff no longer arranged new hosting sites. Only a re-invitation from a prior host would bring a teenager to the country.[61] Few administrators spoke publicly about their attitudes regarding the extension option, but in 1978 Carolyn O'Keefe, a host placement volunteer, let slip that "older children are the subject of debate among" Fresh Air officials because "[a]t 13 or so, unless they've had a lot of positive summer experiences, a kid in the Bronx is on the streets for life."[62] O'Keefe perceived widespread distrust of teenagers and, strikingly, a lack of faith in the efficacy of the summer hosting program itself. But such candid comment was rare. Rather than discuss the tensions present in hosting teens, administrators instead fostered an informal screening mechanism to ensure that children would not introduce too much of those streets into the hosting environment.

Hosts expressed a preference for younger children within the prescribed age range. Administrators complained that the children "between the ages of 10 and 12 . . . we find hardest to place."[63] Echoing mid-century professional and legal shifts that treated childhood as a time of freedom from adult knowledge and responsibilities, hosts had begun asking for younger and purportedly less worldly wise visitors.[64] A 1954 Pennsylvania host requested "the youngest you can get but not an older one."[65] As a 1978 report on the evening arrival of a group of thirty-five Fresh Air children in the north-central Pennsylvania town of Clearfield noted, "the children are younger this year because sponsors requested them."[66] One year later, a local Fresh Air representative bemoaned that hosts "would rather have the younger ones," which meant "the only way to get the older ones is to get families to re-invite them."[67] Given the widespread preference for younger children, even those children fortunate enough to be placed at a young age could not count on re-invitations (see figure 8). Camps did provide opportunities for some older children, but here again registration rates dropped precipitously once the children became teenagers.[68]

The preference for younger children led to problems arising from immaturity and homesickness. Upon returning to New York, one young child did not know where he lived, insisting that he came from Alabama rather than Brooklyn, a discrepancy cleared up only when his mother arrived to claim him.[69] Mary

FIGURE 8. "Mrs. Dale Cooper of Linville (right) welcomes her guest, Tangiere Walker" (original caption). Used by permission of the *Daily News-Record*, Harrisonburg, VA ("Holiday Begins," *Daily News-Record*, July 14, 1978, 13).

Ann Strawn, a host mother in the northwest Illinois suburb of Rolling Meadows, dubbed her five-year-old guest Yvette the "Princess of the magic tennis shoe" because she could not keep her shoelaces tied.[70] In contrast to these and other minor problems arising from preschoolers traveling away from their families, homesickness traumatized far more children. Although children who complained of homesickness in camp settings often did so to resist authority, Fresh Air children visiting host homes seemed more set on simply extracting themselves from a strange environment.[71] Most common among children ages five to nine, homesickness could be triggered by something as simple as a neighbor's dog barking "just like" a pet at home or the cumulative effect of travel. Upon exiting the bus transporting him from New York City to Wicomico, Maryland, five-year-old Edward Phillips demanded, "I wann' to go home, and I am hungry to [sic]."[72] Amid tears and inconsolable heartache, some children did return home early.[73]

Fresh Air administrators responded to recurring bouts of homesickness by instituting new procedures rather than raising entry ages. Other than a few programs such as the United Way initiative in Minneapolis that stopped sending five- and six-year-olds to camp, administrators chose to manage homesick children rather than remove homesick conditions.[74] At point of departure, Fresh Air staff focused on separating the children from the parents as quickly as possible. In 1968 one reporter observed two staff members "practically shoving" two sobbing girls, ages five and six, on to the train while their parents watched.[75] Once in the home, hosts could call a "24 hour emergency number" if homesickness or other "adjustment problems" emerged.[76] If in need of help, hosts received advice on how to keep the homesickness at bay.[77] If such advice proved ineffective, organizers shifted children over to experienced hosts with reputations for providing solace to homesick children or, in extreme cases, sent the children back on an "early return."[78]

The drive to keep children in homes despite the prevailing issue of homesickness attests to the organizers' dependence on full-length visits. Organizers described homesickness as the "major" or "biggest" problem faced by hosts and made sure to mention those instances when children "were not even homesick."[79] Moreover, although organizers frequently claimed a re-invitation rate of 50 to 60 percent, they never released statistics on how many children became homesick or went home early.[80] Motivated by a desire to provide the best possible experience for the city travelers and to give donors more success stories than tales of homesick woe, organizers pursued robust strategies to comfort distraught children. The difficulty of arranging travel logistics, contacting parents, and appropriating funds for an early return pressured organizers to keep homesick children in guest homes, but concern for long-term program success also factored in their calculation.

Children again exercised significant influence over their hosts and Fresh Air movement organizers. They could make their hosts start "climbing the walls" in frustration over persistent homesickness or become despondent, as in the case of one host whose first guest left the same day she arrived and whose second guest left after she stayed only half the time.[81] Only on the third try did the guest not claim to be homesick and stayed the full two weeks, thereby, in the host's words, proving "satisfactory."[82] Hosts fretted over their charges, changed their bedtime routines, and arranged for visits with other Fresh Air children in the vicinity.[83] They scheduled phone calls home, prepared the children's favorite foods, and tried to keep the children so busy that they would not think of an early departure. Regardless of whether the children intended to manipulate their hosts through claims of homesickness, their actions nonetheless triggered time-consuming emotional and procedural responses from their adult hosts.

Homesick-prone children fulfilled hosts' desires only if the children conformed to their hosts' expectations for age-appropriate behavior. By the end of the 1970s, hosts began to comment on the conduct of their young guests. Even a five-year-old might shatter host expectations. When five-and-a-half-year-old Troy traveled from Bell Harbor, New York, to the Eberhart household in Huntingdon, Pennsylvania, he surprised his hosts by nonchalantly "blurting out a curse word if the mood struck."[84] Other hosts noted that their young guests were "street-wise" or found that the children brought "the agnosticism and sophistication of the city and the profanity of the streets" into their homes.[85] Again echoing Laurence Mickolic's comment about Fresh Air girls over the age of twelve, a host in Friedens, Pennsylvania, by the name of Karen Gibson noted that many of the children came to her community "like little adults, very sophisticated."[86]

A conclave of Fresh Air representatives in the mid-1960s sheds light on the frequent use of the term *sophisticated* to describe urban children. Seventy administrators, volunteers, and staff people gathered in New York City to share ideas and address issues arising from hosting "Inner-City" youths.[87] In the midst of a wide-ranging discussion, a participant asked "why new invitations are limited to 12 year olds." In response, an unidentified conference member noted, "Generally youngsters over 12 years are more sophisticated than children of the same age in Friendly Town communities." As a result, the conference goer added, "adjustments are difficult."[88] Other correspondence from adults involved in hosting attributed the sophistication to the children's exposure to television.[89] Regardless of the source of the differing experiences, in this instance the adults used a term usually reserved to describe upper-class refinement as a euphemism for knowledge about sexual relations. Hosts desired children who remained ignorant of such intimate matters—another participant at the New York conference noted that "invitations for children 10 and over are minute compared to younger age groups"—but spoke about that preference in the most oblique manner possible.[90]

Older children no longer desired by hosts could take their vacations at a number of sex-segregated camping facilities. As early as 1950, the New York City

Mission Society began scheduling a "pioneer unit" for teenage boys, a model of primitive camping that numerous camps began implementing at the time.[91] Separate camping programs for teenage girls focused on "homemaking" skills like sewing, cooking, personal grooming, and child care but could also include carpentry and woodcraft.[92] Although by the 1960s a few camps did run coed programs for teens, including a work camp for well-behaved campers over the age of fourteen, more commonly Fresh Air camps either discontinued camp offerings for girls once they became teenagers or offered sex-segregated programs for adolescents.[93] Primitive camping continued to be popular through the 1970s, but the opportunity for Fresh Air girls to "rough it" remained rare.[94]

Despite age caps and gender selection, hosts spoke of their guests as family. From the 1940s through the 1970s, hosts delighted in guests who called them "Mommy" and "Daddy," referred to their host siblings as "sister" and "brother," and welcomed being treated "like a member of the family."[95] Yet the vast majority of the hosts stopped hosting children once they turned thirteen. In most cases, even those families that re-invited the same guest each year eventually broke off connection. Even though hosts asserted that guests were like "one of the family," only in the rare instances when hosts adopted or assumed legal guardianship did Fresh Air children truly become family after their teen years.[96]

Those programs that offered both home-based and camp hosting found it difficult to reconcile the two approaches. From the 1940s through 1970s, program administrators stressed that they and the children they served preferred home visits over camp stays. According to a promoter in the 1940s, homes offered a "feeling of belonging that the best camp cannot duplicate."[97] Thirty years later, another promoter echoed that sentiment when he claimed that Fresh Air children enjoyed home visits the most "because of the closeness and the lasting bond that often result."[98] At the same time, organizations such as the Fresh Air Fund invested far more per camp visit than home stay. In 1969, for example, the Fund invested $157 for each of the 2,550 campers it served while only $27 for each of the 15,700 Friendly Town visitors on its roster.[99] By 1977, the Fund served 2,700 campers but only 14,000 home visitors, a number that continued to decline through the 1970s and beyond.[100] Two years later, as economic pressures forced mothers to enter the workforce, only 10,600 children ended up in homes.[101] At the same time, the Fund continued to invest hundreds of thousands of dollars in its camp facilities. In all, the Fund constructed 356 buildings, 3 artificial lakes, and 17.5 miles of roads as well as a $90,000 planetarium.[102] The considerable investment in age-capped campgrounds revealed core priorities.

The channeling of funds to camping programs stemmed first from fund-raising strategies. Fund-raisers have long noted that donors respond well to building projects. Development officers at the Fund capitalized on this tendency by inviting major donors to contribute to camp projects like a planetarium or new lodges, the latter of which received positive acclaim—and more publicity—from other architects.[103] Donors responded. Already by 1967, they had contributed over three million dollars to camp development.[104] Although contributors also gave money every year for program costs, the largest donations went to buildings and property.

The Fund also adapted camp infrastructure to serve a growing number of physically handicapped children. Unable to find hosts willing to take children with physical disabilities, Fund director Frederick Lewis allowed the Polio Parents Club of Westchester, New York, to make use of the Hidden Valley camp on the Fund's Sharpe Reservation in 1951. The club ran a two-week program for children "who had been handicapped by polio, cerebral palsy, muscular dystrophy, and rheumatic fever."[105] Within a few years, the Fund had begun scheduling camp sessions that integrated both physically handicapped and able-bodied children.[106] By the mid-1960s, the Fund served "children with handicaps ranging from blindness to diabetes."[107] Along with "conservation" and "interracial harmony," Lewis listed service to the physically handicapped among the Fund's top three outreach opportunities.[108] Although by 1974, the Fund served only 180 handicapped children per summer, its publicity staff ensured that reporters featured the handicapped program on an annual basis.[109]

The reporters who wrote articles about Camp Hidden Valley emphasized the children's independence. In contrast to a prevailing twentieth-century camping trend to reduce opportunities for self-directed play, Hidden Valley staff challenged campers to push their limits on their own.[110] A camper with cerebral palsy who had to wear leg braces surprised his mother by climbing a rock wall. When she expressed concern to a nearby staff person, the Fresh Air staffer replied, "Don't worry. We've got Band-Aids."[111] Rather than protect the children, staff encouraged the campers to hike, play baseball, and dance in wheelchairs. Geraldine Hill, a camper born with "a club foot and seven fingers," attested that camp staff "showed me I could do things I never thought I could do—they made me feel like an able-bodied person."[112] In 1973 the Fund began experimenting with sending children with handicaps to the homes of willing hosts.[113] A few responded, but in the main service to physically disabled children took place on camp property.[114]

A sprawling, well-funded camping facility capable of serving able-bodied and physically handicapped children alike undercut the program's interest in long-term relationships. Children did return to camps and in a limited number of instances came back to serve as counselors or summer program directors. Given high turnover rates among the largely college-age counseling staff, long-term sustainable relationships seldom developed in the camp setting. By investing so much of their fortune in camp facilities, the Fund's board members made clear where their longest-term interests remained. As families stopped re-inviting children at the end of the 1970s, Fresh Air Fund directors poured ever more money into their camping facility. Host interest may have waned, but camps thrived. The one component of their program in which there could be no re-invitations and, for girls, no participation at all once they reached their teen years continued to grow.

Yet 50 percent of those who visited homes did return at least one additional summer. Across the country, that figure remained consistent until the very end of the 1970s. For the space of nearly four decades, about half of all hosts invited their guests back. The largest of the programs noted that the average length of stay of a child in a given host home lasted just under five consecutive summers.[115] Some children took special trips during the school year or at other points in the summer to participate in host family events like weddings, birthday parties, and vacation trips.[116] One even moved in with her former hosts in order to find a local job when she turned eighteen.[117] Although Fresh Air promoters rarely stopped to explain why half of the children did not receive re-invitations or that in many areas only a third or even as few as 10 percent of the children went back to the same family three or more times, many children did anticipate returning to the same family more than once.[118]

Even such long-term relationships can appear quite different from the perspectives of the children. Some, such as Luis and Nilson Diaz, two brothers from New York who participated as guests in the programs in the 1970s, lost track of their hosts once they became teenagers but felt positive about the experience as a whole. As an adult, Luis even reconnected with his original host family via a social media site.[119] Others, such as a group of teenage girls from Gulfport, Mississippi, who traveled to Newton, Kansas, to attend school at Bethel College, discovered that the warm welcome they remembered from their experiences as Fresh Air children had cooled considerably upon their return as young adults. In addition to being denied the privilege of associate church membership, the young women confronted racial epithets, found dating difficult, and received unequal treatment in host homes when on choir tour.[120] Most commonly, older Fresh Air guests recognized that once they became teenagers, they could not venture back. As sixteen-year-old James Murray lamented in a 1976 letter to his former host, "I can't go because I'm too old."[121] The author of a letter to the editor in Bennington, Vermont, observed that hosts found their former guests to be threatening when they returned as teens or adults.[122]

Cindy Vanderkodde's experience confirms the observation. Like so many other Fresh Air children, she was African American, hailed from New York City, and first visited a host at the age of five. Traveling under the auspices of a Fresh Air program run by the Christian Reformed Church, she felt welcomed and included by her hosts and the surrounding community in the 1950s and 1960s. Yet

Vanderkodde stayed long enough with Helen and Roger Vandervelde, her hosts from Grand Rapids, Michigan, that she learned the embrace eventually turned cold. When she was younger, the former Fresh Air child thought, "Oh wow! This is family. They love me." Yet once she graduated from college, established a career, and had "become an equal" to the hosts, Vanderkodde observed that her hosts' affections cooled. "There was just no interest there," she lamented.[123]

Many other former Fresh Air children reported a similar sense of alienation upon becoming an adult or even entering adolescence. Glenda Adams, a participant in the same program as Vanderkodde, recognized a former host sister when she arrived as a first-year student at Calvin College but received no acknowledgment in return.[124] Peggy Curry, the mother of a Fresh Air child in Harrisonburg, Virginia, noted that her daughter never received another invitation to visit a host family in Pennsylvania once she became a teenager.[125] The list goes on of former Fresh Air children who felt cut off by their hosts or simply lost contact for decades.[126] Notably, all the examples identified here came from situations where white hosts brought African American children into their homes. Although some children did maintain connections with former hosts into adulthood, most participants enjoyed short interactions without the benefit of long-term relationships.

A recurrent desire for naïve, prepubescent children again shaped age limits built into the programs. Seven-year-old children had far less trouble finding a welcome at camps and homes than did seventeen-year-olds. The younger children still embodied the themes of innocence long promoted by Fresh Air programs: lack of sexual knowledge, naïveté about worldly affairs, and absence of both physical and moral contagion. Likewise, Fresh Air Fund administrators' interest in serving the handicapped dovetailed well with the overall attraction to desexualized, unaware, cooperative children. Although camps did promote the children's independence to a degree, that support focused more on freedom of mobility than independence from adult authority. As long as the children accepted a subservient role, they had the full support and affection of their hosts. Once they became sophisticated or equal to their hosts, many fewer found a ready welcome.

Age caps and sex segregation proved effective. They quelled much of the children's dissent. Yet wrapping the Fresh Air movement in an antiseptic gown did even more. By carefully screening all potential guests for contagious disease, Fresh Air programs protected hosts from the threat of the city's sickness entering their homes.

Sick

Fresh Air programs guaranteed that every child sent to the country had a clean bill of health. Recruitment notices assured hosts that all children had to pass at least one and most often two medical examinations prior to departure. Only discussion of transportation received more consistent and widespread attention. At the same time, not a single program required that hosts also receive medical examinations in order to participate. Like the programs themselves, the threat of contagion went only one way.

Administrators initially focused on tuberculosis cures. In the earliest years of the programs, Fresh Air administrators sought to cure children by exposing them to fresh country air—hence the fresh air label. After 1944, however, the discovery of antibiotics dramatically altered that practice.[127] A course of isoniazid, and later rifamycin, rendered fresh air cures obsolete. Rather than bring children who had a communicable disease to the country, program administrators made certain that no child who left the city ever had a disease.

The screening continued even after the children left the city as program staff and volunteers measured the children's weight. Through the mid-1950s, hosts commented on the amount of food their guests consumed, kept statistics on average weight gain, and exclaimed over children who individually ate "more than one loaf of bread per day."[128] A 1948 report from a Fresh Air camp noted "a gain of 257 pounds . . . , four and one half pounds to the boy" and "a gain of 71 pounds" by the thirty-eight girls attending the camp.[129] The children likewise paid attention to their weight. In 1950 Anne O'Hagan, a New Yorker visiting the island town of Jamestown, Rhode Island, expressed concern that if she gained too much weight, she would not "be undernourished anymore" and thus ineligible to return.[130] With the advent of federal food subsidies, free breakfast programs, and greater attention to children's nutrition, however, concern about weight gain during Fresh Air visits waned in the later half of the 1950s until, by the beginning of the 1960s, comments on the children's poundage rarely appeared in the written record.

Interest in tuberculosis cures and weight gain may have dissipated, but assurances about the children's health remained. Time and again, recruitment notices emphasized that children received two medical exams, one by a doctor a week or so before departure and one by a nurse the day before they left or as they boarded the bus or train.[131] In the words of a local chairperson, sponsors did "everything possible" to assure that the children arrived "in perfect health."[132] The long-standing reputation of the city as an environment filled with disease—evangelist Billy Sunday once warned that God should "wear rubber gloves" when dealing with urban dwellers—fostered this intense and sustained concern about contagion from the city.[133] Since the 1920s, some clinic personnel had even tested Fresh Air participants for venereal disease without explaining how such a test might be relevant to hosting programs.[134] In one instance, Mennonite Fresh Air program administrator Paul N. Kraybill contacted Bud Lewis at the Fresh Air Fund in 1952 to see whether Lewis's organization ever gave blood tests to Fresh Air participants so as to "determine the incidence of venereal disease."[135] Hosts had apparently contacted Kraybill to express concern that some of the children might "spread the disease to others in the country through drinking glasses, toilets, etc."[136]

A few programs promoted the medical exams as free health care for the children. A report on Dr. Frank A. Manzella, a physician who gave more than 15,000 medical examinations to Fresh Air children in the course of his fifty-year career, emphasized that all the exams had been offered free of charge.[137] The Cleveland Fresh Air program in particular touted its comprehensive pre-trip physical exams and, by 1971, its "year-round medical care."[138] That same year, the Fresh Air Fund in New York also made attempts to extend health care to children in their programs when physicians discovered that between "50 and 90 per cent" of the children had never previously been to a doctor.[139]

The provision of free checkups did not change the fundamental equation. From the perspective of the rural hosts, the city bred sickness, and the country bore health. In contrast to the unhealthy, disease-ridden city, promoters and hosts viewed the suburbs and country as inherently salubrious. In addition to the ameliorative benefit of clean air, good food, and cool nights, promoters highlighted the country's psychiatric restorative properties, the healing power of space for children to "run around" and "let off steam," and the reparative value of "placing cool bare feet on the green grass of a meadow."[140] As a result of the one-way equation, although the city children endured medical scrutiny that at times included humiliating delousing in the presence of local hosts, Fresh Air host families never had to contend with questions about their physical condition.[141]

Assertions about the benefits of country living obscured health hazards regularly faced by the children while on their visits. Transportation to the rural locations could leave the children "confused, tired, dirty, hot, and hungry" and, in at least one instance, "in tears" upon arrival.[142] In another instance, a car accident left several children injured while on their Fresh Air vacation.[143] Many Fresh Air children returned home with injuries ranging from bee stings to broken bones.[144] Those placed on farms faced the real threat of death or dismemberment from working around and riding on farm machinery.[145] Each year some did tumble from hay lofts, get kicked by a draft animal, or find their fingers cut by a blade.[146] Although the Fresh Air Fund began an awareness campaign that resulted in fewer accidents and injuries, by 1966, 634 children still experienced an accident or became ill during their stays.[147] The insurance provided by most Fresh Air programs covered the resulting medical expenses, but the risk that a child traveling on a vacation would return home in poorer health than when she or he left belied the claims that country visits only improved the children's physical condition.

Program administrators like Kraybill and Lewis paid attention to health concerns because they and their staff genuinely cared for the children, but also because they wanted to protect hosts from contagion. In the programs' early years, only a third of the children examined traveled to the country.[148] Even so, hosts complained that children still brought lice and impetigo with them.[149] Some children did test positive for tuberculosis.[150] It seems that no one, from the Fresh Air children and their families to the hosts themselves, registered the possibility that contagion could as easily flow back to the city from the country if a member of a host family came down with measles or was already infected with tuberculosis. The assumption that only urban residents could spread disease blinded all involved to alternate vectors of contagion and obscured the record of rural injuries, farm accidents, and travel trauma.

The medical vetting process thus set apart Fresh Air children from other urban dwellers. Unlike their counterparts back in the city found to be contagious, the young travelers who arrived on the doorsteps of suburban and country homes brought no disease with them and therefore posed no medical threat. The children could bring stories and perspectives of the city into their host homes, but program administrators exerted every effort to ensure that nothing more dangerous came with them. In effect, the programs sanitized the children as they vetted them. Paul Kraybill's 1952 query about testing children for sexually transmitted disease was not unique. As late as 1971, medical professionals engaged by the Cleveland Fresh Air program screened potential participants for sexually transmitted diseases.[151] Although they offered little or no explanation to the children or their parents, the medical staff indicated that at least these children of the city would bear no medical threat and, presumably, would less likely be sexually active. Program administrators sold Fresh Air programs with a guarantee that a measure of the urban world would enter host homes, but it would not be contagious.

Innocence and Power

Fresh Air administrators did their job well. By curtailing romance, focusing on preadolescents, and ensuring clean bills of health, those in charge continued to define their programs by the images of innocence that they projected. Fresh Air staff succeeded in promoting their programs as sexless, nonthreatening, and contagion free.

The narrative that fueled this presentation centered fundamentally on power. As historian E. Melanie DuPuis contends, "Stories about perfection are in fact acts of power."[152] The reporters, administrators, hosts, boosters, and endorsers of every stripe used the privileges afforded them by virtue of class, status, wealth, and often race to assert that Fresh Air trips were not only a good way to respond to the apparent plight of children stuck in the city but also, as one booster claimed, "the best thing that could happen to a child" in those circumstances.[153] Unblemished children sent to a superior setting by flawless supporters told a perfect story. But as critics had begun to note by the 1970s, that Fresh Air narrative, regardless of the individual motives of those involved in telling it, powerfully devalued and diminished the children's capacity. At the same time, by emphasizing the children's poverty and need, promoters—perhaps inadvertently—highlighted their own wealth and ability. A few activists rejected the assertion that the Fresh Air hosts and administrators offered viable solutions to the children's problems, ones that even the children's parents could not solve.[154] The activists recognized that to host a Fresh Air child may have been an act of kindness, but it was also an act of power.

From the perspective of the ever more trenchant critics, children brought to the country counted more as passive recipients than capable actors. In rural communities afraid of interracial romance, in camps and homes where age caps limited long-term relationships, or in the examining rooms of health clinics where medical professionals asked questions about STDs, administrators limited the children's initiative. Although the young sojourners challenged stereotypes, talked back, rejected doctrine, swam to suit themselves, and celebrated the city, Fresh Air critics held that program promoters cast the children as passive recipients of charitable largesse.

In the end, the Fresh Air hosting programs centered on an exchange between children and adults. Race, class, and gender always shaped and molded those interactions, but at root Fresh Air organizers sent children rather than their parents outside the city. As the following chapter makes clear, Fresh Air lasted so long and reached so many because its leaders had found a way to encourage giving based on presenting the children—not their parents—as deserving of pastoral salubrity. By the middle of the twentieth century, the adults who had participated as travelers in the early years of the program had long since been left behind. They had lost their cachet. Only those children who remained mattered.

MILK, MONEY, POWER

How Fresh Air Sold Its Programs

Bryant Fearon and Danford Mojica carried milk pails from cows to containers with pleasure. Even though they struggled to keep the milk from slopping, the two young Harlemites took to their task with gusto. They worked all the harder given that a photographer from the Associated Press had come to visit the farm of J. B. Vaughn in Hinesburg, Vermont, where the two boys vacationed in 1950 (see figure 9). In the photo that preserves a moment of their dairy chore, the boys appear satisfied, proud even, of their ability to work in a barn with cows.[1] Photos like this one documented for interested donors that Fresh Air staff did what they claimed. They brought children into close contact with the smells, sounds, and symbols of the country. Amid the bellowing of cattle, the rich odors of bovine lactation, and the photographer's flashbulbs, Fearon and Mojica learned firsthand about milk's origins. The two African American boys did their part to make Fresh Air programs into some of the wealthiest and most well-known charities in the nation.

The photo of Fearon and Mojica tending to dairy chores resulted from careful Fresh Air marketing. Administrators, hosts, celebrities, and politicians made Fresh Air ventures relevant by crafting highly successful promotional campaigns. The adults who ran the programs linked the summer sojourns with pristine symbols of the country like cows and the milk they produced, pursued donors with some of the most sophisticated publicity measures available, and fostered relationships with some of the country's most powerful individuals. By using milk, money, and power, they created a thoroughly American institution. Combining volunteerism, charity, agrarian husbandry, and patriotism, Fresh Air made a long-term home in the United States.

FIGURE 9. "Invited to spend a couple of weeks vacationing in the hills of Vermont, these Negro youths from Harlem gladly lend a helping, if inexperienced, hand at milking time on the farm operated by J.B. Vaughn (left) and his son Roger (center) at Hinesburg, VT. Boys are Bryant Fearon (right) and Danford Mojica, who were part of a group of 79 children from Harlem invited to visit in Vermont homes" (from label on back of 1950 original photo). New York Public Library, Schomburg Collection, Children, 23–012.

Milk

A Hinesburg, Vermont, dairy barn opens a door into the cultural, financial, and civic themes of the Fresh Air movement. The photographer who captured Fearon and Mojica carrying milk pails in 1950 depicted a quintessential rural scene. In a state known for its dairy industry and a town known for its cheddar cheese, cows dominated the landscape, work flow, and economy. In 1946 the state listed 370,800 human residents and 296,000 bovine inhabitants.[2] Amid this dairy-intensive culture, the two young Harlemites, like the seventy-seven others who had traveled with them and the thousands who visited New England each summer, knew farm life by getting close to cows.[3]

More so than silos, tractors, pitchforks, or horses, the cow evoked the country. Because of efforts of the dairy industry to create a "dairy-consuming culture" and of reformers to ensure proper nutrition, North Americans perceived milk as a dietary necessity by the 1930s.[4] Many milk advertisers initially avoided using cows in promotional campaigns, opting instead for babies and, curiously, birds. Borden bucked the trend by introducing Elsie the cow in the 1930s.[5] Because of advertising campaigns like Borden's and the proliferation of pastoral images depicting cows grazing in a field or chewing their cud while a suspender-wearing farmer squirted milk into a tin pail, cows came to represent both the place and practice of rural life. As represented in a host of commercial and decorative products, by the middle of the twentieth century animal husbandry defined the country as much as did open fields.[6] Cows had come to stand in for what one saw and what one did when outside the city.

By the end of World War II, Fresh Air programs had been devastated. Having sent out more than 14,000 children each year between 1923 and 1934, by 1947 the number had dropped to 3,118. Communities that had hosted children for as long as six decades were no longer participating.[7] Both hosting and hosted families had seen sixteen million of their sons, brothers, and fathers march to war. Women who had been available to host had joined the paid workforce.[8] Children had answered the call to support the war effort by collecting scraps of metal, bits of rubber, old newspapers, and tin cans.[9] Cows helped restore Fresh Air in the midst of this disruption. As males returned from the battlefield, women left the workshop, and children traded recycling tasks for playground games, Fresh Air programs ramped up their efforts by riding on the backs of cows.

Fresh Air promoters used bovine references in the 1940s to emphasize the abundant food made available to children who traveled to the country. Cut off from the largely urban-focused milk delivery industry, the residential homes that hosted children from the city frequently featured a small herd of cows to ensure that young visitors received "plenty of milk and cream."[10] Likewise, Fresh Air camps during the same period boasted of the volume of milk used to feed the children and mandated up to one quart of milk per camper per day for use in cooking and drinking, nearly four times the average consumption in the United States during the 1940s.[11] One reporter noted that kitchen staff at a camp run by the Fresh Air Fund "used 75,000 quarts of milk" in 1947 to "keep the small fry full." Another camp run by the Salvation Army offered three pints of milk each day for every child that it hosted.[12] The children who went to the country could expect to both see cows and be fed by them.

The children often had to travel far to visit such milk-infused locales. Early on, staff at the Fresh Air Fund began to recognize that costs increased as children traveled greater distances. Although the cows looked the same in Pittstown, New Jersey, as they did in Hinesburg, Vermont, it cost nearly ten times as much to travel to the latter as it did the former. Fund staff responded by instituting zones encircling New York City at 150-, 250-, and 350-mile increments. A higher proportion of Fresh Air children traveled to the nearer zones than those farther away.[13] As Fearon and Mojica traveled to Hinesburg, they joined a privileged group carefully selected to represent the Fund at such choice, remote locales.

Those who enthused about the milk supplied for the children did not appear to notice the irony that this cherished symbol of health made some children worse rather than better. Although generally unacknowledged at the beginning of this period, lactose intolerance affected as significant a portion of the children brought to the country as it did the entire population.[14] Over time, as more children of African descent participated in the program, a greater percentage of Fresh Air children were lactose intolerant.[15] Thus, a significant percentage of the children brought to the country could not tolerate the dairy products so amply provided. The very product said to improve the children's health left some of them with a stomachache.

The same Fresh Air promoters who referred to cows as signs of rural abundance also used the animals to emphasize the children's ignorance. As had been the case prior to World War II, boosters continued to stress how little the children knew. At base, published accounts highlighted the children's lack of knowledge about cows' appearance. From the 1940s through the 1970s, hosts and reporters exclaimed that the children had "never seen a cow."[16] The reports also poked fun at the uninformed guests. In 1963 two Puerto Rican children asked to ride the "horses"—in actuality, Angus cattle—they saw grazing.[17] Fifteen years later another guest, only five years old, exclaimed, "[L]ook at the doggies" upon encountering a herd of cows.[18] Promoters also made light of the children's lack of knowledge about milk production. One reporter quoted a "darling boy" in 1948 who wished to find his way to a farm so that "he could milk a horse."[19] Another related the story of a young guest who, in 1972, came upon a case of milk bottles and rushed to tell her host that she had found "the cow's nest!"[20] A year earlier, another booster quoted five-year-old Herbert King's retort to his friend's assertion that milk came from cows: "'Don't give me that,' said Herbie in great contempt. 'Milk comes from the store.'"[21] In every case, the accounts emphasized that the children knew less about cows, and by extension life in the country, than did their hosts.

Declarations of simple ignorance shifted by the 1970s to more frequent claims of sheer wonder. Although promoters continued to note that children like a Fresh Air guest named Orlando Correa "had never seen a cow milked or known where milk came from except from a bottle," the program boosters also began to emphasize the children's awe in the face of their natural surroundings.[22] Already in the 1950s, one reporter related a young boy's simple query—"What color is a cow?"—to emphasize his and others' "wide-eyed wonder" rather than their ignorance.[23] By the early 1960s, boosters had begun to entice new hosts with the promise of "pure enjoyment" gained from watching a "little fellow" encounter a cow for the first time.[24] A decade later, reporters and program promoters emphasized the children's fascination with milk production and other "minor miracles" of the countryside.[25] One host claimed that the children loved learning about "how milk comes out of a cow" so much that they "would rather watch the farming than eat."[26] As with other charities active in the 1970s, program promoters became more sophisticated in their publicity and drew on modern psychological theories to design their promotional campaigns.[27] Having learned of the relative ineffectiveness of ridicule as a marketing strategy and having become sensitized to the racial stereotypes underlying depictions of black children as naïve and uneducated, boosters invested more heavily in nostalgic representations of nature. They began to tell a story of children who were not just ignorant about cows and the country but truly "awed by the dairy cattle" they encountered.[28]

The addition of wonder and awe to ignorance in the Fresh Air presentation of children in the country allowed promoters to emphasize the educational value of the vacation trips. Hosts and camp counselors first made sure that the children knew how to identify a cow and other farm animals. By the 1960s and 1970s, when farm stays had become a rare treat because of the increasing disappearance of small-scale, family-run agriculture, camps and local hosting committees planned visits to dairy barns so that the children could encounter cows firsthand.[29] Staff from the Fresh Air Fund collaborated with Cornell University and a nonprofit organization known as New York Farmers to construct a fully functional, twenty-acre farm on the grounds of their Sharpe Reservation camping center in 1966.[30] In addition to seeing where eggs came from, tasting fresh cucumbers off the vine, and learning that popcorn "grew on trees"—i.e., corn stalks—the campers got close enough to touch and brush livestock.[31] As one Fresh Air promoter noted, "It is one thing to read about cows . . . but it is another to actually see them."[32] Various Fresh Air directors made sure their supporters knew that children would no longer confuse cows with doggies thanks to their educational initiatives.

Some children even took their turn at milking. As indicated in the anecdote that opens this chapter, children like Fearon and Mojica readily participated in dairy culture. Their eagerness increased when they actually got a chance to squat down and squeeze milk into a tin pail. A 1957 annual report from the Fresh Air Fund featured a photo of a small boy smiling as he leaned into a large cow and pulled on her udder.[33] By the 1970s, reporters regularly referred to children who had "overcome their fears enough to try milking a cow."[34] Emphasizing the children's response to the tactile experience also proved popular. As one child noted in 1978, the cow's teat felt "sort of rubbery at first."[35] Although boosters clearly used the children's enthusiasm to their own promotional ends, the young visitors who got to try their hand at milking seldom forgot the experience.

Fresh Air cow stories also highlighted the children's curiosity. Some hosts spun yarns about former guests that again emphasized their ignorance. Although Fearon and Mojica appear fairly relaxed as they stood next to a row of cows, other Fresh Air children received a big surprise when they first encountered the large animals. A rural host from Michigan related the story, told by his father, of a Fresh Air guest who "wandered into the barn" only to hear a cow moo. The unexpected sound so startled the young boy that he "came flying out of the barn" with "eyes as big as saucers."[36] In 1962 another guest, visiting a farm in Port Royal, Virginia, ventured into the barn against the advice of his host mother. While unknowingly watched by his host father, the young boy lost his composure as a cow "rolled her eyes and let out a terrific 'Moo.'" Although startled, the boy stayed to introduce himself. "Hello. I'm Marty," he declared.[37] Other children held their curiosity in check enough to avoid solo barn ventures but still impressed their hosts with their cow fixation. A twelve-year-old named Jack even became "fascinated by certain aspects of the private lives of cows," none of which the reporter specified.[38]

The cows the children encountered also represented work. In many children's telling, both at the time and in later recollections, getting to milk cows seldom seemed burdensome. For example, Fearon and Mojica appear to be enjoying themselves as they hauled cans in the milking parlor. Having not grown up with the routine demands of farm labor, Fresh Air children often found milking and other tasks like gathering eggs, herding cows, or sweeping the barn quite novel.[39] In some areas of the country, children earned money during their stay by performing odd jobs or working alongside the children of their host family picking berries, harvesting onions, or gathering other cash crops (see figure 10).[40] By the latter part of the 1970s, when most farm families found children to be an economic drain rather than a supplement to farm labor, the Fresh Air Fund sent older Fresh Air alums to work on country farms, some of them Amish, as hired hands in exchange for room, board, and a stipend of fifty dollars each week.[41] A few older Fresh Air children worked on the cattle farm of Franklin D. Roosevelt's son, Franklin D. Roosevelt Jr., for the same weekly stipend, and at least one guest

FIGURE 10. A boy identified only as "Ervin Krehbiel's son" of the Newton, Kansas, area (left) and Johnny Jefferson of Gulfport, Mississippi, with a young calf on the Krehbiels' farm (1960). Used by permission of the Mennonite Library and Archives, Bethel College, North Newton, KS (Mennonite Library & Archives, Bethel, Kansas: Photo collection; folder: "Mississippi—Gulfport").

assured a reporter that he did "not resent Mr. Roosevelt's wealth."[42] Many children from the city embraced the demands of farm work as a unique opportunity.

Yet not all found work obligations so appealing. Alanzo, a child who visited Hesston, Kansas, in 1961, refused to meet his hosts' expectations. Despite acknowledging that his trip from Gulfport, Mississippi, was a "vacation," his hosts nonetheless asked Alanzo to put on an apron and get to work.[43] In this instance, Alanzo took off the apron and left the store. As his host mother later complained, he would not "fit himself into the program."[44] At a time when most youths sought employment in order to participate more fully in the consumer culture, Alanzo's refusal to cooperate makes sense.[45] He had nothing to gain by laboring without pay. In another instance ten years before, a host wrote to the program administrator that she couldn't get her guest to work.[46] Other more oblique references to guest children's "lack of cooperation" may also refer to children refusing to work given how often rural families relied on their own children to provide no-cost or low-cost labor.[47] Most children traveled to the country to swim, ride bikes, and enjoy themselves around animals. Spending their trip caring for livestock or harvesting crops was not a priority.

Such varied work expectations speak to class tensions around the extent and reach of vacations. Even though the number of poor people in the United States had decreased between 1960 and 1969, the economic gap between hosts and guests remained wide during this period of especially intense Fresh Air activity.[48] Despite that gap, the children reached across to claim a symbol of wealth and privilege, a vacation away from the city. Children who refused to work during their vacation stressed that their visit would center on recreation rather than remuneration and so gave notice that they deserved just as much of a break as did the wealthy urban dwellers who flocked to the Adirondacks or the New Jersey shore during the summer months. Although they seldom referred to the class differences between hosts and guests in their promotional materials, program boosters such as Executive Director Lewis consistently referred to the children's trips as vacations.[49] By so doing, they too participated in the project of extending leisurely respites to the masses, an effort that held more in common with labor unions than charity organizations by the middle of the twentieth century.

The themes of wonder, work, and curiosity that cows came to represent in the Fresh Air programs contained a racial subtext especially evident by the 1960s. The AP photographer described Fearon and Mojica in 1950 as "Negro youths."[50] The host who related the story of the young boy flying out of the barn with "eyes as big as saucers" also reported that his "kinky hair" tried "to straighten itself" as he ran, a description reminiscent of racist tropes marketed in vaudeville shows, slapstick comedy, and cartoons.[51] When describing Marty's self-introduction to a dairy cow in 1962, his host specified him as a "little Negro boy."[52] Likewise, the description of two boys asking to ride the Angus "horses" referenced their Puerto Rican ancestry.[53] As was common practice during the breadth of the twentieth century, white children in the same accounts received no such racial designation. As the nation turned its collective attention to the racial foment of the era, hosts looked for ways to encourage positive race relations—a theme explored at length in chapter 3. From the hosts' perspective, the lessons they offered in agrarian husbandry and the Protestant work ethic bridged the racial divide to correct what they saw as racially determined deficiencies in the children's upbringing. By educating the children, they sought to decrease the racial distance between them. Yet each time they told a story about a child of African American and Latino descent who needed guidance and correction, whether about cows or chores, the hosts also demonstrated both their superior knowledge and their good intentions, a pattern visible in multiple Fresh Air programs. In this, as was the case in most white-led, mission-focused enterprises of the post–World War II era, the message sent said more about white superiority and racial separation than it did about black and brown equality and racial integration.[54]

An even more common pattern twined through the programs as cows and nature became synonymous. Children, according to boosters in 1945, got to see "lakes and woods and cows."[55] They laid eyes on "grass, trees, cows, grasshoppers."[56] And they moved among "grazing cows" and "tree-lined streams" and looked at "cows milling about" next to a "waterfall and a bridge."[57] Across a span of more than thirty years, the pairing of rural vistas and dairy animals continued unabated. In each decade analyzed in this book, the children followed suit by likewise referring to "cows and cornfields" and mentioning cows when they described their country vacations.[58] From the perspective of both boosters and the guest children, to see a grazing cow was to encounter resplendent nature.

The children and the cows that they so adored thus infused the country with wonder by way of the city. Although few involved with Fresh Air promotion at the time acknowledged or knew the history, one of the reasons cows proliferated in rural settings was that the city demanded milk. Consumption of cow's milk as a breast milk replacement and dietary supplement for young children began in urban centers and thereby created the modern dairy industry.[59] Although some city children like Herbie had forgotten milk's origins, dairy farmers had not. They knew that urban centers provided the market they needed to maintain their large dairy herds. In essence, dairy cows and Fresh Air children originated in the city. Thus, these two urban products—children and cows—renewed hosts' appreciation for nature. The adults found their wonder renewed as they watched the children delight in encountering cows and other country sights for the first time. The very program designed to take city children into the country depended on the city to promote the country. In short, city cows and city children kept rural communities fresh. Children like Fearon and Mojica and the placid cows they came to see kept the programs running and the connection between city and country ever more apparent.

Money

Introducing children to cows and country depended on money. The photographer who took Fearon's and Mojica's picture as they worked in the barn participated in a long-standing arrangement between reporters and Fresh Air boosters. Pictures like that of the two boys publicized the programs and offered proof of their integrity. The photos demonstrated that Fresh Air initiatives did what they claimed: send children to the country. Without the publicity and the money that it generated, the two boys would never have left the city to meet cows in a dairy barn.

As more and more children like Fearon and Mojica sought country vacations, the work of raising funds to send children to the country came to overshadow the work of actually sending children to the country. More than hosting, donating defined Fresh Air by the 1970s. Far more groups and individuals connected to the programs through fund-raising ventures than through actual hosting. In 1971, for example, an estimated 20,600 individuals donated more than $700,000 to the Fund's unrestricted operating budget, thirty gave endowment bequests totaling more than a half million dollars, and nineteen contributed a total of $33,000 to the Fund's endowment for "vacations-in-perpetuity."[60] By contrast, only 13,832 actually hosted children in their homes.[61] Although some hosts also contributed financially, most gave through the act of hosting. Moreover, the Fund concentrated its fund-raising efforts on those who lived in New York City and who thus, by definition, could not themselves host a child. Subsequently, Fresh Air boosters developed an extensive, creative, and effective fund-raising machine rivaled by only a few other charities and dependent upon class contrast and comparison. As in the case of the American Red Cross or the Salvation Army, many more constituents participated by letting go of money than letting in the less fortunate.

Those contributors who kept Fresh Air coffers flush participated in a remarkable array of civic, religious, educational, social, and business groups. The diversity of contributing organizations peaked during the 1950s, with volunteer service groups such as the Elks, Jaycees, Kiwanis, Optimists, and Rotary being joined by the Women's Christian Temperance Union, local mothers' clubs, congregations from nearly every mainline denomination and the Salvation Army, as well as newspapers, business clubs, and, somewhat unexpectedly, labor unions.[62] Yet even as volunteerism flourished in the 1950s, more people donated money than hosted children.[63] In what proved the decade's high point, in 1955 an estimated 25,000 donors contributed to the annual fund while well under 10,000 opened their homes to children.[64] Although critics and changing demographics would somewhat dampen the enthusiasm for Fresh Air in the subsequent two decades, the innocuous vision of children like Fearon and Mojica encountering cows kept donor dollars flowing.[65]

The donor-friendly profile of the various Fresh Air programs at times attracted particularly novel contributors. In the 1950s, contributions from a parent teacher association at a private Catholic school in Maryland or a high school Spanish club in New York drew little attention.[66] When fraternity brothers held a Fresh Air fund-raiser in 1972, however, reporters' interest increased.[67] Five years later, a group of recovering alcoholics stepped forward with a contribution of $57 from the sale of their leather craft that again drew press attention.[68] Both reporters and administrators highlighted a $50 check received from the Pennsylvania Lifer's Association in 1979. The group's president, Gerard McKenna, explained that the incarcerated members of his group hailed from "areas similar to the home cities of the fresh air children" and believed in the benefit of offering summer visits to the country.[69] In these cases the sentimental coverage of rowdy frat boys, sober recovering alcoholics, and rueful life prisoners played well with the public and prompted others to give.

Reporters in the 1970s also favored stories of wealthy children giving to poor children for similar sentimental reasons. Sixth-grade students at a well-funded public school in Howard Beach, New York, held an annual carnival fund-raiser for the Fresh Air Fund and, according to the school's principal, wrote "themes about" and discussed the Fund to get the "affluent" children to "learn to share."[70] In an example of the prevailing pattern among post–World War II 501(c)(3) nonprofits, the elite children from Queens P.S. 232 apparently never met Fresh Air participants. By the 1970s, most voluntary organizations had no clear social dimension. Although prior to World War II, membership in groups like the Fresh Air Fund meant meeting with other people, after that point membership meant making a donation.[71] And so, rather than meeting Fresh Air participants, the Howard Beach students saw films, read handouts about the program, and explained to the "smaller children" participating in the carnivals that the proceeds "sent youngsters from poor districts" on country vacations.[72] Likewise, in 1975 a group of young women from another elite school, this one in Long Island, washed cars to raise $200 for the Fund, again lacking direct contact with the program or its participants.[73] In 1979 publicists for the Fresh Air Fund highlighted a Brooklyn third-grade class along with a "group of naval reservists" and a business executive in a list of loyal donors.[74] At a time when many adults expressed anxiety about a rapidly shifting moral and cultural terrain, stories of gifts from young people allayed fears that the young had lost their moral footing and spurred others to offer financial gifts as well.[75]

Yet the fund-raising efforts extended beyond youthful donors to encompass a broad range of participants. From the 1940s through the 1960s, local committees sponsored hot dog roasts, fashion shows, vaudeville performances, and tag days, the latter a fund-raising practice in which donors received a small card or tag to indicate their support of the sponsoring charity.[76] The community-based efforts continued though the 1970s, although tagging no longer proved viable as shop owners expressed concern that overeager fund-raisers beleaguered their customers.[77] The summer residents of Fire Island, a resort community off the coast of New York, held fairs to support Fresh Air.[78] Farther west in Guthrie County, Iowa, a Fresh Air committee recruited the county extension agent to select hosts and publicize the program.[79] And in a rare example of African American parents becoming involved in Fresh Air fund-raising, in Cleveland the women of an historic African American congregation, the Mount Zion Congregational Church, held a Friendly Town Day to sponsor children's visits to homes outside the city.[80] Although the local events seldom brought in substantial funds, they connected a striking array of donor groups to the Fresh Air movement regardless of whether individual members actually hosted children.

Staff at the various Fresh Air headquarters developed much more sophisticated methods than carnivals and hot dog roasts to meet their development goals. Although centralized fund-raising campaigns like those run by the United Way had become increasingly common, most Fresh Air initiatives conducted their own campaigns.[81] Like other charities with roots in the Progressive Era, the Fresh Air Fund and its many imitators had become larger, more bureaucratic, and more specialized in the course of the twentieth century.[82] Yet Fresh Air boosters had found a way to make their appeals personal and connect donors to the program even though most of them would never host children. From the inception of the movement, the public learned about Fresh Air by reading newspapers. Building on Willard Parsons' long-term relationship with the *Herald Tribune*, Fund staff enjoyed free and unfettered access to the paper's publicity machine. In 1953 alone, the *Herald Tribune* ran more than 150 Fresh Air stories and photos.[83] By the 1960s, Fund staff fostered relationships with regional and local newspapers by handing out awards for best local coverage of Fresh Air programs. In 1963, for example, the *Bennington Banner* (Vermont) won the Fresh Air newspaper award for its coverage of visiting children like Fearon and Mojica.[84] By 1966, 300 local newspapers ran Fresh Air stories.[85] Although the *Herald Tribune* and the Fresh Air Fund parted ways in 1966, the Fund built on past positive relationships with the *New York Times* and received editorial and reporting coverage from it through the 1970s.[86] To make its programs personal, Fresh Air first turned to print.

The newspapers that gave such positive coverage to country visits also lavished attention on sports fund-raisers. Although they generated more income from newspaper-based appeals, Fund staff still took full advantage of Americans' love of sport. By 1939, the Fund had been sponsoring an annual all-star football game for four years that regularly drew in excess of 40,000 fans.[87] Despite the commentator who criticized the annual event for lackluster showmanship in 1947, crowds continued to gather through 1951 and generated media coverage across the country from Connecticut to Kansas, a national reach uncommon for a program run out of a single city.[88] Fund staff extended the All-Star concept to the basketball court in 1946 by bringing top-tier collegiate players to Madison Square Garden. Through 1958, more than 13,000 fans gathered for each game.[89] Although the Cleveland-based Friendly Town program arranged a fund-raiser at a 76ers–Cavaliers game in 1976, development officers in that program preferred baseball tie-ins.[90] Back in New York, the Fresh Air Fund arranged for its children's chorus to perform at Yankee Stadium, sent thousands of children to Mets and

Yankees games, and persuaded embattled New York Mayor Abraham Beame to leave his financial worries long enough to make a pronouncement in honor of the Fund's centennial at Shea Stadium in 1977.[91] In these latter instances, the Fund had moved away from using sports events for direct revenue, choosing instead to generate publicity by associating with popular athletes.

The same staff members who used newspaper coverage so effectively turned their attention to electronic media as well. Already in 1939, *Herald Tribune* staff members arranged for Fresh Air children to appear on the CBS radio junior quiz show *March of Games*.[92] Ten years later, a Fresh Air committee in Hagerstown, Maryland, scheduled radio interviews for Fresh Air hosts.[93] Soon after the 1941 founding of the first U.S. television station, Fresh Air staff produced and distributed promotional films.[94] Through the 1970s, local television affiliates aired *Holiday for Danny* (1955), *For All the Children* (1959), *Spud's Summer* (1965), and *Summer's Children* (1965).[95] Although other charities and social service groups also made ready use of emerging electronic media to promote their programs, the Fresh Air Fund in particular latched on to the power of moving images to make the children's stories personal and immediate. Children walked into donors' lives through stories in the newspaper, but they leapt off the screen into donors' hearts through stories on the television. As they had throughout the history of the Fresh Air movement, adult promoters used every available technology to distribute their message.

High-society charity events also drew media attention. As fund-raisers have long realized, gala events make only about thirty cents on the dollar and require extensive volunteer hours to organize. Yet such events engage elite donors and confirm the status of those involved and of the organization they promote.[96] Like many other charitable organizations in the middle of the twentieth century, Fresh Air boosters recognized the benefits of engaging the elite and did so with abandon. In the early 1940s, the Harlem Children's Fresh Air fund proved particularly adept at hosting gala events. Demonstrating the cross-racial appeal of the Fresh Air model to donors in the city, the Harlem group drew in the wealthy to socialize and support children's country vacations. From fashion shows to cocktail parties—one that featured an African American ice skater doing tricks on a six-foot square "midget ice rink"—the Harlem initiative brought black and white elites together for this charitable cause.[97] However, the Fresh Air Fund brought out even more socialites to galas at the well-appointed Hotel Astor on Times Square in the 1950s, including one in which heiresses and business magnates alike "swiveled . . . deluxe, red, yellow and blue" hula hoops in a benefit that raised $25,000.[98] Although the Fund did have its limits, having rejected a staff proposal to sell tickets to a preview of the violent World War II film *The Dirty Dozen* in 1967, both board and staff members happily accepted income from the sale of a Renoir painting and an original Jamie Wyeth graphic, the latter at a 1977 fund-raiser at the Tavern on the Green in Central Park, where entertainment stars mixed with wealthy donors.[99]

Corporations also saw the benefit of offering both in-kind and financial support to the Fresh Air movement. In keeping with a larger trend of business leaders becoming involved in civic pursuits during the twentieth century, Fresh Air administrators called on corporate interests.[100] Having drawn business executives such as investment banker and American Stock Exchange governor Blancke Noyes to their board, the Fresh Air Fund eagerly cultivated corporate sponsors during the 1960s and 1970s.[101] In 1966, Lord and Taylor, Johnson & Johnson, Pfizer, Spalding, and Elmer each offered trademark items such as shopping bags, bandages, motion sickness pills, footballs, and arts and crafts materials.[102] Thirteen years later, corporations pursued a similar strategy as Barney's men's clothing store donated sneakers, Burlington textile manufacturers offered arts and crafts fabric, and the aptly named Popsicle Industries contributed five thousand popsicles to Fresh Air camps.[103] Although in-kind donations helped summer camp programming, they did not go as far as did the thousands of dollars contributed by blue-chip corporations such as American Express, Coca-Cola, IBM, Mobil, Sony, and Western Electric.[104]

The elite who contributed to the Fresh Air Fund went against typical twentieth-century fund-raising patterns. In the aftermath of the Great Depression, most philanthropists assumed that the government should supply a social safety net for the poor and needy.[105] They turned their attention to museums, colleges, hospitals, and civic pursuits that ultimately served themselves and members of their class more than the poor and oppressed.[106] In the case of Fresh Air, however, the involvement of upper-class figures like *Herald Tribune* chairman Whitelaw Reid and Museum of Modern Art president John Hay Whitney ensured other elite donors of the organization's credentials. Likewise, the Fresh Air model dovetailed well with the post–World War II shift toward a more conservative political agenda among philanthropists that emphasized the values of self-help and individual responsibility.[107] Although at root it operated as a charity, the Fresh Air program expected children to do something with the opportunity they had received in the form of a summer vacation. Although they could not offer the personal gratification available by supporting a museum or the symphony, Fresh Air fund-raisers did provide donors the assurance that their investment would pay dividends in the form of more well-adjusted and cooperative citizens.

The combination of local events, newspaper coverage, sports contests, socialite galas, corporate sponsorship, and contributions from major donors built large reserves for the Fresh Air Fund. Despite a series of recessions in the latter part of the 1960s and a major financial collapse in New York City from 1974 through 1978, the

Fund steadily expanded its financial base.[108] By the end of 1955, the Fund's assets had risen to excess of 2.3 million dollars.[109] By the middle of the following decade, the figure had risen to over 5.5 million.[110] By the 1970s, the Fund reported assets in excess of 8.6 million.[111] Even though the Fund ran deficit budgets upon occasion, its considerable reserves allowed the financial picture to improve even in years when individual donors gave less than the organization spent.[112] The mid-1950s claim that the Fund was "unable to dramatize their needs to the public as readily as" other charities rang hollow in light of its long-term fund-raising success.[113] In an era that saw the collapse and disappearance of a host of charity organizations, the Fund's long-term financial success stands out as remarkably consistent.[114]

Such robust financial development hinged on emphasizing the children's poverty. Hosts opened their homes and donors offered their dollars to support children constantly described as poor. Summarizing her experience as a long-time Fresh Air area coordinator, Anna Buckwalter opined that the children and their families "have lived on welfare for so long that they have lost their self respect." She asserted that the urban parents "should have to do something to get that welfare check."[115] Although Buckwalter's comments may reveal more about her and other hosts' urban stereotypes than the statistical reality of urban poverty, children did face harsh class realities. In the United States as in most of the world, class determines a child's well-being more than any other factor.[116] A large percentage of U.S. children learned the truth of that assertion in poor families. During the postwar era in the nation as a whole, almost one-third of children grew up in families with incomes near or under the poverty line.[117]

Urban environments concentrated that poverty, racial disparity intensified it, and Fresh Air programs exposed hosts to its effects. Even though black family income improved overall between 1947 and 1977, African American children remained disproportionately poor and, along with Latino children, overrepresented among those selected for Fresh Air visits.[118] Of course, some children never made it out of the city because of their poverty. Some parents simply could not afford to pay registration fees or the cost of clothing for camp.[119] But given that most hosting programs had dropped or reduced registration fees by the middle of the 1960s, many more children brought evidence of their poverty into host homes. One 1962 account emphasized a young guest's "surprise at being given a toothbrush 'just for myself,'" pleasure in having his own bed, and "horror" at those who fed hot dog ends or ice cream cones to their dogs.[120] In 1977 another host reported that her visitor had a nightmare about losing the one precious dollar that she had brought with her to the country.[121] Long-time Fresh Air Fund executive director Frederick Lewis declared in 1971 that the only eligibility requirement for a child to go on a summer vacation is that she or he be "poor and human."[122]

The long-term emphasis on poverty led to donors and hosts alike defining the children by their impoverished state. Fresh Air programs used a common 1970s strategy of highlighting the children's deficiencies, an approach that attracted donors interested in preparing children for inclusion in a capitalist society rather than in challenging economic systems.[123] Rather than rely on crisis-based requests as did organizations like the Southern Christian Leadership Conference, staff at the Fund based their appeals on enduring poverty.[124] According to published reports during the 1960s and 1970s, the children were "all victims" of poor homes, lived in "miserably closed conditions," and were "extremely needy."[125] In fact, in a shift from prior practice, organizers in the early 1970s advised hosts to invite at least two children at a time because the city visitors were "used to large families and crowded neighborhoods" and therefore would be happiest when surrounded by more children.[126] During the same period, other administrators encouraged giving individualized attention to guests because they came from large families crammed into small quarters.[127] The physical poverty in turn led to emotional neediness as camp counselors in 1964 described Fresh Air participants as "more dependent" and "more insecure" than children hailing from middle-class homes.[128] By the 1970s, reports also emphasized that most of the children came from "broken homes" with only one parent, usually the mother, living with the child.[129] Before the children ever arrived in the country, their hosts had received many messages about the children's material, social, and psychological poverty.

Many hosts offered genuine empathy for the impoverished conditions faced by their temporary charges. At the sight of an undernourished girl getting off the train upon her arrival in Mount Union, Pennsylvania, in 1951, several of the host mothers gathered at the depot let out "sighs of anguish" even as they observed that the Brooklyn youngster "had boundless pep" and "swung like a gymnast on the fence rails."[130] Four years later, Alice Trissel in Harrisonburg, Virginia, expressed concern about the home environment of the two young girls she hosted because their older teenage brothers "lived from house to house with friends, who would let them stay" because of crowded conditions in their family's apartment.[131] By 1976, concern for guests' living conditions remained as Kay Barbel, a host mother in Westbury, New York, expressed delight that the two boys visiting her could each sleep in their own beds; they had to share a single one at home in the Bronx.[132]

Hosts expressed even more concern about the condition of the children's clothing. Although Fearon and Mojica appear outfitted in dapper and durable clothes, others arrived dressed in a manner deemed unsuitable. One host mother in the mid-1960s described her eight-year-old charge who arrived with an "old leather 'strap'" wrapped twice around "his tiny waist."[133] During the same decade, state policies aimed at removing unwed mothers from federal welfare programs such as Aid to Families with Dependent Children increased the number of Fresh Air children struggling with poverty.[134] Piteous descriptions became even more common. Another host detailed the entire contents of the paper bag containing her guest's clothing by listing "a flimsy, ill fitting dress, slip, underwear, torn socks . . . the rundown shoes she wore, . . . one set of underwear, one bathing suit sizes too large, a pair of shorts and a polo shirt."[135] Most dramatically, in 1963 yet another host mother related the story of a guest who refused her host's invitation to stay an additional two weeks because, the young girl admitted in a whisper, "I have to go home and give my sister all my clothes, so that she can go to the country next week for HER vacation."[136] By the 1970s, when even work incentive programs had failed to improve the economic conditions of poor families, many of the Fresh Air programs, including several African American congregations in cities like Cleveland, raised money to supply the children with clothing when they went on their visits.[137] When it came to clothes, white hosting communities and at least a limited number of black congregations found common ground in ensuring that the children arrived in the country looking respectable.

Individual hosts often responded to their guests' poverty by giving gifts. Although organizers frequently cautioned hosts against offering presents, their words had little impact.[138] The children and reporters alike referred to the gifts they brought home. On their return trips, girls frequently wore new dresses given to them by their hosts.[139] Although boys also received new clothing, they more typically described bringing home a frog, bat, or puppy.[140] In contrast to a culture ever more filled with consumer goods, children boasted of receiving homemade presents ranging from toys to snake rattlers and from home-baked bread and jelly to "a large bag of empty butter cartons."[141] Having listened to organizers exclaim over the children's poverty, hosts responded by making sure that children took home some kind of gift from their stay. As one host organizer in Oneonta, New York, noted in 1971, "You can't help laugh sometimes when you see them returning with their arms loaded . . . sometimes you can hardly see the kid through all he carries."[142]

Yet the giving of gifts brought complications. Theorists note that children take part in the gift-giving process by mocking or affirming the gift giver based on their assessment of the gift's quality. The children's response thus either causes embarrassment or satisfaction.[143] Reports about Fresh Air gift giving focused on the kinds of gifts given rather than the emotional dynamics of the exchange, but other evidence makes clear that gift giving could become complex. Johnnie Stanley, a Fresh Air guest in Kansas in 1963, insisted that his host sister had given him a silver dollar that his host parents asserted he had stolen.[144] Another Fresh Air visitor from 1978 packed toys from his host's home in his suitcase under the assumption that, since they had been left out in the yard, no one needed them. The boy's host father complained to the Fresh Air program, making clear he had not thought them gifts.[145] Conversely, in 1963 one host mother arranged a birthday party for Pearl, her young guest, after discovering Pearl had never had one. After the party, the host mother found Pearl dividing up her presents to share with her two host sisters. Despite the host mother's objection that the gifts were intended only for the birthday girl, Pearl insisted that she loved her host sisters and was "going to share with them."[146] Furthermore, children returning from the country with bags full of clothes found themselves ridiculed by neighborhood peers.[147] Only truly poor children needed such gifts. Regardless of what was given, gift giving invariably added complex, often awkward dimensions to the hosting relationship.

Such complexities frequently heightened class differences between host and guest. In the early 1960s a Fresh Air child named Linda brought her host family to tears when they discovered that she had taken a train to an after-school job in order to earn enough money to buy them gifts.[148] A thirteen-year-old girl named Ruth admitted in 1957 that she had gone without lunch at school for two weeks in order to save up enough money to buy flowers for her host mother after Ruth learned that the woman's husband had died.[149] In urban communities where many single mothers had to choose between spending quality time with their children or working to pay the bills, the sacrifice of the children proved even more poignant.[150] In no instance did the giving of gifts diminish the class differences between guest and hosts, and in at least one program by 1970, a program administrator claimed that the children did "not wish to be patronized with gifts or in any other way."[151] Although the administrator may have been reflecting attitudes of parents influenced by the Black Nationalist thought of the day, the comment suggests that gift giving may have done more to appease residual guilt on the part of the host than remove the all-too-apparent class differences between guests and hosts. As one host mother in Pittsfield, Massachusetts, proclaimed with pride, "He arrived in Pittsfield with a half-full suitcase and left with enough for two people to carry."[152]

The children hardly needed gifts to make them aware of the class differences between themselves and their hosts. Most often they commented on two of the most prominent symbols of white-flight fueled suburbanization: houses and cars. In 1959, seven-year-old Deborah Jean Taylor noted that, in comparison to her home in New York City, "[w]e have apartment houses and people here have private houses."[153] By 1966, other children continued to express their amazement that "a single family lives in a single house."[154] In addition to houses, children equated suburban and country wealth with cars. Margie Middleton noted that her hosts "had lots of money" and "big cars."[155] Twelve-year-old Pauline Colon put it bluntly when she said of Bennington, Vermont, "People in New York aren't so good at money that they can afford a car, here everybody has a car."[156]

Attention to those class differences prompted some participants to yearn for a return to rural communities. Despite many boosters' assertions that time in the country did not create unrealistic expectations or change the children's attitudes about their homes, in 1950 nine-year-old Carol Hopewell said that she hoped to someday "live in a lovely house" in the country.[157] Some of the children who grew to love the rural settings they visited as children did return as adults and lived, at least for a short while, outside the city. In a typical example, Elba Rosa traveled from Manhattan each summer to attend the Fresh Air camp in Fishkill, New York, where she met her future husband. The couple then moved to upstate New York and invited Fresh Air children into their home.[158] In other instances, former Fresh Air children stayed to attend high school or find work.[159] The stories that boosters repeated more often focused on those like Rosa or another former Fresh Air child named Orlando Vasquez who considered himself "fortunate to have gotten out" of the "noise and squalor" of the city when he moved his family from the Lower East Side of New York City to Annville, Pennsylvania, a town that had originally impressed him with its quiet streets, plentiful Christmas decorations, and abundant toys in his host home.[160] For the limited number of children who did return as adults, very few of whom were African American, their interest in relocation could not be separated from the material wealth and sense of security they remembered from their youthful visits. No record exists of Fearon and Mojica relocating to Hinesburg, and such a move, even if pursued, would have made them as much an object of curiosity as had been Shubael Clark, a lone "colored man" who attended the Baptist Church in Hinesburg during the nineteenth century.[161]

The Fresh Air program model simply could not support large-scale, permanent relocation to the countryside. In the early 1970s, staff at the Henry Street Settlement House in New York City proposed a far more likely scenario. Staff imagined a program that would transport children from "welfare hotels" to Echo Hill Farm in Yorktown Heights, about an hour north of the city.[162] Funded by New York's Department of Social Services, the day camp trips not only offered "a natural setting, free from the stresses of immediate pressing problems" but also provided both group and one-on-one counseling.[163] The only initiatives that ever saw fruition always returned the children to their families in the city.

The day trip counseling sessions helped children cope with exposure to poverty, not exposure to rural wealth. Reporters and boosters did not speak of negative effects resulting from poor children crossing class lines. In fact, prior to early 1960, hardly anyone criticized the Fresh Air program in print.[164] By 1963, reflecting the liberal turn toward rhetoric that emphasized the damage done to African

American and other victims of social oppression by even well-intentioned social services, some critics asked whether children would be harmed by discovering the "advantages others have and then return[ing] to poorer neighborhoods."[165] Although boosters regularly asserted that no harm took place, they did not develop a uniform response until the later 1970s, when they began to compare Fresh Air visits to amusement park trips.[166] As one host explained in 1976, "It is nice and really special for a while, but it is also nice to come home."[167] From the administrators' perspective, exposure to a stable family, middle-class values, and pristine nature improved the children's chances for success even if they ended up feeling inferior about their homes in the city.

Yet the trade-off had mixed results. In keeping with the myth of American success common from the end of the nineteenth century onward, Fresh Air reporters touted individual achievement.[168] As was the case with most charities, social service agencies, and professional social workers by the 1970s, institutionalized barriers of class or race received at most passing mention.[169] The children would succeed, claimed the reporters, as long as they followed the example set by their rural and suburban hosts. At times, the children agreed. Looking back on their summer vacation trips from their perspective as adults, some former Fresh Air guests appreciated having been prodded to look for options outside their immediate neighborhoods.[170] Others expressed ambivalence over having visited wealthier and whiter homes and criticized the programs for not attending to the systemic roots of poverty.[171] In the end, boosters asserted that country visits led to lifelong success, but they relied almost exclusively on anecdotal evidence to make that claim.

The contrast of wealthy hosts and poverty-stricken guests proved so central to Fresh Air funding that hosts objected when their guests did not seem poor enough. Given the Fresh Air fund-raisers' unrelenting emphasis on providing free summer vacations to poor children, hosts expected that their guests would always arrive in tatters. However, the children sometimes arrived in their Sunday best. Representing the politics of respectability whereby members of the African American community in particular claimed equal status with whites by conforming to middle-class norms of dress, manner, and diction, some girls dressed in frilly skirts and white stockings and boys in dress coats and ties.[172] When the children did not conform to the hosts' expectations of what a child from the "most deserving" poor should look like, the hosts complained.[173] Said one mother of her well-dressed guest in 1961, "She came from too wealthy a home to really appreciate what we had here."[174] Hosts repeated those complaints from the 1950s through the 1970s, with little understanding that parents scraped and saved so that their children could conform to their hosts' dress standards.[175]

Such class pressures eased when hosts came from less wealthy backgrounds. In a few instances, children visited families living in trailer homes. According to at least one local coordinator, some of the "happiest children" he encountered had spent their two-week vacation with a family in a trailer park.[176] Given the physical displacement, unknown surroundings, strange food, and new customs faced by Fresh Air visitors, staying with a poorer family offered welcome familiarity. Such placements were rare, however, as middle- and upper-class families interested in helping the needy populated the hosting ranks.

Hosts thus joined administrators and donors in first viewing Fresh Air ventures as a financial undertaking. Although the pre–World War II programs gave priority to hosting and direct care, by the 1950s programs focused on fund-raising campaigns in order to raise budgets in the hundreds of thousands of dollars and sustain million-dollar endowments. Many postwar charitable organizations made similar shifts to more-professional development efforts that crafted fund-raising appeals supportive of the existing social and financial hierarchy.[177] However, Fresh Air fund-raising campaigns necessitated class comparisons that ratcheted up the attention to money. Staff repeatedly assured hosts that their guests "were from poor families, without question."[178] Along with milk, money mattered to the Fresh Air movement.

Power

Fresh Air programs sought and received support from U.S. power brokers. Drawing on the military, the government, law enforcement, and the entertainment industry, those involved in bringing children to the country infused their rhetoric with central U.S. themes such as patriotism, citizenship, democracy, and equal opportunity for all. Rarely content to limit their efforts to the logistical enterprise of taking children to the country for a summer vacation, program promoters integrated Fresh Air into the very fabric of the nation. Through endorsements from politicians, police, entertainers, and the press, the Fresh Air movement came to represent the hopes of a people for prosperity and fulfillment while legitimizing the possibility that all could succeed. Regardless of their relative penchant for patriotism, the children came to represent a fully democratic, egalitarian, and open society.

Fresh Air boosters first appealed to patriotic themes. Such appeals intensified during World War II. Between 1939 and 1945, the global conflict shaped the lives of children in profound ways, instilling both patriotic values and lasting trauma. In the midst of these formative forces, children eagerly participated in domestic defense activities such as gathering recyclable materials like scrap metal, newspapers, and rubber.[179] Other "nonfarm" youths, often older high school students from the city, answered the government's call to help farmers harvest their crops.[180] As in the case of the privately run Fresh Air programs, some of the youths lived on the farms and others in camps, but all heard adults around them praise the programs "for stimulating mature personality and responsible, democratic character in the lives of average city boys and girls."[181] In many parts of the country, government officials and parents had already encouraged patriotism in the young people before any of them set foot on a Fresh Air farm or rural homestead.

The violence and trauma surrounding the children could be as intense as the patriotism. In schools, art classes turned into spontaneous therapy sessions as young boys drew airplanes strafing the ground. Game playing took on new meaning as "Junior Commando" members received orders to eat lots of carrots so that their night vision would improve as they kept vigil for enemy parachutists, and sandy beaches became potential entry points for invading navies. One adult recalled listening to a soldier at a nearby base instructing a group of five- to seven-year-olds to "maintain frontal fire while using part of your force to encircle and attack from the rear."[182] The violence of a nation at war inundated the children and left vivid impressions of their role—whether real or imagined—in waging war against the enemy.

Fresh Air promoters claimed that their programs could help restore children to an untrammeled state free of worry about war. In 1940 an editorial writer in Altoona, Pennsylvania, proposed bringing European refugee children to country homes in the United States. Although the attack on Pearl Harbor a year later shattered the image of the United States as a haven from wartime violence, at the time she penned her proposal the author claimed that "in this country children are still carefree." Her hope, however unrealized, stemmed from a desire to restore an "innocent childhood" to as many children as possible. Even in the midst of war, she claimed that children still deserved "an untroubled, carefree, happy time."[183] Like hundreds of Fresh Air boosters across the country, the editorial writer looked to the countryside to provide a childhood free of trauma.

The Fresh Air enterprise took on a fresh coat of patriotism during the war years. Hosting children at home came to mean supporting democracy abroad. In 1941 New York Episcopalians advertised their program with a full-color photo of two boys raising an American flag.[184] Two years later, as the war dragged on, promoters in Pittsfield, Massachusetts, implored families with a son or daughter serving in the armed forces to fill their "vacant bed and chair" with a child from the inner city in order to be part of a "patriotic effort."[185] Fresh Air campers planted victory gardens, sent arts and crafts to convalescing soldiers and sailors, and pledged allegiance each evening around the flagpole.[186] In 1945 a Fresh Air home in upstate New York showed children gathered in a circle for "flag-raising time."[187] That same year, Fund staff publicized donations they received from former Fresh Air children then serving in the U.S. Army in China.[188] Like many other social service organizations at the time such as the Boys Club and the Boys Athletic League, Fresh Air programs positioned themselves as part of the war effort, intent upon working with children in order to sustain the nation.[189]

Program administrators continued to resist foreign influences by idealizing rural life. As Fresh Air boosters promoted patriotism during the war, they employed a single phrase, "real America." One particularly enthusiastic supporter wrote in 1942 that Fresh Air vacations showed children "what REAL American home life is like" in order to "make them realize what our country is fighting to preserve."[190] As a booster explained one year later, the "real American" life, people, and ideals that the children experienced during their vacations countered those found in the "foreign quarter of the city" that the children called home.[191] Making his point explicit in 1945, another booster stated that the rural hosts represented "decent, upstanding Americans," whereas the "foreign" urban dwellers lived "in homes that are dirty and smelly from poverty."[192] Although people of color would rapidly take the place of foreigners in Fresh Air discourse, during World War II administrators focused on bringing foreigners into the American fold.

Yet the "real American" rhetoric lingered on for several years past the war's end. As the Cold War settled in and government officials kept alive the threat of foreign infiltration, Fresh Air administrators continued and, in some cases, intensified the idealization of the rural home. At first, they simply repeated the contrast between the life and ideals of real "American folks" and those of the foreign quarter, but by 1948 they had begun to wax even more eloquent about the "great, sunshiny, beautiful, fragrant, wide-spreading altogether glorious" American homes in the country.[193] Likewise, the disparaging of the city grew worse as boosters described in the same year the "unhappy sections" of the city as "breeding places for many movements hostile" to democratic values.[194] Fresh Air administrators continued to employ the "real American" rhetoric through 1956, consistently contrasting rural havens with the less desirable versions of America found in urban tenement districts like Harlem.[195]

Another, even more long-lasting rhetorical strategy focused on democracy and citizenship. For a span of thirty years, at least from 1947 through 1977, Fresh Air program administrators promoted their efforts on the grounds that they instilled in hosted children the ideals of democracy and prepared them to be effective citizens. When visiting homes, the children received "valuable lessons" about getting along with other Americans.[196] Like many other camping programs interested in forming young citizens, Fresh Air campers learned about democracy, patriotism, cooperation, and fair play.[197] In small towns they saw how "Americanism works."[198] The child could "grasp" how democracy unfolded in a town's "government, offices, factories, farms, schools, stores, [and] points of interest."[199] At the height of the discourse in 1963, *Herald Tribune* Fresh Air Fund executive director and former military officer Frederick Lewis proclaimed that programs he oversaw embodied "the essential genius of democracy itself."[200] Although seldom returning to such lofty rhetorical sentiment, Fresh Air staff continued through 1977 to proclaim the value of teaching children "to be good citizens" because they held "the nation's future in their hands."[201]

The pervasive rhetoric influenced the children as well. Felix J. Cuervo, a former Fresh Air child, provides one example of how patriotic messages influenced young program participants. In 1949 Cuervo offered his first testimonial in support of the program when he wrote a sentimental letter in memory of his former host, Mrs. Rena L. Coburn of Croydon, New Hampshire. In his letter, that the Fresh Air Fund then released, Cuervo described his rise from a "little slum kid with a running nose" to a government clerk and navy seaman, a true example of the "decent hard-working and loyal citizens" that Cuervo claimed the Fund sought to create.[202] Nine years later, Cuervo spoke again on behalf of the Fresh Air Fund, noting that the Fund gave him his "first contact with American people, American food, American attitudes," which led him to write an essay that won the prestigious Freedoms Foundation Award.[203] Through the 1960s, Cuervo continued to praise the Fund for making "a better American of me."[204] Although by 1977 he seemed to have reconciled himself to his city—he served as the president of the Native New Yorkers Association and gave historical tours of New York City streets—he supported the Fresh Air fund during its centennial celebrations.[205] Not every alumnus of the program became such a proud, patriotic booster, but those who did, like Cuervo, found much meaning in their assimilation to one version of the American ideal.

The hosts also found patriotic import in the hosting project. Mrs. J. Walter Coleman, a Gettysburg, Pennsylvania, host and local chairperson, asserted in 1948 that Fresh Air hosting helped "preserve the American way of life." Concerned that "un-American" influences in the "crowded unhappy sections of the big cities" threatened the country "from within," she contended that children in Fresh Air programs gained a "new outlook on life" by exposure to "our homes" and "the way Americans live."[206] In the same vein, W. C. "Tom" Sawyer, the executive vice president of the Freedoms Foundation and an active Fresh Air Fund supporter, touted the program for taking children out of highly regimented cities where democracy was "in peril." In the country, city children could immerse themselves in the "American way of life" by encountering chickens and geese, walking "barefoot in the dewy grass," and swimming "au naturel in a pool."[207]

Cuervo's experience dovetailed well with the Cold War anticommunist sentiment that likewise pervaded the Fresh Air programs. Following a lengthy defense

against accusations that communists had "infiltrated" summer camping programs in 1954, Frederick Lewis went on the offense.[208] In addition to emphasizing the benefits of democracy and exposure to "real Americans," Lewis began to
promote rural vacations as "one of the most effective antidotes" to "the spread of
Communistic ideas."[209] Returning again to a favorite source, the executive director quoted Cuervo, who maintained that the love and affection he experienced
in the country allowed him to refute the communists who said that "Americans
were all fat capitalists."[210] Lewis continued to promote an anticommunist agenda
at least through 1963, when he quoted an anonymous Fresh Air alum—most
probably Cuervo again—who said that the promise of annual trips to the "green
fields" of the country kept him from turning into a "criminal, a communist, a
bum."[211] For Lewis and other promoters, their job of sending children from the
city to the country carried the burden of patriotic duty, one that reached out
far beyond the borders of the nation to thwart those perceived to threaten the
foundations of democracy.

Willard Parsons' original goal of nurturing children back to emotional and
physical health through summertime trips to the country had become a much
grander undertaking by the middle of the twentieth century. By the 1960s, promoters no longer stopped after making sure that the children had enough food to
eat and grass to stomp. They now imbued their efforts with patriotic themes that
called hosts and donors to contribute their time and effort for love of country as
much as love of children. As such, promoters positioned the Fresh Air programs
to garner wide publicity and gain the attention of those in power, a particularly adept move as government bodies increasingly sought through the 1970s
to return responsibility for health care and social welfare to the nonprofit sector.[212] By linking urban children's rural summer trips to the popular sentiments
of democracy, citizenship, and anticommunism, Fresh Air boosters wrapped
themselves in patriotic rhetoric and attracted the powerful to their pursuits. In
the process, the interests of the children often took second place.

Fresh Air program supporters thus found willing collaborators in military
officials. Frederick Lewis again led the way. During World War II he served as a
lieutenant commander in the intelligence division of naval air combat in Japan
and then worked for a short time in the Special Devices Division of the Office
of Research and Inventions before turning to youth work with the Fund.[213] His
naval experience helped open doors with funders, board members, and the military itself.[214] Servicemen gave money to the Fund.[215] Former navy officers served
as Fund officials.[216] And, in an example of particular privilege, air force bombers
flew New York City children to Cape Cod on their way to Martha's Vineyard on
July 10, 1958.[217] Lewis even brought in members of the army reserves to complete work on a garbage trench at the Fund's campgrounds.[218] Given such close

connections with the military and the relative lack of employment opportunities for many of the children, Fresh Air alums often ended up in military service following their time in the program, serving in all four branches of the armed forces.[219]

Fresh Air programs also partnered with law enforcement officials. J. Edgar Hoover hosted Fresh Air children at FBI headquarters in 1949.[220] In the 1960s and 1970s, local precincts and officers encouraged youths to take vacations in the country. In some areas, police officers helped select and register children for the summer trips.[221] In others, precinct officers planned and developed summer programs for city youths that included Friendly Town visits as one of many available activities.[222] At least one detective used part of his vacation in 1972 to volunteer at a Fresh Air camp.[223] Police officers also gave talks on drug addiction to visiting Fresh Air hosts, spoke at fund-raisers, and sometimes ran their own Fresh Air programs.[224] Although relationships with local African American communities could still prove tense, as in 1968 when Westchester, New York, police chief Albert Vitolo referred to "you people" in the course of trying to thank African American leaders for "keeping his summer from being too long and hot," the police who partnered with Fresh Air programs gained a measure of goodwill from the families and children who had positive encounters during their rural sojourns.[225] As with the case of the military, a significant number of Fresh Air alums went on to become police officers themselves.[226]

The military and criminal justice network built by staff, board members, and donors extended into the political sphere. At all levels of government, politicians gravitated toward Fresh Air programs. Mayors such as John V. Lindsay of New York City and Oscar V. Newkirk of Kingston, New York, as well as New York governors Thomas E. Dewey and Nelson A. Rockefeller, gained political capital by associating with Fresh Air from the 1940s through the 1970s.[227] At the presidential level, Eleanor Roosevelt promoted the Fund during the 1950s, and Vice President Richard Nixon recognized the advantage of publicly supporting the programs when he and his wife contributed more than $1,000 to the Fund in 1957.[228] A decade later, President Lyndon Johnson praised the Fund through comments made by Sargent Shriver of the Office of Economic Opportunity in thanks for Fresh Air's support of the War on Poverty, and then, in 1967, Johnson used the Fund's slogan—to "share summer" with "disadvantaged children"—in urging his fellow citizens to host city children.[229]

Politicians paid their highest compliment to the Fresh Air concept by cribbing from the program. In 1968 New York City mayor John Lindsay and Vermont governor Philip H. Hoff, a liberal Democrat concerned about racial integration, brought African American youths from New York City and white youths from Vermont to live together for extended summer stays at colleges and camps.[230]

Although controversial, the 1969 Vermont-New York Youth Project garnered more than $400,000 in federal, city, and private funds and brought more than 300 New York children to Vermont for six-week visits.[231] The project copied the Fresh Air model in all but name and budget. Most Fresh Air programs sent several thousand children to the country for what it cost the politicians to send fewer than 500.

The combined roster of military, law enforcement, and political Fresh Air supporters fell far short of the list of celebrities who endorsed the programs. During the 1940s, performers from "stage and screen" frequently appeared at fund-raisers.[232] Although few held the national profile of later boosters, singers like the Peters Sisters and performers like Etsy Cooper and Tommy Watkins drew local crowds nonetheless.[233] As the Fund's profile rose in the 1950s, so did the caliber of its celebrity support. Internationally respected writer and editor Norman Cousins penned a thoughtful defense of the Fresh Air Fund in 1955 in which he proclaimed that he had "decided to run, not walk, to the nearest telephone to get a child."[234] During the same years, performers like Benny Goodman, Mary Martin, Ethel Merman, the Radio City Rockettes, and the Von Trapp family also lent their support.[235] Building on past enthusiasm, celebrity involvement reached a new high in the 1960s. In addition to ongoing support from Martin, Merman, and others, A-list celebrities including Ginger Roberts, Joan Crawford, and Harry Belafonte joined in Fresh Air promotion, as did Steve Lawrence and Eydie Gorme.[236] Playwright Paddy Chayefsky, actress Lauren Bacall, jazz legend Duke Ellington, novelist James A. Michener, and songwriters Richard Rodgers and Oscar Hammerstein also helped promote summer vacations.[237] Although the Fund continued to draw celebrities to its promotional ranks well beyond this era, the 1960s lineup shone with a particular brilliance. In addition to new actors and artists, the Fund also recruited athletes such as Willie Mays and Arthur Ashe in the 1970s to further extend its reach.[238] In particular, the support of black celebrities like Ashe, Belafonte, Ellington, and Mays endowed the Fund with a modicum of racial legitimacy during a time of racial unrest and criticism of white-run social programs.

The social and cultural reach of the Fresh Air Fund became evident with the addition of corporate executives to the group's promotional ranks. A fund-raiser in 1959 featured a "walking pilgrimage" to the private offices of "some of the world's most famous figures." The itinerary included visits to the "inner sanctums" of the chairman of RCA, Pakistan's ambassador to the United Nations, the director of the Museum of Natural History, the president of the real estate firm Webb and Knapp, and the chair of the powerful bank Manufacturers Trust Company.[239] In addition to such influential supporters, the floor traders of the New York and American Stock Exchanges emptied the trading room in 1972 to play stickball, handball, and stoopball in a fund-raising stunt for Fresh Air on Broad and Wall streets.[240]

At a time when the number of nonprofit organizations nationwide had increased from 12,000 in the 1940s to 600,000 in the 1970s, the Fresh Air Fund rose above the competition and found its base among the wealthy and elite.[241]

High-profile contacts infused Fresh Air in popular culture. Already in 1949, a local newspaper editor wrote that a visitor would "probably feel like a Fresh Air."[242] He took for granted that his readers would understand the reference. Two years later, a columnist featured in a North Carolina newspaper described the antics of a group of reporters who established a "Fresh Air Fund for Stray Cats."[243] Again, the writer offered no background on Fresh Air funds. In 1956 the nationally distributed Steve Roper comic strip made a reference to boys posing with a starlet for a "fresh air fund poster."[244] In 1969 a reporter for the *Chicago Tribune* made the point that a juvenile detention center was not "something out of a fresh air fund." Even the meticulous columnist William Buckley dropped in a reference to "the local fresh air fund" in 1978 without comment.[245] The Fresh Air Chorus, a racially integrated group of past and current participants in the Fund's programs—ages six to sixteen—appeared on the *Today* show and at prestigious venues such as the Pan Am Building, Yankee Stadium, and Madison Square Garden.[246] As a result, the term *fresh air* became synonymous with more than a quality of the climate. Although less well known in the South and Southwest, in the Northeast, upper Midwest, and parts of the Northwest, Fresh Air meant summers in the country.

Such well-known, politically connected, celebrity-promoted, militarily supported, patriotic organizations had situated themselves at the center of society. In exchange for their endorsement, Fresh Air boosters received public thanks and association with a "feel-good" project. By seeking out high-status, powerful, and famous supporters, Fresh Air Fund staff members ensured a strong and sustainable organization. Even in the midst of the stagflation of the 1970s, when other nonprofits struggled to survive and many smaller Fresh Air programs collapsed, the Fresh Air Fund in New York City thrived. Connections with the elite, the influential, and the wealthy made that stability possible. As was the case with most successful nonprofits in the middle of the twentieth century, fostering such high-profile, elite connections required a conservative, charity-based, individualized outlook on poverty and oppression.[247]

Yet these powerful supporters who so eagerly associated themselves with Fresh Air often had the least amount of contact with the children or the environment from which they came. Other than congratulating Fresh Air chorus singers after a performance or appearing with a child in a television promotional, most of the highest-profile donors had little interaction with the children who traveled each summer to the country. Although a few, like Norman Cousins, did themselves host children, most of the celebrities, politicians, and writers who supported Fresh Air with such enthusiasm did not fit the profile of hosts who lived on farms or in walking distance from streams, ponds, and grassy lawns. Many of the promoters thus endorsed a program with which they had little or no practical experience.

Marketing Innocence

If Fresh Air programs sold anything, they sold the idea of innocence. Program boosters' promotional rhetoric wove together milk's purity, poverty's virtue, and power's decency to convince donors and hosts alike that children from the city posed no threat. When promoters described children who drank milk and stared at cows, they evoked the same sort of wonder that had countered the jaded cynicism of an industrializing nation since the end of the nineteenth century. When reporters through the 1970s described children arriving in tatters and departing in new shirts and dresses, they echoed the Progressive Era conviction that well-intentioned do-gooders could save the deserving poor. Like most philanthropists involved in charitable pursuits in the post–World War II period, those who supported the Fund and other Fresh Air programs with major gifts asserted they knew best how to solve the problems of the poor.[248] When recruiters attested to the program's connections to the powerful, they claimed that the city-bred unseemliness could, at least temporarily, be overcome. To the public, the Fresh Air movement fostered only innocent children: bearers of awe, stripped of all wealth, correct and respectable.

Yet more striking than the promotional content of Fresh Air publicity was its reach. During the Cold War, adults cultivated an image of children unburdened with adult knowledge by producing movies such as *Bambi* and television shows that featured Bozo the Clown and Lassie.[249] However, the narrative developed in Fresh Air programs from the onset of World War II through the end of the 1970s extended beyond the realm of popular culture to the spheres of agriculture, finance, and medicine. It was not just entertainment moguls like Walt Disney or television producers like Robert Maxwell and Larry Harmon who marketed the image of uncorrupted children; social service providers did as well. In the case of Fresh Air programs, executive directors like Frederick Lewis marketed adorable children rather than adorable fawns, collies, or clowns.

And the rhetoric used to promote the image of golden childhood lasted a long time. Although the racial demographics shifted from Italians, Slavs, and other European ethnics to African American and Latino youths during the 1950s, the rhetorical strategies remained remarkably consistent. As is evident in chapter 3's treatment of "grass, color, and sass," Fresh Air promoters and hosts—who themselves remained white—focused on the children's unblemished state in much the same way regardless of the children's racial profiles. By linking the children with symbols of the pristine countryside, establishing the faultlessness of their poverty, and stamping them with politicians' and celebrities' seal of approval, the promoters used such time-tested strategies to overcome widespread racial prejudice against hosting children of color.

Those promotional efforts found their staying power in the era's rising expectations. During the Cold War, many Americans believed that the United States would improve the international community even while creating a better society within its borders.[250] By shaping the world around them to match their ideals and by fostering a nation grounded in equal opportunities and unbound by class, all would benefit. In particular, white Americans held a profound belief that the U.S. class structure was both flexible and permeable.[251] Anyone could succeed. The tripartite presentation of Fresh Air children as milk-pure, wealth-deprived, and power-approved dovetailed with these widespread expectations. Organizers sent children like Fearon and Mojica on Fresh Air trips to be improved in body and mind, taken out of poverty, and given the opportunity to rise—like the country itself—to new heights. During a time when so many saw their fortunes improve over that of the generation before them, few felt the need to assess whether the programs achieved the ends they sought. To the promoters and those who joined them in the Fresh Air effort, the belief that children from the city could transcend class via two-week stays in the country mattered more than did the actual outcome.

The binding of milk, money, and power contextualizes the intense criticism that surfaced in the 1960s and 1970s. Those who said the programs "did more harm than good" knew of the trauma experienced by young children separated from their families.[252] They knew of the disparaging remarks made about the children's neighborhoods. Although at times staff would assert that the children came "from good homes" and had parents who "love[d] them dearly, and wish[ed] them the best on their vacation," more often staff derided the children's home communities.[253] As one booster explained in 1955, the Fund sought to "rescue" children from their "substandard homes, and substandard neighborhoods" by providing them with the "comfort and enjoyment of a real home."[254] Critics like Ellen Delmonte, the editorial writer at the *Cleveland Post* who observed that white suburban hosts locked out Fresh Air children "the other 51 weeks of the year," recognized the underlying philosophy of the hosting programs: The children's home environments—including their parents—held them back; they needed to be distant from, and therefore different from, their families to succeed.[255]

The marketing of innocence thus came with a trade-off. Children got trips to the country. They learned about new ways of living. They got to milk cows and drink milk. The evidence suggests that Fearon and Mojica smiled because they genuinely enjoyed carrying cans of milk around a dairy barn. They did not just grin for the photographer. Likewise, the children's parents cooperated with the programs and ultimately gave permission for their offspring to travel to the country for the summer vacations. As New York City parent Margaret Joyner said in 1979, "They get to meet new people, it breaks their daily sometimes monotonous summer vacations in the city."[256] Yet, as critics pointed out to leaders of many mid-twentieth-century social service agencies, neoliberal programming came at a cost.[257] In exchange for summer vacations, the children and their parents listened to promotions that criticized their home communities and often muted their voices.

But that is not all that happened. Somewhere between the greeting and the good-bye, hosts and children experienced transformation. Not always. Not in overwhelming numbers. But in many instances, adults and children left their two-week visits changed. Chapter 6 calls for a more thorough examination of the breadth of that change because the Fresh Air movement could instill both despair and delight.

GREETING, GONE, GOOD
Racialized Reunion and Rejection in Fresh Air

Luis Diaz felt like a member of the Cooley family because of diabetes. Not his—his host brother's. In the middle of the 1970s, at the age of ten or eleven, Diaz told his host mother, Anne Cooley, that he did not mind spending his vacation in the hospital, not if his host brother Timothy needed medical treatment. Diaz told Anne that he wanted to be at the hospital also. He was willing to give up his summer to be with Timothy. As he told Mrs. Cooley, "If Timothy is hurting, I feel like I should be in the hospital with the rest" of the family. He could tell that this made her happy. Even if it meant shortening his summer-long visit to three weeks or, in subsequent summers, learning to give insulin shots to his host brother, he "felt like he was part of the family" by spending his Fresh Air days breathing hospital air.[1] He had been greeted well.

Diaz crossed multiple boundaries to spend time with the Cooleys. Born in San Juan, Puerto Rico, in 1965, Diaz moved with his family to New York City, where both his mother and father found jobs out of the home. The first time he visited Anne and Roger Cooley and their three sons, David, Bradley, and Timothy, in Califon, New Jersey, in 1974, he became aware that some families earned enough income to allow the mother to stay home full time. Roger Cooley's job at the World Trade Center allowed Anne to focus on the three boys. Diaz crossed over from relative poverty into wealth every time that he traveled to Califon. He also entered Lutheran territory as a Roman Catholic and stayed with white people as a Latino. Even so, he called his host parents "mom and dad" and his host brothers' grandmother "Grandma Rich."[2]

Greeting

The Cooley family greeted Diaz each summer in the context of a shrinking program. Even though children across the country continued to clamor for Fresh Air vacations, the number of available slots had begun to diminish. As an organizer in Cleveland had already noted in 1971, "There are always more children who want to come than we can accommodate."[3] Through the 1970s, other program administrators attributed the drop-off in host volunteers to the economy, mothers working outside the home, time-consuming work assignments, and "a rising tide of suburban apathy."[4] Between 1969 and 1979, the number of Fresh Air Fund annual placements in camps and homes dropped from a high of almost 18,000 to 13,000, a number that would continue to decline through the 1990s until stabilizing in the range of 8,000–9,000 summer placements. The Cleveland program dropped from a high of 2,000 down to 900 placements by 1979. Other programs simply stopped sending children altogether, shortened stays to a week's time, or, in one instance, arranged only weekend trips.[5] Return visits also began to disappear as organizers tried to cycle as many children as possible through the program.[6] Unlike so many other children interested in rural vacations, Diaz not only got to be greeted by the same family each summer; he also got to stay for weeks on end.

The Cooley family strengthened Diaz's sense of belonging by integrating him into all their routines. When he stayed in Califon, Diaz had his own bed and received new clothes. Like his host brothers, he earned an allowance by doing chores. He had his own bike when he visited and used it to ride around in a "bicycle gang" with his host brothers and their cousins.[7] They spent their allowances at a nearby country store on sweets and snacks that they would then trade with one another. When Anne and Roger Cooley went on a date, they left Diaz, as the oldest of the four boys, in charge. The Cooleys also disciplined Diaz like they did their own children. On one occasion, Diaz got into a fight with an older cousin who had been bothering his host brothers. Although Mrs. Cooley docked his allowance, in private she thanked him for intervening on behalf of her children. Diaz felt so welcomed by the Cooleys that one year he spent two winter weeks with his summer hosts.[8]

Yet the warm greeting Diaz received from the Cooley family came with caveats. Even though he stayed longer than most Fresh Air children, he had to return home in the fall. Only once did he spend time with the Cooleys in the winter. With the exception of an afternoon the Cooleys spent visiting Diaz in New York City, Diaz always had to travel in their direction. When life in Califon got too stressful, as when Timothy's medical condition required professional attention,

Diaz's stay shortened. He had a bike when he visited, but he could not bring it back to New York City.

He also became a teacher to his adopted family. Like so many other Fresh Air children before him, Diaz taught racial lessons to his hosts. As a light-skinned Puerto Rican, he helped his hosts learn about the tremendous racial diversity within the Latino community. As his younger brother Nilson explained about his white hosts, we "changed their minds around" because they "had never seen an Hispanic before."[9] Diaz also interpreted the city to his host family. The Cooley brothers thought he came from a "concrete jungle" devoid of vegetation and expressed amazement at his ability to climb trees. He explained to them that "of course" he knew how to climb trees. Just because he lived in the city did not mean that "absolute concrete" surrounded him. He also taught Anne Cooley about the men who partnered with men and the women who partnered with women in his home community.[10] He expanded the worldview of his hosts simply by telling them about his life.

Along with teacher, he played the role of a grateful recipient. The Cooley family gave him the run of their extensive property and that of a nearby pond that Grandma Rich kept stocked for the boys' fishing expeditions. While living with the Cooleys each summer he learned how to swim, build a fort, play tennis, compete in dodgeball, outrun a bull, and toss cowpucks—dried cow manure—in country fields. He ate a yam for the first time as well as a potato with the skin still on it. One summer he even joined his host siblings at 4-H camp. Another time, he accompanied the Cooley family on their summer vacation.[11] As long as he expressed appreciation, cooperated, and did not sass back, he had a summer home.

That is until he turned sixteen. The Fresh Air Fund would send re-invited children to their hosts only until that age. Thirteen-year-olds, as already noted, who did not get re-invited could no longer participate. For example, Luis's brother Nilson did not return to his host family after his twelfth birthday.[12] However, Luis had found a family willing to extend their invitations through 1979, the year of his sixteenth birthday. That summer, or perhaps the one before—the details blurred in Diaz's memory—he had a crush on an older girl in the community. Although his affection remained unrequited, he did briefly date another local girl in one of those last summers. Given his light skin and long-term connection to the community, no one seemed to mind. He did remember with much greater clarity an argument he had with Anne Cooley that last summer. They discussed religion. It did not go well. He never went back. The greetings had ended.

The family that had welcomed him so well for six consecutive summers lost touch with Diaz. After he served in the Marine Corps and returned home to build a life as an adult in New York City, more than a decade passed before Diaz looked up the Cooleys in the phone book and gave the family a call. Although the timing of the contact found his former host family in a crisis that left them with little time to reconnect with their former Fresh Air guest, he did try again several years later and reconnected via a social networking site. At the time of this writing, Diaz hoped to someday greet Anne, Roger, and a few of their children in New York City, where he would take them to dinner and a Broadway show.

Diaz had nothing but praise to offer his former host family despite their relative lack of contact. The summers he spent in Califon made him "into the man that I am now." The care and inclusion he felt from his host parents and brothers kept him from a life of drugs and crime. He stated, "I never had a drug problem and I have never been arrested." Moreover, because of the example set by the Cooley family, he felt challenged to improve his life condition. "I bettered myself," he said, "by being around people" like the Cooleys.[13] The Fresh Air program worked for Luis Diaz. He had, indeed, been greeted well.

Gone

Janice Batts could not claim the same. One summer in the latter part of the 1960s, Batts stayed with a Fresh Air host family in the Midwest. Batts had been traveling to towns in Iowa, Illinois, and Indiana from her home in the Pilsen neighborhood on Chicago's Near West Side since 1962, when she turned four (see figure 11).[14] About six years later her hosts took her and another guest, a young boy from a different church in Chicago than the one she attended, to a public swimming pool.

When her hosts announced the plans for the day's recreation, she remembered exchanging a nervous glance with the other guest. Both of them knew that black children like themselves could not go to public swimming pools in Chicago. They assumed that they would experience the same kind of harassment in the country that they did in the city. Unfortunately, they assumed all too correctly. On their way into the pool, a group of boys started calling out, "Look at the niggers." Rather than turning back to the car and leaving or confronting the boys to make them stop, Batts's hosts told the children to ignore the chanting even as it escalated and the boys repeated "nigger" over and over again. Batts and her hosts stayed until it became too uncomfortable for the hosts, and they finally went back to the car.[15] Her hosts never discussed the incident with her.

Batts connected with the Fresh Air movement through the Mennonite Community Chapel on 18th Street in Chicago. Since 1957, white Mennonites had gone door to door in an effort to bring local community members into their largely white congregation.[16] Unlike many members of the Pilsen community,

FIGURE 11. Four-year-old Janice Batts holds a kitten while on a 1962 Fresh Air visit to the farm of Earl Gingerich in West Chester, Iowa. Used by permission of Janice Batts.

Batts's foster mother welcomed the visitors into her home and soon took her young daughter to the storefront church building. Because she was one of the few black residents to do so, Batts's mother received special attention and invitations to visit sister congregations in downstate Illinois. While on those visits, Janice Batts endured humiliating stares, unwanted touching, and inappropriate questions about the size of her nostrils and the texture of her hair.[17] Even before she arrived on one of the visits, she wanted to be gone.

Her Fresh Air visits included some of the same treatment but also had some benefits. For example, the train rides to Iowa provided much excitement, as did getting to run barefoot in the grass. She got to connect with other children her own age and, as she later recalled, enjoyed being somewhere other than the city. In addition, she had two weeks in the country away from the beatings she received at the hands of her foster mother, who would force Batts to strip naked before she would beat her, and her alcoholic foster father, who would often beat her in the middle of the night. When she first started participating in the program—and for several years to follow—she looked forward to going to the country.

Yet racial and sexual land mines riddled the terrain frequented by Batts and other African American children from Chicago. Although the train rides excited them, they also found the 2:00 or 3:00 A.M. arrival process in Iowa City unsettling. "It was like a slave auction," Batts explained. The local organizers called out the names of the white hosts followed by the names of the black children. Although eventually discontinued, the practice of draping identification tags around the children's necks enhanced the image of children being distributed to the highest bidder in the hope that she or he would get, as a host in Kansas once wrote, "the best one" of the group.[18] Although sponsoring organizations experimented with various transportation methods, most programs arranged for the children to be picked up at a train station or large parking lot, a practice that led invariably to auction-like scenes. The hosts came, picked up their charges, and were gone.

The hosting environment itself proved even more challenging for Batts. During the mid-1960s she spent many summers with the Troyer family in Kalona, Iowa. Although Batts remembered with fondness unusual events like living in a turkey shed while the Troyers built a new house, she vacillated between boredom at being the only child with an older host couple and terror at the possibility of being assaulted by one of the Troyers' grandsons. A year or two older than Batts, the grandson hit her without fear of reprisal. When she complained, the adults explained that the boy had "problems" and just needed to take a nap.[19] In the process, no one protected her from physical harm.

Batts also learned to expect inappropriate questions and racial ignorance. Like the children she met on church visits in downstate Illinois, children in Kalona and other Fresh Air sites asked her, "Why is your nose so wide? Do you sunburn?

Why is your hair curly? How [do] you know when you are dirty?" Her hosts, as well as the hosts of the other girls who traveled with Batts, had no knowledge of how to care for a black girl's hair. Consistent with the experience of many other Fresh Air children across the country, the girls in Batts's group returned home at the end of the two-week visit looking "hideous" because their host mothers had not even touched their hair, let alone treated it properly.[20] Her own hair would get matted and foul smelling for lack of someone to help her care for it. Batts recalled, "Some of them would say, 'I just don't like the way it feels.' . . . We're kids. Why would you say that to us?"

The worst had yet to come. She finally found the courage to ask for different hosts. In the summer of 1969, Batts, an eleven-year-old veteran of seven years of Fresh Air hosting, traveled to northern Indiana to stay with an older couple. In this instance, the host mother worked outside the home during the day, and the host father worked from their home, the parsonage of the church where he was pastor. On the first day of her arrival, the pastor gave Batts a tour of the property. In their garage, he invited Batts to sit on the seat of a John Deere riding mower while he climbed on the hitch behind her and put both of his hands on her breasts. Years later she remembered, "It felt like a bolt of electricity had hit me. And I just froze. I did not know what to do. I immediately knew I had no power in this situation. I was totally out of my element. I'm black. I'm a kid. These people have invited me to my home. And for Christ's sake, the man is a minister."[21] She knew no one would listen to her.

The abuse continued through that visit and that of the following summer. With the host mother out of the house during the day, the host father had no reason to limit his access. Feeling trapped, Batts learned to reciprocate his touching. When the couple invited her for a third visit, Batts knew that if she went back again, she and the host father would start having sex, so she told her mother that she had outgrown the program and no longer wanted to participate. It was time to be gone from Fresh Air. Batts carried the secret of the abuse until she finally told someone while at college. To her knowledge, the host father never received any penalties for his actions.

Batts never again participated in Fresh Air visits but did return to Kalona to attend high school. Sponsored by a church-run program known as High Aim that brought "minority" youths to Mennonite schools, Batts experienced what most Fresh Air children could not, living in a former host community as an adolescent.[22] She soon realized that the local community had never fully accepted her. Young women she had played with during Fresh Air visits refused to socialize with her. Her host mother accused her of stealing a ring only to apologize a few days later after finding it between the floorboards of her own bedroom. However, romance brought the most heartache. Some of the young men at Iowa

Mennonite School told her they could not date her because their "friends and family [would] quit talking" to them. But one young man did invite her on a date. Two days later, he walked past her on the school bus and sat down without saying a word. When she confronted him at school, he explained that his father had told him he could not see her anymore because she was black. "Those words hurt so bad," Batts said, "because that was one thing I couldn't change. If [he] said because you smell or something like that, I could take a bath. Anything else I could change if I still wanted to. And I just took off running and ran the length of the school down to the girls' bathroom. I just cried and cried."[23]

Batts assesses her Fresh Air experience bluntly. Memories of inhaling fresh air and of running barefoot in the grass stayed with her, "but the rest of it can go to hell. . . . I wish I had not had that experience because it was two weeks of being afraid, two weeks of people staring at us, poking at us, asking us ludicrous questions."[24] At the end, she wanted it all to go away.

Good

Two stories from former Fresh Air children cannot represent the entirety of the Fresh Air movement from 1939 through 1979. Given that hundreds of thousands of children participated during that period, even a book based on thousands of written reports and dozens of oral histories can claim only to identify the broadest of trends. However, Diaz and Batts do represent the two most influential legacies of the mid-twentieth-century Fresh Air movement: the greeting and the gone or, to be more specific, racialized reunion and racialized rejection.

Diaz's story captures the theme of racialized reunion. During this period of racial transformation, when programs shifted from serving mostly white ethnic children to serving African American and Latino children, leaders of the Fresh Air movement promoted the idea that all racial problems could and would be solved if only the rest of society got along as well as did the children of color and their white hosts. Diaz and the Cooley family embodied this ideal. Even though they had never before met a Puerto Rican, the family greeted Diaz without reservation. Despite hints of paternalism and the inherent limits of distance, age caps, and length of stay, Diaz and the Cooley family did as best they could to reconnect each summer, upon occasion even during the year. Diaz did lose touch with the family after he turned sixteen, but his host family accepted his phone call years later and responded positively to his request to connect via e-mail.

Batts's story illuminates the second central theme: racialized rejection. In this instance, Fresh Air movement leaders built a program on the idea that interracial relationships were not worth supporting once children of color became adolescents. Batts's experience in high school made evident that hosting a teen-ager interested in romance introduced numerous complications that most white, rural, and suburban communities would not confront. The multiple problems she faced as a preteen including physical and sexual abuse as well as overt racial harassment only underscore how unwilling and ill equipped most hosting com-munities were to truly welcome children of color even before puberty became an issue. As Fresh Air alum Cindy Vanderkodde explains in chapter 4, "[O]nce I became an equal . . . there was just no interest there."[25]

The two legacies intertwined. As leaders of the Fresh Air movement sought to remain relevant, they developed both themes. Images of racialized reunion peppered publicity materials; age caps fostered racialized rejection. Despite the goodwill generated by the programs, the person-to-person connections they supported, and the initiative displayed by the children in educating their elders, the Fresh Air movement could not escape these two legacies. Racialized rejection invariably compromised racialized reunion. Some former Fresh Air children did go on to successful careers as attorneys, CEOs, actors, police officers, teachers, and national magazine editors.[26] Several of them credited their experience with Fresh Air for their achievements.[27] Yet the bulk of the success stories told by eager press agents for the various Fresh Air ventures came from children in the era prior to the racial shift. Fewer of the African American and Latino alums who had been rejected once they became teenagers told such stories.

Racialized reunion and rejection connect at the point where the rhetoric of innocence employed by Fresh Air promoters—the "good" of this chapter's title—defines them both. A fictionalized anecdote distributed widely by Fresh Air staff first reiterates the centrality of innocence in the movement's promotional efforts.

In 1962 Richard Crandell tried to subvert racism by writing a story about an urban child and a frog log. Crandell, the public relations director of the Fresh Air Fund, had penned a story of a black child teaching a white adult; "Carol" led "Bill Stout" by the hand into the wilderness. The frog log of Carol's and Stout's interest jutted through algae-covered water into a pristine lake. Carol did not let go of Stout's hand until they arrived at a muddy shore, where Carol stretched on a log to peer into the water. After reporting that she had seen only "a water snake . . . and a minna," Carol invited her white visitor to take a turn but to be careful because he was "too heavy." Despite Carol's warning to the contrary, Stout stepped on a tuft of grass and promptly fell face first in the mud. With Carol's encouragement, he then cleaned himself as best he could and ventured out to the frog log. As he gazed beneath the surface of the water, Stout saw "another world" filled with bright pebbles, flashing sunfish, swimming frogs, and "waterbugs that pirouetted like some aquatic ballet." A poor, eight-year-old African American camper at the Fund's reserve in Dutchess County, New York, had opened the eyes of a white adult visitor bused in to see the Fund's work firsthand. In gratitude for his new appreciation of nature, Stout made his way back to the muddy lakeshore, where, in Crandell's words, Carol waited for him with "innocence and love and faith."[28]

Many others joined Crandell in celebrating the children's innocence. While World War II raged on, Ruth Millett from Altoona, Pennsylvania, sought to initiate a new Fresh Air program in 1940 that would ensure a "happy, innocent childhood" for children affected by the trauma of combat.[29] In 1953 a host wrote an entire article describing the wide-eyed wonder and innocence of a New York City youngster who built a birdhouse and "showed stars in his eyes" as he displayed it to his host mother.[30] In 1969 a Chicago reporter described youthful Fresh Air participants as "innocent victims of poverty and legalized racism."[31] Veronica Anthony, the Friendly Town Program director in 1971, stressed "these are little children, innocent kids."[32] As long as they remained young enough for the programs, up until they entered adolescence, the children's innocence featured prominently in boosters' rhetoric.

The rhetoric of innocence did change somewhat with time. In the immediate aftermath of World War II, innocence came to mean freedom from cares and worries. By the 1960s, program promoters shifted away from a long-standing emphasis on children's openness to religious instruction. More importantly, in response to the mid-1950s demographic shift from a predominantly white corps of visitors to a predominantly black and brown one, boosters intensified their rhetoric in part to compensate for the perception that children of color did not belong in white rural and suburban communities. Promotional copy began to feature stories stressing the children's obedience, their respectable appearance, their ability to foster friendship across racial lines, and their never—under any circumstances—posing a danger or threat to their hosts. While still emphasizing the previous qualities of innocence, by the 1970s promoters added the wrinkle that, although the children knew little of the country, they knew much of the city and could instruct their hosts about that world.

Crandell's focus on Carol's ability to renew Stout also demonstrates how the newly minted idea of black children free of moral contagion served white ends. Up to the middle of the twentieth century, childhood innocence had only one color: white.[33] It took the civil rights movement to establish that black children could also be innocent.[34] In the process, racial innocence became a "form of deflection, a not-knowing or obliviousness that can be made politically useful."[35] In the context of Fresh Air, the perceived faultlessness and naïveté of African American children like Carol made white adults like Stout feel good. By twice referring to Carol's "brown hand" and describing Stout as "settler" and "Dan'l

Boone," Crandell made sure that his readers understood the racial terrain.[36] In Crandell's account, the unfamiliar territory of black innocence moved Stout nearly to tears.

A thorough exploration of the innocence rhetoric exemplified in Crandell's story begins with the work of Shelby Steele. Steele made much of innocence as faultlessness in his 1990 book on race in the United States. He contended that white guilt for black victimization kept the two groups mired in "racism and racial disharmony" as they struggled over who got to claim more innocence and therefore more power.[37] "Innocence is power," explained Steele, because "our innocence always inflates us and deflates those we seek power over. Once inflated we are entitled; we are in fact licensed to go after the power our innocence tells us we deserve."[38] As a result, blacks sought to maintain their guiltlessness by focusing on racism rather than "individual initiative," and whites sought to reclaim a blameless state by "helping the disadvantaged."[39] According to Steele, in a world of such racialized blame swapping, no one escaped his or her assigned roles.

Steele failed first by ignoring the initiative the children took while on their trips. Steele claimed that a theme like racialized rejection furthered victimization and maintained the status quo. According to his analysis, focusing on racism led only to a community remaining mired in poverty and oppression. However, the African American and Latino children who participated in Fresh Air programs faced down the racism they encountered and established themselves as teachers, not victims, of their adult hosts. Children like Diaz and Batts taught their hosts how to negotiate racial minefields, a process that revealed much more about the children's expertise than their victimization. Steele did not take into account children who never thought of themselves as victims and confounded prevailing expectations about who should be teaching and instructing whom.

Fresh Air children also complicate Steele's argument as purveyors of blamelessness rather than guilt. Other charity-based programs predicated white innocence on black victimization. In the Fresh Air movement, by taking children out of the communities where the victimization occurred, organizers could, at least for a short while, drape a new racial mantle over the children. Rather than being trapped in victim status, the children found natural wonder, color-blind friendship, and barefoot bliss. Promoters and publicists thus tried to have it both ways. By emphasizing racialized reunion, they presented hosts who bore no blame for racial strife because of their willingness to invite a black or brown child into their home. The discourse about the hosting ventures likewise depicted fault-free children enraptured with nature and eager to make friends with white people. Steele's formula breaks down when everyone gets to be innocent.

The boosters' presentation of that all-embracing faultlessness thus grounded Fresh Air. One of the central reasons that programs proliferated throughout the

Northeast, the Midwest, and the West Coast during the 1960s and 1970s was that, in the recurrent and consistent Fresh Air rhetoric, everyone involved got to be free of blame for racial strife. Fresh Air publicists and boosters actively promoted ideas about the children's blameless state while also lauding the fault-free hosts who opened their homes during a time of racial foment. Reporters and publicity staff praised the adults for hosting a Fresh Air child and for their selfless sacrifice. Involving little of the controversy of a sit-in but offering all of the decency of an adoption, a Fresh Air visit simply made the hosts look good in the eyes of other white liberals. White suburbanites or rural farmers interested in doing the right thing about race had only to invite a child into their home for a two-week stay to participate in one of the few programs of the civil rights period that enhanced the reputation of all involved. The critics who called the programs into question rarely penetrated the publicity shield maintained each summer by heartwarming stories in the national press.

Fresh Air programs attracted so much attention for so long for two other central reasons. First, summer hosting ventures offered symbolic relief to collective concern about urban growth. From the end of the 1930s to the end of the 1970s, the United States had shifted from a country evenly split between rural and urban communities to one dominated by city centers. That shift engendered widespread fear about the deleterious effects of urban living on the young. Sending children from the city to rural communities assuaged those fears on an annual basis. The Fresh Air program promised that two weeks surrounded by nature would make up for fifty more surrounded by concrete. Moreover, program promoters avowed that they would insert children into rural environs in a way that would promote democracy. The Cold War environment fostered keen interest in any program that countered assertions of American hypocrisy. A country that supported democracy abroad often failed to do so at home in the face of widespread racial and class inequities. Bringing poor black and brown children to the country demonstrated the values of liberty and democracy in action.

A pervasive rhetoric of innocence undergirded the program's long-term success. The greeting and the gone turned on the good. Hosts appeared faultless because of racialized reunion. If they embraced a dark-skinned child, they had no need to do anything else to demonstrate their concern about racial inequality. If they rejected that child once she or he entered adolescence, the hosts remained blameless because they had simply followed program guidelines. The Fresh Air promoters who told story after story of racialized reunions wove the themes of sexual ignorance, worldly inexperience, natural wonder, racial openness, and overall decency into their tales. The critics who countered that narrative did so by noting that racialized rejection corrupted those same exact themes. Both promoters and critics relied on innocence to make their case.

Yet an analysis of the rhetoric of innocence cannot explain all the historical dynamics of Fresh Air. For example, the work of anthropologist Mary Douglas offers purity as an interpretive trope. Douglas notes that when members of a group differentiate between the pure and impure, they define boundaries and create order and security. That which they define as impure or dirty is nothing more than matter out of place. It is dirt because it does not belong.[40] And that which does not belong is dangerous because it threatens order in society.[41] From this perspective, the children, no matter how young, represented danger from the very start because they were out of place. Hosts ameliorated that danger by limiting the amount of time the children spent in their homes and using age and gender preferences to get them to fit in with their families. As the children grew older, they fit in less and less, the desire to maintain boundaries grew more urgent, and the danger expanded. Hosts rid themselves of the impurity they had tolerated for a short while. Fears born of urbanization and the Cold War could overcome concerns about purity for a short time only.

A focus on nature provides additional insight. The idea of nature itself as a social construct imbued with the hopes of days past and those to come, especially as expressed in the concept of wilderness, has defined the difference between civilized and uncivilized in the twentieth century.[42] In the process, nature in its pristine state has been highly racialized and treated as a paradise for white people.[43] The Fresh Air children soaked up the possibility of becoming civilized by immersing themselves in natural surroundings. They became a kind of noble savage—in tune with nature, capable of instructing white people, possessing insight even at their young age.[44] Nature, as a restorative force, cured them of the ills of modernity and corruption found in the urban environment. Yet they could revel in nature for only so long. Once the children became jaded about nature, they no longer received a welcome. The racial paradise returned to its previous state.

Yet attention to the construct of innocence used by Fresh Air boosters enhances these and other interpretive approaches. Where analysis based in purity unearths the boundaries that separate clean from unclean, interpretation grounded in innocence reveals those boundaries' permeability. In the midst of the multiple pressures of the Cold War era, Fresh Air children reached out from the city to push through the dividing wall of race, class, and status separating them from their hosts to influence the adults even as the adults influenced them. Where analysis based in nature lays bare the irony of wilderness civilizing urban residents, interpretation grounded in innocence shows why that civilizing impulse so often alienated those it sought to serve. Amid urbanization's corrosive effects, Fresh Air children shrugged off the mantle of innocence by expressing disdain for streams, woods, and grassy fields because they found little of value in water, leaf, and blade, preferring instead the pulse and quickstep of city streets. Likewise, a study of the rhetoric of innocence also allows for a more rigorous interpretation of the relationship of the center and periphery. By attending to innocence, the constant exchange between the core and the margin in the midst of historical change becomes evident.[45] Leaders in the Fresh Air movement refreshed and rearticulated their innocence-focused narratives by physically transporting children from the center city to the suburban and rural margins. The physical relocation made possible the figurative connection between country and city.

Civil Rights and Childhood

In the midst of this recurring fixation on innocence, the black and brown freedom struggle unfolded in Fresh Air camps and homes. Both historians and the broader public have underestimated the efforts of black and brown urban children who negotiated the racial problems of their day in the living rooms and backyards of suburban and rural homes. Yet, as acknowledged here, children like Batts may have made small gains in reducing individual prejudice, but many adult hosts offset those advances when they used their participation in Fresh Air to distance themselves from the systemic adjustments sought by street-based civil rights activists. So how can the children then be called freedom fighters for racial justice?

The answer turns on an evaluation of failure. The civil rights campaigns in Albany, Georgia, in 1961–1962 and in St. Augustine, Florida, in 1963–1964 saw few immediate gains, which led many at the time to deem them failures. Historians now note that in the long run, both campaigns bore significant fruit. In the same way, despite ongoing racial subordination at Fresh Air hosting sites, the children entered important battlegrounds in the black and brown freedom struggle. That Fresh Air children still faced racism before, during, and after their rural vacations does not negate that they took part in a movement to redefine racial freedom. The crossing of racial lines itself established the historical significance of Fresh Air hosting grounds as a site of civil rights activism.

Fresh Air sites become even more historically significant when we consider not just racialized rejection and reunion but their interdependence. In his work with the Southern Christian Leadership Conference, Martin Luther King Jr. extolled the vision of a "beloved community."[46] Despite the prominence of Black Power and separatism after 1966, the idea that the civil rights movement was predicated upon its own form of racialized reunion remained long after King's death in 1968. The images of whites and blacks walking hand in hand down the streets of Washington, Selma, and Detroit remain powerfully evocative even today. But just as those who marched together almost always separated when they finished walking, so too did Fresh Air children return to their racially segregated homes after visiting the suburbs. With the exception of integrated communities such as Koinonia Farms in Americus, Georgia, and Mennonite House in Atlanta, most civil rights movement participants did not live in integrated settings.

If we accept Fresh Air hosting sites as battlegrounds in the struggle for racial freedom, a central irony becomes evident. The programs relied on both integration and separation. Far fewer hosts would have signed up if they would have been required to host a child of another race all year round or after they became teenagers. Only by guaranteeing that the visits would not last too long did the programs last so long. Little bits of integration worked better than the long-term kind.

The broader black and brown freedom struggle contained a similar irony. There, too, little bits of integration worked better than the long-term kind. Marching hand in hand made for arresting photo ops. Longer-term relationships across racial and gender lines rarely offered dramatic tableaus. King himself emphasized that the "Negro's primary aim is to be the white man's brother, not his brother-in-law."[47] Some integration proved necessary; too much would bring even more wrath than the activists already faced. SCLC leaders did their best to avoid the specter of interracial romance from the late 1950s through the 1970s, and so did Fresh Air leaders. Regardless of how problematic such assumptions may appear to contemporary readers, leaders of both groups came to similar conclusions. They depended just as much on the idea of separation as they did on integration to pursue their organizations' goals.

The Fresh Air movement also defined key elements of childhood between 1939 and 1979. Contrary to the message sent by Crandell's frog log story, childhood has rarely offered a perfectly innocent, protected state. In the late nineteenth and early twentieth century, children labored in the workforce or cared for younger siblings.[48] In the latter part of the twentieth century, children dealt with divorce, increasing isolation from adults, and ever more standardized, impersonal academic instruction.[49] In the process, even the perception of childhood innocence grew shorter.[50] In the main, as Steven Mintz has written, "Childhood has never been insulated from the pressures and demands of the surrounding society, and each generation of children has had to wrestle with the social, political, and economic constraints of its own historical period."[51] Fresh Air promoters predicated their programs on a state of innocence that simply did not exist.[52]

As an exploration of the rhetoric of innocence has made evident, the programs set limits on the duration of childhood for African American and Latino children by placing and enforcing age caps. In addition, the programs linked childhood with nature. Even before the onset of World War II, Fresh Air promoters sent the message that a child truly experienced childhood only when given a chance to connect with the natural world. The program boosters stuck to that script for the next four decades. And, by corollary, the adult promoters convinced many that those children confined to the city lost an irretrievable portion of their childhood by staying inside city limits. Through their fund-raising efforts, program promoters also treated childhood as a commodity used to garner funds. Likewise, Fresh Air policies made childhood more feminine in the earliest years as hosts expressed their preferences for girls over boys.

Yet the children themselves participated in defining childhood. During the same four-decade time span, the children linked childhood with independence as they sought spaces to swim. Many children made childhood a time of teaching adults rather than being taught as they instructed their hosts on the realities of racism and cross-cultural connection. And the children overturned the idea of childhood compliance by exercising their own power as they made trouble in homes and camp environments.

The most enduring message about childhood sent by those involved in the movement dealt with sex. To be a child, as defined by the mid-century parameters of Fresh Air, one could be neither sexually active nor aware. Sophisticated girls lost their bid at summer camp and their childhood because they knew too much. Boys who showed signs of interest in the girls they encountered on their trips never got asked back, their childhood revoked. As Fresh Air children walked through green grass, they pounded into place many childhood markers; sex was the most central. Initial vetting, age caps, gender selection, publicity material—each of these major design elements winnowed out children who did not conform to the sexually innocent image of childhood that so many in the movement cherished.

Such desexualized notions of childhood and the rhetoric of innocence they fostered held social purchase long after the 1970s. Yet those notions of children's sexual naïveté, awe of nature, unsophistication, malleability, and racial acceptance helped shape the racial order in a far different manner than suggested by Shelby Steele. Steele claimed that the desire to escape blame—to be seen as innocent of racial fault—encouraged white paternalism and black victimization and thereby kept racial inequity in place. But Steele missed the point so glaringly evident in this, the largest, longest-lasting, and most influential racial exchange program the country had ever seen. Fresh Air program supporters made the claim that if black and brown adults were taken out of the equation, it could be an innocent exchange. Everyone could be innocent. There would be no guilty parties. In the midst of intense racial pressures across the country, Fresh Air promoters treated black and brown children as innocent while also cutting their parents out of the picture. In so doing, many people felt good, but the fundamental inequities of access to housing, education, job opportunity, and health care remained the same. The innocence narrative, in this case, allowed those inequities to remain in place untouched and uninterrupted.

The story that Luis Diaz told about his Fresh Air experience dovetailed with that told by promoters from the end of the 1930s to the end of the 1970s. However, the one told by Janice Batts did not fit. Few wanted to hear about rejection, corrupted hosts, or children far more aware of sex than anyone would desire. Yet to understand the persistence of racial inequality in the middle of the twentieth century, the stories told by Diaz and Batts are both necessary. Only by attending to the ways in which children charmed their adult hosts and suffered at the hands of the same, prompted those around them to deal more directly with race, and yet were ultimately kept in check by the stories of innocence told about them will the legacies of that time become apparent. The Fresh Air children may here, yet again, serve as instructors.

CHANGING AN INNOCENCE FORMULA

[T]he New York kids receive a feeling of security and exposure to such simple pleasures as 'what green grass is like to run on barefooted.'

Barbara Horst, Fresh Air Fund coordinator, Lancaster County, Pennsylvania, 1996

The Fresh Air formula had remarkable staying power. The instructions were simple. First, filter out those most likely to make trouble before they arrived at camps or homes. Second, limit the ages of those who could return. Next, allow hosts to determine the gender of their guest. Follow this by transporting the children from the city to the suburbs or country but rarely if ever in the reverse direction. Let everyone know that the children will be able to run barefoot in the grass for the first time. Finally, tell the hosts at every opportunity that they undermined racism by hosting black and brown children. Fresh Air programs had settled on all but the last step by the beginning of the 1940s. The racial transformation of the program over the next two decades completed the instructions. Other nonprofit service agencies could only wish for such staying power.

And what a shelf life. Although only a few programs survived the significant decline in host participation and camp programming by the end of the 1970s, the Fresh Air Fund continued.[1] Stabilizing at around 9,000 participants a year being placed in approximately 4,000 host homes and the rest in camps, the Fund went on to report over fifteen million dollars in annual income in 2014 and net assets worth more than 138 million.[2] Although it had been tweaked along the way, the Fresh Air formula still worked.

A 1996 report demonstrates the remarkable staying power of the Fresh Air prescription. Since the 1930s, reporters had emphasized many of the same themes. A regional newspaper in southeastern Pennsylvania, the *New Era*, stressed that Fresh Air children arriving in the town of Ephrata had come from New York City, where cabs careened past X-rated movie theaters, noises proved deafening,

streets filled with filth, and concrete soaked up heat. In contrast to the sweltering city, the cool countryside of Lancaster County provided healthy, wholesome
fun. The young visitors, noted the reporter, shared a "near-unanimous desire to
swim." He also quoted Jeane Flood, who, at nine years of age, had already traveled out of the city for five years, indicating that she had first arrived when only
four. Beneath a photo of African American children embracing their white host
sibling, the reporter also highlighted the "good relationship[s]" made possible
by the program. Although one host hinted at some disciplinary challenges when
she noted that "the children don't come tranquilized," no other hints of discord
appeared.[3] All the children quoted were under the age of twelve, except for a lone
thirteen-year-old who had been invited back by his host. Every major element of
the Fresh Air formula from age to race remained in place.

This approach persisted because the rural hosting model had survived the
most dramatic demographic shift of the twentieth century. The same movement that had served few children of color at the onset of World War II came
to serve few white children by the end of the 1970s. That stunning demographic
shift—one fueled by the Great Migration of blacks to cities and white flight to
suburbs—transformed many other urban programs. Settlement houses dis-
banded. The YWCA adopted a central imperative to eliminate racism. Urban
churches changed the style of their preaching, the mode of their music, and the
breadth of their programming.[4] The Fresh Air model stayed the same. Children
still traveled to the country for limited summer stays in homes and camps.

However, the guests' complexion had changed. Bringing poor black or brown
children into white middle-class communities opened up an entirely different
set of social dynamics than did bringing poor white children into the same settings. Yet administrators did not alter the programs' parameters. Although they
recognized the racial shift and discussed its implications, they stayed true to their
model in hopes of including all the children and challenging those hosts not
ready to cross the color line in their living rooms. Yet the administrators had to
stifle more and more of the children's disruptions of a model that did not work
as it had prior to the shift in racial demographics. Even when race compounded
class, the adults kept telling the same story.

The Fresh Air Fund in particular remained invested in its rural and suburban
hosting formula, one that was guarded with great jealousy. Readers will have
noted by this point what has and has not been included in the body of evidence
that supports this study. More than 1,500 newspaper articles from a diverse array
of publications, including regional weeklies, national dailies, and historic black
newspapers, provided the basis for the public story of the Fresh Air movement.
A body of fictional literature about Fresh Air children expanded that public narrative. Memoirs by and interviews with more than forty-five Fresh Air hosts,

guests, administrators, and supporters provided essential anecdotal material.[5] In addition, over 5,000 pages of minutes, promotional brochures, correspondence, financial reports, staff memos, and photographs from eighteen archives offered insight into the internal workings of the sponsoring organizations. Other than annual reports available on its website, however, none of these materials came directly from the Fresh Air Fund.

Unfortunately, the Fund refused to open its records to me. Although I conducted research at many other archives, administrators at the Fund turned down repeated requests for access to theirs. Despite initial enthusiasm and support for this project and a warm welcome when I visited their offices, once they heard about the race-focused nature of my work, they informed me that they had had a bad experience with a master's student and had decided to close their archives to all researchers.[6] Fortunately, I was able to gain a clear picture of the internal workings of the organization thanks to financial records, board reports, and correspondence donated to the Library of Congress by Helen Rogers Reid, a long-time Fresh Air Fund board member and supporter. Given the picture of an institution deeply concerned about its public image that emerged from the Reid files, the Fund's decision to close its archives to outside researchers raises a host of questions that will only be answered by reversing that decision at some point in the future. As history has shown, secrets will not remain hidden forever.

One element of the Fresh story had never been stashed away. The crowd that gathered to greet the 150 children bused in from New York City in 1996 would have known about the wonders of grass. Or at least how much Fresh Air children purportedly loved to run in it. Barbara Horst, the local coordinator for the Fresh Air program in Lancaster, emphasized that children participating in the program received a "feeling of security" through their summer vacations. Horst also extolled the simple pleasures that awaited the children such as learning "what green grass is like to run on barefooted."[7] Here was the image that promoters had been returning to time and again for well over a hundred years, a child running innocent, free, and unencumbered by shoes. Although few children ever actually fit that image, the icon still evoked enough nostalgia and good feeling that Horst returned to it with ease when approached by an eager reporter.

And that image of grassy green proved even more long lasting. A 2013 feature in the *New York Times* on the Fresh Air Fund extolled the pleasure of running in grass. The same article returned to other familiar themes as well by celebrating swimming, contrasting the city's heat with the country's shade, highlighting host amazement at children's manners, featuring city children's dislike of bugs, and noting age caps set at twelve.[8]

In 2013 as in 1943—or 1953 or 1963 or 1973, for that matter—the image of children running in grass without shoes on their feet captured the story that promoters wanted to tell better than any other. But entrenched racial inequity in the United States has never been—and almost certainly never will be—solved by depictions of black and brown children running through white-owned lawns. Although by no means the principle cause of racism in the United States, the Fresh Air program remains a powerful indicator of racism's persistence and an enduring symbol of the prevalence of neoliberal approaches to social inequity.

Perhaps a change in the formula might be in order. Youthful idealism about grass and innocence—even in an organization with more than 140 years of experience—has done little to change the racial order. Perhaps the Fresh Air Fund, and all white-led social service organizations and related nonprofits, might start that change process simply by being more honest and open about their past. The monolith of racial inequity and subordination will not change if the past does not inform the present. And we cannot understand that past if it remains shrouded in secrecy.

History calls us to the future. Formulas are meant to be modified. Perhaps someday the Fresh Air Fund will help answer history's call. Like the green grass so loved by Fresh Air boosters, good growth needs open air, clean sunlight, and new rain. The Fresh Air Fund could also grow by opening its archives to the light and watering its organization with new ideas for bringing adults together without paternalism, speaking directly about racism, and finally realizing that, no matter how attractive, calling everyone innocent will never change injustice.

FRESH AIR ORGANIZATIONS

Oral histories, records, reports, and articles from and about the following organizations informed this book.

California
    Friendly Town Program, Friendly Town, Inc. (Oakland)
Connecticut
    Fresh Air Fund, *Life* (Branchville)
    Fresh Air Fund, *New Haven Register* (New Haven)
Iowa
    Fresh Air Camp, Red Cross (Des Moines)
    Friendly Town (Ames)
Illinois
    Farm Vacations, People's Organization of the Cabrini-Green Housing Development (Chicago)
    Fresh Air Fund, *Chicago Daily News* (Chicago)
    Fresh Air Fund, Hull House (Chicago)
    Friendly Town Program, Chicago City Missionary Society/Community Renewal Society (Chicago)
    Home Mission Fresh Air Program, Old Mennonite Church (Chicago)
    Newberry-Dubuque Project, Newberry Avenue Center (Chicago)
Indiana
    Fresh Air Camp, Girl Scouts (Hammond)

Fresh Air Fund, *Indianapolis News* and *Star* (Indianapolis)
Fresh Air Fund of Winona (Winona)
Massachusetts
Friendly Town, City Missionary Society (Boston)
Operation Discovery (Sharon/Boston)
Selma, AL, youth hosting venture, Ipswich residents (Ipswich/Selma)
Maryland
Children's Fresh Air Society/Fresh Air Fund (Baltimore)
Minnesota
Camp Manakiki, Pillsbury Settlement House (Minneapolis)
Minnesota Vacation Visits, Minnesota Council of Churches and the Catholic
Interracial Council of the Twin Cities (Winona)
United Way (Minneapolis)
Mississippi
Camp Landon, Fresh Air Program, General Conference Mennonite Voluntary Service (Gulfport)
Montana
Friendly Town Program (Kalispell)
North Carolina
Fresh Air Fund, *Charlotte Observer* (Charlotte)
Fresh Air Fund, Lions Club (Statesville)
Nebraska
Kathy Tyler Farm visits, Kathy Tyler—a junior at Nebraska Wesleyan University in 1965—and nine farm families (Omaha)
New Jersey
Fresh Air Fund for Anemic Children (Trenton)
New York
Camp Fund, Community Service Society (New York City)
Camp Nathan Hale, Union Settlement House (New York City)
Echo Hill Farm, Henry Street Settlement House (New York City)
Ethical Humanist Society home stays, Ethical Humanist Society of Long Island (New York City)
Fresh Air Fund for Greenwich Village Children, Greenwich Village Association and *The Villager* (New York City)
Grosevenor Neighborhood House (New York City)
Harlem Children's Fresh Air Fund/Colored Children's Fresh Air Fund (New York City)
Herald Tribune Fresh Air Fund/The Fresh Air Fund/Friendly Town (New York City)
Hudson Guild Farm (New York City)
Friendly Town Program, Inner City Protestant Parish (New York City)

Fresh Air Fund, *Troy Times* (Troy)

Fresh Air Programs, Episcopal Diocese of New York (New York City)

Friendly Town, Manhattan Christian Reformed Church (New York City)

La Guardia Memorial House (New York City)

United Neighborhood Houses of New York (New York City)

Youth Services Agency Vermont Visit; Astor Fund (private), Office of Economic Opportunity (federal), President's Commission on Youth Opportunity (federal), State of Vermont, Urban Task Force (New York City), Welfare Department's National Institute of Mental Health (New York City/Vermont towns)

Ohio

Fresh Air Camp, Salvation Army (Canton)

Friendly Town Program (Columbus)

Fresh Air Fund, Radio Neighbors (Lima)

Friendly Town Program, Cleveland Inner-city Protestant Parish (Cleveland)

Pennsylvania

Children's Visitation Program, Mennonite Board of Missions and Charities (Salunga)

Fresh Air Fund, *The Mercury* (Pottstown)

Friendly Town, Inter-Church Ministries of Northwestern Pennsylvania (Erie)

Lillian Taylor Fresh Air Camp (Pittsburgh)

Pittsburgh Association for the Improvement of the Poor (Pittsburgh)

South Carolina

Florence Fresh Air Fund (Florence)

Fresh Air Fund for Girls (Florence)

Wisconsin

Lake Geneva Fresh Air Fund (Lake Geneva)

Washington

Friendly Town, Ecumenical Metropolitan Ministry and Seattle Public Schools (Seattle)

West Virginia

Fresh Air Camp, Union Mission (Charleston)

Ontario, Canada

Bolton Fresh Air Camp, Neighborhood Workers' Association (Toronto)

Manitoba, Canada

Associated Fresh Air Camp (Winnipeg)

Fresh Air Fund and Social Services (Gimli)

Great Britain

Pearson's Fresh Air Fund (London)

DOCUMENTED FRESH AIR HOSTING TOWNS, 1939–1979

California
Concord
El Centro
Hayword
Mill Valley
Montclair Hills
Redondo Beach
Ross
San Alsemo
San Diego
San Francisco
Santa Cruz
Sleepy Hollow
Walnut Creek
Colorado
Greeley
Connecticut
Botsford
Branchville
Bridgeport
Bridgewater
Burlington
Canterbury

Coventry
Danbury
Darien
Easton
Edmond
Fairfield
Georgetown
Greenwich
Kent
Litchfield
Milford
New Britain
New Canaan
New Haven
New Milford
New Preston
Newtown
North Haven
Norwalk
Ridgefield
Rocky Hill
Roxbury
Stratford

Westport
Willimantic
Illinois
Aledo
Arlington Heights
Baileyville
Bensenville
Buffalo Grove
Chicago Heights
Dakota
DeKalb
Danvers
Des Plaines
Dixon
Elburn
Elk Grove Village
Elmhurst
Forreston Grove
Franklin Grove
Freeport
Genoa
Glen Ellyn
Grand Detour

Harvey

Hoffman Estates

Inverness

Kingston

LaSalle

Lena

Maple Park

Marengo

Milledgeville

Mount Prospect

Northlake

Orland Park

Palatine

Palos Park

Park Forest

Pearl City

Peru

Polo

Pontiac

Prospect Heights

Ridott

Rolling Meadows

Saint Charles

Schaumburg

Shannon

Spring Valley

Sterling

Stockton

Wheaton

Wheeling

Wood Dale

Woodstock

Indiana

Berne

Charleston

Elwood

Goshen

Hammond

Kokomo

Oaklandon

Terre Haute

Tipton

Topeka

Wolcottville

Iowa

Albia

Algona

Ames

Ankeny

Arcadia

Avery

Bagley

Blairsburg

Boone

Buffalo Center

Carroll

Clear Lake

Columbus Junction

Coon Rapids

Corwith

Cresthaven

Cylinder

Depew

Emmetsburg

Estherville

Fenton

Greenbrier

Harlan

Humboldt

Iowa City

Joice

Kalona

Lake City

Lakota

Ledyard

Lenox

Livermore

Lucas

Madrid

Mason City

Moravia

Muscatine

Nashua

Oelwein

Omaha

Ottosen

Panora

Ringsted

Rock Valley

Rose Mary

Rutland

Saint Joe

Salem

Silver City

Storm Lake

Swea City

Terril

Waterloo

Wayland

Wellington

Wellman

Kansas

Abilene

Buhler

Burdick

Burrton

Carlton

Chapman

Effingham

Elbing

Galva

Goessel

Herington

Hesston

Hillsboro

Hope

Hutchinson

Inman

Junction City

Kansas City

Lincolnville
Lyona
Moundridge
Newton
Pawnee Rock
Pretty Prairie
Salina
Talmage
Topeka
Troy
Whitewater
Wichita
Woodbine

Louisiana
Hammond

Maine
Alfred
Arundel
Biddeford
Biddeford-Saco
Bryant Pond
Cape Neddick
Cape Porpoise
Dayton
Eliot
Ferry Beach
Goodwins Mills
Hollis Center
Kennebunk
Kennebunkport
Kezar Falls
Kittery Point
Maplewood
Moody
North Berwick
Old Orchard Beach
Portland
Saco
Sanford
Scarborough

South Berwick
Springvale
Wells

Maryland
Bedford
Bel Air
Bowling Green
Bridgeville
Cambridge
Cresaptown
Crisfield
Cumberland
Delmar
Denton
Ellerslie
Federalsburg
Flintstone
Frostburg
Grantsville
Hagerstown
Harrington
Hyndman
Keyser
La Vale
Lonaconing
Midland
Mount Savage
Oldtown
Petersburg
Pocomoke City
Ridgeley
Salisbury
Seaford
Severna Park
Street
Town Creek
Wellersburg
Westernport
Wiley Ford
Willards

Massachusetts
Action
Adams
Ashburnham
Ashby
Athol
Baldwinville
Becket
Bedford
Brattleboro
Cape Cod
Carlisle
Centerville
Chelmsford
Cheshire
Clarksburg
Concord
Coventry
Dalton
Dunstable
East Brookfield
Edgewood
Egremont
Fitchburg
Granville
Great Barrington
Greater Gardner
Greenfield
Groton
Headsboro
Hinsdale
Hoosac Tunnel
Lanesboro
Lee
Lenox
Leominster
Lowell
Monroe Bridge
New Bedford
North Adams

Northfield
North Pownal
Pepperell
Pittsfield
Plymouth
Pownal
Reading
Readsboro
Richmond
Rowe
Salem
Shaftsbury
Sharon
Sheffield
Sherbourne
South Berkshire
Southbridge
Stamford
Stockbridge
Templeton
Tewksbury
Townsend
Tyngsboro
Westminster
West Stockbridge
Williamstown
Wilmington
Winchendon
Winchester
Worthington
Michigan
Ann Arbor
Benton Harbor
Brighton
Cassopolis
Detroit
Devils Lake
Douglas
Dowagiac
Graafschap
Little Pine Island

Patterson Lake
Piatt Lake
Pinckney
Portage Lake
Saginaw
Minnesota
Battle Lake
Columbia Heights
Erhard
Fergus Falls
Henning
Lake City
Minneapolis
Minnesota City
Mountain Lake
Perham
Saint Peter
Talmadge Hanson
Underwood
Winona
Missouri
Bourbon
Montana
Big Fork
Bitterroot Lake
Bozeman
Kalispell
Marion
Missoula
Polson
Thompson Falls
Nebraska
Beatrice
Henderson
Lincoln
North Platte
Omaha
Plattsmouth
New Hampshire
Abbot Hill
Abbot Hill Acres

Alstead
Amherst
Brookline
Chester
Concord
Derry
Dover Point
Dublin
Durham
Eliot
Exeter
Fitzwilliam
Goffsville
Greenfield
Greenland
Greenville
Hampton
Hanover
Hollis
Hudson
Keene
Kittery
Kittery Point
Litchfield
Londonderry
Manchester
Mason
Merrimack
Milford
Moody
Mount Vernon
Nashua
New Castle
New Dunstable
Newfields
Newington
New Ipswich
New Market
Pelham
Port City
Portsmouth

Rindge
Rochester
Round Island
Rye
Wilton
Windham
York
York Beach
New Jersey
Atlantic Highlands
Basking Ridge
Bedminster
Belvidere
Bernardsville
Bridgeton
Brookside
Bungalow Terrace
Caldwell
Chatham
Chester
Englewood
Far Hills
Gladstone
Green Village
Hackensack
Lake Mohawk
Liberty Corner
Little Falls
Livingston
Madison
Maplewood-Oranges
Martinsville
Mendham
Millington
Millville
Morris Plains
Morristown
Mount Kemble Lake
North Branch
   Station
Oldwick

Orange
Peapack
Pottersville
Red Bank
Somerset Hills
Somerville
Sparta
Summit
Teaneck
Twin Lakes
White Meadow Lake
New York
Alaben
Albany
Alfred
Alleghany
Almond
Altamont
Amsterdam
Andes
Andover
Ardsley
Auburn
Babcock Lake
Bainbridge
Baldwinsville
Ballsion
Ballston Lake
Ballston Spa
Barnard
Beaumont
Beech Hill
Belfast
Bellona
Belmont
Bemis Heights
Bennington
Bloomington
Bloomville
Blue Mountain
Bolivar

Bollton Landing
Bovina
Bovina Center
Bradley Brook
Brewster
Briarcliff
Bristol
Burlington Flats
Burnt Hills
Buskirk
Cambridge
Camden
Camillus
Canandaigua
Canaseraga
Carmel
Cazenovia
Cheektowaga
Cherry Valley
Chittenango
Circleville
Clintondale
Cohoes
Colliers
Colonie Village
Colts Neck
Constantia
Cooperstown
Cooperstown
   Junction
Cornwall
Cortland
Croton-on-Hudson
Cuba
Cuba Lake
Darien
Davenport
De Kalb Junction
Delancey
Delhi
Delhi Stage

Deposit	Grand George	Lowville
DeWittt	Granville	Lycoming
Downsville	Greene	Malone
Dresden	Greenwich	Manlius
Dunkirk	Groveside	Marbletown
Eagle Bridge	Halcyon Park	Marcellus
East Bloomfield	Hale Eddy	Margaretville
East Greenbush	Hancock	Maryland
East Hoosick	Hanover Hill	Masonville
East Meredith	Harpersfield	Mechanicville
East Springfield	Hartwick	Meredith
Edmeston	Highland	Middletown
Elbridge	Holcomb	Milford
Ellenville	Homer	Montgomery
Elmira	Honeoye Falls	Morris
Endicott	Hoosick Falls	Morristown
Esopus	Hornell	Mountainville
Fayetteville	Horseheads	Mount Union
Fillmore	Houghton	Mount Vision
Fishkill	Hudson Valley	Naples
Flax Island	Hurley	Nassau
Fly Creek	Ilion	Neahwa Park
Forestport	Jefferson	Nedrow
Fort Ann	Johnsonville	Newburgh
Fort Plain	Katonah	New Hamburg
Franklin	Kerhonkson	New Lebanon
Fredonia	Kingston	New Paltz
Fruit Valley	Knapp Creek	Newtonville
Fulton	LaFayette	North Adams
Gansevoort	Lake	North Hoosick
Garden City	Lake Ronkonkoma	North Petersburg
Garraitsville	Lake Seneca	North Syracuse
Genesee	Larchmont	Norwood
Geneva	Latham	Oaksville
Gilbertsville	Laurens	Olean
Gilboa	Liberty	Oneonta
Glens Falls	Lima	Oswego
Goodyear Lake	Liverpool	Otego
Gorham	Long Island	Penn Yan
Grafton	Loudonville	Petersburg

Phoenix
Pine Plains
Pittstown
Plattsburgh
Poestenkill
Portlandville
Portville
Potsdam
Poughkeepsie
Poughquag
Pownal
Prattville
Pulaski
Raymertown
Red Hook
Rensselaer
Rhinebeck
Richfield Springs
Ridgefield
Ridgewood
Riverside
Rochester
Rockdale
Rome
Roscoe
Rosendale
Roxbury
Rushville
Sand Lake
Saratoga Springs
Saugerties
Sauquoit
Schaghticoke
Schenevus
Schnectady
Schuylerville
Sennett
Shongo
Sidney
Sidney Center

Skaneateles
Slingerlands
Smithtown
Somers
South New Berlin
Springfield Center
Staatsburg
Stamford
Stannards
Stephenstown
Stillwater
Stone Ridge
Syracuse
Tenafly
Thornwood
Treadwell
Troy
Ulsterville
Unadilla
Valatie
Valley Falls
Vernon
Victor
Walden
Walton
Waterford
Watertown
Webster
Weedsport
Wells Bridge
Wellsville
West Bainbridge
West Bloomfield
West Burlington
West Davenport
West Eaton
Westford
West Hoosick
West Sand Lake
White Creek

Wilton
Wolcott
Woodstock
Woodville
Worcester

North Carolina
Asheboro
Charlotte
Cherryville
Clover
Gastonia
Graham
Iredell
Statesville

North Dakota
Cavalier
Grassy Butte
Hettinger

Ohio
Ashland
Ashtabula
Athens
Berea
Butler
Cincinnati
Cleveland
Coshocton
Dover
East Liverpool
Elyria
Fredonia
Hillsboro
Jeromesville
Lancaster
Mansfield
Marion
Massillon
Mentor
Millersburg
Newark

Newcomerstown
New Philadelphia
Nova
Piqua
Portsmouth
Salem
Savannah
Steubenville
Uhrichsville
Warren
Zanesville
Pennsylvania
Ardsley
Alexandria
Allensville
Altoona
Annville
Ashland
Atglen
Athens
Barton
Belle Vernon
Bellevue
Bellwood
Bendersville
Biglerville
Bird-in-Hand
Black Log Valley
Blairs Mills
Bonneauville
Boothwyn
Boyertown
Bradford
Bristol Township
Brownsville
Butler Township
Butler Valley
Camp Hill
Carlisle
Centerville

Chambersburg
Chester
Chicora
Clearfield
Cleona
Coalmont
Collegeville
Concord
Conyngham
Corning
Cornwall
Cornwall-Quentin
Coudersport
Danville
Delaware Water Gap
Dover
Doylestown
Drums
DuBois
Dudley
Earlville
East Berlin
East Bissett
East Coventry
    Township
East Hickory
Edie
Elam
Elizabethtown
Ellisburg
Ellwood City
Elverson
Ephrata
Erwina
Evansburg
Fairfield
Fleetwood
Folsom
Ford City
Forks

Fox Valley
Frackville
Franklin
Fredericksburg
Friedens
Friedensburg
Genesee
Gettysburg
Gilbertsville
Girardville
Glen Holden
Glen Mills
Glen Rock
Grantville
Hanover
Harrisburg
Haverford
Havertown
Hazelton
Hegins
Henryville
Hershey
Hesston
Hollidaysburg
Houstontown
Hummelstown
Huntingdon
Indiana
Indiantown Gap
Intercourse
Jersey Shore
Johnsonburg
Jonestown
Jutland
Kane
Kishacoquillas
Kis-Lyn
Knowltonwood
Knox
Lancaster

Langhorne	Newfoundland	Shippensburg
Lebanon	Newton Hamilton	Somerset
Leeper	Nichols	South Park
Lehighton	Norwood	Spring City
Levittown	Oil City	Springfield
Littlestown	Orbisonia	Spring Grove
Lock Haven	Orrstown	Strausstown
Loganton	Orrtanna	Stroudsburg
Logantown	Orwigsburg	Sugarloaf
Lurgan	Palmyra	Sunbury
Manheim	Paoli	Three Springs
Mapleon	Paradise	Tidioute
Marshall	Perkasie	Tionesta
Martinsburg	Petersburg	Titusville
McVeytown	Phoenixville	Tunkhannock
Meadville	Pikestown	Tylersburg
Mechanicsburg	Pine Grove	Tyrone
Media	Pittsburgh	Upland
Melville	Pittsfield	Upper Bald
Meyersdale	Pittston	Eagle
Middleton	Pleasantville	Upper Chichester
Middletown	Port Matilda	Upper Darby
Mifflintown	Pottstown	Upper Providence
Mill Creek	Punxsutawney	Valencia
Millerstown	Quarryville	Wagontown
Mill Hall	Quentin	Wallingford
Millheim	Reading	Wapwallopen
Montoursville	Reamstown	Warren
Morris Cove	Rexmont	Warrendale
Morton	Riddlesburg	Warriors Mark
Mountain Grove	Rockhill Furnace	Washington Boro
Mountaintop	Ronks	Waverly
Mount Jewett	Saint Marys	Wellsboro
Mount Joy	Saxton	West Chester
Mount Union	Sayre	Westfield
Mowry	Scarsdale	West View
Myersdale	Sellersville	Williamsport
Myerstown	Sheakleyville	Woodland
New Bethlehem	Shenandoah	Wrightsville
Newburg	Sherman	York

Youngstown
Youngsville
Rhode Island
Jamestown
Middletown
Newport
Portsmouth
Tiverton
South Carolina
Cleveland
Florence
Greenville
Kings Mountain
    Battleground Park
South Dakota
Freeman
Grand Forks
Marion
Texas
Dallas
Vermont
Arlington
Barre
Bellows Falls
Bennington
Brattleboro
Burlington
Cambridge
Castleton
Derby
Dorset
East Arlington
East Dorset
East Manchester
East Pownal
Hanover
Hinesburg
Johnson
Ludlow

Manchester
Manchester Depot
Middlebury
Monroe Bridge
Montpelier
Morrisville
New Haven
North Adams
North Bennington
Northfield
North Pownal
Norwich
Pawlet
Peru
Pittsfield
Pownal
Pownal Center
Readsboro
Rupert
Rutland
Saint Johnsbury
Salisbury
Sandgate
Shaftsbury
South Barre
South Pownal
South Shaftsbury
Springfield
Stamford
Sunderland
Wells
West Hoosick
White Creek
Whitingham
Williamstown
Wilmington
Virginia
Bridgewater
Charlotte

Dayton
Elkton
Front Royal
Harrisonburg
Linville
Norwich
Rawley Springs
Saint George
Shenandoah
Staunton
Stuarts Draft
Timberville
Waynesboro
Washington
Centralia
Chehalis
Forks
Oakville
Port Angeles
Rochester
Sequim
West Virginia
Wheeling
Weirton
Wisconsin
Army Lake
Fond du Lac
Hillsboro
Janesville
Lake Geneva
Lima Center
Mondovi
Nashotah
Neenah
Oshkosh
Platteville
Rhinelander
Sheboygan
Whitehall

Notes

ARCHIVAL ABBREVIATIONS

CUA:	Columbia University Archives (New York, NY)
EDNY:	Episcopal Diocese of New York (New York, NY)
ELAA, UMN:	Elmer L. Andersen Archives, University of Minnesota (Minneapolis, MN)
EMM:	Eastern Mennonite Missions Record Room (Salunga, PA)
FAFR:	Fresh Air Fund Records, Library of Virginia (Richmond, VA)
GNHR:	Grosvenor Neighborhood House Records, Columbia University Archives (New York, NY)
HGR:	Hudson Guild Records, Columbia University Archives (New York, NY)
HSSR:	Henry Street Settlement Records, Columbia University Archives (New York, NY)
LGMHR:	La Guardia Memorial House Records, Columbia University Archives (New York, NY)
LMHS:	Lancaster Mennonite Historical Society (Lancaster, PA)
LOC-MC:	Library of Congress, Manuscript Collection (Washington, DC)
LOC-PPD:	Library of Congress, Prints and Photographs Division (Washington, DC)
LVA:	Library of Virginia (Richmond, VA)
MLABC:	Mennonite Church USA Library Archives—Bethel College (Newton, KS)
MLAGC/AMC:	Mennonite Church USA Library Archives—Goshen College (Goshen, IN)
MSHL:	Menno Simons Historical Library (Harrisonburg, VA)
NYCPL-BRARR:	NYC Public Libraries, Stephen A. Schwarzman Building, Manuscripts and Archives Division, Brooke Russell Astor Reading Room (New York, NY)
NYCPL-PARC:	NYC Public Libraries, Performing Arts Research Collections (New York, NY)
NYCPL-SC:	NYC Public Libraries, Schomburg Center for Research in Black Culture (New York, NY)
NYHS:	New York Historical Society (New York, NY)
NYUA:	New York University Archives (New York, NY)
PHS:	Presbyterian Historical Society (Philadelphia, PA)
PNHA:	Presbyterian National Historical Archives (Philadelphia, PA)
PRF, HRR:	Papers of Reid Family, Helen Rogers Reid, Library of Congress, Manuscript Collection (Washington, DC)
UIL, MNC:	University of Illinois at Chicago, Marcy Newberry Collection (Chicago, IL)
USAR:	Union Settlement Association Records, Columbia University Archives (New York, NY)
UTA, CCAH:	University of Texas at Austin, Collections in the Center for American History (Austin, TX)
WRSH:	Western Reserve Historical Society Library (Cleveland, OH)

PREFACE

1. Memorandum by Ira J. Buckwalter, "Colored Workers Committee Notes 1947–1953," EMM—Record Room, drawer: "Home Missions Locations and Other General 1956–1964."

2. Janice Batts, Iowa City, IA, telephone, interview by the author, 2012.

3. A few outside groups did conduct at least partial studies of Fresh Air ventures through the years, but even these failed to introduce dependable means of quantifying the effects of the visits. See Loren C. Dunn, "Analysis of the Effectiveness of the Friendly Town Publicity Program of the *Herald Tribune* Fresh Air Fund" (master's thesis, Boston University, 1966); Robert M. Vanderbeck, "Inner-City Children, Country Summers: Narrating American Childhood and the Geographies of Whiteness," *Environment and Planning* 40, no. 5 (2008): 1132–50; Christine Horace, "One Group's Journey from Camp to College," *Social Work with Groups* 27, no. 4 (2005): 31–50. In 1980 the Fresh Air Fund asked Dr. Michael Phillips of Fordham University to conduct a survey of hosts, sponsors, parents, and children about their opinions of the program. The "self-study" found overwhelming support for the program but did not offer evidence regarding its long-term effects. See the memorandum by Michael Phillips, "Report of the Fresh Air Fund Friendly Town Study Undertaken by the Long Range Planning Committee," April 1980, LVA, FAFR, 1949–1999, accession number 36407, box 31, folder 2: "Reports, Friendly Town Study, 1979–1980."

4. Bartlett Hendricks, "Three Boys, Two Weeks and No Worries at All," *Berkshire Eagle* (Pittsfield, MA), August 4, 1956.

5. I echo the work of historian Thomas Sugrue, who follows a similar line of inquiry. He argues that an influential strand of activism in modern America has proposed that the solution to racial inequality lies in ridding individuals of their prejudices and convincing white people to respect black people as equals. In contrast to those who organized against racism in the systems of finance, law, and politics, Fresh Air promoters joined those who argued that changing individual beliefs and attitudes through education and the press came first. See Thomas J. Sugrue, *Sweet Land of Liberty: The Forgotten Struggle for Civil Rights in the North* (New York: Random House, 2008), xxvi.

INTRODUCTION

1. Paul E. Warfield, "The Whole Story," *Bennington (VT) Banner*, September 6, 1963.

2. Edith Simonds, "Letter to a Suburban Church," *Presbyterian Life*, September 1, 1966, 19–21, 40.

3. Memorandum by Ted Dubinsky, "Minutes of the 'Committee to Consider the Minority Group Male's Self-Image'—8/21/67," 3, CUA, HGR MS#1465, Series III: Hudson Guild Files, box 13, folder 21: "Committee to Consider the Minority Group Male's Self-Image, 1967–1968."

4. Rita J. Simon, Howard Altstein, and Marygold S. Melli, *The Case for Transracial Adoption* (Washington, DC: American University Press, 1994), 40.

5. Lynford Hershey to Leon Stauffer, July 18, 1971, AMC—IV-21-4, box 1, MBM, Minority Ministries Council, Data Files 1, A–K, folder: "Education Program 1970–72, Lynford Hershey"; Lacey Fosburgh, "Director of the Fresh Air Appeal Retiring after 25 Years in Post," *New York Times*, August 1, 1971.

6. Ellen Delmonte, "An Editorial Feature," *Call and Post* (Cleveland, OH), July 3, 1971.

7. Although the voices and perspectives of the suburban and rural children who assisted in hosting also appear in this narrative, the children who traveled from the city to the country as guests in the Fresh Air program figure most prominently because they served as the program's raison d'être.

8. Author's estimate based on available data.

9. Memorandum by Frederick Howell Lewis, "Iconography of a Wilderness," 1962, copied from the CCAH, UTA.

10. Memorandum, "Registrar's Interview—Duckworth—Trip A," 1949, CUA, USAR, 1896–1995 MS#1149, Series VII: Programs and Services, box 53, folder 5: "Camp-Children's Records (D–E), 1945–57"; Memorandum, "Camp Intake Form—Rupel, Eileen," June 30, 1955, CUA, USAR, 1896–1995 MS#1149, Series VII: Programs and Services, box 53, folder 8: "Camp-Children's Records (R), 1950–58." Here and throughout the book, I place home and camp visits under the same analytical umbrella. Although I do note a recurring preference by children for camp stays over home visits and highlight the structural and programmatic differences between the two sub-models, I treat camp and home visits as two expressions of a single movement because Fresh Air participants and their supporters did the same.

11. Memorandum by Frederick H. Lewis, "What Am I Doing Here?: Remarks at Friendly Town Spring Planning Conference Held at Sharpe Reservation," February 20, 1963, LOC, PRF D224, HRR, file 12568: "Fresh Air Fund."

12. "Narrow World Big Threat to 'Fresh Air' Children," *Huntingdon (PA) Daily News*, May 19, 1973.

13. Eleanor Charles, "Apathy Endangers Fresh Air Fund," *New York Times*, May 20, 1979.

14. Robin Bernstein, *Racial Innocence: Performing American Childhood and Race from Slavery to Civil Rights* (New York: New York University Press, 2011), 41.

15. Jim Banman, "Integration Comes to Central Kansas as Mennonites Are Hosts to Negroes," *Hutchinson (KS) News*, 27, in MLABC: MLA.VII.R GC Voluntary Service, Series 11 Gulfport VS Unit, box 4, folder 123, Fresh Air, 1961.

16. Civil rights historians have failed to examine the off-street actions of the purportedly innocent children who ventured into the suburbs and the country. Despite the excellent, children-centered work of Robert Coles, few texts examine children's participation in the civil rights movement. See Robert Coles, *Children of Crisis: A Study of Courage and Fear* (Boston: Little, Brown, 1967). The few that do include children in their civil rights narratives nonetheless miss the exploits of children in the confines of white homes and summer camps even though thousands more African American and Latino children participated in Fresh Air programs than marched in the streets. See Taylor Branch, *Parting the Waters: America in the King Years 1954–63* (New York: Simon & Shuster, 1988); Branch, *Pillar of Fire: America in the King Years 1963–65* (New York: Simon & Schuster, 1998); Branch, *At Canaan's Edge: America in the King Years 1965–68* (New York: Simon & Schuster, 2006); James Farmer, "The March on Washington: The Zenith of the Southern Movement," in *New Directions in Civil Rights Studies*, ed. Armstead L. Robinson and Patricia Sullivan, Carter G. Woodson Institute Series in Black Studies (Charlottesville: University Press of Virginia, 1991), 30–37; David Halberstam, *The Children* (New York: Fawcett, 1998); Andrew B. Lewis, *The Shadows of Youth: The Remarkable Journey of the Civil Rights Generation* (New York: Hill and Wang, 2009); Robert J. Norrell, "One Thing We Did Right: Reflections on the Movement," in *New Directions in Civil Rights Studies*, 65–80; Daniel Perlstein, "Teaching Freedom: SNCC and the Creation of the Mississippi Freedom Schools," *History of Education Quarterly* 30, no. 3 (1990): 297–324; "Fresh Air Work Humor," *Fitchburg (MA) Daily Sentinel*, July 27, 1907; Barbara Ransby, *Ella Baker and the Black Freedom Movement: A Radical Democratic Vision* (Chapel Hill: University of North Carolina Press, 2003). Historians have also missed children's contributions by stretching the notion of childhood. Matthew Delmont, Aldon Morris, and Charles Payne all speak of the prominent role that teenagers played in local civil rights campaigns, as do Anne Moody and Tracy Sugarman in their autobiographies, but there is no singular study of the role of preadolescent children in the movement. See Matthew F. Delmont, *The Nicest Kids in Town: American Bandstand, Rock 'n Roll, and the Struggle for Civil Rights*

in 1950s Philadelphia (Los Angeles: University of California Press, 2012); Anne Moody, *Coming of Age in Mississippi* (New York: Dell, 1976); Aldon D. Morris, *The Origins of the Civil Rights Movement: Black Communities Organizing for Change* (New York: Free Press, 1984); Charles M. Payne, *I've Got the Light of Freedom: The Organizing Tradition and the Mississippi Freedom Struggle* (Berkeley: University of California Press, 1995). Alisa Harrison begins to incorporate African American girls into her work but only inasmuch as they participated in public efforts led by African American women. See Alisa Y. Harrison, "Women's and Girls' Activism in 1960s Southwest Georgia: Rethinking History and Historiography," in *Women Shaping the South: Creating and Confronting Change,* ed. Angela Boswell and Judith N. McArthur (Columbia: University of Missouri Press, 2006), 229–58. Even Wilma King's treatment of the 1960 New Orleans school integration effort and the 1963 Birmingham children's crusade depicts children like the iconic Ruby Bridges as innocents swept up by history, with little agency of their own. See Wilma King, *African American Childhoods: Historical Perspectives from Slavery to Civil Rights* (New York: Palgrave Macmillan, 2005).

17. A note on childhood: Although scholarly definitions of childhood vary widely, with some starting just after infancy and ending well after adolescence, the Fresh Air movement generally focused on the ages between four and twelve. See Marta Gutman and Ning De Coninck-Smith, "Introduction: Good to Think with—History, Space, and Modern Childhood," in *Designing Modern Childhoods: History, Space, and the Material Culture of Children,* ed. Marta Gutman and Ning De Coninck-Smith (Newark, NJ: Rutgers University Press, 2008), 1–19. The latter time frame suits the purposes of this study well in that it separates adolescence as a distinct development phase that rarely bears the marks of innocence. Adolescents become sexually aware and enter the world of work; they begin to shoulder adult responsibility. I draw on the following works for my segmentation of adolescence from childhood in this study: Steven Mintz, *Huck's Raft: A History of American Childhood* (Cambridge, MA: Belknap Press of Harvard University Press, 2004), 3–4; Jennifer Ritterhouse, *Growing up Jim Crow: How Black and White Southern Children Learned Race* (Chapel Hill: University of North Carolina Press, 2006), 20–21; R. P. Neuman, "Masturbation, Madness, and the Modern Concepts of Childhood and Adolescence," *Journal of Social History* 8, no. 3 (1975): 1–27. During the period of this study, adults structured programs based on the ready assumption that childhood ended in the teen years.

18. Joe R. Feagin, *Racist America: Roots, Current Realities, and Future Reparations* (New York: Routledge, 2000); J. Morgan Kousser, *Colorblind Injustice: Minority Voting Rights and the Undoing of the Second Reconstruction* (Chapel Hill: University of North Carolina Press, 1999); Joe Pettit, "The Persistence of Injustice: Challenging Some Dominant Explanations," *Journal of the Society of Christian Ethics* 25, no. 1 (2005): 197–218.

19. Kenneth T. Jackson, *Crabgrass Frontier: The Suburbanization of the United States* (New York: Oxford University Press, 1985); Renee Christine Romano, *Race Mixing: Black-White Marriage in Postwar America* (Cambridge, MA: Harvard University Press, 2003); Ritterhouse, *Growing up Jim Crow.*

20. Sarah Burns, "Barefoot Boys and Other Country Children: Sentiment and Ideology in Nineteenth-Century American Art," *American Art Journal* 20, no. 1 (1988): 25–50.

21. Ibid., 25, 48.

22. Memorandum by Richard F. Crandell, "Public Information: The Year a Landmark," 1962, LOC, PRF D224, HRR, file 12568: "Fresh Air Fund."

23. Colin Heywood, *A History of Childhood: Children and Childhood in the West from Medieval to Modern Times* (Cambridge: Polity, 2002), 40, 170; Marina Warner, *Six Myths of Our Time: Little Angels, Little Monsters, Beautiful Beasts, and More* (New York: Vintage, 1994), 54–55.

24. The literature on interracial marriage is robust. See, for example, Peggy Pascoe, *What Comes Naturally: Miscegenation Law and the Making of Race in America* (New York:

Oxford University Press, 2009); Fay Botham, *Almighty God Created the Races: Christianity, Interracial Marriage, and American Law* (Chapel Hill: University of North Carolina Press, 2009); Jane Dailey, "Sex, Segregation, and the Sacred after *Brown*," *Journal of American History* 91, no. 1 (2004): 119–44; Charles F. Robinson, *Dangerous Liaisons: Sex and Love in the Segregated South* (Fayetteville: University of Arkansas Press, 2003); Rachel F. Moran, *Interracial Intimacy: The Regulation of Race and Romance* (Chicago: University of Chicago Press, 2001); Maria P. P. Root, *Love's Revolution: Interracial Marriage* (Philadelphia: Temple University Press, 2001); Peter Wallenstein, *Tell the Court I Love My Wife: Race, Marriage, and Law* (New York: Palgrave Macmillan, 2002). Historians have been particularly adept at parsing changes in law and social custom. Those texts have focused on efforts to keep white people separate from people of color. Much less has been written about the sexual dynamics of efforts to bring together white and black people, with even less attention given to interracial attraction among children. (For a notable exception, see King, *African American Childhoods*.) I argue that the control mechanisms instituted by Fresh Air administrators to reduce the possibility of interracial romance—most notably the right to choose the gender of the hosted child—were the single most important policy component of the Fresh Air model. If administrators could not guard against interracial sex, the program would collapse. Indeed, program administrators invested far more resources in ensuring that the children would not enter into romantic liaisons across racial lines than they did in protecting children from sexual and physical abuse by their hosts.

25. Stuart C. Aitken, *Geographies of Young People: The Morally Contested Spaces of Identity*, ed. Tracey Skelton and Gill Valentine (New York: Routledge, 2001), 94; Bernstein, *Racial Innocence*, 4.

26. Martin Luther King, *Stride toward Freedom: The Montgomery Story* (New York: Harper, 1958), 207; Memorandum, "Host Parents Summary—1960," MLABC: MLA.VII.R GC Voluntary Service, Series 11 Gulfport VS Unit, box 4, folder 122: "Fresh Air, 1960."

27. Memorandum, "The Church Facing the Race Crisis," December 4, 1963, AMC, CESR papers I-3–7, box 5, folder 168.

28. David Sibbet, "City Children Visit Suburbs," *Chicago Tribune*, July 14, 1968.

29. "The Project Is Sponsored by," *Daily Sentinel* (Rome, NY), 1962.

30. Few historians—or scholars from other disciplines—have examined the Fresh Air movement at any length. This book provides a much more thorough and historically specific study of the initiatives and places them in the context of the story of race in America. Those who have addressed the movement in some form include Loren C. Dunn, "Analysis of the Effectiveness of the Friendly Town Publicity Program of the *Herald Tribune* Fresh Air Fund" (master's thesis, Boston University, 1966); Julia Guarneri, "Changing Strategies for Child Welfare, Enduring Beliefs about Childhood: The Fresh Air Fund, 1877–1926," *Journal of the Gilded Age and Progressive Era* 11, no. 1 (2012): 27–70; David Hechler, *The Battle and the Backlash: The Child Sexual Abuse War* (Lexington, MA: Lexington Books, 1988); Christine Horace, "One Group's Journey from Camp to College," *Social Work with Groups* 27, no. 4 (2005): 31–50.

31. A note on children's agency: As numerous historians and other childhood scholars have shown, children shape the world around them. Historian Stephen Mintz asserts that children enter into "conflicts with adults who seek to regulate and direct kids' activities." See Steven Mintz, "The Changing Face of Children's Culture," in *Reinventing Childhood after World War II*, ed. Paula S. Fass and Michael Grossberg (Philadelphia: University of Pennsylvania Press, 2012), 38–50. Rather than passive recipients of adults' machinations, children act on others even as others act on them. See Heywood, *A History of Childhood*, 3–4; Patrick J. Ryan, "How New Is the 'New' Social Study of Childhood? The Myth of a Paradigm Shift," *Journal of Interdisciplinary History* 38, no. 4 (2008): 553–76; Sharon Stephens, "Children and the Politics of Culture in 'Late Capitalism,'" in *Children and the Politics of Culture*, ed. Sharon Stephens (Princeton, NJ: Princeton University Press,

1995), 3–48; Bonnie J. Miller-McLemore, "'Let the Children Come' Revisited: Contemporary Feminist Theologians on Children," in *The Child in Christian Thought*, ed. Marcia J. Bunge (Grand Rapids, MI: W.B. Eerdmans, 2000), 446–73. As employed in this book, *agency* then refers to the ability of the children to set adult agenda, influence their hosts' worldview, and initiate action in an unfamiliar environment. Given that children entered dangerous territory, domestic environs that childhood historian John Gillis has called "the single most dangerous place for both women and children," where adults could and did mistreat children with few repercussions, the actions chronicled in the chapters to follow prove all the more bold and incisive. See John R. Gillis, "Epilogue: The Islanding of Children—Reshaping the Mythical Landscapes of Childhood," in Gutman and De Coninck-Smith, *Designing Modern Childhoods*, 316–30.

32. Even those texts that address themes similar to those found in the Fresh Air movement miss the breadth of children's contributions. Already in 1969, Peter Schmitt included Fresh Air camps in his treatment of the Arcadian myth in U.S. history. See Peter J. Schmitt, *Back to Nature: The Arcadian Myth in Urban America* (New York: Oxford University Press, 1969). However, his analysis fails to include the children's perspectives and treats them as passive recipients of adults' largesse. Phyllis Palmer's study of interracial camps sponsored by the National Conference of Christians and Jews in the post–World War II era again focuses on teens. See Phyllis M. Palmer, *Living as Equals: How Three White Communities Struggled to Make Interracial Connections during the Civil Rights Era* (Nashville: Vanderbilt University Press, 2008). Leslie Paris offers a masterful analysis of the racial and social dynamics of the camping experience and incorporates the perspectives of preadolescent children but fails to connect camp activities with social change movements, a link that Palmer establishes much more directly. See Leslie Paris, *Children's Nature: The Rise of the American Summer Camp* (New York: New York University Press, 2008).

33. Memorandum by Frederick H. Lewis, "Annual Report for 1968: A Reappraisal," 11, copied from CCAH, UTA.

34. Martin Luther King Jr., "The Birth of a New Nation," www.africanamericans.com/MLKjrBirthofANewNation.htm.

1. KNOWLEDGE, GIRL, NATURE

1. "Fresh Air Days," *Galveston (TX) Daily News*, April 30, 1910.

2. Alexander Hynd-Lindsay, "A Memorial Address on the Life and Work of Rev. Willard Parsons, Founder of the Tribune Fresh-Air Work," *Sunday Afternoon*, 1912, copied from the CCAH, UTA.

3. Robert H. Wiebe, *The Search for Order: 1877–1920* (New York: Hill and Wang, 1967); Kenneth Cmiel, "Destiny and Amnesia: The Vision of Modernity in Robert Wiebe's *The Search for Order*," *Reviews in American History* 21, no. 2 (1993): 352–68.

4. Julia Guarneri, "Changing Strategies for Child Welfare, Enduring Beliefs about Childhood: The Fresh Air Fund, 1877–1926," *Journal of the Gilded Age and Progressive Era* 11, no. 1 (2012): 27–70.

5. LeRoy Ashby, *Endangered Children: Dependency, Neglect, and Abuse in American History* (New York: Twayne, 1997), 40.

6. Marilyn Irving Holt, "Adoption Reform, Orphan Trains, and Child-Saving, 1851–1929," in *Children and Youth in Adoption, Orphanages, and Foster Care: A Historical Handbook and Guide*, ed. Miriam Foreman-Brunell (Westport, CT: Greenwood, 2006), 222.

7. Marilyn Irvin Holt, *The Orphan Trains: Placing out in America* (Lincoln, NE: University of Nebraska Press, 1992), 62.

8. Hugh D. Hindman, *Child Labor: An American History* (Armonk, NY: M.E. Sharpe, 2002), 37.

9. Sarah Burns, "Barefoot Boys and Other Country Children: Sentiment and Ideology in Nineteenth-Century American Art," *American Art Journal* 20, no. 1 (1988): 25–50.

10. Chuck Austin, "The History of the Fresh Air Fund" (1981), C9–2, LVA, FAFR, 1949–1999, accession number 36407, box 22, folder 2: "Histories 1977."

11. Loren C. Dunn, "Analysis of the Effectiveness of the Friendly Town Publicity Program of the *Herald Tribune* Fresh Air Fund" (master's thesis, Boston University, 1966), 8–9.

12. Michael B. Smith, "'The Ego Ideal of the Good Camper' and the Nature of Summer Camp," *Environmental History* 11, no. 1 (2006): 70–101; James Marten, *Childhood and Child Welfare in the Progressive Era: A Brief History with Documents* (Boston, MA: Bedford/ St. Martin's, 2004), 3.

13. Dunn, "Analysis of the Effectiveness of the Friendly Town Publicity Program," 20–22.

14. Steven Mintz, *Huck's Raft: A History of American Childhood* (Cambridge, MA: Belknap Press of Harvard University Press, 2004), 215.

15. Dunn, "Analysis of the Effectiveness of the Friendly Town Publicity Program," 10–11.

16. Norris Magnuson, *Salvation in the Slums: Evangelical Social Work, 1865–1920* (Metchuen, NJ: Scarecrow Press, 1977), 61–62.

17. Kenneth L. Kusmer, "The Functions of Organized Charity in the Progressive Era: Chicago as a Case Study," *Journal of American History* 60 (1973): 657–78.

18. Magnuson, *Salvation in the Slums*, 62.

19. Peter J. Schmitt, *Back to Nature: The Arcadian Myth in Urban America* (New York: Oxford University Press, 1969), 97.

20. Ibid., xix.

21. Guarneri, "Changing Strategies for Child Welfare."

22. Robert M. Vanderbeck, "Inner-City Children, Country Summers: Narrating American Childhood and the Geographies of Whiteness," *Environment and Planning* 40, no. 5 (2008): 1132–50.

23. Memorandum by Robert Heasman, "Pearson's Holiday Fund, 1892 to 1980, with a Summary from 1980 to 2000: Archive Research Undertaken (June 2000)," 2000, author's personal collection.

24. C. Arthur Pearson, "An Old Country Appeal," *Manitoba Free Press* (Winnipeg), April 7, 1913.

25. Guarneri, "Changing Strategies for Child Welfare."

26. Magnuson, *Salvation in the Slums*, 64–65.

27. "Fresh Air Fund," *Chicago Defender*, July 9, 1927.

28. Ruth Hutchinson Crocker, "Making Charity Modern: Business and the Reform of Charities in Indianapolis, 1879–1930," *Business and Economic History* 12 (1983): 158–70.

29. Vanderbeck, "Inner-City Children, Country Summers."

30. Holt, *The Orphan Trains*, 5–6. Some of the earlier Fresh Air ventures, particularly those focused on camps, did include mothers of young children, and a few even focused on bringing the elderly to the country, but these efforts quickly died out as donors proved far more interested in supporting initiatives focused on children.

31. Vanderbeck, "Inner-City Children, Country Summers."

32. Guarneri, "Changing Strategies for Child Welfare."

33. Walter Shephard Ufford, *Fresh Air Charity in the United States* (New York: Bonnell, Silver & Co., 1897), 11–12.

34. "The New York Tribune and Fresh Air Fund," *Christian Recorder* (Philadelphia), August 10, 1882.

35. "England and America Have Had Their John Browns . . . ," *Christian Recorder* (Philadelphia), April 26, 1883; "Spring Is at Hand; Summer Will Soon Be Here . . . ," *Christian Recorder* (Philadelphia), March 27, 1884.

36. Holt, *The Orphan Trains*, 71.

37. "'All the Milk You Want' Turns Camp into Paradise for Urchin," *Telegram* (Bridgeport, CT), August 3, 1937.

38. Susan D. Carle, *Defining the Struggle: National Organizing for Racial Justice, 1880–1915* (New York: Oxford University Press, 2013), 2.

39. William Johnson, "Wanted—A Fresh Air Guild," *Freeman* (Indianapolis), August 11, 1896.

40. "African Orthodox Church," *Pittsburgh Courier*, August 2, 1924; "Fresh Air Fund Workers Busy," *Chicago Defender*, March 1, 1924; "Fresh Air Fund."

41. Abigail A. Van Slyck, *A Manufactured Wilderness: Summer Camps and the Shaping of American Youth, 1890–1960* (Minneapolis: University of Minnesota Press, 2006), xxvi.

42. "Weekly Comment," *Chicago Defender*, July 5, 1919.

43. Ibid.

44. Darrell Michael Scott, *Contempt and Pity: Social Policy and the Image of the Damaged Black Psyche, 1880–1996* (Chapel Hill: University of North Carolina Press, 1997), 2.

45. Mintz, *Huck's Raft*, 3.

46. Marten, *Childhood and Child Welfare in the Progressive Era*, 13.

47. David Glassberg, "Restoring a 'Forgotten Childhood': American Play and the Progressive Era's Elizabethan Past," *American Quarterly* 32, no. 4 (1980): 351–68.

48. Peter N. Stearns, *Childhood in World History* (New York: Routledge, 2006), 93–94.

49. Colin Heywood, *A History of Childhood: Children and Childhood in the West from Medieval to Modern Times* (Cambridge: Polity, 2002), 171.

50. "Only Six Days More to Help 200 Poor Kiddies; Church Players to Aid," *Trenton (NJ) Evening Times*, May 26, 1914; Alan Dawley, *Struggles for Justice: Social Responsibility and the Liberal State* (Cambridge, MA: Belknap Press of Harvard University Press, 1991), 160; Wiebe, *The Search for Order*; Marten, *Childhood and Child Welfare in the Progressive Era*, 2–3.

51. "80 Children to Spend Two Weeks at Girls' Camp," *Hammond (IN) Times*, August 3, 1937; "Fresh Air Children Leave Local Hosts," *Hagerstown (MD) Morning Herald*, August 3, 1945.

52. C. A. Holton, "Camp Endeavor, Belair, MD," in *Eleventh Annual Report of the Children's Fresh Air Society of Baltimore City* (Baltimore, MD: Children's Fresh Air Society, 1901), 15.

53. Mintz, *Huck's Raft*, 219.

54. Marta Gutman and Ning De Coninck-Smith, "Introduction: Good to Think with—History, Space, and Modern Childhood," in *Designing Modern Childhoods: History, Space, and the Material Culture of Children*, ed. Marta Gutman and Ning De Coninck-Smith (Newark, NJ: Rutgers University Press, 2008), 1–19.

55. "150 Kiddies Frolic in Park at Fund Outing," *Lima (OH) News*, July 15, 1937.

56. "Fresh Air Kiddies Will Be Cared for This Year," *Daily Messenger* (Canandaigua, NY), June 13, 1934.

57. Rebecca Stiles Onion, "Picturing Nature and Childhood at the American Museum of Natural History and the Brooklyn Children's Museum, 1899–1930," *Journal of the History of Childood and Youth* 4, no. 3 (2011): 434–69.

58. "City Children in the Country," *American Citizen* (Kansas City, KS), February 3, 1899.

59. "Fresh Air Work Humor," *Fitchburg (MA) Daily Sentinel*, July 27, 1907.

60. "32 New York City Children Arrive for Farm Holiday," *Syracuse Herald*, July 17, 1935.

61. "12 Tenement Children Here: Brought from New York Slums for Vacation in Frederick County," *Frederick (MD) Post*, July 17, 1934.

62. Herbert Allan, "Harlem Runs Night (and Day) Club for Youngsters in Own Backyard," 1935, in NYHS, Children's Aid Society Collection, volume 489, 1935–1941, and addendum 1929–1937; "They Won't Forget This Day: Hudson Trip Spells Joy," *Evening Journal and American* (New York, NY), July 24, 1937.

63. "Fresh Air Fund Representative Arrives," *Portsmouth (NH) Herald*, June 1, 1933; "Seek Home for Summer Camp for Poor Kiddies," *Chicago Defender*, February 4, 1928.

64. "Harlem Ready to Play Santa Role for Needy," *New York Amsterdam News*, December 20, 1933.

65. Isaac S. Field, "President's Report," in *Eleventh Annual Report of the Children's Fresh Air Society of Baltimore City* (Baltimore, MD: 1901), 7–10; C. Arthur Pearson, "Help Wanted for Children: An Appeal for the English Fresh Air Fund," *Gleaner* (Kingston, Jamaica), June 18, 1906; Pearson, "An Old Country Appeal."

66. Guarneri, "Changing Strategies for Child Welfare."

67. Vanderbeck, "Inner-City Children, Country Summers."

68. All of the following sources refer only to girls as re-invited guests: "Fourteen Will Have Vacation from Big City," *Daily Messenger* (Canandaigua, NY), August 1, 1932; "Homes Opened to Youngsters: 71 Fresh Air Kiddies Arrive for Vacation in Ontario County," *Daily Messenger* (Canandaigua, NY), July 27, 1933; "Appeals Made for Children," *Daily Messenger* (Canandaigua, NY), July 12, 1935; "14 Children to Arrive Tuesday," *Daily Messenger* (Canandaigua, NY), July 25, 1935.

69. "Fresh Air Children Return to Homes," *Newport (RI) Mercury and Weekly News*, August 5, 1932; "12 Tenement Children Here."

70. "12 Tenement Children Here."

71. "Blue Coats Will Be in Charge of Outing for 200 Boys on Thursday," *Lima (OH) News*, July 26, 1937.

72. "Brooklyn Notes," *Chicago Defender*, August 7, 1926.

73. "Boys' Camp Registration Now on," *Chicago Defender*, June 28, 1919.

74. "League Youths Back from Camp," *New York Amsterdam News*, September 17, 1938.

75. Steven L. Schlossman, "G. Stanley Hall and the Boys' Club: Conservative Applications of Recapitulation Theory," *Journal of the History of the Behavioral Sciences* 9, no. 2 (1973): 140–47.

76. Van Slyck, *A Manufactured Wilderness*, 8–9.

77. Gail Bederman, *Manliness & Civilization: A Cultural History of Gender and Race in the United States, 1880–1917* (Chicago: University of Chicago Press, 1995), 106; Thomas Fallace, "Recapitulation Theory and the New Education: Race, Culture, Imperialism, and Pedagogy, 1894–1916," *Curriculum Inquiry* 42, no. 4 (2012): 510–33.

78. Pamela Riney-Kehrberg, *The Nature of Childhood: An Environmental History of Growing up in America since 1865* (Lawrence: University Press of Kansas, 2014), 74.

79. Van Slyck, *A Manufactured Wilderness*, xxiii, xxiv.

80. Glassberg, "Restoring a 'Forgotten Childhood.'"

81. Van Slyck, *A Manufactured Wilderness*, 99.

82. "Negro Children in New York," *Nation*, May 25, 1933.

83. S. R. Briggs, *Dot: A Story of the Fresh Air Fund* (Toronto, Ontario: Toronto Willard Tract Depository, 1883), 13.

84. Vanderbeck, "Inner-City Children, Country Summers."

85. Field, "President's Report," 8.

86. Lulu Johnson, "Fresh Air Fund," *Denton (MD) Journal*, September 19, 1908.

87. "The Thrill of a Lifetime," *Oneonta (NY) Star*, July 10, 1924.

88. Evan Berry, *Devoted to Nature: The Religious Roots of American Environmentalism* (Oakland: University of California Press, 2015), 2–3, 5, 21.

89. Marten, *Childhood and Child Welfare in the Progressive Era*, 4.

90. Kusmer, "The Functions of Organized Charity in the Progressive Era."

91. Leslie Paris, *Children's Nature: The Rise of the American Summer Camp* (New York: New York University Press, 2008), 9; Onion, "Picturing Nature and Childhood."

92. Briggs, *Dot*, 13.

93. Epes W. Sargent, "Perkins' Fresh Air Fund," *Daily Northwestern* (Oshkosh, WI), June 29, 1904; Johnson, "Fresh Air Fund"; "Fresh Air Fund Needs More Money," *Afro-American* (Baltimore), July 17, 1909; "Fresh Air Funds Glorious Career," *Lincoln (NE) Evening News*, December 27, 1917.

94. "Club Arranges Card Tourney," *New York Amsterdam News*, June 22, 1935.

95. David Nasaw, *Children of the City: At Work and at Play* (New York: Anchor, 1985), 9.

96. Christine Stansell, *City of Women: Sex and Class in New York, 1789–1860* (New York: Knopf, 1986), 10.

97. Paul S. Boyer, *Urban Masses and Moral Order in America, 1820–1920* (Cambridge, MA: Harvard University Press, 1978), 240; Marten, *Childhood and Child Welfare in the Progressive Era*, 3.

98. "The Thrill of a Lifetime."

99. Van Slyck, *A Manufactured Wilderness*, xxiii.

100. Kenneth T. Jackson, *Crabgrass Frontier: The Suburbanization of the United States* (New York: Oxford University Press, 1985), 181.

101. "Seeks La Guardia Aid for Children's Camp," *New York Amsterdam News*, February 2, 1935.

102. Lloyd Burgess Sharp, *Education and the Summer Camp: An Experiment* (New York: Teacher's College, Columbia University, 1930), 7–8.

103. "The Tribune Fresh-Air Fund Society: Articles of Incorporation Filed with the Secretary of State at Albany," *New York Herald Tribune*, December 13, 1888; Nasaw, *Andrew Carnegie* (New York: Penguin, 2007), 292–93.

104. Stuart M. Blumin, *The Emergence of the Middle Class: Social Experience in the American City, 1760–1900* (New York: Cambridge University Press, 1989).

105. Vanderbeck, "Inner-City Children, Country Summers."

106. Ufford, *Fresh Air Charity in the United States*, 50.

107. Ibid.

108. "Will Help the Kiddies: Rotary Club Back Movement to Secure Hosts for Tribune Fresh Air Fund Children—When a Fellow Needs a Friend," *Oneonta (NY) Star*, July 22, 1922; "Rotarians Seek Homes Here for Underprivileged Children of N.Y.," *Gettysburg (PA) Times*, July 7, 1925; "Will Seek Homes for N.Y. Children in This County: Lions Club Fostering Plan to Give Youngsters Fresh Air Outing," *Frederick (MD) Post*, July 24, 1925; "Plan Vacation for Children: 10 Applications Received for New York Fresh Air Kiddies," *Daily Messenger* (Canandaigua, NY), June 21, 1934; "Chairman of Group Named," *Daily Messenger* (Canandaigua, NY), May 20, 1937.

109. Paris, *Children's Nature*, 123; Mrs. Clayton Shaub, "An Unfinished Story," *Missionary Messenger*, June 1965, 14–15; "2 Boys Go to Camp and Keep 6 Puppies," *New York Times*, August 21, 1937.

110. "The World's Healthiest Kids—on the Sidewalks of New York!" *Sunday Mirror Magazine*, 1936.

111. "Child Convalescents Go to the Country: Where It's Quiet and Pleasant with Fresh Air," *New York Sun*, August 22, 1937.

112. Van Slyck, *A Manufactured Wilderness*, 45.

113. Marten, *Childhood and Child Welfare in the Progressive Era*, 14.

114. Eleanor I. Lovett, "One Summer's Work" ([reprinted from *Sunday Afternoon*], 1878), 7.

115. "Your Money Will Send Undernourished Kiddies to This Fresh Air Home," *Des Moines News*, June 20, 1913.

116. Lovett, "One Summer's Work"; F. R. Chandler, *The Story of Lake Geneva or, Summer Homes for City People* (Lake Geneva, WI: Lake Geneva Villa Association, 1898); Sargent, "Perkins' Fresh Air Fund"; "Your Money Will Send Undernourished Kiddies to This Fresh Air Home"; "Fresh Air Fund for Kiddies," *Chicago Defender*, June 27, 1925; "Camp Algonquin Putting Zip into Underfed Bodies," *Chicago Daily Tribune*, June 23, 1935.

117. Magnuson, *Salvation in the Slums*, 66.

118. Deborah Valenze, *Milk: A Local and Global History* (New Haven, CT: Yale University Press, 2011), 253.

119. C. Arthur Pearson, "The Fresh Air Fund," *Manitoba Free Press* (Winnipeg), March 31, 1909.

120. William Allen, "Fresh Air Work," *Annals of the American Academy of Political and Social Science* 23 (1904): 464–71; Johnson, "Fresh Air Fund"; Hynd-Lindsay, "A Memorial Address on the Life and Work of Rev. Willard Parsons"; "Fresh Air for Mothers," *Waukesha (WI) Daily Freeman*, August 4, 1922; "Mission to Hold Fund Campaign," *Charleston (WV) Gazette*, June 4, 1924; Altair, "Sunshine for the Slums."

121. Briggs, *Dot*, 21.

122. Untitled news item, *Freeman* (Indianapolis), August 5, 1905.

123. Hynd-Lindsay, "A Memorial Address on the Life and Work of Rev. Willard Parsons."

124. Briggs, *Dot*, 2; Holt, *The Orphan Trains*, 15.

125. Briggs, *Dot*, 21; Hynd-Lindsay, "A Memorial Address on the Life and Work of Rev. Willard Parsons."

126. "Fresh Air Fund Representative Arrives"; "Camp Algonquin Putting Zip into Underfed Bodies"; Virginia Gardner, "Algonquin Set for Season of Happy Outings," *Chicago Daily Tribune*, June 16, 1937.

127. "Plan Vacation for Children"; "Fresh Air Kiddies Will Be Cared for This Year."

128. C. A. Holton, "Camp Endeavor—Belair, Md," in *Eleventh Annual Report of the Children's Fresh Air Society of Baltimore City* (Baltimore, MD: 1901), 12–17.

129. "Salvation Army to Open in $20,000 Drive: City Canvass for Fresh Air Camp Fund Will Be Started Today," *Indianapolis Star*, May 7, 1923; Paris, *Children's Nature*, 184–85.

130. Gardner, "Algonquin Set for Season of Happy Outings," 17.

131. Dunn, "Analysis of the Effectiveness of the Friendly Town Publicity Program," 11–12.

132. "Fresh Air Work Humor."

133. "Plan Vacation for Children."

134. Ibid.

135. "The Thrill of a Lifetime."

136. Hynd-Lindsay, "A Memorial Address on the Life and Work of Rev. Willard Parsons."

137. Viviana A. Zelizer, *Pricing the Priceless Child: The Changing Social Value of Children* (New York: Basic Books, 1985), 10; "Harlem Ready to Play Santa Role for Needy," *New York Amsterdam News*, December 20, 1933; Sandra M. O'Donnell, "The Care of Dependent African-American Children in Chicago: The Struggle between Black Self-Help and Professionalism," *Journal of Social History* 27, no. 4 (1994): 763–76; "Harlem Ready to Play Santa Role for Needy."

138. Sadie Van Veen, "Give City Kids a Break," *N.Y.C. Daily Worker*, August 15, 1937.

2. CHURCH, CONCRETE, POND

1. Childhood historian Howard Chudacoff notes that children have historically created play spaces in three settings: nature, public space, and the home. Notably, these three spaces roughly correspond to this chapter's three themes: nature as found in ponds, public space as found in cities, and church instruction in the home. See Howard P. Chudacoff, *Children at Play: An American History* (New York: New York University Press, 2007), 4.

2. Lloyd deMause, "The Evolution of Childhood," in *The History of Childhood*, ed. Lloyd deMause (New York: Psychohistory Press, 1974), 1–73.

3. Colin Heywood, *A History of Childhood: Children and Childhood in the West from Medieval to Modern Times* (Cambridge: Polity, 2002), 33.

4. Keith Graber Miller, "Complex Innocence, Obligatory Nurturance, and Parental Vigilance: 'The Child' in the Work of Menno Simons," in *The Child in Christian Thought*, ed. Marcia J. Bunge (Grand Rapids, MI: W.B. Eerdmans, 2000), 194–226.

5. Henry Louis Gates Jr., "(Annotations)," in *The Annotated Uncle Tom's Cabin*, ed. Henry Louis Gates Jr. (New York: W.W. Norton, 2007); Stuart C. Aitken, *Geographies of Young People: The Morally Contested Spaces of Identity*, ed. Tracey Skelton and Gill Valentine (New York: Routledge, 2001), 31.

6. John Wall, "Fatherhood, Childism, and the Creation of Society," *Journal of the American Academy of Religion* 75, no. 1 (2007): 52–76.

7. Linda A. Pollock, *Forgotten Children: Parent-Child Relations from 1500 to 1900* (Cambridge University Press, 1984), 140; Bonnie Miller-McLemore, "Whither the Children? Childhood in Religious Education," *Journal of Religion* 86, no. 4 (2006): 635–57; John R. Gillis, "Epilogue: The Islanding of Children—Reshaping the Mythical Landscapes of Childhood," in *Designing Modern Childhoods: History, Space, and the Material Culture of Children*, ed. Marta Gutman and Ning De Coninck-Smith (Newark, NJ: Rutgers University Press, 2008), 316–30; Aitken, *Geographies of Young People*, 33.

8. Sara M. Keily to Sylvia Leshowitz, July 21, 1948, CUA, USAR, 1896–1995 MS#1149, Series VII: Programs and Services, box 53, folder 5: "Camp-Children's Records (D–E), 1945–57."

9. Norman G. Shenk to Lancaster Conference Mission Superintendents, June 27, 1956, EMM Record Room, folder: "MCVP—1956."

10. Margie Middleton and Ruth Y. Wenger, "Fresh Air Reminiscences," *Missionary Messenger*, July 1977, 12–13, 21; Luis Diaz, New York, NY, telephone interview by the author, May 4, 2010; Cindy Vanderkodde, Grand Rapids, MI, telephone interview by the author, March 7, 2010.

11. "Fresh Air Kids to Vacation Here This Year," *Wellsboro (PA) Gazette*, June 7, 1951.

12. Richard F. Crandell, ed., *The Frog Log and Other Stories about Children* (New York: Herald Tribune Fresh Air Fund, 1962), 23; "Sermon Inspired Fresh Air Fund," *New York Amsterdam News*, June 24, 1967.

13. Representative accounts referring to Parsons include "Tablet to Willard Parsons Unveiled at Franklin," *Middletown (NY) Daily Times-Press*, September 26, 1912; "Fresh Air Funds Glorious Career," *Lincoln (NE) Evening News*, December 27, 1917; "Fresh Air Fund: Rev. Dr. H. L. G. Keiffer Refers to Vacation of Tenement Children," *Frederick (MD) Post*, June 10, 1929; Lloyd Burgess Sharp, *Education and the Summer Camp: An Experiment* (New York: Teacher's College, Columbia University, 1930); "Franklin Native Originated Idea of Rural Vacations for Fresh Airs: Rev. Parsons Memorialized for Program," *Oneonta (NY) Star*, July 29, 1949; "District Homes Needed for Fresh Air Children," *Daily News* (Huntingdon and Mount Union, PA), May 18, 1959; John Kord Lagemann, "Something Special in Vacations: A *Reader's Digest* Reprint," *Reader's Digest*, June 1963; Linda Vosburgh, "Religion, 'Street' Meet in 'Fresh Air,'" *Sunday Herald* (Chicago), September 16, 1979.

14. David Nasaw, *Children of the City: At Work and at Play* (New York: Anchor, 1985), 138–43; Norris Magnuson, *Salvation in the Slums: Evangelical Social Work, 1865–1920* (Metchuen, NJ: Scarecrow Press, 1977).

15. Julia Guarneri, "Changing Strategies for Child Welfare, Enduring Beliefs about Childhood: The Fresh Air Fund, 1877–1926," *Journal of the Gilded Age and Progressive Era* 11, no. 1 (2012): 27–70.

16. Memorandum, "A Recreational and Educational Project through Churches to Help Meet Youth Needs in Brooklyn," March 1945, 2–3, PNHA, NCC, Home Missions Council of North America, 1903–1951, RG26, box 16, folder 11: "Negro Work Brooklyn Project, March 1945–June 1949."

17. Carol Van Horn, "The Inner City: Elective in Understanding," *Presbyterian Life*, October 15, 1963, 25–27.

18. Fresh Air programs also made sure that religious instruction was done by adherents. For example, promotional materials from Camp Nathan Hale, a New York settlement house Fresh Air retreat, indicated that counselors should be persons "of religious convictions": Memorandum, "Union Settlement Camp Nathan Hale Counselor's Informant," May 23, 1944, CUA, USAR, 1896–1995 MS#1149, Series VII: Programs and Services, box 40, folder 11: "Camp-Film, 1944–49."

19. "Boro to Host 20 Fresh Air Fund Children," *Wellsboro (PA) Gazette*, May 27, 1948; "Yates to Invite City Children for Vacation," *Chronicle-Express* (Penn Yan, NY), May 26, 1949; "Chinatown Youngsters to Come Here," *Cumberland (MD) Sunday Times*, May 31, 1959; George Cornell, "Get Acquainted Process New Phase of Relationship of Negroes, Whites," *Post-Crescent* (Appleton, WI), August 9, 1965; Joan Monaco, "City Kids Get Chance for Some Friendly Adventures," *Lowell (MA) Sunday*, August 22, 1971.

20. Jo Cullson, "Fire Threatens 'Friendly Town' Visit," *Coshocton (OH) Tribune*, June 16, 1968.

21. "Revive Friendly Town Program," *Lowell (MA) Sunday*, April 22, 1966; "100 Inner City Kids to Visit in Glen Ellyn," *Chicago Tribune*, April 25, 1966; "Children from Waterloo in Ames Program," *Waterloo (IA) Sunday Courier*, June 27, 1971.

22. "June Means Vacation to City Children Too," *Olean (NY) Times Herald*, June 11, 1948.

23. "Wellsboro Is Friendly Town: Twenty Children to Be Invited Here for Two Weeks," *Wellsboro (PA) Agitator*, May 26, 1948; "Kingston Included as Friendly Town to Aid Children," *Kingston (NY) Daily Freeman*, June 8, 1949; "Will Hear of Air Plan," *Troy (NY) Record*, June 12, 1969.

24. Memorandum, "Herald Tribune Fresh Air Fund 81st Year Annual Report," 1957, LOC, PRF D224, HRR, file 12567: "The Fresh Air Fund."

25. Elizabeth Douvan, "The Age of Narcissism, 1963–1982," in *American Childhood: A Research Guide and Historical Handbook*, ed. Joseph M. Hawes and N. Ray Hiner (Westport, CT: Greenwood, 1985), 587–617.

26. Walter I. Trattner, *From Poor Law to Welfare State: A History of Social Welfare in America* (New York: The Free Press, 1984), 257.

27. Shirley Maye Tillotson, *Contributing Citizens: Modern Charitable Fundraising and the Making of the Welfare State, 1920–66* (Vancouver: UBC Press, 2008), 7; Alice O'Connor, "Neither Charity nor Relief: The War on Poverty and the Effort to Redefine the Basis of Social Provision," in *With Us Always: A History of Private Charity and Public Welfare*, ed. Donald T. Critchlow and Charles H. Parker (New York: Rowman & Littlefield, 1998), 191–210.

28. "Friendly Town Program in This Area Explained," *Derrick* (Oil City, PA), April 27, 1970.

29. "Bring Children to New Homes," *Chicago Tribune*, July 14, 1963; "1,100 Deprived Children Go on Trip Today," *Chicago Tribune*, July 16, 1966.

30. "Storefront Churches Organize for Youth," *New York Amsterdam News*, August 1, 1970, 31.

31. "Camping Is Fun," *Call and Post* (Cleveland, OH), July 3, 1971.

32. Pete Mekeel, "Local Mennonite Missionaries Run 5 Churches in Slums of N.Y.," *New Era* (Lancaster, PA), May 25, 1976; Paul N. Kraybill to John H. Garber, June 25, 1952, EMM Record Room, folder: "F–J."

33. Bob Zanic, "Friendly Town Works 2 Ways," *Palatine (IL) Herald*, June 10, 1969.

34. "More Hosts Needed to Keep Our Community on 'Friendly List,'" *Hagerstown (MD) Daily Mail*, June 7, 1946.

35. "Martinsburg," *Altoona (PA) Mirror*, June 16, 1955.

36. Jo McMeen, "Along the Juniata: Wanted: Homes for Fresh Air Kids," *Daily News* (Huntingdon and Mount Union, PA), April 18, 1962.

37. "In Brief . . . ," *Berkshire Eagle* (Pittsfield, MA), June 6, 1975.

38. "Friendly Town Program Seeks Homes for Youths," *Evening Observer* (Dunkirk, NY), May 4, 1965; "Chicago Core Children Visiting at Whitehall," *Eau-Claire (WI) Leader*, July 20, 1967; Eleanor Charles, "Apathy Endangers Fresh Air Fund," *New York Times*, May 20, 1979.

39. Edna K. Wenger, "Children Are People Too," *Missionary Messenger*, March 9, 1941, 2.

40. Memorandum, "Through Decisive Years: New York Protestant Episcopal City Mission Society One-Hundred-Thirtieth Anniversary Report 1831–1961," 1961, EDNY, Episcopal Missional Society Mission News 1923–1976: "Misc. loose reports & pamphlets."

41. "Friendly Town Time Once Again in the Oneonta Area," *Oneonta (NY) Star*, May 25, 1955.

42. Lacey Fosburgh, "Fresh Air Homes for Boys Needed," *New York Times*, June 27, 1971.

43. Lee Edwards, "All Their World Is Asphalt and Farms Are Only in Stories," *Oneonta (NY) Star*, July 12, 1971.

44. "Rotary Backs Friendly Town," *Wellsboro (PA) Agitator*, May 11, 1949.

45. "Churches Will Sponsor Friendly Town Program," *Fitchburg (MA) Sentinel*, April 30, 1966.

46. "1,000 Inner-City Youths to Vacation in Suburbs," *Chicago Tribune*, June 2, 1968.

47. Joan Skidmore, "Fresh Air Fund: Give a Child a Chance," *Delaware County Daily Times* (Chester, PA), June 7, 1974.

48. "New York Youngster Adjusts Rapidly to Life in the Country," *Daily News-Record* (Harrisonburg, VA), August 2, 1973; Leslie Maitland, "Rural Vacations a Joy to Children," *New York Times*, July 27, 1975.

49. Johanna M. Lindlof et al., *Adventures in Camping* (New York: Johanna M. Lindlof Camp Committee for Public School Children, 1943), 18; Memorandum, "Union Settlement Camp Nathan Hale Counselor's Informant"; Memorandum, "Camp Manakiki," 1953, ELAA, UMN, United Way of Minneapolis records (SW 70), box 74, folder 1: "Camps-Study 1953, 1958"; Memorandum, "Herald Tribune Fresh Air Fund Annual Report on Camping," 1954, LOC, PRF D223, HRR, file 12560: "The Fresh Air Fund, 1953–54"; Memorandum, "Camp Information for Parents," [n.d.], ELAA, UMN, United Way of Minneapolis records (SW 70), box 72, folder 5: "Camps General 1953–55."

50. "Friendly Town Project Set Again by Fredonians," *Dunkirk (NY) Evening Observer*, April 19, 1956; "17 Fresh Air Visitors Arrive and Get Acquainted in County," *Lock Haven (PA) Express*, July 1, 1958; Anna Buckwalter, "Johnny Says," *What's in the Air*, Spring 1965; Jo Cullson, "52 Cleveland Youngsters Will Find Coshocton 'Friendly Town,'" *Coshocton (OH) Tribune*, June 12, 1968; "Narrow World Big Threat to 'Fresh Air' Children," *Huntingdon (PA) Daily News*, May 19, 1973; Maitland, "Rural Vacations a Joy to Children"; Janice Batts, "Discovering Me," http://themommastrikesback.blogspot.com.

51. "Lancaster Helps Needy Children," *New York Times*, June 13, 1976; Maitland, "Rural Vacations a Joy to Children."

52. "Narrow World Big Threat to 'Fresh Air' Children"; "New York Youngster Adjusts Rapidly to Life in the Country"; Rachel [no surname listed in source] to Alice Trissel, October 28, 1975, LVA, FAFR, 1949–1999, accession number 36407, box 21, folder 1: "Correspondence—FAF children—1959–1984."

53. "Narrow World Big Threat to 'Fresh Air' Children."

54. Sara Ann Freed, "Mennonites in the Fresh Air Program: An Early Expression of the Mennonite Social Conscience" (research paper, Goshen College, 1967), 14.

55. J. Lester Brubaker, "Editorial," *Missionary Messenger*, October 1950, 3.

56. Orlo Kaufman to Erwin Krehbiel, April 28, 1959, MLABC: MLA.VII.R GC Voluntary Service, Series 11 Gulfport VS Unit, box 1, folder 28: "Correspondence—misc."

57. John H. Kraybill, "The Mission Field Brought to You," *Missionary Messenger*, July 1956, 5.

58. Barbara L. Little, "Helps New York City Children to a Vacation in the Country," *Lancaster (PA) Intelligencer-Journal*, July 31, 1958; Frederick Howell Lewis, "Tribute to Fresh-Air Worker," *Daily Intelligencer Journal* (Lancaster, PA), January 16, 1959.

59. "Lancaster Holds Film Premier," *What's in the Air*, fall 1964.

60. Fred W. Miller, "What about Fresh Air Host Families," *Valley Mennonite Messenger*, July 7, 1966; Ronald L. Trissel, "The Fresh Air Child's Urban Influence on Rural Shenandoah and Rockingham County" (term paper, Eastern Mennonite College, 1967), 4–5; Renee M. Savits, "A Guide to the Fresh Air Fund Records, 1949–1999" (Richmond, VA: Library of Virginia, 2002); Laurel Wissinger, "Fields and Dreams," *Curio* 14, no. 1 (1991): 40–42.

61. "Fresh Idea in '77 Becomes Fun Fund for City Children," *New York Times*, May 23, 1976; Jennifer Dunning, "Last Day to Register for Fresh Air Fund Camp Is a Big Day for Little Ones," *New York Times*, June 18, 1978.

62. Unattributed article clipping, June 1976; Jane Blanksteen, "A Refreshing Experience," *New York Times*, June 19, 1977; "Lancaster Helps Needy Children."

63. "Deputy Police Chief Aids Fresh Air Fund," *New York Times*, May 15, 1977; "12,000 Families Aid the Fresh Air Fund," *New York Times*, June 25, 1978.

64. Julia Spicher Kasdorf, "'Why We Fear the Amish': Whiter Than White Figures in Contemporary American Poetry," in *The Amish and the Media*, ed. Diane Zimmerman Umble and David Weaver-Zercher (Baltimore: Johns Hopkins Press, 2008), 67–90.

65. Ami Regier, "Revising the Plainness of Whiteness," *Mennonite Life* 57, no. 2 (2002); Kasdorf, "Why We Fear the Amish," 69.

66. Memorandum, "Host Parents Summary—1960," [1], MLABC: MLA.VII.R GC Voluntary Service, Series 11, Gulfport VS Unit, box 4, folder 122: "Fresh Air, 1960."

67. Middleton and Wenger, "Fresh Air Reminiscences."

68. Memorandum, "Host Parents Summary—1960."

69. "Lancaster Helps Needy Children."

70. Lawrence Wright, *City Children, Country Summer* (New York: Scribner, 1979), 80.

71. Middleton and Wenger, "Fresh Air Reminiscences."

72. Norman G. Shenk, Salunga, PA, telephone interview by the author, March 22, 2005; Peggy Curry, Harrisonburg, VA, interview by the author, March 29, 2005; Thomas W. Brock, Harrisonburg, VA, telephone interview by the author, May 17, 2005.

73. Janice Batts, Iowa City, IA, telephone interview by the author, February 15, 2012; Paul N. Kraybill to Robert R. Bender, M.D., February 13, 1957, EMM Record Room, folder: "Mission Children's Visitation Program—1957."

74. Laurie Johnston, "Fresh Air Fund Launches Drive," *New York Times*, May 14, 1972.

75. Ari L. Goldman, "Fresh Air: A Together Atmosphere," *New York Times*, June 27, 1976.

76. For a few examples of the dozens of references to children getting homesick, see: "7 Fresh Air Children Write of Newport Visit," *Newport (RI) News*, January 19, 1950; "Fresh Air Girl Wants Sister Here," *Oneonta (NY) Star*, June 4, 1954; Bill Draves Jr., "Inner-City Children from Chicago Bring Surprises to 'Friendly Town' Parents," *Commonwealth Reporter* (Fond du Lac, WI), 1968; Monaco, "City Kids Get Chance for Some Friendly Adventures"; Lynne Ames, "The Fresh Air Fund: Summers of Sharing," *New York Times*, May 20, 1979.

77. "21 More Fresh Air Fund Children Arrive," *Salisbury (MD) Times*, July 28, 1957.

78. Chudacoff, *Children at Play*, 107; Maude Hines, "Playing with Children: What the 'Child' Is Doing in American Studies," *American Quarterly* 61, no. 1 (2009): 151–61.

79. Abigail A. Van Slyck, *A Manufactured Wilderness: Summer Camps and the Shaping of American Youth, 1890–1960* (Minneapolis: University of Minnesota Press, 2006), 49; Peter J. Schmitt, *Back to Nature: The Arcadian Myth in Urban America* (New York: Oxford University Press, 1969), xvi.

80. Robert A. Orsi, "Introduction: Crossing the City Line," in *Gods of the City: Religion and the American Urban Landscape*, ed. Robert A. Orsi (Bloomington: Indiana University Press, 1999), 1–78.

81. Guarneri, "Changing Strategies for Child Welfare, Enduring Beliefs about Childhood."

82. Orsi, "Introduction: Crossing the City Line," 11.

83. "Friendly Town Program in This Area Explained"; Cornell, "Get Acquainted Process New Phase of Relationship of Negroes, Whites." The only exception I can find to the urban origination pattern in the Fresh Air movement is the program run by General Conference Mennonites that brought children from the relatively small town of Gulfport, Mississippi, to rural towns in Kansas, South Dakota, and Michigan. Interestingly, the originators of the Gulfport program based their initiative on a Mennonite program that was centered in Chicago. In this instance the Gulfport administrator substituted racial idioms for urban ones in describing the program. See Delton Franz to Orlo Kaufman, February 1, 1960, MLABC: MLA.VII.R GC Voluntary Service, Series 11 Gulfport VS Unit, box 1, folder 4: "Correspondence—General Conf. 1960"; Orlo Kaufman, "A New Venture," *Gulfbreeze*, July–August, 1960, 1.

84. "Fresh Air Kids to Vacation Here This Year"; "Fresh Air Kids," *Evening Banner* (Bennington, VT), July 6, 1955; "Kiwanis Club Sponsors Friendly Town Program," *Daily News* (Huntingdon and Mount Union, PA), June 14, 1954; "Ticket to Happiness," *New York Times*, May 20, 1973; "Funding Fresh Air," *New York Times*, July 4, 1969; ". . . And a Greater Need," *New York Times*, June 1, 1975; "Summer in the City? No Fun!" *Daily News* (Huntingdon, Mount Union, and Saxton, PA) *News*, May 12, 1978.

85. "'Friendly Town' Needs 32 Homes," *Buffalo Grove (IL) Herald*, July 7, 1970; "Tribune Fresh Air Fund," *Kingston (NY) Daily Freeman*, June 9, 1949; "Their Yard Is Concrete," *Oneonta (NY) Star*, May 14, 1953.

86. Shelby M. Howatt, "From Concrete to Country," *Bulletin*, May 1960, 4–6, EPNY, Episcopal Missional Society, Publications et al., 1930s–1970s; James M. Markham, "Hunts Point Youths Draw Gang Battle Lines," *New York Times*, September 2, 1971; "Seek Families for Friendly Town Program," *Rock Valley (IA) Bee*, July 9, 1975.

87. Howatt, "From Concrete to Country"; "Wide-Open Spaces," *Aiken (SC) Standard and Review*, October 14, 1964; "Mrs. Motley Offers Her Tribute to Fresh Air's Friendly Towns," *New York Herald Tribune*, February 18, 1966; "A Fresh Air Child, Now 30, Returns to Settle in His 'Friendly Town,'" *New York Times*, July 23, 1978; Jerry Kelly, "Hosts Are Sought for Fresh Air Vacationists," *Salisbury (MD) Times*, May 20, 1959; "City Youngsters Will Need Homes," *Hagerstown (MD) Morning Herald*, May 29, 1945; Crandell, ed., *The*

Frog Log and Other Stories about Children; "Summer Camping Lures Young of All Ages," *Episcopal New Yorker,* May 1969.

88. "Read Story of Fresh Air Fund—Then Be Host to City Youngsters," *Huntingdon (PA) Daily News,* June 21, 1945; "Your Help Is Needed for Fresh Air Vacations," *Portsmouth (NH) Herald,* July 29, 1954.

89. Memorandum, "Fresh Air Fund's Newest Unit, Camp Hayden for Boys, Joins Group at Sharpe Reservation," July 6, 1962, copied from the CCAH, UTA; "A Special Appeal to Depression Babies Who Made Good," *Herald Tribune Fresh Air Fund,* 1962.

90. Trissel, "The Fresh Air Child's Urban Influence on Rural Shenandhoah and Rockingham County," 2.

91. Witold Rybczynski, *City Life: Urban Expectations in the New World* (New York: Scribner, 1995), 160–61.

92. Howard P. Chudacoff and Judith E. Smith, *The Evolution of American Urban Society* (Upper Saddle River, NJ: Prentice Hall, 2000), 268–69.

93. Rybczynski, *City Life,* 166; Katharine G. Bristol, "The Pruitt-Igoe Myth," in *American Architectural History: A Contemporary Reader,* ed. Keith L. Eggener (New York: Routledge, 2004), 352–64.

94. "Everybody Wins," *New York Amsterdam News,* June 21, 1952; Memorandum by Frederick H. Lewis, "Executive Director's Annual Report to the Board of Directors, for the Fiscal Year 1963–1964," 1964, LOC, PRF D225, HRR, file 12572: "The Fresh Air Fund 1965"; "'Poor Kid,'" *Tyrone (PA) Daily Herald,* May 28, 1974.

95. Leo J. Heffernan, "By Bus to a New World" (New York: Union Settlement Association, 1944).

96. Bruce Kenrick, *Come Out the Wilderness: The Story of East Harlem Protestant Parish* (New York: Harper and Brothers, 1962), 70.

97. Nathan Manning to Howard Kaplan, 1952, CUA, USAR, 1896–1995 MS#1149, Series VII: Programs and Services, box 41, folder 3: "Camp-Reports, 1948–53."

98. Lacey Fosburgh, "Fresh Air Fund's Children Dazzled by Rural Marvels," *New York Times,* July 4, 1971.

99. Stephen H. Goldstein, "Jacqueline's Back for Summer Fun," *Times Record* (Troy, NY), July 3, 1975.

100. Jane Blanksteen, "Summer Visitors from the City," *New York Times,* June 12, 1977; "A Fresh Air Child, Now 30, Returns to Settle in His 'Friendly Town,'" 31; Diaz interview.

101. Marjorie Miller, 1956, LVA, FAFR, 1949–1999, accession number 36407, box 19, folder 6: "Contest Entries—1956, Essays (Contest #2)."

102. Helen Busuttil Regenbogen, Bainbridge, NY, telephone interview by the author, March 10, 2010.

103. "Fund Pal Revisits Md. Site," *New York Herald Tribune,* September 13, 1966.

104. Anne Mancuso, "Boy from Brooklyn Is at Home in Croton," *New York Times,* May 14, 1978.

105. Diaz interview; Melody M. Pannell, Harrisonburg, VA, interview by the author, January 20, 2016.

106. Marjorie Miller, 1956.

107. Middleton and Wenger, "Fresh Air Reminiscences."

108. Darrell Michael Scott, *Contempt and Pity: Social Policy and the Image of the Damaged Black Psyche, 1880–1996* (Chapel Hill: University of North Carolina Press, 1997), xiii, 190–91; Edith Simonds, "Letter to a Suburban Church," *Presbyterian Life,* September 1, 1966, 19–21, 40; Lacey Fosburgh, "Director of the Fresh Air Appeal Retiring after 25 Years in Post," *New York Times,* August 1, 1971; Lynford Hershey to Leon Stauffer, July 18, 1971,

AMC—IV-21-4, box 1, MBM, Minority Ministries Council, Data Files #1, A–K, folder: "Education Program 1970–72, Lynford Hershey."

109. Memorandum by Ted Dubinsky, "Minutes of the 'Committee to Consider the Minority Group Male's Self-Image'—8/21/67," CUA, HGR MS#1465, Series III: Hudson Guild Files, box 13, folder 21: "Committee to Consider the Minority Group Male's Self-Image, 1967–1968"; Simonds, "Letter to a Suburban Church"; Paul E. Warfield, "The Whole Story," *Bennington (VT) Banner*, September 6, 1963.

110. "100 Inner City Kids to Visit in Glen Ellyn."

111. "Welcome Inner City Child," *Arlington Heights (IL) Herald*, August 17, 1971.

112. Fosburgh, "Director of the Fresh Air Appeal Retiring after 25 Years in Post."

113. Memorandum by Michael Phillips, "Report of the Fresh Air Fund Friendly Town Study Undertaken by the Long Range Planning Committee," April 1980, 8, LVA, FAFR, 1949–1999, accession number 36407, box 31, folder 2: "Reports, Friendly Town Study, 1979–1980."

114. Lena Williams, "Full of Fresh Air, They Return Home," *New York Times*, August 7, 1977.

115. Goldman, "Fresh Air: A Together Atmosphere."

116. "Friendly Town Is Set up by Pennsylvania Couple," *New York Times*, August 19, 1979.

117. "The Fresh Air Fund Focuses on Culture," *New York Times*, June 12, 1977.

118. (Untitled Photo of Two Boys—One White, One Black—in Relay Race in Playground of a School—Circa Mid-1970s) (Grosvenor Neighborhood House, [n.d.]), CUA, GNHR, 1916–1990s MS# 1433, Series IV: Photographs, folder 27643–27655: "Children Outdoors, 1960s–1970s."

119. "East Side Hikers Climb Stair Mountains . . . ," *PM's Weekly*, September 1, 1940.

120. Joe A. Pissarro, (Untitled Photo of Young African American Boys Walking Past Graffiti on Building Which Says Summer in the City Is Fun), NYCPL-SC: "Children, 13–487."

121. "Two Who Make Fresh Air Fund Campers Happy," *New York Times*, May 6, 1979.

122. "A Fresh Air Fund Vacation Delights a Child," *New York Times*, May 14, 1978; David Stewart Hudson, "Family Hosts Enjoyed 'Fresh Air' Visits, Too," *Daily News-Record* (Harrisonburg, VA), May 10, 1973.

123. "To Kids from Kids," *New York Amsterdam News*, May 27, 1978.

124. Memorandum by Agnes Louard, "Summer Day Camp—Report 1953," August 26, 1953, CUA, USAR, 1896–1995 MS#1149, Series VII: Programs and Services, box 41, folder 3: "Camp-Reports, 1948–53"; The Merry Mermaids, "The Merry Mermaids," *Day Camp News* 1957, 2, CUA, USAR, 1896–1995 MS#1149, Series VII: Programs and Services, box 42, folder 2: "Day Camp, 1955–62"; Freddy Mercer, "The Lions," *Day Camp News* 1957, 2, CUA, USAR, 1896–1995 MS#1149, Series VII: Programs and Services, box 42, folder 2: "Day Camp, 1955–62."

125. Mary Cole, *Summer in the City* (New York: P. J. Kenedy and Sons, 1968), 56.

126. Ibid., 56, 72, 96.

127. Chudacoff and Smith, *The Evolution of American Urban Society*, 289.

128. Frederick H. Lewis, "Time to Blow . . . Not to Pull in Our Horns: Welcoming Observations by Frederick H. Lewis, Executive Director of the Fresh Air Fund, at Opening of Friendly Town Planning Conference, February 16, 1970, Brotherhood-in-Action Building, New York City" (Washington, D.C., 1970), LOC, PRF D225, HRR, file 12576: "The Fresh Air Fund 1968–70."

129. Johnston, "Fresh Air Fund Launches Drive."

130. Chuck Austin, "The History of the Fresh Air Fund" (1981), C9–2, LVA, FAFR, 1949–1999, accession number 36407, box 22, folder 2: "Histories 1977."

131. "How Friendly Is This Country?" *Daily News* (Huntingdon, Saxton, and Mount Union, PA), June 7, 1979.

132. George J. Gordodensky, "Fresh Air Children, Co-Hope," *Daily News Record* (Harrisonburg, VA), April 12, 1979.

133. Gene Rondinaro, "A Change of Pace in the Sun," *New York Times*, June 3, 1979.

134. Robert M. Vanderbeck, "Inner-City Children, Country Summers: Narrating American Childhood and the Geographies of Whiteness," *Environment and Planning* 40, no. 5 (2008): 1132–50. A 2010 ad by the Fresh Air Fund in *Vanity Fair* magazine continued the theme by noting that children in the city were deprived of "a safe, fun summer." See "The Only Thing More Fleeting Than Summer Is Childhood," *Vanity Fair*, June 2010.

135. Thomas J. Sugrue, *Sweet Land of Liberty: The Forgotten Struggle for Civil Rights in the North* (New York: Random House, 2008), 351; Simon Wendt, "The Roots of Black Power? Armed Resistance and the Radicalization of the Civil Rights Movement," in *The Black Power Movement: Rethinking the Civil Rights-Black Power Era*, ed. Peniel E. Joseph (New York: Routledge, 2006), 145–65; Peniel E. Joseph, *Waiting 'Til the Midnight Hour: A Narrative History of Black Power in America* (New York: Holt Paperbacks, 2007), 289.

136. "Friendly Towns Play Host to the Fresh Air Needy," *New York Times*, July 8, 1979.

137. Linda Punch, "Friendly Town: A Family Affair," *Arlington Heights (IL) Herald*, August 20, 1971.

138. Jeff Wiltse, *Contested Waters: A Social History of Swimming Pools in America* (Chapel Hill: University of North Carolina Press, 2007), 2–5.

139. Ibid., 158.

140. Ibid., 182.

141. Ibid.

142. Ibid., 199–201.

143. Wilbert Marcellus Leonard II, *A Sociological Perspective of Sport* (Minneapolis, MN: Burgess Publishing Company, 1980), 173, 180; John J. Gnida, "Teaching 'Nature Versus Nurture': The Case of African-American Athletic Success," *Teaching Sociology* 23, no. 4 (1995): 389–95; David W. Hunter, "Race and Athletic Performance: A Physiological Review," in *African Americans in Sport*, ed. Gary A. Sailes (New Brunswick, NJ: Transaction Publishers, 1989), 85–101; Gary A. Sailes, "The African American Athlete: Social Myths and Stereotypes," in *African Americans in Sport*, 183–98.

144. Wiltse, *Contested Waters*, 141.

145. Ibid., 188.

146. Blanksteen, "A Refreshing Experience," 401.

147. Dee Wedemeyer, "Farm Plan Extends Fresh Air Program," *New York Times*, July 31, 1977.

148. Draves, "Inner-City Children from Chicago Bring Surprises to 'Friendly Town' Parents"; Glenda Adams, New York, NY, telephone interview by the author, March 28, 2010; "Fresh Air Fund Summer Offers Widened Outlook," *New York Times*, June 3, 1979; "Inquiring Photographer," *Evening Banner* (Bennington, VT), July 18, 1959; "Journey into Another World," *Call and Post* (Cleveland, OH), August 2, 1969.

149. Vanderkodde interview; Joseph Gibbons, Tallahassee, FL, telephone interview by the author, March 17, 2010.

150. "A Friendly Note—to Some of the Friendliest People in the World" (New York, 1953 [circa]), LOC, PRF D223, HRR, file 12560: "The Fresh Air Fund, 1953–54."

151. Kathleen Floyd, October 14, 1969, Mansucripts, Archives and Rare Books Division, NYCPL-SC, Robert & Anita Stein Papers, SCM 87–20, box 2, folder 19: "Summer Programs—1971, Proposals, Children's Letters, etc."

152. "Fund Camp Is Family Tradition for 2 Boys," *New York Times*, June 24, 1979.

153. Memorandum by Frederick H. Lewis, "Annual Report to the Board of Directors by the Executive Director of the Herald Tribune Fresh Air Fund," January 28, 1949, 16, LOC, PRF D222, HRR, file 12557: "The Fresh Air Fund, 1950–51."

154. "Camp Inquiry," *Camp Nathan Hale Echo*, August 12, 1948, 5, CUA, USAR, 1896–1995 MS#1149, Series VII: Programs and Services, box 41, folder 2: "Camp-Publications, 1948–49."

155. Memorandum by Ellen Marvin, "Brescia, Anthony, Age: 5," 1951, CUA, USAR, 1896–1995 MS#1149, Series VII: Programs and Services, box 53, folder 3, "Camp-Children's Records (A-B), 1945–57."

156. Wiltse, *Contested Waters*, 29, 34.

157. "Little Fresh Air Girl Won't Be Here but Her Brother Will," *Oneonta (NY) Star*, June 3, 1953.

158. Arlene Feinstein, "The Athlete's Feet," *Echo*, 1944, ELAA, UMN, HSSR (SW0058), Activities Reports, 1941, box 49, folder 3: "Camps and Camping—Echo Hill Farm, Newsletter—The Echo—1944"; Beverly Glasser, Harriet Gleich, and Ida Sokoloff, "Suggestion Box," *Echo*, 1944, 11, ELAA, UMN, HSSR (SW0058), Activities Reports, 1941, box 49, folder 3: "Camps and Camping—Echo Hill Farm, Newsletter—The Echo—1944"; Phyllis M. Palmer, *Living as Equals: How Three White Communities Struggled to Make Interracial Connections during the Civil Rights Era* (Nashville: Vanderbilt University Press, 2008), 230, 255–56, 278.

159. Lacey Fosburgh, "18,000 Plan on Fresh Air Vacations," *New York Times*, May 23, 1971.

160. "Fresh Air Fund Giving Children Country Holiday," *New York Herald Tribune*, November 22, 1966.

161. Lena Williams, "Disabled Enjoy Fresh Air Camp," *New York Times*, July 10, 1977.

162. "Fresh Air Fund Presses Appeal," *New York Times*, May 10, 1970.

163. Williams, "Disabled Enjoy Fresh Air Camp."

164. Memorandum, "Annual Report to the Board of Directors," 1951, 10, LOC, PRF, HRR, file 12558: "The Fresh Air Fund, 1951"; Memorandum by Ralph B. Dwinell, "Friendly Towns," 1962, LOC, PRF D224, HRR, file 12568: "The Fresh Air Fund"; Memorandum by Richard F. Crandell, "Report on the Death of Genevieve Turner, Fresh Air Child, 6, in Columbia Lake, Near Hale Eddy, Delaware County, New York, Sunday Afternoon, July 28, 1963," 1963, LOC, PRF D225, HRR, file 12569: "The Fresh Air Fund 1963"; Memorandum by Ralph B. Dwinell, "Friendly Town, Summer 1967," 1967, [2], NYCPL-BRARR, Series I—Grant Files, box 2, folder: "Fresh Air Fund 1962," Whitney North Seymour Papers, 1930–1983, box 114—Subject Files: "Fresh Air Fund, 1962–1983, January 1965–June 1967."

165. "Accidental Drowning," *Statistical Bulletin—Metropolitan Life* 53 (1972): 6–8.

166. Leanna Kauffman, 1956, LVA, FAFR, 1949–1999, accession number 36407, box 19, folder 6: "Contest Entries—1956, Essays (Contest #2)."

167. Vanderkodde interview.

168. Donald W. Hastings, Sammy Zahran, and Sherry Cable, "Drowning in Inequalities: Swimming and Social Justice," *Journal of Black Studies* 36, no. 6 (2006): 894–917.

169. Van Slyck, *A Manufactured Wilderness*, 94–95; Memorandum by Dr. R.N. Barr, "How We Keep Camps Healthy," 1950, ELAA, UMN, United Way of Minneapolis records (SW 70), box 72, folder 1: "Camps—general 1950."

170. Memorandum by Mary E. Smith, "Minutes 1964 Friendly Town Planning Conference, February 18, 19, 20," 1964, 9, UIL, MNC, box 99, folder 1505: "Fresh Air Fund, University of IL at Chicago Special Collection."

171. Memorandum by Dwinell, "Friendly Town, Summer 1967," [2].

172. Gerald (Gunny) Gunthrup, "The Gunny Sack," *Oneonta (NY) Star*, June 9, 1954; Betty Joyce, "York County Towns Welcome Fresh Airs and Lewises," *York County Coast Star* (Kennebunk, ME), August 3, 1966; David Sibbet, "City Children Visit Suburbs," *Chicago Tribune*, July 14, 1968; Draves, "Inner-City Children from Chicago Bring Surprises to 'Friendly Town' Parents"; "Young Campers in Fresh Air Fund Learning Canoeing," *New York Times*, August 21, 1970; Lacey Fosburgh, "Fresh Air Fund Puts 2,800 in Camp," *New York Times*, July 11, 1971; "Swimming Key Part of Fresh Air Camps," *New York Times*, July 24, 1977; Carol Rabasca, "Speaking Personally," *New York Times*, June 26, 1977; Joan Bastel, "Portrait of a 'Fresh Air' Family," *Daily Intelligencer* (Doylestown, PA), July 9, 1979; "Fresh Air Fund Is Magic Carpet for Urban Children," *New York Times*, July 1, 1979; "City Youngsters Planned Summer Vacations," *Daily News Record* (Harrisonburg, VA), June 14, 1979; Adams interview; Diaz interview.

173. "Fresh Air Fund Camp Buses Liberate 750 City Youths," *New York Times*, July 2, 1978.

174. Wiltse, *Contested Waters*, 3–4.

175. James C. Lont, Meeting to Discuss "Friendly Town" Project in the 60's, Graafschap, MI: 2010.

176. Cornell, "Get Acquainted Process New Phase of Relationship of Negroes, Whites"; Rabasca, "Speaking Personally"; Batts interview.

177. Joe R. Feagin, "The Continuing Significance of Race: Antiblack Discrimination in Public Places," *American Sociological Review* 56, no. 1 (1991): 101–16.

178. Paul Parker, (Untitled Photo of Integrated Groups of Elko Lake Campers at Lakeside before or after Swimming) ([1949–1958]), EDNY, Episcopal Missional Society, Summer Camp Photos, 1940's–1960's, folder: "Elko Lake Boys Camp—1949–1958"; Memorandum, "1952 Annual Report [proof]," 1953, LOC, PRF D223, HRR, file 12559: "The Fresh Air Fund, 1952"; Memorandum, "Herald Tribune Fresh Air Fund 81st Year Annual Report"; Memorandum, "Annual Report—Reviewing 1958," 1959, LOC, PRF D224, HRR, file 12567: "The Fresh Air Fund"; Mrs. Gerald Steger, "Enlightening Summer," *What's in the Air*, 1963; Cornell, "Get Acquainted Process New Phase of Relationship of Negroes, Whites"; Memorandum, "Eighty-Ninth Annual Report: Herald Tribune Fresh Air Fund," 1967, [5], copied from the CCAH, UTA; Memorandum, "1971 Annual Report," 1971, NYHS, F128HV 938.N5 F74.

179. Robert Goldstein, (unlabeled contact sheet) ([circa 1953]), EDNY, Episcopal Missional Society, Summer Camp Photos, 1940's–1960's (2922–2951—from folder "Elko Lake Camps—1950s,'60s & '70s"); "The Experience of Beauty" in Coatesville, Pa. (What's in the Air: Herald Tribune Fresh Air Fund, 1965), 3, LOC, PRF D224, HRR, file 12568: "The Fresh Air Fund."

180. Wiltse, *Contested Waters*, 201; "Fresh Air," *Daily News* (Huntingdon and Mount Union, PA), June 28, 1968.

181. Fosburgh, "18,000 Plan on Fresh Air Vacations"; Monaco, "City Kids Get Chance for Some Friendly Adventures"; Randy Wynn, "Children Find New Homes during Week in Ashland," *News Journal* (Mansfield, OH), July 4, 1971; Edward Hudson, "City Youths Find Country Delight," *New York Times*, July 22, 1973; Joan Cook, "Fresh Air Fund Gets Helping Hand," *New York Times*, August 7, 1977; Wedemeyer, "Farm Plan Extends Fresh Air Program," 33; Peg Hurd, "Tony Campano Picks Upper Bald Eagle over the Bronx," *Tyrone (PA) Daily Herald*, July 22, 1978; "Two Young Brothers Are Ready for a Fresh Air Fund Adventure," *New York Times*, May 21, 1978; "How Friendly Is This Country?"

182. Marie Winn, *Children without Childhood* (New York: Pantheon, 1983), 114.

183. Thomas A.P. van Leeuwen and Helen Searing, *The Springboard in the Pond: An Intimate History of the Swimming Pool* (Cambridge, MA: MIT Press, 1998).

184. "Be a Host Family to an Inner City Child," *Call and Post* (Cleveland, OH), March 26, 1977; Rabasca, "Speaking Personally"; "Community Activities," *Call and Post* (Cleveland, OH), March 24, 1979, 12A.

185. Trattner, *From Poor Law to Welfare State*, 293, 294.

186. "Fresh Air."

187. Hudson, "City Youths Find Country Delight."

188. Cook, "Fresh Air Fund Gets Helping Hand."

189. "Country Life New World to City Boy," *New York Herald Tribune*, November 29, 1966; "Fresh Air Fund Notes," *Bennington (VT) Banner*, June 4, 1976; Rondinaro, "A Change of Pace in the Sun."

190. "First Woman Executive Director Takes Helm for Fresh Air Fund Tomorrow," *New York Times*, October 26, 1975.

191. "Ticket to Happiness"; Michael Burns et al., *Fresh Air Don't Smell Like That* (Boyd Malloy, 1973), [34]; "Fresh Air Fund Enables 14,000 to Enjoy Fresh Air," *New York Amsterdam News*, August 14, 1976; Anne-Gerard Flynn, "Breath of Fresh Air for Everyone," *New York Times*, May 21, 1978; Rondinaro, "A Change of Pace in the Sun"; James C. Lont to Tobin Miller Shearer, July 24, 2010, paper copy in author's personal collection.

192. "Fresh Air Fund Is a Ticket for a Real Vacation," *Pottstown (PA) Mercury*, May 10, 1948.

193. Goldman, "Fresh Air: A Together Atmosphere."

194. Kenrick, *Come Out the Wilderness*, 106–07.

195. "Many Offer Help to Fresh Air Fund," *New York Times*, July 28, 1974.

196. Wiltse, *Contested Waters*, 185–88.

197. Mary Douglas, *Purity and Danger: An Analysis of the Concepts of Pollution and Taboo* (New York: Routledge, 1966), 2, 5, 44.

3. GRASS, COLOR, SASS

1. Lacey Fosburgh, "Fresh Air Fund Puts 2,800 in Camp," *New York Times*, July 11, 1971.

2. "Friendly Town Offers Suburban Vacation for Inner City Kids," *Call and Post* (Cleveland, OH), June 26, 1971; Sally Mulligan, "Subtle Racism," *Call and Post* (Cleveland, OH), May 16, 1970; Eleanor Charles, "Apathy Endangers Fresh Air Fund," *New York Times*, May 20, 1979.

3. Memorandum, "Annual Report—Reviewing 1958," 1959, 9, LOC, PRF D224, HRR, file 12567: "The Fresh Air Fund."

4. Richard F. Crandell, ed., *The Frog Log and Other Stories about Children* (New York: Herald Tribune Fresh Air Fund, 1962), 19.

5. "Turn Kids on to Real Grass," *Forbes*, July 1, 1974, 81.

6. "They're Off!" *Turning Points*, May, 1956, EDNY, box—Episcopal Missional Society, Turning Points Publ. 1950s–1970s, folder: "Turning Points, 1952, 1966–'68."

7. Robert Messia, "Lawns as Artifacts: The Evolution of Social and Environmental Implications of Suburban Residential Land Use," *Suburban Sprawl: Culture, Theory, and Politics*, ed. Matthew J. Lindstrom and Hugh Bartling (Lanham, MD: Rowman & Littlefield, 2003), 69–83.

8. Robert Fishman, *Bourgeois Utopias: The Rise and Fall of Suburbia* (New York: Basic Books, 1987), 147; Messia, "Lawns as Artifacts."

9. Kenneth T. Jackson, *Crabgrass Frontier: The Suburbanization of the United States* (New York: Oxford University Press, 1985), 59.

10. Messia, "Lawns as Artifacts"; Adam Rome, *The Bulldozer in the Countryside: Suburban Sprawl and the Rise of American Environmentalism* (New York: Cambridge University Press, 2001), 13.

11. Messia, "Lawns as Artifacts."

12. Jackson, *Crabgrass Frontier*, 133.

13. Ibid., 208.

14. Michael J. Klarman, *From Jim Crow to Civil Rights: The Supreme Court and the Struggle for Racial Equality* (New York: Oxford University Press, 2004), 261; Wendy Plotkin, "'Hemmed In': The Struggle against Racial Restrictive Covenants and Deed Restrictions in Post–WWII Chicago," *Journal of the Illinois State Historical Society (1998–)* 94, no. 1 (2001): 39–69.

15. "Will You Do Me a Favor?" *Oneonta (NY) Star*, June 10, 1954.

16. "Children Source of Entertainment," *Hagerstown (MD) Daily Mail*, August 2, 1943; "As Fresh Air Special Arrives in the Area," *Daily News* (Huntington and Mount Union, PA), July 15, 1953 (emphasis added).

17. "Friendly Town Is Set up by Pennsylvania Couple," *New York Times*, August 19, 1979.

18. "Children Source of Entertainment."

19. "38 Fresh Air Children Taken by Bradford, Area Residents," *Bradford (PA) Era*, July 29, 1948; "The Goal: 100 Children," *Bennington (VT) Banner*, May 8, 1963.

20. Leo J. Heffernan, "Chariot to a New World" (New York: Union Settlement Association), 9, CUA, USAR 1896–1995 MS#1149, Series VII: Programs and Services, box 40, folder 11: "Camp-Film, 1944–49."

21. Sarah Burns, "Barefoot Boys and Other Country Children: Sentiment and Ideology in Nineteenth-Century American Art," *American Art Journal* 20, no. 1 (1988): 25–50; Hazel Bowers, "Fresh Air Boy," *What's in the Air*, autumn 1955.

22. George A. Edmonds, "Friendly Town Program Molds Young Lives," *Bennington (VT) Banner*, July 27, 1963.

23. "Fresh-Air Families Recall 'City Brothers,'" *New York Times*, August 6, 1978; "Fresh Air Fund Kids Have Picnic," *New York Herald Tribune*, September 29, 1966; Dorothy Belle Pollack, "Pearl and Ebony," *What's in the Air*, summer vacation edition, 1963.

24. Crandell, ed., *The Frog Log and Other Stories about Children*.

25. "A Child's Look of Amazement," *New York Times*, April 29, 1979.

26. Abigail A. Van Slyck, *A Manufactured Wilderness: Summer Camps and the Shaping of American Youth, 1890–1960* (Minneapolis: University of Minnesota Press, 2006), 45–49.

27. Fred W. Hohloch to Frederick H. Lewis, November 30, 1960, LOC, PRF D224, HRR, file 12566: "The Fresh Air Fund, 1960"; Crandell, ed., *The Frog Log and Other Stories about Children*, 2; Richard F. Crandell, "Fresh Air Fund—Birth of an Idea," *New York Herald Tribune*, October 30, 1966.

28. Burns, "Barefoot Boys and Other Country Children."

29. Memorandum, "Eighty-Ninth Annual Report: Herald Tribune Fresh Air Fund," 1967, [4], copied from the CCAH, UTA; Cathy Aldridge, "Herald Tribune Fresh Air Fund Continues despite Long Strike," *New York Amsterdam News*, August 13, 1966; Memorandum, "Eighty-Ninth Annual Report: Herald Tribune Fresh Air Fund," [4]; Aldridge, "Herald Tribune Fresh Air Fund Continues despite Long Strike"; Memorandum by Nelson A. Rockefeller, "On the Occasion of Dedicating a New Lake and Model Farm at Sharpe Reservation, East Fishkill, N.Y.," 1967, LOC, PRF D225, HRR, file 12575: "The Fresh Air Fund 1967."

30. Aldridge, "Herald Tribune Fresh Air Fund Continues despite Long Strike"; "Conservation Work at Fishkill Is Aided by Fresh Air Fund," *New York Times*, July 5, 1970.

31. Memorandum, "My Vacation in the Country," November 28, 1947, LOC, PRF D222, HRR, file 12556: "The Fresh Air Fund, 1942–49."

32. Helen Busuttil Regenbogen, Bainbridge, NY, telephone interview by the author, March 10, 2010.

33. "10 Children from New York's East Harlem Visiting Leominster Homes for Two Weeks," *Fitchburg (MA) Sentinel*, July 22, 1954.

34. Barbara L. Little, "Helps New York City Children to a Vacation in the Country," *Lancaster (PA) Intelligencer-Journal*, July 31, 1958; "Trees and Open Spaces a Treat for Youngsters," *Emmetsburg (IA) Democrat*, August 31, 1967; MaryBeth Wagner, "Manheim Couple Hosts Fifty Phila. Children," *Intelligencer Journal* (Lancaster, PA), August 11, 1978; "A Small Harlem Boy and 'All That Green Stuff,'" *Berkshire Eagle* (Pittsfield, MA), July 31, 1956, 7.

35. "No Place to Play," *Bennington (VT) Evening Banner*, June 22, 1957.

36. Paul S. Boyer, *Urban Masses and Moral Order in America, 1820–1920* (Cambridge, MA: Harvard University Press, 1978), 236–37.

37. Ibid., 239–40, 279.

38. Wade Barnes, "Washington Square" (New York: Shelley Music Co., 1962), NYUA, Washington Square Association Activities, MC 94, Series 6, box 20, folder 7: "Fresh Air Fund: 1962"; Frederick Kelly, "Trees against Light Bryant Park" (1961), NYHS, Department of Prints, Photographs, and Architectural Collections, Frederick Kelly Photograph Collection, PR 246, box 1, folder 2: "Bryant Park"; Kelly, "Three Girls Washington Square" (1962), NYHS, Department of Prints, Photographs, and Architectural Collections, Frederick Kelly Photograph Collection, PR 246, box 2, folder 19: "Washington Square People."

39. Ari L. Goldman, "Fresh Air: A Together Atmosphere," *New York Times*, June 27, 1976.

40. Bartlett Hendricks, "Three Boys, Two Weeks and No Worries at All," *Berkshire Eagle* (Pittsfield, MA), August 4, 1956.

41. Leanna Kauffman, 1956, LVA, FAFR, 1949–1999, accession number 36407, box 19, folder 6: "Contest Entries—1956, Essays (Contest #2)"; Memorandum by Ralph B. Dwinell, "Friendly Town," 1966, LOC, PRF D224, HRR, file 12567: "The Fresh Air Fund"; Fosburgh, "Fresh Air Fund Puts 2,800 in Camp"; Edward Hudson, "Fresh Air Goal: 19,000 Vacations," *New York Times*, May 20, 1973.

42. Mrs. Raymond E. Carr, 1956, LVA, FAFR, 1949–1999, accession number 36407, box 19, folder 6: "Contest Entries—1956, Essays (Contest #2)"; Louise A. Sweeney, "Designed for Women," *Berkshire Eagle* (Pittsfield, MA), June 5, 1959.

43. Perfinax, "Experiment in Humanity," *Lowell (MA) Sun*, July 26, 1961.

44. Crandell, ed., *The Frog Log and Other Stories about Children*, 9.

45. Ibid., 5.

46. Anonymous Fresh Air participant, New York, NY, interview by the author, September 15, 1995.

47. "A Small Harlem Boy and 'All That Green Stuff.'"

48. "Couple Recall Their Early Days as Fresh Air Fund Hosts," *New York Times*, April 30, 1978; "Deadline Tonight for Fresh Air Guests," *Portsmouth (NH) Herald*, July 9, 1956.

49. "Mrs. Pavlis Takes Her Fresh Air Footprint to the Royal Wedding," *What's in the Air*, fall 1964.

50. "Turn Kids on to Real Grass."

51. Leon Dash, "Leaders Arrested in Camp Drug Raid," *Journal News* (Hamilton, OH), August 25, 1972.

52. E. R. Braxton and R. J. Yonker, "Does Being Urban, Poor, Black, or Female Affect Youth's Knowledge and/or Attitudes Relating to Drugs?" *Journal of School Health* 43 (1973): 185–88; Department of English, *Current Slang* (Vermillion, SD: University of South Dakota, 1966–1967); Stephen Dill and Donald Bebeau, *Current Slang* (Vermillion, SD: University of South Dakota, 1968–1970); Carry Cowherd, "The Following List Was Gathered from the Seven Male Black Undergraduates at the University of South Dakota," *Current Slang: A Quarterly Glossary of Slang Expressions Presently in Use* 5, no. 2 (1970): 5–14; R. S. P. Weiner, *Drugs and Schoolchildren* (New York: Humanities Press, 1970), 62.

53. Frederick H. Lewis, "Integration, Then What?" *American Unity: An Education Guide*, September–October, 1954, 3–9, LOC, PRF D223, HRR, file 1562: "The Fresh Air Fund, 1954–55."

54. Tom Jachimiec, "Suburbs' War on Prejudice: Big Response to Friendly Town," *Bensenville (IL) Register*, May 10, 1968.

55. Crandell, ed., *The Frog Log and Other Stories about Children;* Jonathan R. Dwyer, "God and Cows," *Bennington (VT) Banner*, April 30, 1968.

56. Mrs. Gerald Steger, "Enlightening Summer," *What's in the Air*, 1963.

57. Rita J. Simon, Howard Altstein, and Marygold S. Melli, *The Case for Transracial Adoption* (Washington, DC: American University Press, 1994), 41.

58. Julia Guarneri, "Changing Strategies for Child Welfare, Enduring Beliefs about Childhood: The Fresh Air Fund, 1877–1926," *Journal of the Gilded Age and Progressive Era* 11, no. 1 (2012): 27–70; H. Addington Bruce, "The Story of the Great Fresh Air Movement," *Lowell (MA) Sun*, August 14, 1903; "Fresh Air Work Humor," *Fitchburg (MA) Daily Sentinel*, July 27, 1907; "Fresh Air Days," *Galveston (TX) Daily News*, April 30, 1910.

59. Paul C. Mishler, *Raising Reds: The Young Pioneers, Radical Summer Camps, and Communist Political Culture in the United States* (New York: Columbia University Press, 1999).

60. "Lions Launch Campaign for Fresh Air Camp," *Statesville (NC) Daily Record*, May 28, 1946; "Florence Fresh Air Fund Group to Meet Tomorrow," *Florence (SC) Morning News*, May 15, 1949.

61. Lillian Scott, "Gotham Kiddies Back after Summer Vacation," *Chicago Defender*, September 13, 1947.

62. Memorandum, "A Recreational and Educational Project through Churches to Help Meet Youth Needs in Brooklyn," March, 1945, PNHA, NCC, Home Missions Council of North America, 1903–1951, RG26, box 16, folder 11: "Negro Work Brooklyn Project, March 1945–June 1949"; Tarrance, Amateur Boxing Tournament Finalists (1949), NYCPL-SC, Children, 13–491; *Friendship Frontiers 1949–1950: A Complete Listing of All Frontiers for Children and Young People* (Presbyterian Church, USA, General Council, Youth Budget Office, 1949), PHS, PAM-FOL VB 2616, V6 F7 1949 UF33P Y87f.

63. Marian E. McKay, "Free Seaboard Camps Offer Summer Fun to Children of All Races," *Chicago Defender*, September 18, 1948.

64. Steven Mintz, *Huck's Raft: A History of American Childhood* (Cambridge, MA: Belknap Press of Harvard University Press, 2004), 257–58.

65. Ai-min Zhang, *The Origins of the African American Civil Rights Movement, 1865–1956*, ed. Graham Russell Hodges (New York: Routledge, 2002), 90.

66. Walter I. Trattner, *From Poor Law to Welfare State: A History of Social Welfare in America* (New York: The Free Press, 1984), 298.

67. Howard P. Chudacoff and Judith E. Smith, *The Evolution of American Urban Society* (Upper Saddle River, NJ: Prentice Hall, 2000), 270.

68. Leslie Paris, *Children's Nature: The Rise of the American Summer Camp* (New York: New York University Press, 2008), 268.

69. Lewis, "Integration, Then What?"

70. Memorandum, "Annual Report to the Board of Directors," 1951, LOC, PRF D223, HRR, file 12558: "The Fresh Air Fund, 1951."

71. Paris, *Children's Nature*, 72–73.

72. "Improvement of Poor Integrates Fresh Air Camp," *Pittsburgh Courier*, June 20, 1953, 5.

73. Memorandum, "Annual Report to the Board of Directors," 1953, 4, LOC, PRF D223, HRR, file 12560: "The Fresh Air Fund, 1953–54."

74. "Seek County Homes for 'Fresh Airs,'" *Evening Banner* (Bennington, VT), June 12, 1956; "Exchange Club Will Sponsor Fresh Air Fund Program Again," *Bridgeport (CT) Post*, June 5, 1957; "20 Homes in Newtown on 'Fresh Air' List," *Bridgeport (CT) Sunday Post*, June 22, 1958.

75. "Friendly Town Project Set Again by Fredonians," *Dunkirk (NY) Evening Observer*, April 19, 1956.

76. Memorandum, "Friendly Town—1965—Summary of Children Sent," 1965, LOC, PRF D224, HRR, file 12568: "The Fresh Air Fund."

77. "Spring Conference Reviews a Joyful Year," *What's in the Air*, spring 1966.

78. Memorandum by Frederick H. Lewis, "Annual Report for 1968: A Reappraisal," 1968, 5, copied from the CCAH, UTA.

79. Irvana Wilks, "Project Friendly Town Described as Coin with Two Sides," *Iowa City Press-Citizen*, July 26, 1968; "Welcome Mat Out," *Arlington Heights (IL) Herald*, April 17, 1969.

80. Aldridge, "Herald Tribune Fresh Air Fund Continues despite Long Strike."

81. "Journey into Another World," *Call and Post* (Cleveland, OH), August 2, 1969.

82. Dwyer, "God and Cows."

83. Blancke Noyes to Alan W. Betts, April 22, 1968, NYCPL-BRARR, Series I—Grant Files, box 14: "Grants Files, 1968, Fresh Air Fund."

84. "Fresh Air for Sale," *New York Times*, April 30, 1978; "Church Promotion Due in Onalaska Services," *Centralia (WA) Daily Chronicle*, June 4, 1971; "Girl, 9, Learns New View of Life," *Chicago Tribune*, August 4, 1971.

85. Marian Abbott, "Cultural Exchange Program," *Daily Inter Lake* (Kalispell, MT), July 10, 1970; "Girl, 9, Learns New View of Life"; Excitement and Confusion . . ." (*Ephrata Review*, 1971), LMHS, Newspaper Clippings Collection: "Fresh Air Program"; "'Fresh Air' Welcome," *Bennington (VT) Banner*, June 30, 1976; "Elko Lake Camps," *Episcopal New Yorker*, spring 1976.

86. "'Fresh Air' Children Due Here on June 29," *Tyrone (PA) Daily Herald*, June 14, 1978; "New York Youngsters Due," *Tyrone (PA) Daily Herald*, June 28, 1978; "Give a Fresh Air Kid a Boost," *Progress* (Clearfield, PA), May 25, 1978.

87. "Fresh Air Hosts May Not Specify Race, Religion," *Oneonta (NY) Star*, April 20, 1971; "Fresh Air Fund Seeks Hosts Here," *Tyrone (PA) Daily Herald*, April 13, 1976.

88. "Friendly Town Opens Drive," *Call and Post* (Cleveland, OH), March 24, 1973; "Friendly Town Vacation Visits," *Call and Post* (Cleveland, OH), May 4, 1974; "More Host Families Are Needed," *Call and Post* (Cleveland, OH), May 8, 1976; Lynne Ames, "The Fresh Air Fund: Summers of Sharing," *New York Times*, May 20, 1979.

89. Phyllis M. Palmer, *Living as Equals: How Three White Communities Struggled to Make Interracial Connections during the Civil Rights Era* (Nashville: Vanderbilt University Press, 2008), 6, 27.

90. Joseph Owens, "Little Town with a Big Heart," *Afro-American* (Baltimore), July 30, 1955; Sweeney, "Designed for Women"; Edmonds, "Friendly Town Program Molds Young Lives"; Ethel Hanson Wood, "Adirondack Wood-Cuttings," *What's in the Air*, spring 1966.

91. Carr, 1956.

92. David Sibbet, "City Children Visit Suburbs," *Chicago Tribune*, July 14, 1968; Edward Hudson, "City Youths Find Country Delight," *New York Times*, July 22, 1973; Jane Blanksteen, "A Refreshing Experience," *New York Times*, June 19, 1977.

93. Paris, *Children's Nature*, 269.

94. J. Wayne Burrell, "Harlem Social Whirl," *Afro American* (Baltimore), July 11, 1936.

95. "Fresh Air Fund Benefit," *New York Amsterdam Star-News*, March 28, 1942; Gladys January Willis, *Faith against the Odds: A Memoir of My Journey from Mississippi to the Ivy League and Beyond* (Bloomington, IN: WestBow Press, 2014), 7–8.

96. Elwood Watson, "Camp Atwater (1921–)," BlackPast.Org, www.blackpast.org/aah/camp-atwater-1921; Henry M. Thomas, III, "Camp Atwater: Building Tomorrow's Leaders," *Camping* (1993), 29–31.

97. "Entertaining Guests from Wilmington, Nashville," *New York Age*, September 9, 1939; "By Way of Mention," *New York Age*, August 8, 1942; "Youthful Floridians to Attend College," *New York Age*, September 14, 1946; "Welcoming Champion Camper," *Pittsburgh Courier*, July 17, 1965; Hazel Garland, "Things to Talk About," *Pittsburgh Courier*, January 29, 1977; William N. DeBerry, "Camp Atwater Offers Many Recreational Advantages," *Pittsburgh Courier*, April 26, 1941; "Toki Types," *Pittsburgh Courier*, August 18, 1951.

98. Toki Schalk Johnson, "Toki Types," *Pittsburgh Courier*, August 7, 1954.

99. "Traditional Atwater: A Legend for Boys and Girls," *Pittsburgh Courier*, June 3, 1961.

100. Johnson, "Toki Types," *Pittsburgh Courier*, January 29, 1966; "Former Springfield Athlete in Camp Work," *Pittsburgh Courier*, June 22, 1940; Toki Schalk Johnson, "Woman of the Week," *Pittsburgh Courier*, February 3, 1951.

101. DeBerry, "Camp Atwater Offers Many Recreational Advantages"; Memorandum, "Camp Atwater for Boys and Girls," 1948, Papers of the NAACP, Part 26: Selected branch files, 1940–1955, Ser. B: The Northeast, Reel 2 of 11, Micro E, 185.5. N273x Pt. 26 Ser. B. Reel 2.

102. Deberry, "Camp Atwater Offers Many Recreational Advantages"; "Apex Head Fetes Palmer Memorial Thanksgiving," *Pittsburgh Courier*, November 28, 1942; David Johnson, "Teen Age," *New York Age*, December 10, 1949; "Fifth Annual Reunion Finds Charles Hill Re-Elected Prexy," *Pittsburgh Courier*, August 22, 1953; "Atwater Alumni Reunion in Picturesque Setting," *New York Age*, August 13, 1955; Lucille Cromer, "Lucille Cromer's Society Script," *New York Age*, June 16, 1956; Al Dumore, "Toki Types," *Pittsburgh Courier*, July 25, 1958; Toki Schalk Johnson, "Toki Types," *Pittsburgh Courier*, July 11, 1958; "Traditional Atwater: A Legend for Boys and Girls"; Memorandum, "Camp Atwater for Boys and Girls."

103. "Sunday Church Services," *Kingston (NY) Daily Freeman*, August 20, 1966; "Sunday Church Services," *Kingston (NY) Daily Freeman*, July 1, 1967; "Sunday Church Services," *Kingston (NY) Daily Freeman*, July 20, 1968; Lionel C. Herron, "Book—from Harlem to Broad St Hollow," www.gofundme.com/campbrytonrock. First Emmanual held worship services at 105 West 130th Street in Harlem at least through 1950 but then appears to have relocated to 50 Abeel Street in Kingston from 1959 onward.

104. Lionel Herron, Cabo, Mexico, telephone interview by the author, June 9, 2015.

105. Herron, "Book—from Harlem to Broad St Hollow"; Herron interview; "Visit Sojourner Truth's Birthplace," *Kingston (NY) Daily Freeman*, August 10, 1968.

106. Lionel Herron, "Life at the Camp," http://campbrytonrock.com/joomla/index.php?option=com_content&view=article&id=46&Itemid=53.

107. George S. Schyler, "Views and Reviews," *Pittsburgh Courier*, January 16, 1965.

108. "Send Your Children to Camp Bryton Rock," *Kingston (NY) Daily Freeman*, July 1, 1960.

109. DeBerry, "Camp Atwater Offers Many Recreational Advantages"; "Traditional Atwater: A Legend for Boys and Girls."

110. Memorandum, "Friendly Town—1965—Summary of Children Sent."

111. "550 Children to Get Special Vacation Trip," *Chicago Tribune*, July 9, 1965; George Cornell, "Get Acquainted Process New Phase of Relationship of Negroes, Whites," *Post-Crescent* (Appleton, WI), August 9, 1965; Mrs. Clayton Shaub, "An Unfinished Story," *Missionary Messenger*, June 1965, 14–15.

112. DeBerry, "Camp Atwater Offers Many Recreational Advantages"; Memorandum, "Camp Atwater for Boys and Girls"; "Traditional Atwater: A Legend for Boys and Girls."

113. Johnson, "Toki Types," January 29, 1966.

114. "Go to Friendly Town," *Call and Post* (Cleveland, OH), July 1, 1967.

115. Frederick H. Lewis, "Amsterdam News Aids Fresh Air Fund," *New York Amsterdam News*, June 17, 1967; "Sermon Inspired Fresh Air Fund," *New York Amsterdam News*, June 24, 1967; "Presentation," *New York Amsterdam News*, October 26, 1968; "Fresh Air Fund Sends over 2,000 to Camp," *New York Amsterdam News*, July 13, 1968.

116. "Planning Evening," *New York Amsterdam News*, July 12, 1969; Memorandum, "Minutes of Meeting of the Board of Directors of Herald Tribune Fresh Air Fund Held April 21, 1966," April 21, 1966, 5, LOC, PRF D224, HRR, file 12567: "The Fresh Air Fund."

117. "Negro Mother Cites Son's Vermont Vacation from Brooklyn 'Summer of Hate,'" *Bennington (VT) Banner*, September 14, 1964. In the midst of similar urban unrest, a host mother echoed Kirton's comments when she explained her motives for hosting African American fourth-grader Lue Bertha by claiming in 1968, "I wanted the opportunity to show at least one Negro child that not all white people hate them." See Kathy Begley, "Haverford Family to Welcome Two-Week 'Fresh Air' Visitor," *Delaware County Daily Times* (Chester, PA), June 10, 1968.

118. Palmer, *Living as Equals*, 29.

119. Joan McKinney, "When Kids Trade Places," *Oakland (CA) Tribune*, May 17, 1971; E. J. Dionne Jr., "The Fresh Air Fund: 100 Years of Success," *New York Times*, May 8, 1977.

120. Janet Shertzer, "Gift from the City," *Missionary Messenger*, April 1968, 2–3; Orlo Kaufman, "Kansas Homes Become Mission Outposts," *Gulfbreeze*, July–August, 1961, 2; Orlo Kaufman to Andrew Shelly, August 10, 1960, MLABC: MLA.VII.R GC Voluntary Service, Series 11 Gulfport VS Unit, box 1, folder 4: "Correspondence—General Conf. 1960."

121. (Photo of Boys Waving from inside of Bus) (New York: Union Settlement Association, 1949), CUA, USAR, 1896–1995 MS#1149, Series VIII: Audio-Visual Materials, box 46, folder 3: "Camp Nathan Hale, ca., 1900, 1940s, 1990s"; (Photo of Boys Sitting out Front of Teepee Reading) (New York: Union Settlement Association, n.d.), CUA, USAR, 1896–1995 MS#1149, Series VIII: Audio-Visual Materials, box 46, folder 3: "Camp Nathan Hale, ca., 1900, 1940s, 1990s"; (Photo of Boys Sitting in Cabin on Bunks) (New York: Union Settlement Association, n.d.), CUA, USAR, 1896–1995 MS#1149, Series VIII: Audio-Visual Materials, box 46, folder 3: "Camp Nathan Hale, ca., 1900, 1940s, 1990s."

122. "Staff of Fresh Air Camps Trained in Racial Amity," *Herald Tribune*, July 6, 1954; Lewis, "Integration, Then What?"

123. Lewis, "Integration, Then What?"

124. Memorandum, "Report on Ponomok Community Center Day Camp—1954," 1954, ELAA, UMN, United Neighborhood Houses of New York Records (SW0005), box 221, folder 442: "Pomonok Community Center Day Camp, Flushing, New York, 1954–1955."

125. Camp discussions of race relations focused exclusively on white/black dynamics; the idea of Native American race relations were generally rendered moot as if the Native community was no longer present even at those camps that celebrated Native lore. See Van Slyck, *A Manufactured Wilderness*, 212–13. For evidence of publicity focusing on interracial contact, see *Dancing at the Girls Camp* (New York: Union Settlement Association, 1950), CUA, USAR, 1896–1995 MS#1149, Series VIII: Audio-Visual Materials, box 46, folder 5: "Camp Gaylord White, ca., 1950"; Memorandum, "Herald Tribune Fresh Air Fund 81st Year Annual Report," 1957, LOC, PRF D224, HRR, file 12567: "The Fresh Air Fund"; "Boys and Girls Offered Vacation at Camp Incarnation," *Bulletin of the Diocese of New York*, February 1959, 8–9; Memorandum, "Through Decisive Years: New York Protestant Episcopal City Mission Society One-Hundred-Thirtieth Anniversary Report 1831–1961," 1961, EDNY, Episcopal Missional Society Mission News 1923–1976: "Misc. loose reports & pamphlets"; Crandell, ed., *The Frog Log and Other Stories about Children;*

"Snapshot Winners," *What's in the Air*, Spring 1964; Cornell, "Get Acquainted Process New Phase of Relationship of Negroes, Whites"; Memorandum, "Eighty-Ninth Annual Report: Herald Tribune Fresh Air Fund."

126. Fosburgh, "Fresh Air Fund Puts 2,800 in Camp"; "Former 'Worst Kid' Helps Fresh Air Fund," *New York Times*, May 20, 1979.

127. Paris, *Children's Nature*, 186, 190–93, 196, 198–99, 203, 205, 207, 212, 219, 220, 224, 225.

128. Memorandum, "Camp Standards," December 15, 1920, 10, ELAA, UMN, United Neighborhood Houses of New York Records (SW0005), box 223, folder 471: "Summer Camps, 1920–1923."

129. Van Slyck, *A Manufactured Wilderness*, 51.

130. Memorandum by Edd Lee, "Summer Camp Registrations and Placements," October 1958, CUA, HGR MS#1465, Series I: Board of Directors, folder 7: "Committees—Hudson Guild Farm, 1948–1964."

131. Andrew Wiese, *Places of Their Own: African American Suburbanization in the Twentieth Century* (Chicago: University of Chicago Press, 2004).

132. Carol Van Horn, "The Inner City: Elective in Understanding," *Presbyterian Life*, October 15, 1963, 25–27; Lee Edwards, "'Friendly Town' Chairman: Fresh Air Fund Matchmaker," *Oneonta (NY) Star*, July 14, 1971; "Ashland to Host City Teenagers," *News Journal* (Mansfield, OH), July 10, 1972; Joan Cook, "City Youths Discover Joy of Suburbs," *New York Times*, May 9, 1976; Ames, "The Fresh Air Fund: Summers of Sharing."

133. Ames, "The Fresh Air Fund: Summers of Sharing"; Stephen H. Goldstein, "Jacqueline's Back for Summer Fun," *Times Record* (Troy, NY), July 3, 1975.

134. Unattributed article clipping, June 1976, author's personal collection.

135. "190 Inner-City Youngsters Go on a One-Week Vacation," *Call and Post* (Cleveland, OH), July 20, 1974.

136. Wilma King, *African American Childhoods: Historical Perspectives from Slavery to Civil Rights* (New York: Palgrave Macmillan, 2005), 123, 128.

137. Clare B. Wood to New York Times Publisher, August 3, 1979, NYCPL-BRARR, Series I—Grant Files, box 2—folder: "Fresh Air Fund 1962," Whitney North Seymour Papers, 1930–1983, box 114—Subject Files—Fresh Air Fund, 1962–1983, folder: "Fresh Air Fund 1976 Life Director."

138. See, for example, Thomas W. Brock, Harrisonburg, VA, telephone interview by the author, May 17, 2005; Janice Batts, Iowa City, IA, telephone interview by the author, February 15, 2012.

139. James C. Lont, Meeting to Discuss "Friendly Town" Project in the 60's, Graafschap, MI: 2010.

140. Joan M. Jacobus, "Our Summer House Guests," *Redbook*, July 1964.

141. Memorandum, "Hudson Guild Farm," 1964, CUA, HGR MS#1465, Subseries IV.3: Hudson Guild Farm, box 24, folder 11: "Reports, 1963–1968 nd."

142. Bill Draves Jr., "Inner-City Children from Chicago Bring Surprises to 'Friendly Town' Parents," *Commonwealth Reporter* (Fond du Lac, WI), 1968; Memorandum by Marchand Chaney and Mimi Vernon," Evaluation of Newberry-Dubuque Project for 1962," 1962, UIL, MNC, box 99, folder 1505: "Fresh Air Fund, University of IL at Chicago Special Collection"; Randy Wynn, "Children Find New Homes during Week in Ashland," *News Journal* (Mansfield, OH), July 4, 1971; Mary Ann Strawn, "Friend of Friendly Town," *Arlington Heights (IL) Herald*, August 17, 1972, 6.

143. Glenda Adams, New York, NY, telephone interview by the author, March 28, 2010; Luis Diaz, New York, NY, telephone interview by the author, May 4, 2010; Nilson Diaz, New York, NY, telephone interview by the author, May 12, 2010; Joseph Gibbons, Tallahassee, FL, telephone interview by the author, March 17, 2010.

144. "Quentin WCTU Has Guest Speaker," *Lebanon (PA) Daily News*, July 31, 1957; "Haverford Family to Welcome Two-Week 'Fresh Air' Visitor," *Daily News* (Huntingdon and Mount Union, PA), June 29, 1966; Draves, "Inner-City Children from Chicago Bring Surprises to 'Friendly Town' Parents."

145. "Fresh Air Kiddies Arrive Tomorrow for Two-Week Visit," *Daily News* (Huntingdon and Mount Union, PA), July 12, 1955; "Homes Opened to Fresh Air Children," *Oneonta (NY) Star*, June 16, 1956; "Newark Valley Tourists," *Syracuse Herald-American*, August 11, 1957; "Six Chinese Children Due to Visit Here: Fresh Air Kids from New York Sponsored by PETA," *Cumberland (MD) Evening Times*, July 10, 1958; "24 Fresh Air Fund Children on Visit," *Lebanon (PA) Daily News*, July 29, 1959; Crandell, ed., *The Frog Log and Other Stories about Children*, 9; "Host Snapshots," review of LOC, PRF D225, HRR, file 12569: "The Fresh Air Fund 1963"; *What's in the Air*, Spring 1963, 3; Memorandum by Mary E. Smith, "Minutes 1964 Friendly Town Planning Conference, February 18, 19, 20," 1964, 7, UIL, MNC, box 99, folder 1505: "Fresh Air Fund," University of IL at Chicago Special Collection; "Friendly Town Children Coming," *North Adams (MA) Transcript*, July 17, 1967.

146. For evidence of children's separatist culture during the Cold War era, see Mintz, *Huck's Raft*, 282. For evidence of children resisting adult supervision of their play, see Maude Hines, "Playing with Children: What the 'Child' Is Doing in American Studies," *American Quarterly* 61, no. 1 (2009): 151–61. For discussion of "hidden transcripts" among oppressed groups, see James C. Scott, *Domination and the Arts of Resistance: Hidden Transcripts* (New Haven, CT: Yale University Press, 1990).

147. Perfinax, "Experiment in Humanity," 7.

148. Beverly Daniel Tatum, *"Why Are All the Black Kids Sitting Together in the Cafeteria?" and Other Conversations about Race* (New York: Basic Books, 1997), 32; Jennifer Ritterhouse, *Growing up Jim Crow: How Black and White Southern Children Learned Race* (Chapel Hill: University of North Carolina, 2006), 17.

149. Draves, "Inner-City Children from Chicago Bring Surprises to 'Friendly Town' Parents"; Cornell, "Get Acquainted Process New Phase of Relationship of Negroes, Whites."

150. Betty Joyce, "York County Towns Welcome Fresh Airs and Lewises," *York County Coast Star* (Kennebunk, ME), August 3, 1966.

151. Rebecca de Schweinitz, *If We Could Change the World: Young People and America's Long Struggle for Racial Equality* (Chapel Hill: University of North Carolina Press, 2009), 106; Pamela E. Klassen, "The Robes of Womanhood: Dress and Authenticity among African American Methodist Women in the Nineteenth Century," *Religion and American Culture* 14, no. 1 (2004): 39–82; Evelyn Brooks Higginbotham, "The Black Church: A Gender Perspective," in *African-American Religion: Interpretive Essays in History and Culture*, ed. Timothy E. Fulop and Albert J. Raboteau (New York: Routledge, 1997), 202–25.

152. Marisa Chappell, Jenny Hutchinson, and Brian Ward, "'Dress Modestly, Neatly ... as if You Were Going to Church': Respectability, Class and Gender in the Early Civil Rights Movement," in *Gender in the Civil Rights Movement*, ed. Peter J. Ling and Sharon Monteith (New York: Garland, 1999), 69–100.

153. Bernie Greenfield, Newark, NJ, telephone interview by the author, April 13, 2010; "73 Chicago Children Quickly Make New Friends, See Fair," *Fond Du Lac (WI) Commonwealth Reporter*, August 4, 1968, 14.

154. Mary Ullrich, "Friendly Towns Spur Tots' Holiday," *Chicago Tribune*, July 16, 1967; "Happiness Is a Beautiful Summer Day . . . ," *Biddeford-Saco (ME) Journal*, July 27, 1967.

155. Memorandum, "Camp Registrar's Report 1957," 1957, CUA, USAR, 1896–1995 MS#1149, Series VII: Programs and Services, box 41, folder 3: "Camp-Reports, 1948–53."

156. Hendricks, "Three Boys, Two Weeks and No Worries at All"; "Westport Seeks Fresh Air Hosts," *Bridgeport (CT) Sunday Post*, June 1, 1958; Mrs. Charles M. Lucas, "Testimo-

nial," *What's in the Air*, fall 1965; Draves, "Inner-City Children from Chicago Bring Surprises to 'Friendly Town' Parents"; Memorandum by Ronall Halloway, "Union Settlement Camps—Report on Camper—Ernest Hobbs," August 28, 1956, CUA, USAR, 1896–1995 MS#1149, Series VII: Programs and Services, box 53, folder 7: "Camp-Children's Records (H–M), 1955–57"; Memorandum by Dolores Lill and Mary Lill, "Yvette Airmis, Age 5," n.d., CUA, USAR, 1896–1995 MS#1149, Series VII: Programs and Services, box 53, folder 3: "Camp-Children's Records (A–B), 1945–57."

157. Wilks, "Project Friendly Town Described as Coin with Two Sides."

158. Wood, "Adirondack Wood-Cuttings"; Joan K. Kahler, "Fresh Air Child Finds Real Home with Rome Family," *Daily Sentinel* (Rome, NY), 1961; Shelby M. Howatt, "From Concrete to Country," *Bulletin*, May 1960, 4–6, EDNY, Episcopal Missional Society, Publications et al., 1930s–1970s.

159. Sweeney, "Designed for Women."

160. Draves, "Inner-City Children from Chicago Bring Surprises to 'Friendly Town' Parents"; John Green, "Friendly Town Afterthoughts: 'Felt So Depressed after He Left,'" *Fond du Lac (WI) Commonwealth Reporter*, August 22, 1968.

161. Margie Middleton and Ruth Y. Wenger, "Fresh Air Reminiscences," *Missionary Messenger*, July 1977, 12–13, 21.

162. Jill Quadagno, *The Color of Welfare: How Racism Undermined the War on Poverty* (New York: Oxford University Press, 1994), 193.

163. A 1982 study found that a Fresh Air child did "not wish to talk about his/her life in the city until he/she knows the host well, believing that their comments will reflect badly on their own family." See Michael Phillips, "Motivation and Expectation in Successful Volunteerism," *Nonprofit and Voluntary Sector Quarterly* 11, no. 2–3 (1982): 118–25.

164. "Visitor, Seven, Gets Lost: 'Fresh Air' Boy Returned," *Syracuse Herald-Journal*, July 10, 1965.

165. Martha Biondi, *To Stand and Fight: The Struggle for Civil Rights in Postwar New York City* (Cambridge, MA: Harvard University Press, 2003), 62; Gerald Horne, *Fire This Time: The Watts Uprising and the 1960s* (Charlottesville: University Press of Virginia, 1995).

166. Jacobus, "Our Summer House Guests."

167. Memorandum by Mary Rohrer and Anna Rohrer, "Mennonite Mission Children's Visitation Program, Visitation Record," 1951, EMM Record Room, folder: "F–J"; Harold Regier to Ervin P. Krehbiel, September 23, 1963, MLABC: MLA.VII.R GC Voluntary Service, Series 11 Gulfport VS Unit, box 4, folder 125: "Fresh Air, 1963"; Ervin Krehbiel and Melva Krehbiel to Harold Regier, October 27, 1964, MLABC: MLA.VII.R GC Voluntary Service, Series 11 Gulfport VS Unit, box 2, folder 36: "Correspondence—non-conf, 1964"; Lawrence Wright, *City Children, Country Summer* (New York: Scribner, 1979), 45.

168. Krehbiel and Krehbiel.

169. Luis Diaz interview.

170. Molly Wiseman, "Kids Are Kids—'Friendly Town' Message," *Paddock Publications* (Arlington Heights, IL), July 24, 1968.

171. Catherin M. Troost, *Catskill Mountain Memories* (Longwood, FL: Xulon Press, 2008), 16.

172. Melody M. Pannell, Harrisonburg, VA, interview by the author, January 20, 2016.

173. Robin Bernstein, *Racial Innocence: Performing American Childhood and Race from Slavery to Civil Rights* (New York: New York University Press, 2011), 63; Georgene Faulkner, *Melindy's Happy Summer* (New York: Julian Messner, 1949).

174. Lewis, "Integration, Then What?"; Begley, "Haverford Family to Welcome Two-Week 'Fresh Air' Visitor"; Florence Steuerwald, "New York Children Coming to County for 'Fresh Air,'" *Delaware County Daily Times* (Chester, PA), July 14, 1972; George

Dugan, "Fresh Air Fund Begins 98th Summer of Taking City Youngsters to Country," *New York Times*, June 8, 1975; Jane Blanksteen, "Summer Visitors from the City," *New York Times*, June 12, 1977; "Fresh-Air Families Recall 'City Brothers,'" 44; Memorandum by Michael Phillips, "Report of the Fresh Air Fund Friendly Town Study Undertaken by the Long Range Planning Committee," April 1980, 9, LVA, FAFR, 1949–1999, accession number 36407, box 31, folder 2: "Reports, Friendly Town Study, 1979–1980."

175. "City Kids Visit Country Homes; Beneficial to All," *Chicago Tribune*, July 22, 1965.

176. Vera M. Revoir, "Welcome Children for Summer Fun," *Post-Standard* (Syracuse, NY), June 6, 1952; Lont, Meeting to Discuss "Friendly Town" Project in the 60's; Horn, "The Inner City: Elective in Understanding"; John Kord Lagemann, "Something Special in Vacations: A *Reader's Digest* Reprint," *Reader's Digest*, June 1963; Ronald L. Trissel, "The Fresh Air Child's Urban Influence on Rural Shenandoah and Rockingham County" (term paper, Eastern Mennonite College, 1967); Wiseman, "Kids Are Kids—'Friendly Town' Message"; Jo Cullson, "52 Cleveland Youngsters Will Find Coshocton 'Friendly Town,'" *Coshocton (OH) Tribune*, June 12, 1968; "Fresh Air Family in Bay State Finds Room despite 6 Children," *New York Times*, August 5, 1970; Margie Clinger and Tom Clinger, "Public Letter," *News Journal* (Mansfield, OH), July 11, 1971.

177. Cathy Aldridge, "Wanted: Black Neighbors!" *New York Amsterdam News*, September 7, 1968.

178. Edith Simonds, "Letter to a Suburban Church," *Presbyterian Life*, September 1, 1966, 19–21, 40.

179. Owens, "Little Town with a Big Heart"; Sweeney, "Designed for Women"; "State 'Fresh Air Fund' Chairmen Hear Reports on Future Plans," *Bennington (VT) Banner*, May 2, 1966.

180. Memorandum by Eve Wiejec, "Rome Fresh Air Program Report," 1963, 4, UIL, MNC, box 99, folder 1505: "Fresh Air Fund, University of IL at Chicago Special Collection."

181. Faulkner, *Melindy's Happy Summer*, 13–14.

182. "Friendly Town Project Meeting Set for April 28," *Pontiac (IL) Daily Leader*, April 15, 1969.

183. "Fresh Air Fund Enables 14,000 to Enjoy Fresh Air," *New York Amsterdam News*, August 14, 1976.

184. "Ashland to Host City Teenagers."

185. Walt Juhnke and Esther Juhnke to Orlo Kaufman, August 20, 1961, MLABC: MLA. VII.R GC Voluntary Service, Series 11 Gulfport VS Unit, box 4, folder 123: "Fresh Air, 1961."

186. John Eby, Philadelphia, PA, telephone interview by the author, February 28, 2003.

187. Blanksteen, "A Refreshing Experience"; Lont, Meeting to Discuss "Friendly Town" Project in the 60's; Rosella Regier, "Fourth Successful 'Fresh Air' Year Completed," *Gulfbreeze*, September–October, 1963, 6.

188. "Athens Families Enrolled in 'Friendly Town' Program," *Messenger* (Athens, OH), April 10, 1967.

189. Carol Rabasca, "Speaking Personally," *New York Times*, June 26, 1977.

190. Regier, "Fourth Successful 'Fresh Air' Year Completed."

191. Memorandum by Ted Dubinsky, "Minutes of the "Committee to Consider the Minority Group Male's Self-Image 8/21/67," August 21, 1967, CUA, HGR MS#1465, Series III: Hudson Guild Files, box 13, folder 21: "Committee to Consider the Minority Group Male's Self-Image, 1967–1968."

192. "Two Summer Projects Share Cathedral Grounds, Facilities," *Cathedral News*, October 1966.

193. Frederick H. Lewis, "Where Do We Go from Here?" (New York: Fresh Air Fund, 1968), LOC, PRF D225, HRR, file 12576: "The Fresh Air Fund 1968–70."

194. Memorandum by Lewis, "What Am I Doing Here?: Remarks at Friendly Town Spring Planning Conference Held at Sharpe Reservation," February 20, 1963, LOC, PRF D224, HRR, file 12568: "The Fresh Air Fund"; Ronald P. Formisano, *Boston against Busing: Race, Class, and Ethnicity in the 1960s and 1970s* (Chapel Hill: University of North Carolina Press, 1991); "Narrow World Big Threat to 'Fresh Air' Children," *Huntingdon (PA) Daily News*, May 19, 1973.

195. Memorandum by Smith, "Minutes 1964 Friendly Town Planning Conference, February 18, 19, 20," 6; "Fund Pal Revists Md. Site," *New York Herald Tribune*, September 13, 1966.

196. "1,000 Inner-City Youths to Vacation in Suburbs," *Chicago Tribune*, June 2, 1968.

197. "100 Inner City Kids to Visit in Glen Ellyn," *Chicago Tribune*, April 25, 1966; "1,000 Inner-City Youths to Vacation in Suburbs."

198. Aldridge, "Herald Tribune Fresh Air Fund Continues despite Long Strike"; Lagemann, "Something Special in Vacations: A *Reader's Digest* Reprint."

199. Cindy Vanderkodde, Grand Rapids, MI, telephone interview by the author, March 7, 2010.

200. Sel Yackley, "Wheaton, Glen Ellyn Participate in Program for Integration," *Chicago Tribune*, April 27, 1967.

201. Lynford Hershey to Leon Stauffer, July 18, 1971, AMC—IV-21-4 box 1, MBM, Minority Ministries Council, Data Files #1, A–K, folder: "Education Program 1970–72, Lynford Hershey."

202. Fosburgh, "Fresh Air Fund Puts 2,800 in Camp."

203. Lawrence W. Levine, *Black Culture and Black Consciousness: Afro-American Folk Thought from Slavery to Freedom* (New York: Oxford University Press, 1977), 132; Deborah Gray White, *Ar'n't I a Woman: Female Slaves in the Plantation South* (New York: W.W. Norton, 1985), 76; Earl Lewis, *In Their Own Interests: Race, Class, and Power in Twentieth-Century Norfolk, Virginia* (Berkeley: University of California Press, 1991), 188; Annelise Orleck, *Storming Caesar's Palace: How Black Mothers Fought Their Own War on Poverty* (Boston, MA: Beacon, 2005), 96.

204. Daniel J. Monti Jr., *The American City: A Social and Cultural History* (Malden, MA: Blackwell, 1999), 190.

205. Charles E. Strickland and Andrew M. Ambrose, "The Changing Worlds of Children, 1945–1963," in *American Childhood: A Research Guide and Historical Handbook*, ed. Joseph M. Hawes and N. Ray Hiner (Westport, CT: Greenwood, 1985), 533–85; Mintz, *Huck's Raft*, 214.

206. Strickland and Ambrose, "The Changing Worlds of Children, 1945–1963," 566.

207. Monti, *The American City*, 191.

208. Trattner, *From Poor Law to Welfare State*, 299.

209. Mintz, *Huck's Raft*, 340.

210. "Tribune Fresh Air Fund Appeals to Kind, Friendly People Here," *Hagerstown (MD) Daily Mail*, June 15, 1948.

211. Paula S. Fass, *Children of a New World: Society, Culture, and Globalization* (New York: New York University Press, 2007), 178; "Groton Hosts Youngsters from Boston," *Fitchburg (MA) Sentinel*, July 12, 1966.

212. Charles, "Apathy Endangers Fresh Air Fund."

213. Bob Zanic, "Friendly Town Works 2 Ways," *Palatine (IL) Herald*, June 10, 1969.

214. Memorandum, "32,391 Turning Points," 1950, EDNY, Episcopal Missional Society Mission News 1923–1976: "Misc. loose reports & pamphlets."

215. C.A. Cooper, "Child Delinquency," *Missionary Messenger*, July 1950, 2.

216. Jack Tait, "1,000-Acre Fresh Air Campsite Is Dedicated," *New York Herald Tribune*, July 26, 1953; "Juvenile Delinquency Going up," *Galveston (TX) News*, July 28, 1953.

217. Frederick H. Lewis to Brown Reid, July 5, 1955, LOC, PRF D223, HRR, file 12561: "The Fresh Air Fund, 1954–55."

218. William J. Colmey, "Help Yourself to Joy," *Daily Sentinel* (Rome, NY), 1960.

219. Frederick H. Lewis to A.W. Betts, May 18, 1962, NYCPL-BRARR, Series I—Grant Files, box 2—folder: "Fresh Air Fund 1962"; Memorandum, "A Report Prepared for the Vincent Astor Foundation on the 1962 Activities of the Herald Tribune Fresh Air Fund," 1962, NYCPL-BRARR, Series I—Grant Files, box 2—folder: "Fresh Air Fund 1962."

220. Memorandum by Lewis, "Executive Director's Annual Report to the Board of Directors, for the Fiscal Year 1963–1964," 1964, LOC, PRF D225, HRR, file 12572: "The Fresh Air Fund 1965"; "3 Churches to Sponsor Friendly Town Program," *Nashua (NH) Telegraph*, May 2, 1966.

221. "Detective Helps Fresh Air Camp," *New York Times*, September 10, 1972.

222. "First Woman Executive Director Takes Helm for Fresh Air Fund Tomorrow," *New York Times*, October 26, 1975; "Fresh Air Fund Camp Buses Liberate 750 City Youths," *New York Times*, July 2, 1978.

223. Mathew L. Wald, "Need for Fresh Air Fund Increases with Inflation," *New York Times*, August 21, 1977.

224. "73 Chicago Children Quickly Make New Friends, See Fair."

225. Higginbotham, "The Black Church: A Gender Perspective," 216; Klassen, "The Robes of Womanhood: Dress and Authenticity among African American Methodist Women in the Nineteenth Century"; Schweinitz, *If We Could Change the World*, 19; Kahler, "Fresh Air Child Finds Real Home with Rome Family"; Howatt, "From Concrete to Country"; Wood, "Adirondack Wood-Cuttings."

226. Memorandum by Antoinette Grighto, "(Day Camp Report)," 1958, CUA, USAR, 1896–1995 MS#1149, Series VII: Programs and Services, box 54, folder 1: "Day Camp-Reports, 1958"; Memorandum by Dorothy Michael, "(Day Camp Report)," 1958, CUA, USAR, 1896–1995 MS#1149, Series VII: Programs and Services, box 54, folder 1: "Day Camp-Reports, 1958"; Memorandum by Donald Moeser, "(Day Camp Report)," 1958, CUA, USAR, 1896–1995 MS#1149, Series VII: Programs and Services, box 54, folder 1: "Day Camp-Reports, 1958"; Memorandum by Yoichi Nishimoto, "(Day Camp Report)," 1958, CUA, USAR, 1896–1995 MS#1149, Series VII: Programs and Services, box 54, folder 1: "Day Camp-Reports, 1958"; Memorandum by Margaret Williams, "(Day Camp Report)," 1958, CUA, USAR, 1896–1995 MS#1149, Series VII: Programs and Services, box 54, folder 1: "Day Camp-Reports, 1958."

227. Memorandum, "Camp Intake Form—Denise Duckworth," May 1, 1956, CUA, USAR, 1896–1995 MS#1149, Series VII: Programs and Services, box 53, folder 5: "Camp-Children's Records (D–E), 1945–57."

228. Mrs. Raymond E. Carr, 1956, LVA, FAFR, 1949–1999, accession number 36407, box 19, folder 6: "Contest Entries—1956, Essays (Contest #2)"; James A. Murray to Alice Trissel, March 26, 1976, LVA, FAFR, 1949–1999, accession number 36407, box 21, folder 1: "Correspondence—FAF children—1959–1984."

229. Memorandum by Ellen Marvin, "Duckworth, Dierdre," 1951, CUA, USAR, 1896–1995 MS#1149, Series VII: Programs and Services, box 53, folder 5: "Camp-Children's Records (D–E), 1945–57"; Sara M. Keily to Sylvia Leshowitz, July 21, 1948, CUA, USAR, 1896–1995 MS#1149, Series VII: Programs and Services, box 53, folder 5: "Camp-Children's Records (D–E), 1945–57"; Memorandum by W. Rivera, "Camp Nathan Hale—Fernandez, John," 1950, CUA, USAR, 1896–1995 MS#1149, Series VII: Programs and Services, Camp-Children's Records (F), 1950–56, box 53, folder 6.

230. Paris, *Children's Nature*, 135, 144, 145, 146, 148.

231. Juhnke and Juhnke.

232. Cook, "City Youths Discover Joy of Suburbs."

233. "Fresh Air Children Will Arrive at Station Tuesday, July 23rd," *Hagerstown (MD) Daily Mail*, July 18, 1946.

234. "Your Help Is Needed for Fresh Air Vacations," *Portsmouth (NH) Herald*, July 29, 1954.

235. Lont, Meeting to Discuss "Friendly Town" Project in the 60's.

236. Lagemann, "Something Special in Vacations: A *Reader's Digest* Reprint."

237. Luis Diaz interview.

238. Regier, "Fourth Successful 'Fresh Air' Year Completed"; Orlo Kaufman to Elva Schrag and Ellen Schrag, February 24, 1961, MLABC: MLA.VII.R GC Voluntary Service, Series 11 Gulfport VS Unit, box 2, folder 32: "Correspondence—non-conf, 1961."

239. Memorandum by Lewis, "What Am I Doing Here?" 2–3.

240. Sol Padlibsky, "Of All Things: Camp Discipline Big Woe," *Charleston (WV) Daily Mail*, September 8, 1964.

241. "Whitewashed," *Times Herald Record* (Middleton, NY), November 30, 1971.

242. "Lehmans Directing Penna. Youth Camp," *Daily News Record* (Harrisonburg, VA), June 25, 1955.

243. Fosburgh, "Fresh Air Fund Puts 2,800 in Camp."

244. Lacey Fosburgh, "Fresh Air Fund Camp Improved Vastly over Years," *New York Times*, June 20, 1971.

245. "Fresh Air Fund Aides Training; First Campers to Arrive Friday," *New York Times*, June 22, 1969.

246. "A Fresh-Air Camp Gears for Season," *New York Times*, June 24, 1973.

247. Faulkner, *Melindy's Happy Summer*, 16; "More Host Families Are Needed."

248. H. D. Forbes, *Ethnic Conflict: Commerce, Culture, and the Contact Hypothesis* (New Haven, CT: Yale University Press, 1997), 112.

4. SEX, SEVEN, SICK

1. Lawrence Wright, *City Children, Country Summer* (New York: Scribner, 1979), 23.

2. R. P. Neuman, "Masturbation, Madness, and the Modern Concepts of Childhood and Adolescence," *Journal of Social History* 8, no. 3 (1975): 1–27.

3. Sterling Fishman, "The History of Childhood Sexuality," *Journal of Contemporary History* 17, no. 2 (1982): 269–83.

4. James A. Morone, *Hellfire Nation: The Politics of Sin in American History* (New Haven, CT: Yale University Press, 2003), 17.

5. Stephen Lassonde, "Ten Is the New Fourteen: Age Compression and 'Real' Childhood," in *Reinventing Childhood after World War II*, ed. Paula S. Fass and Michael Grossberg (Philadelphia: University of Pennsylvania Press, 2012), 51–67.

6. Ann Laura Stoler, *Carnal Knowledge and Imperial Power: Race and the Intimate in Colonial Rule* (Berkeley, CA: University of California Press, 2002), 16.

7. Fishman, "The History of Childhood Sexuality."

8. John Cleverley and D. C. Phillips, *From Locke to Spock: Influence Models of the Child in Modern Western Thought* (Carlton: Melbourne University Press, 1976), 52–53.

9. Fishman, "The History of Childhood Sexuality"; Margaret Lamberts Bendroth, *Growing up Protestant: Parents, Children, and Mainline Churches* (New Brunswick, NJ: Rutgers University Press, 2002), 5.

10. Bendroth, *Growing up Protestant*, 5.

11. Steven Mintz, *Huck's Raft: A History of American Childhood* (Cambridge, MA: Belknap Press of Harvard University Press, 2004), 3–4.

12. Morone, *Hellfire Nation*, 17.

13. Wilma King, *African American Childhoods: Historical Perspectives from Slavery to Civil Rights* (New York: Palgrave Macmillan, 2005), 149.

14. Rebecca de Schweinitz, *If We Could Change the World: Young People and America's Long Struggle for Racial Equality* (Chapel Hill: University of North Carolina Press, 2009), 125–26; Neil R. McMillen, *The Citizens' Council: Organized Resistance to the Second Reconstruction, 1954–64* (Chicago: University of Illinois Press, 1971), 185.

15. George Lewis, *Massive Resistance: The White Response to the Civil Rights Movement* (New York: Oxford University Press, 2006), 4, 12; Jason Sokol, *There Goes My Everything: White Southerners in the Age of Civil Rights, 1945–1975* (New York: Knopf, 2006), 14.

16. Jane Dailey, "Sex, Segregation, and the Sacred after *Brown*," *Journal of American History* 91, no. 1 (2004): 119–44.

17. Ronald P. Formisano, *Boston against Busing: Race, Class, and Ethnicity in the 1960s and 1970s* (Chapel Hill: University of North Carolina Press, 1991), 119.

18. "Summer Vacation," *Cleveland Call and Post*, March 17, 1956; "14 Share Children Guests of Honor at Manlius Picnic," *Post-Standard* (Syracuse, NY), July 21, 1953; "Fresh Air Kids Come for Visits on Shore," *Salisbury (MD) Times*, July 11, 1957.

19. Perfinax, "Experiment in Humanity," *Lowell (MA) Sun*, July 26, 1961; George A. Edmonds, "Friendly Town Program Molds Young Lives," *Bennington (VT) Banner*, July 27, 1963; Kathy Begley, "Haverford Family to Welcome Two-Week 'Fresh Air' Visitor," *Delaware County Daily Times* (Chester, PA), June 10, 1968.

20. "Guest Meets Hosts: First-Timers," *Daily News* (Huntingdon and Mount Union, PA), June 28, 1968; Molly Wiseman, "Kids Are Kids—'Friendly Town' Message," *Paddock Publications* (Arlington Heights, IL), July 24, 1968; "Inner City Youths Enjoy Two Weeks of Suburban Life," *Chicago Tribune*, August 17, 1969.

21. "Holiday Begins," *Daily News Record* (Harrisonburg, VA), July 14, 1978; Eleanor Charles, "Apathy Endangers Fresh Air Fund," *New York Times*, May 20, 1979; "Former 'Fresh Air Kid' Remembers Happy Summer," *Tyrone (PA) Daily Herald*, June 28, 1979.

22. Jerry Thornton, "Visitors Find Warmth in West Side Ghetto," *Chicago Tribune*, August 10, 1972.

23. "In Interest of Fresh Air Fund," *Newport (RI) Mercury and Weekly News*, June 27, 1930; "Fresh Air Group Registers Hosts for N.Y. Kiddies," *Altoona (PA) Mirror*, June 24, 1940; Memorandum by Paul N. Kraybill, "Mennonite Mission Children Visitation Program, Report of the Director," 1951, 2, EMM Record Room, folder: "Committee Action"; "Kiwanis Club Sponsors Friendly Town Program," *Daily News* (Huntingdon and Mount Union, PA), June 14, 1954; "Fresh Air Chairman Is Named," *Daily Sentinel* (Rome, NY), 1960; Joan Skidmore, "Fresh Air Fund: Give a Child a Chance," *Delaware County Daily Times* (Chester, PA), June 7, 1974; Sheila Behrend, Tami Hall, and Margo Behrend, "'Friendly Town,'" *Muscatine, Iowa, Journal*, January 9, 1976; "How Friendly Is This Country?" *Daily News* (Huntingdon, Saxton, and Mount Union, PA), June 7, 1979.

24. Memorandum by Esther Eby Glass, "Report of Mission Fresh Air Sponsors' Meeting," March 27, 1962, EMM Record Room, folder: "Eastern Mennonite Board, Fresh Air Program 1962–1963"; Memorandum by Paul N. Kraybill, "Mennonite Mission Children Visitation Program," 1950, EMM Record Room, folder: "testimonies and Misc."

25. "Shaftsbury Couple Honored for Aid to Fresh Air Program," *Bennington (VT) Banner*, April 6, 1965.

26. Lacey Fosburgh, "Fresh Air Homes for Boys Needed," *New York Times*, June 27, 1971.

27. M. Arlene Mellinger, "200 Children Are Hoping . . . ," *Missionary Messenger*, May 1972, 12–13; Anita Duhe, "Westminster Woman Has Hopes for Boosting Fresh Air Fund," *Sentinel-Enterprise* (Fitchburg, MA), August 29, 1975.

28. Maria P. P. Root, *Love's Revolution: Interracial Marriage* (Philadelphia: Temple University Press, 2001), 34, 180; Andrew Wiese, *Places of Their Own: African American Suburbanization in the Twentieth Century* (Chicago: University of Chicago Press, 2004), 9;

Anita Jones Thomas, Karen McCurtis Witherspoon, and Suzette L. Speight, "Toward the Development of the Stereotypic Roles for Black Women Scale," *Journal of Black Psychology* 30, no. 3 (2004): 426–42.

29. Memorandum, "Host Parents Summary—1960," 1960, [2], MLABC: MLA.VII.R GC Voluntary Service, Series 11 Gulfport VS Unit, box 4, folder 122: "Fresh Air, 1960"; George E. Kroecker and Mrs. George E. Kroecker to Orlo Kaufman, August 20, 1961, MLABC: MLA.VII.R GC Voluntary Service, Series 11 Gulfport VS Unit, box 4, folder 123: "Fresh Air, 1961."

30. Rev. Arnold Nickel to Orlo Kaufman, February 27, 1961, MLABC: MLA.VII.R GC Voluntary Service, Series 11 Gulfport VS Unit, box 2, folder 32: "Correspondence—non-conf, 1961."

31. Luis Diaz, New York, NY, telephone interview by the author, May 4, 2010.

32. Wright, *City Children, Country Summer*, 13.

33. Julie Bettie, "Class Dismissed?: Roseanne and the Changing Face of Working-Class Iconography," *Social Text* 14, no. 4 (1995): 125–49.

34. Jean Ait Belkhir, "The Sexual Boundaries of Race and Class in Working-Class Novels: Marrying up and Living It down/Marrying down and Living It up," *Race, Gender & Class* 9, no. 3 (2002): 101–20; Lori Ouellette, "Ship of Dreams: Cross-Class Romance and the Cultural Fantasy of *Titantic*," in Titanic: *Anatomy of a Blockbuster*, ed. Kevin S. Sandler and Galen Sandler (New Brunswick, NJ: Rutgers University Press, 1999), 169–88.

35. Bill Babel, "Off the Beaten Track . . . ," *Oneonta (NY) Star*, November 30, 1949.

36. "A Friendly Note—to Some of the Friendliest People in the World" (New York, NY: 1953 [circa]), LOC, PRF D223, HRR, file 12560: "The Fresh Air Fund, 1953–54."

37. Luis Diaz interview.

38. John D'Emilio and Estelle B. Freedman, *Intimate Matters: A History of Sexuality in America* (New York: Harper & Row, 1988), 293.

39. Janice Batts, Iowa City, IA, telephone interview by the author, February 15, 2012.

40. Marcia J. Bunge, "The Child, Religion, and the Academy: Developing Robust Theological and Religious Understandings of Children and Childhood," *Journal of Religion* 86, no. 4 (2006): 549–79.

41. David Hechler, *The Battle and the Backlash: The Child Sexual Abuse War* (Lexington, MA: Lexington Books, 1988), 35–36.

42. Mrs. Raymond E. Carr, 1956, LVA, FAFR, 1949–1999, accession number 36407, box 19, folder 6: "Contest Entries—1956, Essays (Contest #2)"; Batts interview.

43. Hechler, *The Battle and the Backlash*, 31.

44. Ibid., 29.

45. For examples of Fresh Air children who did relocate, see "Young Woman Returns Home to Fresh Air Fund 'Parents,'" *New York Times*, May 28, 1978; Cindy Vanderkodde, Grand Rapids, MI, telephone interview by the author, March 7, 2010.

46. Unattributed article clipping, June 1976, author's personal collection; "Former 'Fresh Air Kid' Remembers Happy Summer"; William E. Haskell, "Olean a Fresh Air Town Sixty-Six Years," *Olean (NY) Times Herald*, December 22, 1947; "Lives Brightened by Fresh Air Fund," *New York Times*, August 15, 1976.

47. Margaret L. Hunter, *Race, Gender, and the Politics of Skin Tone* (New York: Routledge, 2005), 7.

48. Laurence Mickolic, "The 'Big Plus' in Programming for 1960," *Annual Report—1960*, 1960, 4–5, LOC, PRF D224, HRR, file 12567: "The Fresh Air Fund"; Lacey Fosburgh, "Fresh Air Fund Puts 2,800 in Camp," *New York Times*, July 11, 1971.

49. "Fresh Air Fund Camp Buses Liberate 750 City Youths," *New York Times*, July 2, 1978.

50. Leslie Paris, *Children's Nature: The Rise of the American Summer Camp* (New York: New York University Press, 2008), 157.

51. Walter Shephard Ufford, *Fresh Air Charity in the United States* (New York: Bonnell, Silver & Co., 1897), 86–87.

52. Memorandum by Mary Jane Gooley, "Camper's Name—Marilyn Hobbs," [n.d.], CUA, USAR, 1896–1995 MS#1149, Series VII: Programs and Services, box 53, folder 7: "Camp-Children's Records (H–M), 1955–57."

53. "Homes Are Needed for 'Friendly' Kids," *Waterloo (IA) Sunday Courier*, June 27, 1972.

54. "20 Fresh Air Boys and Girls Start Vacations in the Area," *Kingston (NY) Daily Freeman*, July 7, 1949; "Fresh Air Fund Is Magic Carpet for Urban Children," *New York Times*, July 1, 1979.

55. "'Friendly Town' Topic for Kittery Meeting," *Portsmouth (NH) Herald*, May 21, 1968.

56. Ufford, *Fresh Air Charity in the United States*, 69.

57. "Will Help the Kiddies: Rotary Club Back Movement to Secure Hosts for Tribune Fresh Air Fund Children—When a Fellow Needs a Friend," *Oneonta (NY) Star*, July 22, 1922; "Fresh Air Children to Visit Area," *Troy (NY) Record*, June 7, 1963. By comparison, the oldest children involved in the "placing out" program of the Children's Aid Society—also known as the orphan trains—were also twelve or thirteen by 1920. See Marilyn Irvin Holt, *The Orphan Trains: Placing out in America* (Lincoln, NE: University of Nebraska Press, 1992), 140.

58. I have found only one instance in which a local hosting committee affiliated with the Fresh Air Fund raised the upper age limit: A Friendly Town committee in Coatesville, Pennsylvania, raised the cap to thirteen in 1958. See Etta Stroud, "'Fresh Air Children' of NYC Are Guests in Chester County," *Afro-American* (Baltimore), July 26, 1958.

59. "Ashland to Host City Teenagers," *News Journal* (Mansfield, OH), July 10, 1972.

60. Joan Monaco, "City Kids Get Chance for Some Friendly Adventures," *Lowell (MA) Sunday*, August 22, 1971; "Friendly Town Program Next Month," *Winona (MN) Daily News*, June 30, 1971; "L.H. Streich Chairman of 'Friendly Town,'" *Oelwein (IA) Daily Register*, June 14, 1972; Judy Russell, "Another 'Friendly Town' Year Is Just Ahead for Families in Area," *Daily Northwestern* (Oshkosh, WI), May 5, 1970.

61. Betty Pobanz, "'Friendly Towns' Offer Summer Vacations to Underprivileged New York Children," *Barnard (NY) Bulletin*, April 14, 1947; "Yates to Invite City Children for Vacation," *Chronicle-Express* (Penn Yan, NY), May 26, 1949; "The Goal: 100 Children," *Bennington (VT) Banner*, May 8, 1963; Lee Edwards, "Fresh Air Fund Workers Give Free Time, Effort," *Oneonta (NY) Star*, July 13, 1971.

62. "Fresh Air Fund Work in Bronx a Challenge," *New York Times*, May 7, 1978.

63. "More Fresh Air Children Here; Others Want to Come if Hosts Can Be Found," *Lebanon (PA) Daily News*, July 14, 1960, 23.

64. Phyllis M. Palmer, *Living as Equals: How Three White Communities Struggled to Make Interracial Connections during the Civil Rights Era* (Nashville: Vanderbilt University Press, 2008), 4, 27.

65. Mrs. E. K. Bruckhart to Paul N. Kraybill, May 31, 1954, EMM Record Room, folder: "A–E."

66. "Fresh Air Kids Get Late Start on Country Visit," *Progress* (Clearfield, PA), July 27, 1978.

67. "Former 'Fresh Air Kid' Remembers Happy Summer."

68. Memorandum, "Camping," November, 1950, ELAA, UMN, United Way of Minneapolis records (SW 70), box 72, folder 2: "Camps General 1950."

69. Carey Winfrey, "Blackout a Problem for Fresh Air Group," *New York Times*, July 17, 1977.

70. Mary Ann Strawn, "Friend of Friendly Town," *Arlington Heights (IL) Herald*, August 17, 1972, 6.

71. Leslie Paris, "'Please Let Me Come Home': Homesickness and Family Ties at Early-Twentieth-Century Summer Camps," in *The American Child: A Cultural Studies Reader*, ed. Carolyn F. Levander and Carol J. Singley (New Brunswick, NJ: Rutgers University Press, 2003), 246–61.

72. "7 Fresh Air Children Write of Newport Visit," *Newport (RI) News*, January 19, 1950; "Fresh Air Kids Come for Visits on Shore."

73. Lee Edwards, "'Friendly Town' Chairman: Fresh Air Fund Matchmaker," *Oneonta (NY) Star*, July 14, 1971; "A Homesick Girl Yearns for 1980 Fresh Air Trip," *New York Times*, August 26, 1979; Bill Draves Jr., "Inner-City Children from Chicago Bring Surprises to 'Friendly Town' Parents," *Commonwealth Reporter* (Fond du Lac, WI), 1968.

74. Memorandum, "Minutes of the Meeting of the Camp Committee, Friday, March 23, 1945, Lecture Room, Citizens' and Building—2:00 P.M.," 1945, ELAA, UMN, United Way of Minneapolis records (SW 70), box 38, folder 2: "Group Work and Relief Division 1945."

75. "Fresh Air," *Daily News* (Huntingdon and Mount Union, PA), June 28, 1968.

76. Edwards, "'Friendly Town' Chairman: Fresh Air Fund Matchmaker."

77. Memorandum by Marchand Chaney and Mimi Vernon, "Evaluation of Newberry-Dubuque Project for 1962," 1962, UIL, MNC, box 99, folder 1505: "Fresh Air Fund, University of IL at Chicago Special Collection"; Monaco, "City Kids Get Chance for Some Friendly Adventures"; Lynne Ames, "The Fresh Air Fund: Summers of Sharing," *New York Times*, May 20, 1979; "Country Homes Sought for City Kids," *Daily Intelligencer* (Doylestown, PA), May 21, 1979, 9.

78. Edwards, "'Friendly Town' Chairman"; Norman G. Shenk, Salunga, PA, telephone interview by the author, March 22, 2005.

79. Monaco, "City Kids Get Chance for Some Friendly Adventures"; Edwards, "'Friendly Town' Chairman"; Joan Brown, "Program Offers Chance to Give Child a Memorable Vacation," *News Journal* (Mansfield, OH), April 4, 1970.

80. Martha Fellows, "Hosts Needed," *Daily Messenger* (Canandaigua, NY), June 3, 1976; "June 3rd Marks 100th Anniversary of Fresh Air Fund," *Wellsboro (PA) Gazette*, June 1, 1977, 6.

81. "Friendly Town Couple Enrich Deaf Boy's Life," *New York Times*, August 5, 1979; Chester H. Thomas to Paul N. Kraybill, March 25, 1951, EMM Record Room, folder: "testimonies and misc."

82. Thomas to Kraybill.

83. John Kord Lagemann, "Something Special in Vacations: A *Reader's Digest* Reprint," *Reader's Digest*, June 1963; Memorandum by Chaney and Vernon, "Evaluation of Newberry-Dubuque Project for 1962"; "The Open Door," *Portsmouth (NH) Herald*, June 29, 1951.

84. "Summer in the City? No Fun!" *Daily News* (Huntingdon, Mount Union, and Saxton, PA), May 12, 1978.

85. "Friendly Towns Play Host to the Fresh Air Needy," *New York Times*, July 8, 1979; Linda Vosburgh, "Religion, 'Street' Meet in 'Fresh Air,'" *Sunday Herald* (Chicago), September 16, 1979.

86. "Friendly Town Is Set up by Pennsylvania Couple," *New York Times*, August 19, 1979. Other Fresh Air hosts likewise referred to the "sophisticated" children. See Chuck Austin, "The History of the Fresh Air Fund," (1981), C12–10, 13, LVA, FAFR, 1949–1999, accession number 36407, box 22, folder 2: "Histories 1977."

87. Memorandum by Mary E. Smith, "Minutes 1964 Friendly Town Planning Conference, February 18, 19, 20," 1964, 1, 8–9, UIL, MNC, box 99, folder 1505: "Fresh Air Fund, University of IL at Chicago Special Collection."

88. Ibid., 4.

89. Nan Ickeringill, "Good or Bad?: A Dialogue on Children's Camps," *Nashua (NH) Telegraph*, June 28, 1969, 14.

90. Memorandum by Smith, "Minutes 1964 Friendly Town Planning Conference, February 18, 19, 20."

91. "Children's Aid Society to Find out How Tenant District Boys Will Make out in 'Pioneer' Camp," *New York Age*, July 6, 1940; Peter Kihss, "Girls Have Busy Time at Maple Knoll Camp," *New York World Telegram*, July 23, 1941; Memorandum, "The East Harlem Protestant Parish: Report to the Administrative Board," April 12, 1950, PNHA, NCC, Home Missions Council of North America, 1903–1951, RG26 box 4, folder 17: "East Harlem Protestant Parish, Aug 1949–Dec 1950"; Patricia Henchie, "Howell House Aids Planning Camp Season," *Chicago Daily Tribune*, May 27, 1951.

92. Kihss, "Girls Have Busy Time at Maple Knoll Camp"; Frederick H. Lewis to Ralph Hayes, 1951, LOC, PRF D223, HRR, file 12558: "The Fresh Air Fund, 1951."

93. Carol Van Horn, "The Inner City: Elective in Understanding," *Presbyterian Life*, October 15, 1963, 25–27; "Parental Check on Youths Asked: Rector on Lower East Side to Work with Adults on Program for Young," *New York Times*, August 31, 1959; Ray Bonda and Ben Silber [n.d.], ELAA, UMN, HSSR (SW0058), General, box 48, folder 16: "1951–1961."

94. "A Fresh-Air Camp Gears for Season," *New York Times*, June 24, 1973; Henchie, "Howell House Aids Planning Camp Season."

95. "Children of Manhattan's Slums Spend Happy Christmas in County," *Hagerstown (MD) Daily Mail*, December 28, 1946; Joseph Owens, "Little Town with a Big Heart," *Afro-American* (Baltimore), July 30, 1955; Joan K. Kahler, "Fresh Air Child Finds Real Home with Rome Family," *Daily Sentinel* (Rome, NY), 1961; Charles, "Apathy Endangers Fresh Air Fund"; Ames, "The Fresh Air Fund: Summers of Sharing"; Peg Hurd, "Tony Campano Picks Upper Bald Eagle over the Bronx," *Tyrone (PA) Daily Herald*, July 22, 1978; Gene Rondinaro, "A Change of Pace in the Sun," *New York Times*, June 3, 1979.

96. Dave Shaw, "Dateline: Fulton," *Syracuse Herald-Journal*, June 24, 1976; "Fresh Air Tots Get Oneonta Home," *Syracuse Herald-American*, December 31, 1950; "Area Family 'Adopts' Two Fresh Airs Brought Here for Christmas Vacation," *Oneonta (NY) Star*, December 27, 1950.

97. Pobanz, "'Friendly Towns' Offer Summer Vacations to Underprivileged New York Children."

98. George Goodman Jr., "Chance for a Child to Get out of the City," *New York Times*, May 16, 1976.

99. Memorandum, "The Fresh Air Fund at a Glance," 1969, LOC, PRF D225, HRR, file 12576: "The Fresh Air Fund 1968–70."

100. "Fresh Air Children off to Country," *New York Times*, June 26, 1977.

101. "Fresh Air Vacation Registering Ends; Many Disappointed," *New York Times*, June 17, 1979.

102. "Planetarium Put in Fresh Air Camp," *New York Times*, July 23, 1972; George Dugan, "Fresh Air Camp Adds Attraction," *New York Times*, June 4, 1972.

103. "A Camp Designed for Summer Fun," *Architectural Forum*, July 1962.

104. Memorandum by Frederick H. Lewis, "Executive Director's Report to December 21, 1967 Meeting of the Board of Directors," 1967, LOC, PRF D225, HRR, file 12575: "The Fresh Air Fund 1967."

105. Memorandum, "Annual Report to the Board of Directors," 1951, 16, LOC, PRF D223, HRR, file 12558: "The Fresh Air Fund, 1951."

106. Memorandum, "1952 Annual Report [proof]," 1953, LOC, PRF D223, HRR, file 12559: "The Fresh Air Fund, 1952."

107. "Vacation Homes Needed for N.Y. Needy Children," *Daily Messenger* (Canandaigua, NY), May 1, 1964.

108. Memorandum by Frederick H. Lewis, "Annual Report for 1968: A Reappraisal," 1968, 11, copied from the CCAH, UTA.

109. "Handicapped Campers," *New York Times*, August 7, 1974; ". . . And a Greater Need," *New York Times*, June 1, 1975; unattributed article clipping, 13; "Swimming Key Part of Fresh Air Camps," *New York Times*, July 24, 1977; "Fresh Air Camp Helps Disabled to Gain in Health and Confidence," *New York Times*, June 4, 1978; "Fund Camp Is Family Tradition for 2 Boys," *New York Times*, June 24, 1979.

110. Abigail A. Van Slyck, *A Manufactured Wilderness: Summer Camps and the Shaping of American Youth, 1890–1960* (Minneapolis: University of Minnesota Press, 2006), 38–39.

111. Unattributed article clipping, 13.

112. Lena Williams, "Disabled Enjoy Fresh Air Camp," *New York Times*, July 10, 1977.

113. "Fresh Air Hosts Cited by Speaker at Dinner," *Lebanon (PA) Daily News*, April 28, 1973.

114. "Friendly Town Couple Enrich Deaf Boy's Life."

115. Edward Hudson, "Fresh Air Fund Opens 97th Year," *New York Times*, May 19, 1974.

116. "Here and There," *Bridgeport (CT) Post*, June 24, 1958; "Fund Camp Is Family Tradition for 2 Boys"; "Fresh Air Fund Summer Offers Widened Outlook," *New York Times*, June 3, 1979.

117. Jill Smolowe, "Giving the Gift of Fresh Air," *New York Times*, May 7, 1978.

118. "Host of Two Fresh Air Fund Boys to Pay Their Fare to California," *New York Times*, June 15, 1969; "A Homesick Girl Yearns for 1980 Fresh Air Trip"; "400 Poor Children Leave for Fresh Air Fund Vacations in Cape Cod Homes," *New York Times*, July 25, 1969; "W. Side Kids to Country," *Chicago Daily Defender*, July 8, 1971.

119. Luis Diaz interview; Nilson Diaz, New York, NY, telephone interview by the author, May 12, 2010.

120. Mae Schrag, "Mennonite Prejudice," *Gulfbreeze*, May–June 1963, 5.

121. James A. Murray to Alice Trissel, April 15, 1976, LVA, FAFR, 1949–1999, accession number 36407, box 21, folder 1: "Correspondence—FAF children—1959–1984."

122. Paul E. Warfield, "The Whole Story," *Bennington (VT) Banner*, September 6, 1963.

123. Vanderkodde interview.

124. Glenda Adams, New York, NY, telephone interview by the author, March 28, 2010.

125. Peggy Curry, Harrisonburg, VA, interview by the author, March 29, 2005.

126. See, for example: Marion L. Osborne to Mr. and Mrs. Trissel, 1976, LVA, FAFR, 1949–1999, accession number 36407, box 21, folder 1: "Correspondence—FAF children—1959–1984"; Batts interview; James C. Lont, Meeting to Discuss "Friendly Town" Project in the 60's, Graafschap, MI: 2010.

127. Anne-Marie Châtelet, "A Breath of Fresh Air: Open-Air Schools in Europe," in *Designing Modern Childhoods: History, Space, and the Material Culture of Children*, ed. Marta Gutman and Ning De Coninck-Smith (Newark, NJ: Rutgers University Press, 2008), 107–27.

128. "Mrs. Harry May Is Tribune Host for Eight Consecutive Years," *Hagerstown (MD) Daily Mail*, July 27, 1946; "Final Contingent on Vacation at Fresh Air Home," *Troy (NY) Times Record*, August 5, 1947; Owens, "Little Town with a Big Heart."

129. "1948 Fresh Air Fund Campaign Begins Tomorrow; $6,000 Is Goal Established," *Florence (SC) Morning News*, June 6, 1948.

130. "Fresh Air Guests Express Enthusiasm: Hosts Report Not One Child Has Had to Leave," *Newport (RI) News*, July 20, 1950.

131. "Fresh Air Fund Campaign Sent," *Bridgeport (CT) Telegram*, May 30, 1958; "Friendly Town Sends 20 Children to Area," *Chronicle-Telegram* (Elyria, OH), June 13, 1964; "Inner-City Protestant Parish Work Described," *Chronicle-Telegram* (Elyria, OH), February 4, 1968; "Fresh Air Fund Campaign Sent"; "Friendly Town Sends 20 Children to Area."

132. "Trouble Shooters," *What's in the Air*, Spring 1966.

133. Robert A. Orsi, "Introduction: Crossing the City Line," in *Gods of the City: Religion and the American Urban Landscape*, ed. Robert A. Orsi (Bloomington: Indiana University Press, 1999), 1–78.

134. Paris, *Children's Nature*, 123.

135. Paul N. Kraybill to Frederick Howell Lewis, June 25, 1952, EMM Record Room, folder: "F–J."

136. Ibid.

137. "Fresh Air Fund Helps to Honor Doctor Who Gave Tests Free," *New York Times*, June 29, 1969.

138. Randy Wynn, "Children Find New Homes during Week in Ashland," *News Journal* (Mansfield, OH), July 4, 1971.

139. Lacey Fosburgh, "Medical Aid Given by Fresh Air Fund," *New York Times*, June 6, 1971.

140. "District Homes Needed for Fresh Air Children," *Daily News* (Huntingdon and Mount Union, PA), May 18, 1959; Marilou Hedlund, "'4 Chance to Yell and Scream and Look at Things,'" *Chicago Tribune*, July 26, 1964.

141. "Trouble Shooters"; Mary Childers, *Welfare Brat: A Memoir* (New York: Bloomsbury, 2005), 5; Richard F. Crandell, ed., *The Frog Log and Other Stories about Children* (New York: Herald Tribune Fresh Air Fund, 1962).

142. "Fresh Air Youngsters Arrive in Geneva Friday Night," *Chronicle-Express* (Penn Yan, NY), July 24, 1952.

143. "$22,197 Settlement Approved for Five Injured Children," *Post-Standard* (Syracuse, NY), January 4, 1952.

144. Memorandum, "Annual Report to the Board of Directors"; Memorandum by Ralph B. Dwinell, "Friendly Town, Summer 1967," 1967, NYCPL-BRARR, Series I—Grant Files, box 2, folder: "Fresh Air Fund 1962," Whitney North Seymour Papers, 1930–1983, box 114—Subject Files: "Fresh Air Fund, 1962–1983, January 1965–June 1967."

145. "Sheboygan Girl Dies in Tractor Accident," *Fond Du Lac Commonwealth Reporter*, August 4, 1968; "Tractor Iron Rim Hits Dunstable Boy in Face," *Lowell (MA) Sunday*, May 6, 1968.

146. Wright, *City Children, Country Summer*, 46.

147. Memorandum by Ralph B. Dwinell, "Friendly Town," 1966, LOC, PRF D224, HRR, file 12567: "The Fresh Air Fund."

148. Ufford, *Fresh Air Charity in the United States*, 50.

149. "Trouble Shooters."

150. Fosburgh, "Medical Aid Given by Fresh Air Fund."

151. Ibid.

152. E. Melanie DuPuis, *Nature's Perfect Food: How Milk Became America's Drink* (New York: New York University Press, 2002), 10.

153. Lee Edwards, "All Their World Is Asphalt and Farms Are Only in Stories," *Oneonta (NY) Star*, July 12, 1971.

154. Memorandum by Ted Dubinsky, "Minutes of the Committee to Consider the Minority Group Male's Self-Image, 10/30/67," October 30, 1967, CUA, HGR MS#1465, Series III: Hudson Guild Files, box 13, folder 21: "Committee to Consider the Minority Group Male's Self-Image, 1967–1968."

5. MILK, MONEY, POWER

1. Milking Time (1950), NYCPL-SC, Children, 23–012.

2. Jan Albers, *Hands on the Land: A History of the Vermont Landscape* (Cambridge, MA: MIT Press, 2000), 274.

3. Barbara F. Agnew et al., *Look Around Hinesburg and Charlotte, Vermont* (Burlington, VT: Chittenden County Historical Society, 1973).

4. Andrea S. Wiley, "'Drink Milk for Fitness': The Cultural Politics of Human Biological Variation and Milk Consumption in the United States," *American Anthropologist* 106, no. 3 (2004): 506–17; Deborah Valenze, *Milk: A Local and Global History* (New Haven: Yale University Press, 2011), 253.

5. E. Melanie DuPuis, *Nature's Perfect Food: How Milk Became America's Drink* (New York: New York University Press, 2002), 97–98.

6. Laurie Winn Carlson, *Cattle: An Informal Social History* (Chicago: Ivan R. Dee, 2001), 46–47.

7. Loren C. Dunn, "Analysis of the Effectiveness of the Friendly Town Publicity Program of the *Herald Tribune* Fresh Air Fund" (master's thesis, Boston University, 1966), 23.

8. Steven Mintz, *Huck's Raft: A History of American Childhood* (Cambridge, MA: Belknap Press of Harvard University Press, 2004), 255.

9. Ibid., 258.

10. "Children Leave for Vacation," *Troy (NY) Record*, July 10, 1946; "Final Contingent on Vacation at Fresh Air Home," *Times Record* (Troy, NY), August 5, 1947; DuPuis, *Nature's Perfect Food*, 5.

11. Memorandum, "Meeting of Camp Standards Committee of the Group Work and Recreation Division Held on April 3 and 5, 1945, at 2 P.M. in Room 1 of Citizens Aid Building," 1945, ELAA, UMN, United Way of Minneapolis records (SW 70), box 38, folder 2: "Group Work and Relief Division 1945"; DuPuis, *Nature's Perfect Food*, 6.

12. Marian E. McKay, "Free Seaboard Camps Offer Summer Fun to Children of All Races," *Chicago Defender*, September 18, 1948.

13. Dunn, "Analysis of the Effectiveness of the Friendly Town Publicity Program of the *Herald Tribune* Fresh Air Fund," 37.

14. The National Institute of Health estimates that 30 to 50 million Americans are lactose intolerant, a statistic likely representing a significant portion of the children sent to country farms. See www.nichd.nih.gov/publications/pubs/upload/NICHD_MM_Lactose_FS.pdf.

15. David M. Paige, Theodore M. Bayless, and George G. Graham, "Milk Programs: Helpful or Harmful to Negro Children?" *American Journal of Public Health* 62, no. 11 (1972): 1486–88. Geneticists treat lactose intolerance as the norm across human populations. Lactose tolerance is a rarer trait found among select northern populations. See Valenze, *Milk*, 3.

16. The phrase "never seen a cow" or a close variant appears in each of the following representative sources ranging over four decades: Justine Flint, "Fresh Air Youngsters to Vacation Here Two Weeks in August," *Portsmouth (NH) Herald*, July 2, 1941; "Vacations Planned by Area Families for 'Fresh Airs,'" *Daily Messenger* (Canandaigua, NY), June 12, 1951; William J. Colmey, "Help Yourself to Joy," *Daily Sentinel* (Rome, NY), 1960; Sheila Behrend, Tami Hall, and Margo Behrend, "'Friendly Town,'" *Muscatine, Iowa, Journal*, January 9, 1976.

17. John Kord Lagemann, "Something Special in Vacations: A *Reader's Digest* Reprint," *Reader's Digest*, June 1963.

18. Peter Kondrat, "An Escape from Asphalt to Fresh Country Air," *Gettysburg (PA) Times*, July 1, 1978.

19. "38 Fresh Air Children Taken by Bradford, Area Residents," *Bradford (PA) Era*, July 29, 1948.

20. Laurie Johnston, "Fresh Air Fund Launches Drive," *New York Times*, May 14, 1972.

21. Lacey Fosburgh, "Fresh Air Fund's Children Dazzled by Rural Marvels," *New York Times*, July 4, 1971.

22. "Couple Recall Their Early Days as Fresh Air Fund Hosts," *New York Times*, April 30, 1978.

23. Len Wilson, "What Color Is a Cow? 70 Fresh Air Children Arrived from New York City: Joy, Awe and Expectation Mark Train Trip from City," *Evening Banner* (Bennington, VT), July 22, 1955.

24. Colmey, "Help Yourself to Joy."

25. "Fresh Air Fund Enables 14,000 to Enjoy Fresh Air," *New York Amsterdam News*, August 14, 1976.

26. John C. Devlin, "Farm Jobs to Aid City Youngsters," *New York Times*, July 4, 1976.

27. Lawrence J. Friedman, "Philanthropy in America: Historicism and Its Discontents," in *Charity, Philanthropy, and Civility in American History*, ed. Lawrence J. Friedman and Mark D. McGarvie (New York: Cambridge University Press, 2003), 1–21; Shirley Maye Tillotson, *Contributing Citizens: Modern Charitable Fundraising and the Making of the Welfare State, 1920–66* (Vancouver: UBC Press, 2008), 59–60.

28. Randy Wynn, "Children Find New Homes during Week in Ashland," *News Journal* (Mansfield, OH), July 4, 1971.

29. Helen Husen, "Fresh Air Program," *Bridgeport (CT) Post*, July 23, 1970; "Model Farm Proves Popular among Children at Fishkill Camp," *Poughkeepsie (NY) Journal*, July 17, 1966.

30. "Fresh Air Children to Get Farm-Life Lore First-Hand," *World Journal Tribune* (New York City), November 26, 1966.

31. "Fresh Air Appeal Gives Farm Tour," *New York Times*, August 12, 1970; "Fresh Air Fund Gives Children from the Slums a Taste of Life on the Farm," *New York Times*, August 17, 1969.

32. Memorandum by Mary E. Smith, "Minutes 1964 Friendly Town Planning Conference, February 18, 19, 20," 1964, 6, UIL, MNC, box 99, folder 1505: "Fresh Air Fund, University of IL at Chicago Special Collection."

33. Memorandum, "Herald Tribune Fresh Air Fund 80th Annual Report," 1957, 15, NYCPL-BRARR, Whitney North Seymour Papers, 1930–1983, box 114—Subject Files—Fresh Air Fund, folder: "January 1962 through December 1964."

34. "Fresh Air Appeal Gives Farm Tour"; Joan Brown, "Program Offers Chance to Give Child a Memorable Vacation," *News Journal* (Mansfield, OH), April 4, 1970; "A Fresh Air Fund Vacation Delights a Child," *New York Times*, May 14, 1978.

35. Jennifer Dunning, "Last Day to Register for Fresh Air Fund Camp Is a Big Day for Little Ones," *New York Times*, June 18, 1978.

36. James C. Lont, Meeting to Discuss "Friendly Town" Project in the 60's, Graafschap, MI: 2010.

37. Jo McMeen, "Along the Juniata: Wanted: Homes for Fresh Air Kids," *Daily News* (Huntingdon and Mount Union, PA), April 18, 1962.

38. Bartlett Hendricks, "Three Boys, Two Weeks and No Worries at All," *Berkshire Eagle* (Pittsfield, MA), August 4, 1956.

39. Edith Evans Asbury, "2 Alumni Recall Fresh Air Camp," *New York Times*, May 9, 1976; Memorandum, "My Vacation in the Country," November 28, 1947, LOC, PRF D222, HRR, file 12556: "The Fresh Air Fund, 1942–49"; "Lancaster Helps Needy Children," *New York Times*, June 13, 1976.

40. Joseph Gibbons, Tallahassee, FL, telephone interview by the author, March 17, 2010; Bernie Greenfield, Newark, NJ, telephone interview by the author, April 13, 2010; Elmer Voth and Linda Voth to Orlo Kaufman, September 5, 1961, MLABC: MLA.VII.R GC Voluntary Service, Series 11 Gulfport VS Unit, box 4, folder 123: "Fresh Air, 1961."

41. Devlin, "Farm Jobs to Aid City Youngsters"; Elliott West, *Growing up in Twentieth-Century America: A History and Reference Guide* (Westport, CT: Greenwood, 1996), 210.

42. Dee Wedemeyer, "Farm Plan Extends Fresh Air Program," *New York Times*, July 31, 1977.

43. Mrs. Winton Stucky to Orlo Kaufman, August 12, 1961, MLABC: MLA.VII.R GC Voluntary Service, Series 11 Gulfport VS Unit, box 4, folder 123: "Fresh Air, 1961."

44. Ibid.

45. West, *Growing up in Twentieth-Century America*, 217.

46. Memorandum by Mary Rohrer and Anna Rohrer, "Mennonite Mission Children's Visitation Program, Visitation Record," 1951, EMM Record Room, folder: "F–J."

47. Memorandum by Paul N. Kraybill, "Mennonite Mission Children Visitation Program," 1952, EMM Record Room, folder: "Committee Action."

48. Walter I. Trattner, *From Poor Law to Welfare State: A History of Social Welfare in America* (New York: The Free Press, 1984), 318.

49. Memorandum by Frederick H. Lewis, "Report of the Executive Director on 1947 to the Board of Directors Herald Tribune Fresh Air Fund," 1947, LOC, PRF D222, HRR, file 12556: "The Fresh Air Fund, 1942–49"; Memorandum by Lewis, "Annual Report to the Board of Directors Herald Tribune Fresh Air Fund for the Year 1955," 1955, LOC, PRF D223, HRR, file 12561: "The Fresh Air Fund, 1954–55"; Memorandum by Lewis, "The Fresh Air Fund: Annual Report to the Board of Directors," December 31, 1969, 2, LOC, PRF D225, HRR, file 12576: "The Fresh Air Fund 1968–70."

50. Milking Time.

51. Lont, Meeting to Discuss "Friendly Town" Project in the 60's.

52. McMeen, "Along the Juniata."

53. Lagemann, "Something Special in Vacations."

54. Emily S. Rosenberg, "Missions to the World: Philanthropy Abroad," in *Charity, Philanthropy, and Civility in American History*, ed. Lawrence J. Friedman and Mark D. McGarvie (New York: Cambridge University Press, 2003), 241–57.

55. "Tenement Youths Need Local Hosts," *Hagerstown (MD) Morning Herald*, June 21, 1945.

56. George J. Gordodensky, "Fresh Air Children, Co-Hope," *Daily News Record* (North Hills, PA), April 12, 1979.

57. "Fresh Air Children Here on Vacations," *Lebanon (PA) Daily News*, June 25, 1959; MaryBeth Wagner, "Manheim Couple Hosts Fifty Phila. Children," *Intelligencer Journal* (Lancaster, PA), August 11, 1978.

58. "Inquiring Photographer," *Evening Banner* (Bennington, VT), July 18, 1959; "Danny's Dreaming of Friendly Town," *World Journal Tribune* (New York City), December 15, 1966; Lawrence Wright, *City Children, Country Summer* (New York: Scribner, 1979), 196.

59. DuPuis, *Nature's Perfect Food*, 5.

60. Estimate of 20,600 donors in 1971 determined by extrapolating donor rates and average contributions based on the reported figure of 16,688 having contributed $574,763 to the Fund by November 28 of that year. Total received from the public by the end of the year was $711,228. See "Fresh Air Fund Given $574,763 So Far in '71," *New York Times*, November 28, 1971; Memorandum, "1971 Annual Report," 1971, NYHS, F128HV 938. N5 F74.

61. Memorandum, "1971 Annual Report."

62. "Good Fellows Give 2,091 Gifts, $9,700 to Needy Children," *Chicago Daily Tribune*, December 23, 1946; "Tribune Fund New Drive; Doris Johnson Chairman: Rep Assembly Chooses Tribune Fresh Air Fund to Help Provide Vacations for New York City's Underprivileged Children," *Barnard (NY) Bulletin*, February 20, 1947; "Plan Fresh Air Vacations for City Children," *Gettysburg (PA) Times*, March 24, 1948; "43 Youngsters Open Season's First Week at Community Camp," *Pottstown (PA) Mercury*, July 5, 1948; McKay, "Free Seaboard Camps Offer Summer Fun to Children of All Races"; "Business Club Hears Camp Fund Appeal," *Pottstown (PA) Mercury*, July 15, 1948; "Labor Club Makes $500 Contribution

to Fresh Air Fund," *Pottstown (PA) Mercury*, May 14, 1948; "Fresh Air Fund Enriched by $200 as Gift of Union," *Pottstown (PA) Mercury*, May 20, 1948; "Help Still Needed for Fresh Air Fund," *Pottstown (PA) Mercury*, May 21, 1948; "Fresh Air Fund Gets $100 Boost," *Pottstown (PA) Mercury*, June 8, 1948; "Flag CIO Union Donates $250 to Fresh Air Fund," *Pottstown (PA) Mercury*, June 15, 1948; "Boy Going to Camp on Doe Club Help," *Pottstown (PA) Mercury*, June 18, 1948; "Wellsboro Is Friendly Town: Twenty Children to Be Invited Here for Two Weeks," *Wellsboro (PA) Agitator*, May 26, 1948; "Friendship Plans to Aid Fresh Airs," *Olean (NY) Times Herald*, June 12, 1948; "Florence Civic Clubs Play Big Role in Creating Progressive Attitudes," *Florence (SC) Morning News*, November 5, 1948; "Kingston Included as Friendly Town to Aid Children," *Kingston (NY) Daily Freeman*, June 8, 1949; "Fresh Air Fund Organizes for Season," *Florence (SC) Morning News*, May 31, 1950; "Fresh Air Fund Drive," *Bridgeport (CT) Telegram*, June 18, 1955; "Homes Being Sought for East Harlem Tots on Vacation," *North Adams, Massachusetts, Transcript*, June 22, 1951; "Kiwanis Club Sponsors Friendly Town Program," *Daily News* (Huntingdon and Mount Union, PA), June 14, 1954; "35 Fresh Air Youngsters Are Invited to Area," *Daily News* (Huntingdon and Mount Union, PA), July 3, 1954; "Spanish Club Donates Check to Aid Puerto Rican Child," *Post-Standard* (Syracuse, NY), June 27, 1954; "Fresh Air Fund Drive"; "Quentin WCTU Has Guest Speaker," *Lebanon (PA) Daily News*, July 31, 1957; "Linda Saari Elected by Monday Club," *Portsmouth (NH) Herald*, May 25, 1976.

63. Robert D. Putnam, *Bowling Alone: The Collapse and Revival of American Community* (New York: Touchstone, 2001).

64. Memorandum by R. G. Rankin & Co., "Financial Reports," December 31, 1955, LOC, PRF D223, HRR, file 12561: "The Fresh Air Fund, 1954–55."

65. "Gastonians to Play in 'Messiah' Tonight," *Gastonia (NC) Daily Gazette*, December 17, 1940; "Fresh Air Fund Youngsters," *Bridgeport (CT) Telegram*, August 9, 1951; Sid Feder, "Star-Less All-Squad Wins Where Collections of Famous Players Failed," *Daily Inter Lake* (Kalispell, MT), September 5, 1940.

66. "PTA to Hear Talk on Harold-Trib's Fresh Air Fund Project," *Cumberland (MD) Evening Times*, November 18, 1954; "Spanish Club Donates Check to Aid Puerto Rican Child."

67. "College Mixer," *Black Coalition Weekly* (New Haven, CT), July 14, 1972.

68. Sheila Rule, "Fresh Air Fund Has a Record 100th Year," *New York Times*, August 28, 1977.

69. "Lifers Aid Fresh Air Fund," *Daily News* (Huntington, Saxton, and Mount Union, PA), May 4, 1979.

70. "Pupils Give Help to Fresh Air Fund," *New York Times*, June 16, 1974.

71. Peter D. Hall, "The Welfare State and the Careers of Public and Private Institutions since 1945," in *Charity, Philanthropy, and Civility in American History*, ed. Lawrence J. Friedman and Mark D. McGarvie (New York: Cambridge University Press, 2003), 363–83.

72. Thomas A. Johnson, "6th Grade Raises Fresh Air Funds," *New York Times*, June 20, 1976.

73. "Girls on L.I. Give to Fresh Air Fund," *New York Times*, June 22, 1975; "Donor, 91, Recalls Her Fresh Air Days," *New York Times*, July 3, 1977.

74. "Donors Aid the Fresh Air Fund with Cash and Ballpark Tickets," *New York Times*, July 22, 1979.

75. Mintz, *Huck's Raft*, 342.

76. "Fund Children to Benefit from Hot Dog Roast," *Berkshire Eagle* (Pittsfield, MA), July 18, 1956; Henry L. DeRham to MacNeil Mitchell, May 29, 1962, NYUA, Washington Square Association Activities, MC 94, Series 6, box 20, folder 7: "Fresh Air Fund: 1962"; "Mrs. F. J. Fraser Is Chosen Regent of Winnipeg Chapter," *Winnipeg (Manitoba) Free Press*, February 10, 1944; "Iran Grotto Stages Annual Field Day," *Troy (NY) Record*, July 17, 1944.

77. Tillotson, *Contributing Citizens, 1920–66,* 3.

78. "Donor, 91, Recalls Her Fresh Air Days."

79. "Homes Are Needed for 'Friendly' Kids," *Waterloo (IA) Sunday Courier,* June 27, 1972.

80. "Receives Aid," *Call and Post* (Cleveland, OH), July 13, 1974.

81. Tillotson, *Contributing Citizens,* 4–5, 20, 233, 237.

82. Ruth Hutchinson Crocker, "Making Charity Modern: Business and the Reform of Charities in Indianapolis, 1879–1930," *Business and Economic History* 12 (1983): 158–70.

83. Memorandum, "Annual Report to the Board of Directors," 1953, 5, LOC, PRF D223, HRR, file 12560: "The Fresh Air Fund, 1953–54."

84. "Chronology," *Bennington (VT) Banner,* December 31, 1963.

85. Memorandum by Anthony DeLorenzo and Angela Kochera, "Public Information," 1966, LOC, PRF D224, HRR, file 12567: "The Fresh Air Fund."

86. Memorandum by Frederick H. Lewis, "Executive Director's Report," September 15, 1966, LOC, PRF D224, HRR, file 12567: "The Fresh Air Fund"; Memorandum, "President's Report," April 20, 1967, LOC, PRF D224, HRR, file 12567: "The Fresh Air Fund"; "Campaign Is Begun by Fresh Air Fund," *New York Times,* May 4, 1969; Frederick H. Lewis to Arthur Hays Sulzberger, June 27, 1957, NYCPL-BRARR, New York Times Company Records, Arthur Hays Sulzberger Papers, 1823–1999, MssCol 17782, box 214, folder 11: "New York Herald Tribune 1956."

87. Arch Ward, "Football Giants Tackle Eastern Eleven Tonight," *Chicago Daily Tribune,* September 7, 1939; Arch Ward, "Giants to Meet Eastern Stars before 40,000," *Chicago Daily Tribune,* September 3, 1941.

88. Arch Ward, "In the Wake of the News," *Chicago Daily Tribune,* September 5, 1947; "New York Fans Await First Football Game," *Plaindealer* (Kansas City, KS), June 22, 1951; "Giants, Rams Battle in Grid Tilt Tonight: Pro Rivals Set for Fresh Air Fund Game at Polo Grounds," *Bridgeport (CT) Telegram,* September 20, 1951.

89. "Coaches Are Named for East-West Game," *Mansfield (OH) News-Journal,* February 1, 1949; "East's Rally Beats West in Fresh Air Fund Game in N.Y.," *Progress-Index* (Petersburg, VA), March 31, 1957; "Won't Play Game," *Racine (WI) Sunday Bulletin,* February 1, 1959.

90. "Friendly Town Plans Cavalier Fundraiser," *Call and Post* (Cleveland, OH), March 6, 1976.

91. "Lindsay Proclaims This Week to Honor the Fresh Air Fund," *New York Times,* June 4, 1970; "12 States Observe 100th Anniversary of Fresh Air Fund," *New York Times,* June 5, 1977; "It Was an Afternoon of Basehits . . . ," *New York Amsterdam News,* May 5, 1979.

92. "Fresh Air Kids on Junior Show," *Mason City (IA) Globe-Gazette,* December 9, 1939.

93. "Miss Heinemann to Be Heard on WARK," *Hagerstown (MD) Morning Herald,* July 12, 1949.

94. George J. Lankevich and Howard B. Furer, *A Brief History of New York City* (New York: Associated Faculty Press, 1984), 245.

95. "Fresh Air Tot Movie on TV Friday Six PM," *Daily News-Record* (Harrisonburg, VA), June 16, 1955; Whitelaw Reid to Helen Odgen Reid, May 12, 1959, LOC, PRF D224, HRR, file 12565: "The Fresh Air Fund, 1959"; "Founder's Day Tonight," *Bridgeport (CT) Post,* February 16, 1960; "Fresh Air Hosts Cited by Speaker at Dinner," *Lebanon (PA) Daily News,* April 28, 1973; "Fresh Air Fund Seeks Hosts Here," *Tyrone (PA) Daily Herald,* April 13, 1976; Memorandum by Frederick H. Lewis, "Executive Director's Annual Report to the Board of Directors, for the Fiscal Year 1963–1964," 1964, LOC, PRF D225, HRR, file 12572: "The Fresh Air Fund 1965"; "Lancaster Holds Film Premier," *What's in the Air,* fall 1964.

96. Teresa Odendahl, *Charity Begins at Home: Generosity and Self-Interest among the Philanthropic Elite* (New York: Basic Books, 1990), 42.

97. "Modeled for Charity," *Afro-American* (Baltimore), May 11, 1940; "Benefit for Kiddies," *New York Amsterdam Star-News*, June 7, 1941; "Fresh Air Dance Date Is July 9," *New York Amsterdam News*, June 26, 1943.

98. "Society Hoops It Up!" *Independent* (Humboldt, IA), October 2, 1958; "New York Socialites 'Hoop It Up' in Astor," *Brownwood (TX) Bulletin*, October 2, 1958.

99. Memorandum, "Minutes of Meeting of Board of Directors," April 20, 1967, 5, LOC, PRF D225, HRR, file 12575: "The Fresh Air Fund 1967"; "Renoir Painting to Be Sold to Aid Three Charities," *Chicago Daily Tribune*, December 2, 1962; "Fresh Air Fund to Mark 100th Year with Benefit," *New York Times*, May 18, 1977.

100. Daniel J. Monti Jr., *The American City: A Social and Cultural History* (Malden, MA: Blackwell, 1999), 250, 257, 262, 265.

101. "Fresh Air Fund Elects a Chairman," *New York Times*, December 22, 1967.

102. Memorandum by DeLorenzo and Kochera, "Public Information."

103. "Donors Aid the Fresh Air Fund with Cash and Ballpark Tickets."

104. "Too Many Potential Leaders . . . ," *New York Times*, September 11, 1977.

105. Odendahl, *Charity Begins at Home*, 59; Tillotson, *Contributing Citizens, 1920–66*, 7.

106. Friedman, "Philanthropy in America: Historicism and Its Discontents," 18; Odendahl, *Charity Begins at Home*, 3, 4; David C. Hammack, "Failure and Resilience: Pushing the Limits in Depression and Wartime," in *Charity, Philanthropy, and Civility in American History*, ed. Lawrence J. Friedman and Mark D. McGarvie (New York: Cambridge University Press, 2003), 263–80.

107. Hall, "The Welfare State and the Careers of Public and Private Institutions since 1945," 379; Hammack, "Failure and Resilience: Pushing the Limits in Depression and Wartime," 280.

108. Lankevich and Furer, *A Brief History of New York City*, 264, 294, 297, 303.

109. Memorandum by Rankin & Co., "Financial Reports."

110. Memorandum, "Statement of Operating Fund Income and Expenses for the Year Ended September 30, 1965," November 23, 1965, LOC, PRF D224, HRR, file 12568: "The Fresh Air Fund."

111. Memorandum, "1971 Annual Report," 6–9.

112. Memorandum, "Statement of Operating Fund Income and Expenses for the Year Ended September 30, 1965."

113. "United Fund Campaign Is Explained," *Statesville (NC) Record & Landmark*, September 16, 1955.

114. Tillotson, *Contributing Citizens*, 158–59.

115. Chuck Austin, "The History of the Fresh Air Fund" (1981), C12–12, LVA, FAFR, 1949–1999, accession number 36407, box 22, folder 2: "Histories 1977."

116. Mintz, *Huck's Raft*, ix.

117. Ibid., 276.

118. King E. Davis, "Jobs, Income, Business and Charity in the Black Community," *Black Scholar* 9 (1977): 2–11.

119. Memorandum, "Camp Registrar's Report 1957," 1957, CUA, USAR, 1896–1995 MS#1149, Series VII: Programs and Services, box 41, folder 3: "Camp-Reports, 1948–53"; Memorandum by Frieda Schwenkmeyer, "Stories," 1961, ELAA, UMN, HSSR (SW0058), General, box 48, folder 16: "1951–1961."

120. Richard F. Crandell, ed., *The Frog Log and Other Stories about Children* (New York: Herald Tribune Fresh Air Fund, 1962), 13.

121. Joan Cook, "Fresh Air Fund Gets Helping Hand," *New York Times*, August 7, 1977.

122. Lacey Fosburgh, "Registration to Begin for Fresh Air Fund Summer," *New York Times*, May 9, 1971.

123. Julia Guarneri, "Changing Strategies for Child Welfare, Enduring Beliefs about Childhood: The Fresh Air Fund, 1877–1926," *Journal of the Gilded Age and Progressive Era* 11, no. 1 (2012): 27–70.

124. Rhonda D. Jones, "Tithe, Time and Talent: An Analysis of Fundraising Activity for the Southern Christian Leadership Conference (SCLC), 1957–1964" (dissertation, Howard University, 2003), 137–38.

125. "The Goal: 100 Children," *Bennington (VT) Banner*, May 8, 1963; Bob Zanic, "Friendly Town Works 2 Ways," *Palatine (IL) Herald*, June 10, 1969; Mathew L. Wald, "Need for Fresh Air Fund Increases with Inflation," *New York Times*, August 21, 1977.

126. "Friendly Town Group Seeking Homes," *Arlington Heights (IL) Herald*, August 4, 1971.

127. Florence W. Paparo, "Underprivileged Children Offered New Worlds through Fresh Air Family," *Delaware County Daily Times* (Chester, PA), May 9, 1970.

128. Marilou Hedlund, "'A Chance to Yell and Scream and Look at Things,'" *Chicago Tribune*, July 26, 1964.

129. Anita Duhe, "Westminster Woman Has Hopes for Boosting Fresh Air Fund," *Sentinel-Enterprise* (Fitchburg, MA), August 29, 1975; "Stratford Again to Host N.Y. Fresh Air Children," *Bridgeport (CT) Sunday Post*, April 13, 1975; Asbury, "2 Alumni Recall Fresh Air Camp"; "New York Youngsters Due," *Tyrone (PA) Daily Herald*, June 28, 1978.

130. "40 New York Fresh Air Kiddies: Mount Union," *Daily News* (Huntingdon and Mount Union, PA), July 13, 1951.

131. "Fresh Air Tots Hosts in Appeal," *Daily News-Record* (Harrisonburg, VA), June 8, 1955.

132. "Children Placed by Fresh Air Fund," *New York Times*, May 30, 1976.

133. "Fresh Air Mailbag: 'Loved Him,'" *New York Herald Tribune*, December 12, 1966.

134. Charles E. Strickland and Andrew M. Ambrose, "The Changing Worlds of Children, 1945–1963," in *American Childhood: A Research Guide and Historical Handbook*, ed. Joseph M. Hawes and N. Ray Hiner (Westport, CT: Greenwood, 1985), 533–85.

135. "Fresh Air Fund Helps Give Child New Goals," *World Journal Tribune* (New York City), December 24, 1966.

136. Dorothy Belle Pollack, "Pearl and Ebony," *What's in the Air*, summer vacation edition, 1963.

137. "Women's Fellowship Aid Friendly Town Project," *Call and Post* (Cleveland, OH), June 11, 1977; "Be a Host Family to an Inner City Child," *Call and Post* (Cleveland, OH), March 26, 1977; "Vacation Program Dates Set," *Titusville (PA) Herald*, March 21, 1973; "Women's Fellowship Aid Friendly Town Project"; Trattner, *From Poor Law to Welfare State*, 306.

138. Memorandum by Marchand Chaney and Mimi Vernon, "Evaluation of Newberry-Dubuque Project for 1962," 1962, [3], UIL, MNC, box 99, folder 1505: "Fresh Air Fund, University of IL at Chicago Special Collection"; Brown, "Program Offers Chance to Give Child a Memorable Vacation."

139. "Journey into Another World," *Call and Post* (Cleveland, OH), August 2, 1969; Lena Williams, "Full of Fresh Air, They Return Home," *New York Times*, August 7, 1977.

140. "Fresh Air Guests Leave for Home; Have Glum Look," *Evening Banner* (Bennington, VT), August 20, 1955; Joan Cook, "Fresh Air Fund: Tale of 2 Cultures," *New York Times*, May 28, 1978; Lee Edwards, "Fresh Air Fund Workers Give Free Time, Effort," *Oneonta (NY) Star*, July 13, 1971; "Many Offer Help to Fresh Air Fund," *New York Times*, July 28, 1974.

141. Lizabeth Cohen, *A Consumers' Republic: The Politics of Mass Consumption in Postwar America* (New York: Knopf, 2003), 320; "Girl, 9, Learns New View of Life," *Chicago Tribune*, August 4, 1971; "500 Inner City Youths Return from Country," *Chicago Tribune*,

July 30, 1967; "Many Offer Help to Fresh Air Fund"; "A Homesick Girl Yearns for 1980 Fresh Air Trip," *New York Times*, August 26, 1979; "Fresh Air Children Leave Local Hosts," *Hagerstown (MD) Morning Herald*, August 3, 1945.

142. Edwards, "Fresh Air Fund Workers Give Free Time, Effort."

143. Alison J. Clark, "Coming of Age in Suburbia: Gifting the Consumer Child," in *Designing Modern Childhoods: History, Space, and the Material Culture of Children*, ed. Marta Gutman and Ning De Coninck-Smith (Newark, NJ: Rutgers University Press, 2008), 253–68.

144. Harold Regier to Ervin P. Krehbiel, September 23, 1963, MLABC: MLA.VII.R GC Voluntary Service, Series 11 Gulfport VS Unit, box 4, folder 125: "Fresh Air, 1963."

145. Anne-Gerard Flynn, "Breath of Fresh Air for Everyone," *New York Times*, May 21, 1978.

146. Pollack, "Pearl and Ebony."

147. Melody M. Pannell, Harrisonburg, VA, interview by the author, January 20, 2016.

148. Mrs. Howard Rutz, "Hosts for Fresh Air Child Find Experience Enriching," *Daily Sentinel* (Rome, NY), 1962, UIL, MNC box 99, folder 1505: "Fresh Air Fund."

149. Crandell, ed., *The Frog Log and Other Stories about Children*, 10.

150. Strickland and Ambrose, "The Changing Worlds of Children, 1945–1963," 551–52.

151. Brown, "Program Offers Chance to Give Child a Memorable Vacation."

152. Louise A. Sweeney, "Designed for Women," *Berkshire Eagle* (Pittsfield, MA), June 5, 1959.

153. "Inquiring Photographer."

154. Richard F. Crandell, "Fresh Air Fund to Carry on in Pages of WJT," *World Journal Tribune* (New York City), September 12, 1966.

155. Margie Middleton and Ruth Y. Wenger, "Fresh Air Reminiscences," *Missionary Messenger*, July 1977, 12–13, 21.

156. "Inquiring Photographer."

157. "7 Fresh Air Children Write of Newport Visit," *Newport (RI) News*, January 19, 1950.

158. Michele H. Fleischer, "Two Former Fresh Air Kids Return the Favor," *McCall's*, March 1991, 57.

159. Anne Mancuso, "Boy from Brooklyn Is at Home in Croton," *New York Times*, May 14, 1978; Jill Smolowe, "Giving the Gift of Fresh Air," *New York Times*, May 7, 1978.

160. "A Fresh Air Child, Now 30, Returns to Settle in His 'Friendly Town,'" *New York Times*, July 23, 1978.

161. Leonard E. Carpenter, *Hinesburg, Vermont: From 1762* (Burlington, VT: Sheldon Press, 1961), 29.

162. Memorandum, "Day Camp for Children Living in 'Welfare Hotels,'" 1971, ELAA, UMN, HSSR (SW0058), box 54, folder 4: "Proposal—Day Camp for Children Living in 'Welfare Hotels,' 1971."

163. Ibid.; Jule M. Sugarman to Bertram M. Beck, July 2, 1971, ELAA, UMN, HSSR (SW0058), box 54, folder 4: "Proposal—Day Camp for Children Living in 'Welfare Hotels,' 1971."

164. The first instance of semipublic criticism, other than a 1947 complaint about the quality of halftime entertainment at a Fresh Air football fund-raiser, that I have found appeared in a 1949 annual report. Staff mentioned social workers' critique of the informal vetting system used to determine whether host families could bring Fresh Air Children into their homes. See Ward, "In the Wake of the News"; Memorandum by Frederick H. Lewis, "Annual Report to the Board of Directors by the Executive Director of the Herald Tribune Fresh Air Fund," January 28, 1949, LOC, PRF D222, HRR, file 12557: "The Fresh Air Fund, 1950–51."

165. "100 Inner City Kids to Visit in Glen Ellyn," *Chicago Tribune*, April 25, 1966; Darrell Michael Scott, *Contempt and Pity: Social Policy and the Image of the Damaged Black Psyche, 1880–1996* (Chapel Hill: University of North Carolina Press, 1997), 74, 93–94, 120–21, 138.

166. Eleanor Charles, "Apathy Endangers Fresh Air Fund," *New York Times*, May 20, 1979.

167. Ari L. Goldman, "Fresh Air: A Together Atmosphere," *New York Times*, June 27, 1976.

168. Richard Weiss, *The American Myth of Success: From Horatio Alger to Norman Vincent Peale* (New York: Basic Books, 1969), 231.

169. Harold A. Nelson, "Charity, Poverty and Race," *Phylon (1960–)* 29 (1968): 303–16; Trattner, *From Poor Law to Welfare State*, 327–29.

170. Luis Diaz, New York, NY, telephone interview by the author, May 4, 2010; Gibbons interview.

171. Cindy Vanderkodde, Grand Rapids, MI, telephone interview by the author, March 7, 2010; Middleton and Wenger, "Fresh Air Reminiscences."

172. "Seek Two-Week Homes for 'Fresh Air' Children: Some 100 New York Youngsters Expected to Visit Yates Aug. 4," *Chronicle-Express* (Penn Yan, NY), June 16, 1949; "30 Fresh Air Children Arrive for Vacations: Cars Meet New York Train to Bring Youngsters Here for Two Weeks," *Newport (RI) News*, July 13, 1950; "Happiness Is a Beautiful Summer Day . . . ," *Biddeford-Saco (ME) Journal*, July 27, 1967.

173. "Will Hear of Air Plan," *Troy (NY) Record*, June 12, 1969.

174. Mrs. Dwight Stucky to Orlo Kaufman, August 14, 1961, MLABC: MLA.VII.R GC Voluntary Service, Series 11 Gulfport VS Unit, box 4, folder 123: "Fresh Air, 1961."

175. Wilson, "What Color Is a Cow?" 7; Wright, *City Children, Country Summer*.

176. Memorandum by Eve Wiejec, "Rome Fresh Air Program Report," 1963, 3, UIL, MNC, box 99, folder 1505: "Fresh Air Fund, University of IL at Chicago Special Collection."

177. Rosenberg, "Missions to the World: Philanthropy Abroad," 242–43, 256–57.

178. Wilson, "What Color Is a Cow?" 7.

179. "More Hosts Are Needed for Fresh Air Children," *Portsmouth (NH), Herald*, July 7, 1939.

180. "Guides to Successful Employment of Non-Farm Youth in Wartime Agriculture: For Use in Victory Farm Volunteer Program" (Washington, DC: U.S. Department of Labor Children's Bureau, 1943).

181. *The Church's Responsibility for Youth in Wartime Agriculture* (New York: International Council of Religious Education and the Home Missions Council of North America, 1943), 13.

182. Charles Perkins, ed., *Children of the Storm: Childhood Memories of World War II* (Osceola, WI: MBI Publishing Company, 1998), 55.

183. Ruth Millett, "We—the Women," *Altoona (PA) Mirror*, July 18, 1940.

184. "On the Home Front" (New York: New York Protestant Episcopal City Mission Society, 1941), EDNY, Episcopal Missional Society, box: "Publications et al., 1930's–1970's," folder: "Miscellaneous Publications, Leaflets, etc.—Thru '30s, '40s, '50s, '60s."

185. "Fresh Air Children Are Coming: Mrs. Comstock Heads Committee Seeking Accommodations," *Berkshire Evening Eagle* (Pittsfield, MA), July 9, 1943, 8.

186. Austin, "The History of the Fresh Air Fund."

187. "Fresh Air Home Seeks Funds," *Troy (NY) Record*, June 25, 1945.

188. "'Fresh Air Kids' to Visit Huntingdon, Mount Union," *Daily News* (Huntingdon and Mount Union, PA), May 11, 1945.

189. Memorandum, "It Is Our Hope That the Door of Opportunity," November 3, 1944, NYHS, F128 HV885.N5 B68 1941.

190. "Asking Homes to Entertain Fresh Air Kiddies," *Huntingdon (PA) Daily News*, May 11, 1942.

191. "Will You Take a Fresh Air Kiddie This Year?" *Huntingdon (PA) Daily News*, June 25, 1943.

192. "Read Story of Fresh Air Fund—Then Be Host to City Youngsters," *Huntingdon (PA) Daily News*, June 21, 1945.

193. "Annual Campaign to Begin Here for Aid in the Tribune Fresh Air Fund," *Hagerstown (MD) Daily Mail*, April 18, 1946; "Fresh Air Children to Arrive in Hagerstown July 23rd; Goal Set," *Hagerstown (MD) Daily Mail*, June 3, 1946; "Mount Union—Open Your Homes to Many Fresh Air Youngsters," *Daily News* (Huntingdon and Mount Union, PA), June 20, 1948.

194. "Seek Vacation Homes Here for N.Y. Youngsters," *Gettysburg (PA) Times*, June 18, 1948.

195. "Friendly Town Project Set Again by Fredonians," *Dunkirk (NY) Evening Observer*, April 19, 1956.

196. "28 'Fresh Airs' Have Arrived," *Hagerstown (MD) Daily Mail*, July 23, 1947.

197. Memorandum, "Camp Manakiki," 1953, ELAA, UMN, United Way of Minneapolis records (SW 70), box 74, folder 1: "Camps-Study 1953, 1958"; Memorandum by Mark B. Herman, "Group Report," August 7, 1952, CUA, USAR, 1896–1995 MS#1149, Series VII: Programs and Services, box 53, folder 2: "Camp-Activity Reports, 1952"; Abigail A. Van Slyck, *A Manufactured Wilderness: Summer Camps and the Shaping of American Youth, 1890–1960* (Minneapolis: University of Minnesota Press, 2006), xxvi.

198. "Invitations Open for Needy Children," *Hagerstown (MD) Morning Herald*, July 16, 1949.

199. "Homes for Fresh Air Tots Asked," *Daily News-Record* (Harrisonburg, VA), May 26, 1955; Memorandum, "A Friendly Note to the Friendliest People in the World," n.d., CUA, LGMHR (MS#0376), box 5, folder 1: "Fresh Air Camp—Misc, 1920s–50s."

200. "Out of Winter Snows Came Hope of Spring," *What's in the Air*, spring 1963.

201. Memorandum by Lewis, "The Fresh Air Fund: Annual Report to the Board of Directors"; "Fresh Air Sunday," *Bennington (VT) Banner*, May 28, 1977.

202. "Americanism Is Told by Ex-Fresh Air Boy," *Hagerstown (MD) Morning Herald*, June 23, 1949.

203. Barbara L. Little, "Helps New York City Children to a Vacation in the Country," *Lancaster (PA) Intelligencer-Journal*, July 31, 1958.

204. Crandell, ed., *The Frog Log and Other Stories about Children*, 17.

205. "The Fresh Air Fund Focuses on Culture," *New York Times*, June 12, 1977.

206. "Seek Vacation Homes Here for N.Y. Youngsters."

207. "What's in the Air" (Washington, DC: Herald Tribune Fresh Air Fund, 1952), 6, LOC, PRF D223, HRR, file 12559: "The Fresh Air Fund, 1952."

208. Frederick H. Lewis, "Camping Confronts an American Dilemma," *Camping*, December 1954.

209. Frederick H. Lewis to Brown Reid, July 5, 1955, LOC, PRF D223, HRR, file 12561: "The Fresh Air Fund, 1954–55"; Frederick H. Lewis, "Camping Confronts an American Dilemma."

210. Crandell, ed., *The Frog Log and Other Stories about Children*, 17.

211. Memorandum by Frederick H. Lewis, "What Am I Doing Here?: Remarks at Friendly Town Spring Planning Conference Held at Sharpe Reservation," February 20, 1963, LOC, PRF D224, HRR, file 12568: "The Fresh Air Fund."

212. Hall, "The Welfare State and the Careers of Public and Private Institutions since 1945," 362, 382.

213. "All-College Assembly Opens New Term Drive: Mr. Frederick Lewis Is Guest Speaker; Doris Johnson to Outline Drive Plans," *Barnard (NY) Bulletin*, March 4, 1947.

214. "Fresh Air Fund Elects President," *New York Times*, December 16, 1973.

215. "'Fresh Air Kids' to Visit Huntingdon, Mount Union."

216. "Fresh Air Fund Elects President."

217. "N.Y. Herald Tribune Fresh Air Fund," *Flying*, December 1958; Memorandum, "Annual Report—Reviewing 1958," 1959, 10, LOC, PRF D224, HRR, file 12567: "The Fresh Air Fund."

218. Memorandum by Frederick H. Lewis, "Summer Preview 1970," 1970, LOC, PRF D225, HRR, file 12576: "The Fresh Air Fund 1968–70."

219. Gordodensky, "Fresh Air Children, Co-Hope"; "A Homesick Girl Yearns for 1980 Fresh Air Trip"; "'Fresh Air Kids' to Visit Huntingdon, Mount Union"; "Americanism Is Told by Ex-Fresh Air Boy."

220. Austin, "The History of the Fresh Air Fund."

221. Crandell, ed., *The Frog Log and Other Stories about Children;* "Camp Unit Lives on in Aid to Children by Fresh Air Fund," *New York Times*, May 17, 1970; "Fresh Air Fund Starts Vacation Registrations," *New York Times*, May 6, 1970; Edwards, "Fresh Air Fund Workers Give Free Time, Effort"; Asbury, "2 Alumni Recall Fresh Air Camp."

222. "Fresh Air Fund's Programs Help East Harlem's Children," *New York Times*, May 29, 1969; Lee Edwards, "All Their World Is Asphalt and Farms Are Only in Stories," *Oneonta (NY) Star*, July 12, 1971.

223. "Detective Helps Fresh Air Camp," *New York Times*, September 10, 1972.

224. "Fresh Air Hosts Cited by Speaker at Dinner"; "Deputy Police Chief Aids Fresh Air Fund," *New York Times*, May 15, 1977; Memorandum by Paul G. Burkholder, "Glad Tidings Mennonite Church Herald Tribune Fresh Air Fund Agency Report 1966," March 17, 1967, LMHS—box: "Glad Tidings," folder: "Glad Tidings."

225. Chester West, "What's Happening in Westchester," *New York Amsterdam News*, September 14, 1968.

226. "Fresh Air Fund Enriches Lives," *New York Times*, July 20, 1970; "Lives Brightened by Fresh Air Fund," *New York Times*, August 15, 1976; "Fresh Air Fund Aided in Placing Youngsters by Alumnus, Now 35," *New York Times*, April 29, 1979.

227. "Kingston Included as Friendly Town to Aid Children"; "Dewey Supports Fresh Air Fund," *Daily Messenger* (Canandaigua, NY), June 4, 1952; Memorandum by Frederick H. Lewis, "On to a Million . . . 1962 Annual Report—Herald Tribune Fresh Air Fund," 1962, 3, copied from the CCAH, UTA; "Lindsay Proclaims This Week to Honor the Fresh Air Fund," 85.

228. Frederick Howell Lewis to Richard M. Nixon, July 24, 1957, folder: "Herald Tribune Fresh Air Fund," box 333, series 320: "Richard Nixon Pre-Presidential Materials" (Laguna Niguel), Richard Nixon Presidential Library and Museum, Yorba Linda, CA; Austin, "The History of the Fresh Air Fund."

229. Sargent Shriver to Frederick H. Lewis, April, 1965, LOC, PRF D225, HRR, file 12572: "The Fresh Air Fund 1965"; Memorandum, "Eighty-Ninth Annual Report: Herald Tribune Fresh Air Fund," 1967, copied from the CCAH, UTA.

230. "Bring Negroes to Bennington," *Bennington (VT) Banner*, April 30, 1968.

231. "Slum Youths Begin Visit to Vermont," *New York Times*, July 10, 1969.

232. "Helping 'Fresh Air Fund' Drive," *New York Amsterdam News*, June 3, 1944.

233. "Weight and Humor," *New York Amsterdam Star-News*, May 23, 1942; "Helping 'Fresh Air Fund' Drive"; "Assists Urban Camp Fund," *New York Amsterdam News*, June 10, 1944.

234. Norman Cousins, "Norman Cousins, Editor, Saturday Review," *What's in the Air*, spring 1955.

235. John Chapman, "Critic's Idea: Dope Sheet on Benefit Shows," *Chicago Daily Tribune*, September 2, 1956; "Very Cool," *New York Herald Tribune*, December 11, 1959; "Fresh Air Music in Vermont," in Reid Family Collection (Washington, D.C.: Library of

Congress, 1959); Memorandum, "Annual Report—Reviewing 1958"; Frederick H. Lewis to Mrs. Ogden Reid, April 22, 1959, LOC, PRF D224, HRR, file 12565: "The Fresh Air Fund, 1959"; Austin, "The History of the Fresh Air Fund."

236. "Steve, Eydie Aid Fresh Air," *World Journal Tribune* (New York City), April 19, 1967; Memorandum by DeLorenzo and Kochera, "Public Information"; Austin, "The History of the Fresh Air Fund."

237. Memorandum by Paddy Chayefsky, "Spot Announcement for Paddy Chayefsky," NYCPL-PARC, Paddy Chayefsky Papers, 1907–1998, *T-Mss 2001–040, box 140, folder 10: "Text for Fresh Air Fund radio spots, undated"; "Evening of Elegance for Fresh Air Fund," *New Pittsburgh Courier*, July 12, 1968; "Sanctums," *New Yorker*, May 30, 1959, 20–22; "Set for Evening of Elegance," *New York Amsterdam News*, July 26, 1969; James A. Michener and Alice Vielehr 1949, NYCPL-BRARR, Hudson Park Branch records, 1905–1980, Series 2, Alice Vielehr Files, 1946–1980, box 4, folder 7: "Greenwich Village Fresh Air Fund, 1948–1949."

238. "Billy Rowe's Note Book," *Chicago Metro News*, June 30, 1973; "Exhibition by Ashe to Aid Two Funds," *New York Times*, December 29, 1974.

239. "Sanctums."

240. Michael T. Kaufman, "Traders Play Street Games—on Wall St.," *New York Times*, October 2, 1972.

241. Hall, "The Welfare State and the Careers of Public and Private Institutions since 1945," 363–64.

242. Bill Babel, "Off the Beaten Track . . . ," *Oneonta (NY) Star*, July 9, 1949.

243. George Dixon, "Most Embarrassing of All Things Happens to U.S. Senators, Also," *High Point (NC) Enterprise*, June 6, 1951.

244. "Steve Roper," *San Antonio Gazette*, April 23, 1956.

245. William F. Buckley Jr., "Is Personal Charity on Way Out?" *Kokomo (IN) Tribune*, August 8, 1978.

246. Memorandum, "Mary Martin Stars Again," 1962, copied from the CCAH, UTA; "Carol Time . . . ," *World Journal Tribune* (New York City), December 14, 1966; "Lindsay Proclaims This Week to Honor the Fresh Air Fund"; "Fresh Air Chorus at Season End: Its 45 Members Had Busy Year," *New York Herald Tribune*, June 17, 1955; "Fresh Air Chorus Sings Its Thanks for Program," *New York Herald Tribune*, December 12, 1955; "Chorus of the Young to Perform on Fresh Air Fund's 91st Year," *New York Times*, June 2, 1968.

247. Hammack, "Failure and Resilience," 280.

248. Odendahl, *Charity Begins at Home*, 8.

249. Steven Mintz, "The Changing Face of Children's Culture," in *Reinventing Childhood after World War II*, ed. Paula S. Fass and Michael Grossberg (Philadelphia: University of Pennsylvania Press, 2012), 38–50.

250. James T. Patterson, *Grand Expectations: The United States, 1945–1974* (New York: Oxford University Press, 1996), vii.

251. Ibid., 65.

252. Memorandum by Lewis, "What Am I Doing Here?"

253. "Fresh Air Vacations Have Reached Climax Here with Marked Success," *Hagerstown (MD) Daily Mail*, August 1, 1946.

254. "Friendly Town Time Once Again in the Oneonta Area," *Oneonta (NY) Star*, May 25, 1955.

255. Ellen Delmonte, "An Editorial Feature," *Call and Post* (Cleveland, OH), July 3, 1971.

256. Williams, "Full of Fresh Air, They Return Home."

257. Annelise Orleck, *Storming Caesar's Palace: How Black Mothers Fought Their Own War on Poverty* (Boston: Beacon, 2005), 96; Trattner, *From Poor Law to Welfare State*, 316.

6. GREETING, GONE, GOOD

1. Luis Diaz, New York, NY, telephone interview by the author, May 4, 2010.

2. Ibid.

3. Randy Wynn, "Children Find New Homes during Week in Ashland," *News Journal* (Mansfield, OH), July 4, 1971.

4. Joan Skidmore, "Fresh Air Fund: Give a Child a Chance," *Delaware County Daily Times* (Chester, PA), June 7, 1974; "First Woman Executive Director Takes Helm for Fresh Air Fund Tomorrow," *New York Times*, October 26, 1975; Joan Cook, "City Youths Discover Joy of Suburbs," *New York Times*, May 9, 1976; Eleanor Charles, "Apathy Endangers Fresh Air Fund," *New York Times*, May 20, 1979.

5. "Seattle Youngsters Visiting in Area," *Daily Inter Lake* (Kalispell, MT), July 10, 1970; "Seek Families for Friendly Town Program," *Rock Valley (IA) Bee*, July 9, 1975; "Host Families Sought for 'Friendly Town' Children," *Messenger* (Athens, OH), March 27, 1975; "Community Activities," *Call and Post* (Cleveland, OH), March 24, 1979.

6. Lawrence Wright, *City Children, Country Summer* (New York: Scribner, 1979); Peter Kondrat, "An Escape from Asphalt to Fresh Country Air," *Gettysburg (PA) Times*, July 1, 1978.

7. Luis Diaz interview.

8. Ibid.

9. Nilson Diaz, New York, NY, telephone interview by the author, May 12, 2010.

10. Luis Diaz interview.

11. Ibid.

12. Nilson Diaz interview.

13. Luis Diaz interview.

14. Janice Batts, "Discovering Me," http://themommastrikesback.blogspot.com.

15. Janice Batts, Iowa City, IA, telephone interview by the author, February 15, 2012.

16. Steve Estes, Dennis Stoesz, and Paul L. Weaver, "Mennonite Churches in the Midwest, USA Past and Present, 1807–1998, and Their Archival Records," Mennonite Church USA Historical Committee, www.mcusa-archives.org/Congregations/illinoisindexfinal.html.

17. Batts, "Discovering Me."

18. Otto Voth and Marietta Voth to Orlo Kaufman, August 6, 1969, MLABC: MLA. VII.R GC Voluntary Service, Series 11 Gulfport VS Unit, box 4, folder 130: "Fresh Air, 1969."

19. Batts interview.

20. Ibid.

21. Ibid.

22. Menno S. Harder and Adolf Ens, "Education, Mennonite," Global Anabaptist Mennonite Encyclopedia Online, www.gameo.org/encyclopedia/contents/E383ME.html.

23. Batts interview.

24. Ibid.

25. Cindy Vanderkodde, Grand Rapids, MI, telephone interview by the author, March 7, 2010.

26. John Kord Lagemann, "Something Special in Vacations: A *Reader's Digest* Reprint," *Reader's Digest*, June 1963; "Narrow World Big Threat to 'Fresh Air' Children," *Huntingdon (PA) Daily News*, May 19, 1973; "First Woman Executive Director Takes Helm for Fresh Air Fund Tomorrow"; "Lives Brightened by Fresh Air Fund," *New York Times*, August 15, 1976; Judith Cummings, "Fresh Air Fund Put Many on Right Path," *New York Times*, May 29, 1977.

27. George J. Gordodensky, "Fresh Air Children, Co-Hope," *Daily News Record* (Harrisonburg, VA), April 12, 1979; "Couple Recall Their Early Days as Fresh Air Fund Hosts," *New York Times*, April 30, 1978; "12,000 Families Aid the Fresh Air Fund," *New York Times*, June 25, 1978.

28. Richard F. Crandell, ed., *The Frog Log and Other Stories about Children* (New York: Herald Tribune Fresh Air Fund, 1962).

29. Ruth Millett, "We—the Women," *Altoona (PA) Mirror*, July 18, 1940.

30. Memorandum, "1952 Annual Report [proof]," 1953, LOC, PRF D223, HRR, file 12559: "The Fresh Air Fund, 1952."

31. "37 Kids Taste Farm Life," *Chicago Daily Defender*, July 29, 1969.

32. Lacey Fosburgh, "Fresh Air Homes for Boys Needed," *New York Times*, June 27, 1971.

33. Sarane Spence Boocock, "The Social Context of Childhood," *Proceedings of the American Philosophical Society* 119, no. 6 (1975): 419–29; Robin Bernstein, *Racial Innocence: Performing American Childhood and Race from Slavery to Civil Rights* (New York: New York University Press, 2011), 4.

34. Bernstein, *Racial Innocence*, 241–42.

35. Ibid., 41.

36. Crandell, ed., *The Frog Log and Other Stories about Children*, 2–3.

37. Shelby Steele, *The Content of Our Character: A New Vision of Race in America* (New York: HaperCollins, 1990), 4–6.

38. Ibid., 5.

39. Ibid., 125.

40. Mary Douglas, *Purity and Danger: An Analysis of the Concepts of Pollution and Taboo* (1966; New York: Routledge, 2002), 2, 5, 44.

41. Ibid., 49, 117, 22, 219–20.

42. Roderick Nash, *Wilderness and the American Mind* (New Haven, CT: Yale University Press, 1982).

43. Annie Gilbert Coleman, *Ski Style: Sport and Culture in the Rockies* (Lawrence, KS: University Press of Kansas, 2004), 7, 9; Kevin DeLuca and Anne Demo, "Imagining Nature and Erasing Class and Race: Carleton Watkins, John Muir, and the Construction of Wilderness," *Environmental History* 6, no. 4 (2001): 541–60; Donald S. Moore, Anand Pandian, and Jake Kosek, "Introduction: The Cultural Politics of Race and Nature: Terrains of Power and Practice," in *Race, Nature, and the Politics of Difference*, ed. Donald S. Moore, Anand Pandian, and Jake Kosek (Durham, NC: Duke University Press, 2003), 1–72.

44. Thanks to Sorn Jessen, a graduate student in University of Montana's history program at the time of this writing, for suggesting this insight. Jessen also posited that urban Fresh Air children may have to a degree taken the place of Native Americans in the white community's imagining of the noble savage trope.

45. For examples of postcolonial studies featuring analysis of the center—or metropole—and periphery, see Ann Laura Stoler, *Carnal Knowledge and Imperial Power: Race and the Intimate in Colonial Rule* (Berkeley: University of California Press, 2002); David Chidester, *Savage Systems: Colonialism and Comparative Religion in Southern Africa* (Charlottesville: University Press of Virginia, 1996); Peter van der Veer, *Imperial Encounters: Religion and Modernity in India and Britain* (Princeton, NJ: Princeton University Press, 2001).

46. Jason E. Shelton and Michael O. Emerson, *Blacks and Whites in Christian America: How Racial Discrimination Shapes Religious Conviction* (New York: New York University Press, 2012), 199.

47. Martin Luther King, *Stride toward Freedom: The Montgomery Story* (New York: Harper, 1958), 206.

48. Julia Guarneri, "Changing Strategies for Child Welfare, Enduring Beliefs about Childhood: The Fresh Air Fund, 1877–1926," *Journal of the Gilded Age and Progressive Era* 11, no. 1 (2012): 27–70.

49. Steven Mintz, *Huck's Raft: A History of American Childhood* (Cambridge, MA: Belknap Press of Harvard University Press, 2004), vii.

50. Ibid., 348.

51. Ibid., vii.

52. A further note on innocence: On this topic, Paula Fass and Michael Grossberg advance the argument that state institutions increasingly sought to protect children defined as innocent by the society around them. See Paula S. Fass and Michael Grossberg, "Preface," in *Reinventing Childhood after World War II*, ed. Paula S. Fass and Michael Grossberg (Philadelphia: University of Pennsylvania Press, 2012), ix–xiii. Although the collection of essays they bring together makes a strong case for the necessity of evaluating the role of the state and innocence in the post–World War II era, Grossberg's essay directs readers' attention to those less likely to be seen as innocents—teenagers—when offering evidence that "African-American children were primary actors in the era's fight against racial segregation and not simply the beneficiaries of adult civil rights campaigners" (Grossberg, "Liberation and Caretaking: Fighting over Children's Rights in Postwar America," in *Reinventing Childhood after World War II*), 19–37. Most specifically, cultural historian Robin Bernstein offers an insightful window into the racialization of innocence in nineteenth- and twentieth-century children's play. Echoing Fass and Grossberg, she argues that the black freedom struggle sought to protect suffering innocent children, a point made all the more salient by her treatment of dolls. Yet in the process Bernstein misconstrues the role that the children themselves played in shaping ideas of innocence. Even where she claims to show how the children acted, she evaluates how they were acted upon. See Bernstein, *Racial Innocence*. By contrast, the Fresh Air story demonstrates that the children shaped their hosts in the midst of being deemed innocent by program promoters.

EPILOGUE

1. William Kirk to Joseph K. McManus, January 28, 1959, CUA, USAR, 1896–1995 MS#1149, Series VII: Programs and Services, box 40, folder 9: "Camp-Correspondence, 1956–58, 1964"; Phyllis M. Palmer, *Living as Equals: How Three White Communities Struggled to Make Interracial Connections during the Civil Rights Era* (Nashville: Vanderbilt University Press, 2008), 273.

2. Memorandum, "Signs of Summer: The Fresh Air Fund Annual Report," 2014, http://www.freshair.org/Websites/freshairfund/images/The_Fresh_Air_Fund_-_Annual_Report_-_2014.pdf.

3. Paul Reines, "'No Violence, a Lot of Bugs': Fresh Air Children Arrive Here to Escape Big-City Summer," *New Era* (Lancaster, PA), June 28, 1996.

4. Wallace D. Best, *Passionately Human, No Less Divine: Religion and Culture in Black Chicago, 1915–1952* (Princeton, NJ: Princeton University Press, 2005).

5. I make no claims of complete coverage of the experience of every Fresh Air host and participant. It will remain the work of another historian to conduct the thousands of interviews required to truly represent the full breadth of the children's experience in particular. Moreover, the oral histories that my colleagues and I conducted quickly reached a saturation point as former hosts and guests repeated the same types of stories again and again. Even more importantly, the interviews included here of adults recalling their childhood Fresh Air visits provide broad coverage of a variety of experiences but, given the splintered nature of most childhood memories, often proved less helpful than the perspectives of children recorded at the time of their visits in letters, interviews, and photographs. For discussion of the vagaries of childhood memory, see Hans Werner, *The Constructed Mennonite: History, Memory, and the Second World War* (Winnipeg, Manitoba: University of Manitoba Press, 2013), 30.

6. I have reason to suspect the veracity of this assertion. A researcher from Yale was given access to the Fresh Air Fund's archives and worked there after the Fund had purportedly shut down its archives. Interestingly, this researcher covered the period prior to World War II and, as a result, dealt very little with racial questions.

7. Reines, "'No Violence, a Lot of Bugs.'"

8. "Changing Lives: One Summer at a Time," *New York Times*, 2013 (undated supplement; author's personal collection).

Bibliographic Note

INTERVIEWS, ORAL HISTORIES, AND WRITTEN CORRESPONDENCE/MEMOIRS

Adams, Glenda, New York, NY, March 28, 2010; guest

Anonymous, New York, NY, September 15, 1995; guest

Batts, Janice, Iowa City, IA, February 15, 2012; guest

Berry, Lee Roy, Jr., Lee Heights Fellowship, Cleveland, Ohio, July 17, 2004*; sending community member

Brock, Thomas W., Harrisonburg, VA, May 17, 2005; guest

Brown, Hubert, Lee Heights Fellowship, Cleveland, Ohio, July 17, 2004*; sending community member

Curry, Peggy, Harrisonburg, VA, March 29, 2005; parent of guest

Diaz, Luis, New York, NY, May 4, 2010; guest

Diaz, Nilson, New York, NY, May 12, 2010; guest

Douple, Betty, Long Beach, MS, May 25, 2005; sending community member

Eby, John, Philadelphia, PA, February 28, 2003; member of host family

Geil, Libby, Gulfport, MS, May 25, 2005; sending community member

Genzink, Gladys, Graafschap, MI, May 16, 2010†; host

Gibbons, Joseph, Tallahassee, FL, March 17, 2010; guest

Greenfield, Bernie, Newark, NJ, April 13, 2010; program administrator

Hargrow, Phillip, "I Was a "Fresh-Air" Child," *Missionary Messenger*, May 1976, 15; guest

Herron, Lionel, Cabo, Mexico, June 9, 2015; guest

Hoek, Marilyn, Graafschap, MI, May 16, 2010†; host

Holtgeerts, Lois, Graafschap, MI, May 16, 2010†; host

Horst, Barbara, Ephrata, PA, April 22, 2003; program administrator

Hostetler, Goldie, Lancaster, PA, March 14, 2002; host/program administrator

Hughes, Gerald, Lee Heights Fellowship, Cleveland, OH, July 17, 2004; member of sending community

Hulst, Jean, Graafschap, MI, May 16, 2010†; host

Jackson, Raymond, Lee Heights Fellowship, Cleveland, OH, July 17, 2004*; member of sending community

Kennel, Ron, Goshen, IN, February 26, 2004; supporter

Landis, Paul G., Lancaster, PA, April 28, 2005; supporter/administrator

Larson, Kathy Knoll, Graafschap, MI, May 16, 2010†; host

Lont, James, Graafschap, MI, May 16, 2010†; member of hosting community

Lubbers, Howard, Graafschap, MI, May 16, 2010†; host

Lubbers, Lola, Graafschap, MI, May 16, 2010†; host

Middleton, Margie, "Fresh Air Reminiscences," *Missionary Messenger*, July 1977, 12–13, 21; guest

Muckma, Ron, Graafschap, MI, May 16, 2010†; host

Nikiema, Mattie Cooper, Lee Heights Fellowship, Cleveland, OH, July 17, 2004*; member of sending community

Odom, Mertis, Markham, IL, July 3, 2005; family of guest

Pannell, Melody M., Harrisonburg, VA, January 20, 2016; guest

Peeks, Patty (nee Lubbers), Graafschap, MI, May 16, 2010†; host

Postma, Sally Rutgers, Graafschap, MI, May 16, 2010†; host
Powell, John, Lee Heights Fellowship, Cleveland, OH, July 17, 2004*; member of sending community
Regenbogen, Helen Busuttil, Bainbridge, NY, March 10, 2010; guest (as child) and host (as adult)
Regier, Harold, Newton, KS, July 12, 2005; program administrator
Regier, Rosella Wiens, Newton, KS, July 12, 2005; program administrator
Shenk, Norman G., Salunga, PA, March 22, 2005; program administrator
Sluiter, Joyce, Graafschap, MI, May 16, 2010†; host
Sluiter, Stanley, Graafschap, MI, May 16, 2010†; host
Vanderkodde, Cindy, Grand Rapids, MI, March 7, 2010; guest
Van Kampen, Bernie, Graafschap, MI, May 16, 2010†; host
Van Kampen, Faye, Graafschap, MI, May 16, 2010†; host
Zwiep, Myra (nee Lambers), Graafschap, MI, May 16, 2010†; host

*Interview conducted by John Sharp.
†Interview conducted by James Lont.
All other interviews by author.

NEWSPAPERS AND MAGAZINES

Advance (Algona, Kossuth County, IA)
Advocate (Kansas City, KS)
Advocate and American Tribune (Newark, OH)
Afro-American (Baltimore, MD)
Age (New York, NY)
Agitator (Wellsboro, PA)
American Citizen (Kansas City, KS)
Amsterdam News (New York, NY)
Architectural Forum (New York, NY)
Arizona Republic (Phoenix, AZ)
Banner (Bennington, VT)
Banner (Graafschap, MI)
Bee (Danville, VA)
Bee (Rock Valley, IA)
Black Coalition Weekly (New Haven, CT)
Bulletin (Barnard, NY)
Bulletin (Brownwood, TX)
Bulletin of the Diocese of New York (New York, NY)
Californian (Bakersfield, CA)
Call and Post (Cleveland, OH)
Call-Leader (Elwood, IN)
Camping Magazine (Plainfield, NJ)
Capital (Annapolis, MD)
Chronicle-Express (Penn Yan, NY)
Chronicle-Telegram (Elyria, OH)
Christian Recorder (Philadelphia, PA)
Citizen (Culver, IN)
Coast Star (Kennebunk, ME)
Collier's Magazine (New York, NY)
Colored American (Washington, DC)

Commonwealth Reporter (Fond du Lac, WI)
Community Publications (Chicago, IL)
Compiler (Gettysburg, PA)
Conservationist (Albany, NY)
Constitution (Atlanta, GA)
Constitution (Lawton, OK)
Courier (Charlestown, IN)
Courier (Pittsburgh, PA)
Courier Express (DuBois, PA)
Daily American (Somerset, PA)
Daily Bulletin (Anderson, IN)
Daily Bulletin (Van Wert, OH)
Daily Call (Piqua, OH)
Daily Chronicle (Centralia, WA)
Daily Chronicle (DeKalb, IL)
Daily Courier (Bristol, PA)
Daily Courier (Connellsville, PA)
Daily Courier (Waterloo, IA)
Daily Eagle (Brooklyn, NY)
Daily Facts (Redlands, CA)
Daily Forum (Maryville, MO)
Daily Freeman (Kingston, NY)
Daily Freeman (Waukesha, WI)
Daily Gazette (Gastonia, NC)
Daily Gazette (Janesville, WI)
Daily Globe (Atchison, KS)
Daily Globe (Ironwood, MI)
Daily Herald (Chicago, IL)
Daily Herald (Lethbridge, Alberta)
Daily Herald (Tyrone, PA)

Daily Independent Journal (San
Rafael, CA)
Daily Intelligencer (Doylestown, PA)
Daily Intelligencer Journal (Lancaster, PA)
Daily Inter Lake (Kalispell, MT)
Daily Journal (Fergus Falls, MN)
Daily Leader (Pontiac, IL)
Daily Mail (Charleston, WV)
Daily Mail (Hagerstown, MD)
Daily Messenger (Canandaigua, NY)
Daily News (Estherville, IA)
Daily News (Galveston, TX)
Daily News (Huntingdon and Mt.
Union, PA)
Daily News (Lebanon, PA)
Daily News (Newport, RI)
Daily News (Rhinelander, WI)
Daily News (Winona, MN)
Daily News Record (Harrisonburg, VA)
Daily Northwestern (Oshkosh, WI)
Daily Notes (Canonsburg, PA)
Daily Plainsman (Huron, SD)
Daily Press (Escanaba, MI)
Daily Record (Statesville, NC)
Daily Record (York, PA)
Daily Register (Oelwein, IA)
Daily Reporter (Dover, OH)
Daily Reporter (Wellsville, NY)
Daily Republican (Belvidere, IL)
Daily Republican (Monongahela, PA)
Daily Review Sports (Hayward, CA)
Daily Sentinel (Fitchburg, MA)
Daily Sentinel (Rome, NY)
Daily Telegram (Adrian, MI)
Daily Telegraph (Bluefield, WV)
Daily Times (Carroll, IA)
Daily Times (Chester, Delaware
County, PA)
Daily Times (Portsmouth, OH)
Daily Times (Primos, PA)
Daily Times (Salisbury, MD)
Daily Times (Weirton, WV)
Daily Times-News (Burlington, NC)
Daily Times-Press (Middletown, NY)
Daily Tribune (Greeley, CO)
Daily Tribune (Tipton, IN)
Daily World (Atlanta, GA)
Defender (Chicago, IL)
Delphos Daily Herald (Delphos, OH)
Delta Democrat-Times (Greenville, MS)
Democrat (Emmetsburg, IA)

Derrick (Oil City, PA)
Eagle (Pittsfield, MA)
Eagle Gazette (Lancaster, OH)
Enterprise (High Point, NC)
Episcopal New Yorker (New York, NY)
Era (Bradford, PA)
Evening Banner (Bennington, VT)
Evening Gazette (Reno, NV)
Evening Herald (Shenandoah, PA)
Evening Independent (Massillon, OH)
Evening Journal (Lincoln, NE)
Evening News (Harrisburg, PA)
Evening News (Lincoln, NE)
Evening News (Port Angeles, WA)
Evening News (Ridgeton, NJ)
Evening News (Sault Sainte Marie, MI)
Evening Observer (Dunkirk, NY)
Evening Review (East Liverpool, OH)
Evening Standard (Uniontown, PA)
Evening Star (Franklin, IN)
Evening Sun (Hanover, PA)
Evening Telegraph (Dixon, IL)
Evening Times (Cumberland, MD)
Evening Times (Sayre, PA)
Evening Times (Trenton, NJ)
Evening Transcript (North Adams, MA)
Evening Tribune (Hornell, NY)
Express (Lock Haven, PA)
Farmers Weekly (Sutton, Great Britain)
Farming (Lancaster, PA)
Flying (Winter Park, FL)
Forbes (New York, NY)
Freeman (Indianapolis, IN)
Free Press (Winnipeg, Manitoba)
Gazette (Charleston, WV)
Gazette (Cleveland, OH)
Gazette (Emporia, KS)
Gazette (Indiana, PA)
Gazette (Janesville, WI)
Gazette (Pittston, PA)
Gazette (San Antonio, TX)
Gazette (Wellsboro, PA)
Gazette and Daily (York, PA)
Gleaner (Kingston, Jamaica)
Globe-Citizen (Mason City, IA)
Globe-Gazette (Mason City, IA)
Guthrian (Guthrie Center, IA)
Herald (Anderson, IN)
Herald (Arlington Heights, IL)
Herald (Austin, MN)
Herald (Brownsville, TX)

Herald (Buffalo Grove, IL)
Herald (Elk Grove Village, IL)
Herald (Hopewell, NJ)
Herald (Palatine, IL)
Herald (Portsmouth, NH)
Herald (Titusville, PA)
Herald-American (Syracuse, NY)
Herald Journal (Syracuse, NY)
Herald-Star (Steubenville, OH)
Herald Tribune (New York, NY)
Independent (Gallup, NM)
Independent (Humboldt, IA)
Independent (Long Beach, CA)
Index-Journal (Greenwood, SC)
Intelligencer Journal (Lancaster, PA)
Item (New Oxford, PA)
Journal (Biddeford, ME)
Journal (Denton, MD)
Journal (Muscatine, IA)
Journal (Poughkeepsie, NY)
Journal (Salina, KS)
Journal and News-Tribune (Muscatine, IA)
Journal News (Hamilton, OH)
Journal-Standard (Freeport, IL)
Labor Advocate (La Crosse, WI)
Leader (Eau-Claire, WI)
Leader (Malvern, IA)
Ledger (Gaffney, SC)
Ledger (Mexico, MO)
Ledger Transcript (St. Peterborough, NH)
Mail (Charleroi, PA)
Mail Terrill Record (Milford, IA)
McCall's (Chicago, IL)
Mercury (Pottstown, PA)
Mercury and Weekly News (Newport, RI)
Messenger (Athens, OH)
Metro News (Chicago, IL)
Mirror (Altoona, PA)
Missionary Messenger (Salunga, PA)
Morning Herald (Hagerstown, MD)
Morning Herald (Uniontown, PA)
Morning Journal (Logansport, IN)
Morning News (Danville, PA)
Morning News (Florence, SC)
Morning Times (Kokomo, IN)
Nebraska State Journal (Lincoln, NE)
Negro Star (Wichita, KS)
Nevada State Journal (Reno, NV)
New Era (Lancaster, PA)
New Journal and Guide (Norfolk, VA)
News (Albia, Monroe County, IA)
News (Bayard, IA)

News (Bernardsville, NJ)
News (Cumberland, MD)
News (Des Moines, IA)
News (Frederick, MD)
News (Hutchinson, KS)
News (Kingsport, TN)
News (Lima, OH)
News (New Castle, PA)
News (Newport, RI)
News (Salem, OH)
News Advertizer (Harlan, IA)
News-Chronicle (Shippensburg, PA)
Newsday (New York, NY)
News-Herald (Franklin, PA)
News-Journal (Clovis, NM)
News Journal (Mansfield, OH)
News-Palladium (Benton Harbor, MI)
News-Record (Miami, OK)
News Record (North Hills, PA)
News Sentinel (Fort Wayne, IN)
New Yorker (New York)
Nonpareil (Council Bluffs, IA)
Observer (Dunkirk-Freedonia, NY)
Paddock Publications (Arlington Heights, IL)
Palladium-Times (Oswego, NY)
Parents Magazine (Des Moines, IA)
Pharos-Tribune (Logansport, IN)
Plaindealer (Kansas City, KS)
Plain Speaker (Hazleton, PA)
Pocono Record (Stroudsburg, PA)
Post (Bridgeport, CT)
Post (Frederick, MD)
Post-Crescent (Appleton-Neenah-Menasha, WI)
Post Herald The Raleigh Register (Beckley, WV)
Post-Register (Idaho Falls, ID)
Post-Standard (Syracuse, NY)
Presbyterian Life (Louisville, KY)
Press (Chatham, NJ)
Press (Sheboygan, WI)
Press-Citizen (Iowa City, IA)
Press-Courier (Oxnard, CA)
Press-Gazette (Hillsboro, OH)
Progress (Clearfield, Curwensville, Phillipsburg, Moshannon Valley, PA)
Progress-Index (Petersburg, VA)
Reader's Digest (Pleasantville, NY)
Record (Troy, NY)
Record (Wilkes-Barre, PA)
Record-Argus (Greenville, PA)

Record & Landmark (Statesville, NC)
Record-Herald (Washington Court House, OH)
Redbook (New York, NY)
Register (Bensenville, IL)
Register (Des Moines, IA)
Register (Iola, KS)
Register (Sandusky, OH)
Register-Mail (Galesburg, IL)
Reporter (Des Moines, IA)
Reporter (Emmetsburg, IA)
Reporter (Nashua, IA)
Republican (Humboldt, IA)
Republican (Kane, PA)
Republican (Rushville, IN)
Republican-Herald (Winona, MN)
Review (Decatur, IL)
Review (Ephrata, PA)
Robesonian (Lumberton, NC)
Sentinel (Santa Cruz, CA)
Sentinel: The American Jewish Weekly (Kingsport, TN)
Sentinel-Enterprise (Fitchburg, MA)
Simpson's Leader-Times (Kittanning, PA)
Spokesman-Review (Spokane, WA)
Standard and Review (Aiken, SC)
Standard-Speaker (Hazleton, PA)
Star (Chicago, IL)
Star (Indianapolis, IN)
Star (Lincoln, NE)
Star (Marion, OH)
Star (Oneonta, NY)
Star and Sentinel (Gettysburg, PA)
Sun (Lowell, MA)
Sun (New York, NY)
Sun (San Bernardino, CA)
Sunday (Lowell, MA)
Sunday Afternoon (Springfield, MA)
Sunday Bulletin (Racine, WI)
Sunday Herald (Chicago, IL)
Sunday Star (Lincoln, NE)
Sunday Times (Cumberland, MD)
Sun-Gazette (Williamsport, PA)
Telegram (Bridgeport, CT)
Telegraph (Harrisburg, PA)
Telegraph (Nashua, NH)

Times (Gettysburg, PA)
Times (Hammond, IN)
Times (Ironwood, MI)
Times (Kingsport, TN)
Times (Levitown, PA)
Times (Los Angeles, CA)
Times (New York, NY)
Times (Salisbury, MD)
Times (San Mateo, CA)
Times Herald (Middletown, NY)
Times Herald (Olean, NY)
Times Herald Record (New York, NY)
Times Herald Record (Middleton, NY)
Times Leader (Wilkes-Barre, PA)
Times-Mirror and Observer (Warren, PA)
Times Observer (Warren, PA)
Times Record (Troy, NY)
Times Recorder (Zanesville, OH)
Times-Reporter (Dover, PA)
Times-Reporter (New Philadelphia, OH)
Time Table (Lenox, IA)
Town & Country Church (Lebanon, PA)
Transcript (Morrisville, VT)
Transcript (North Adams, MA)
Tribune (Altoona, PA)
Tribune (Chicago, IL)
Tribune (Coshocton, OH)
Tribune (Great Bend, KS)
Tribune (Kokomo, IN)
Tribune (La Crosse, WI)
Tribune (New York, NY)
Tribune (Oakland, CA)
Tribune (Philadelphia, PA)
Tribune (Terre Haute, IN)
Turning Points (New York, NY)
Union (Moravia, IA)
Upper Des Moines (Algona, IA)
Vanity Fair (New York, NY)
What's In the Air (New York, NY)
Whip (Topeka, KS)
Wisconsin Jewish Chronicle (Milwaukee, WI)
Wisconsin State Journal (Madison, WI)
World Journal Tribune (New York, NY)

Index

abuse, 15; sexual, 41, 90, 96, 148

Adams, Glenda, 106

adolescence and adolescents, 9, 92, 98–99, 105

adoption, 153; opposition to, 1; rarity of, 42, 104

African American children, 7, 19–22, 66–69, 71–76; activists as, 89, 179n16; age caps and, 98–99, 150, 156; isolation of, 81; manners of, 83, 86; nature and, 63; poverty and, 25, 125; publicity about, 59; race relations and, 9; racial code of conduct, 90; racism toward, 52–53, 65, 152; respectability and, 77; shift to serving, 139, 149; intimacy with, 93–94; teachers as, 82

African Methodist Episcopal Church, 19

age caps, 24, 98–99, 102–3, 106, 110, 144, 214n58

Allaben, NY, 72

Altoona, PA, 132, 151

amalgamation. *See* interracial romance

American Stock Exchange, 137

Americus, GA, 156

Ames, IA, 98

Amish people, 34, 36, 38–41, 56

Ammann, Jakob, 39

Amsterdam News, 17, 19, 48, 66, 69, 74

Anabaptists, 39–41. *See also* Mennonites

Annville, PA, 129

Anthony, Veronica, 94, 151

Anti-Defamation League, 74

Antioch Baptist Church, 73

Arenas, Savina, 47

Ashe, Arthur, 137

Asian Americans, 67; children, 20, 65, 66, 76

Athens, OH, 81

Atlanta, GA, 156

Atwater, David Fisher, 72

Atwater, Mary, 72

Bacall, Lauren, 137

Bailey, Lauren "Flip," 50, 71, 81

Baltimore, MD, 2, 21, 25, 64, 69

Barbel, Kay, 126

Barrows v. Jackson, 60

Batts, Janice, 11, 145–50, 152, 155, 158

Beame, Abraham, 123

Belafonte, Harry, 73, 137

Bell Harbor, NY, 102

beloved community, 12, 155

Bennington, VT, 1, 69, 105, 129

Bennington Banner, 122

Bethel College, 105

Bethune, Mary McCleod, 81

black freedom struggle. *See* civil rights movement

Black Nationalists, 56, 82, 83, 88, 128

Black Power, 46, 48, 66, 155

Boll, Edith, viii, ix

Boll, John viii, ix

Bonilla, George, 52

Borden industry, 113

Boston, MA, 18, 36, 38, 43, 62, 93, 99

Boys Athletic League, 133

Boys Club, 133

Boy Scouts, 17, 61

Brace, Charles Loring, 15

Brethren, Church of, 39

Brookfield, MA, 72

Brooklyn Urban League, 24

Brown, Natasha, 41

Brown v. Board of Education, 68, 93

Buckley, William, 138

Buckwalter, Anna, 125

busing, 1, 6, 46, 93

Cabrini-Green Housing Project, 45

Califon, NJ, 142–43, 145

Calvin College, 106

Cambridge, MA, 69

Camp Atwater, 72–73

Camp Bryton Rock, 72–73

Camp Fire Girls, 16–17

Camp Hidden Valley, 51, 104

Camp Pioneer, 71, 88

camps, 5, 16–17, 103, 113; abuse at, 96; age caps for, 99; autonomy of children, 51; black, 71–73; boys at, 24; communists and, 32; disciplinary issues, 86–89, 98; fundraising for, 104; gender and, 25; home visits vs., 179n10; Progressive Era and, 18; race

manners, 2, 7, 10, 56, 74, 77–78; discipline and, 87–89, 160; disruptive behavior and, 35, 40, 57–58, 86, 160; misbehavior and, 32, 37, 40, 56–57, 83, 86–89; politeness and, 2, 80, 86; sass and, 31, 57–59, 83, 90
Manzella, Frank A., 108
marijuana, 59, 64, 90
Martha's Vineyard, 73, 135
Martin, Mary, 137
Maxwell, Robert, 139
Mayes, Roosevelt "Teddy," 49, 50, 55
Mays, Willie, 137
McHugh, Lillybelle, 72–73
McHugh, Reginald, 72–73
McKenna, Gerard, 120
medical examinations, 28, 37, 107, 109
Mennonites, x, 34–41, 56, 68, 85, 87, 145–49, 192n83
Mennonite Community Chapel, 145
Mennonite House, 156
Methodists, 36
Merman, Ethel, 137
Michener, James A., 137
Michigan, 39, 76, 81–82, 87, 116, 192n83
Mickolic, Laurence "Larry," 88, 97–98, 102
Middleton, Margie, 40–41, 46, 128
Midwest, 18, 50, 65–69, 90, 93, 138, 145, 153
military, 6, 11, 46, 65, 131, 136; Air Force, 135; Army, 133; Herald Tribune Fresh Air Fund and, 134; Marines, 144, 146; Navy, 135
milk, 29, 111–16, 119, 139–41; lactose intolerance and, 291n14
Miller, Kevin, 51
Millett, Ruth, 151
Minnesota, MN, 43, 101
Mission/Missionary Society, 90, 103
Mississippi, 82
Mojica, Danford, 111–22, 126, 129, 140
Montana, 69
Montlawn Summer Home, 16–17
mothers of Fresh Air children, 74
Moundridge, KS, 81
Mount Joy, PA, 39
Mount Union, PA, 126
Mount Zion Congregational Church, 121
Murray, James, 105
Myrdal, Gunnar, 67

NAACP, 82
National Association of Black Social Workers, 1
National Black Political Convention, 49
National Council of Churches, 66
National Playground Association, 16
National Social Workers Committee on Camping, 75

Native New Yorkers Association, 134
nature, 2, 4, 8–15, 24–26, 30–32, 58–64, 154, 157; bugs in, 63–64, 161; cows and, 119; wilderness in, 24, 30, 103, 154
neoliberalism, x, 141
Newark, NJ, 69
New Era, 159
New Jersey, 76, 87, 118
Newkirk, Oscar V., 136
newspapers, 4, 13, 120, 131; African American, 19–20; publicity in, 122; sources in, 160. See also individual titles
Newton, KS, 9, 105, 117
New York, 69, 71, 87, 99, 105
New York City, 101, 105, 128–29, 151; Bronx, 45, 48, 50, 126; Brooklyn, 45–46, 50, 53, 58, 74, 79, 83, 99, 121; children from, ix, 15, 63, 135–36, 142–45, 159, 161; fundraising in, 120; Harlem, 40, 47, 50–51, 66, 72, 81, 96; inner-city issues, 102; Manhattan, 1, 47–48, 58, 83; programs in, 17–18; program origin, vii; Queens, 45, 95; recessions in, 124; suburbs of, 44; summer programming in, 48; symbol of danger, 42; travel from, 114
New York Globe, 19
New York Stock Exchange, 137
New York Times, 16, 61, 122, 161
Nixon, Richard, 136
noble savage, 154, 232n44
North, 68, 77, 93, 138
North Carolina, 138
North Dakota, 69
Northeast, 18, 50, 65, 69, 90, 138, 153
Northwest, 138
Noyes, Blanke, 69, 124
Nungesser Chateau, 71

Office of Economic Opportunity, 48
O'Hagan, Anne, 107
O'Keefe, Carolyn, 99
Olean, NY, 36
Oneonta, NY, 37, 127
Optimist Club, 120
orphan trains, 15, 19
Otego, NY, 95

Palmgren, Tom, 88
Paradise, PA, 39
parents of Fresh Air children, vii, 51, 109–10; care for children, 42, 140; cooperation of, 141; finances of, 72; involvement of, 12, 14, 46, 28, 121–22, 157; respectability of, 41, 77–80, 86, 89, 130; separating children from, 101; stereotypes about, 125, 140
parks, 26, 59, 62